Tax Reform in Open Economies

Tax Reform in Open Economies

International and Country Perspectives

Edited by

Iris Claus

Centre for Applied Macroeconomic Analysis (CAMA), Australian National University, Australia and Inland Revenue, New Zealand

Norman Gemmell

University of Nottingham, UK

Michelle Harding

The Treasury, New Zealand

David White

Victoria University of Wellington, New Zealand

Edward Elgar

Cheltenham, UK • Northampton, MA, USA

Published by
Edward Elgar Publishing Limited
The Lypiatts
15 Lansdown Road
Cheltenham
Glos GL50 2JA
UK

Edward Elgar Publishing, Inc.
William Pratt House
9 Dewey Court
Northampton
Massachusetts 01060
USA

A catalogue record for this book
is available from the British Library

Library of Congress Control Number: 2009940657

ISBN 978 1 84844 774 5

Printed and bound by MPG Books Group, UK

Contents

Contributors

Rosanne Altshuler, Rutgers University, New Brunswick, and Urban-Brookings Tax Policy Centre, Washington, USA.

Jens Arnold, OECD Paris, France.

Matt Benge, Inland Revenue, Wellington, New Zealand.

Bert Brys, OECD Paris, France.

Iris Claus, Centre for Applied Macroeconomic Analysis, Australian National University, Canberra, Australia, and Inland Revenue, Wellington, New Zealand.

John Creedy, Department of Economics, University of Melbourne, Melbourne, Australia.

Jacinta Dalgety, Ministry of Social Development, Wellington, New Zealand.

Richard Dorsett, National Institute of Economic and Social Research, London, UK.

John Freebairn, Department of Economics, University of Melbourne, Melbourne, Australia.

Norman Gemmell, School of Economics, University of Nottingham, UK and The Treasury, Wellington, New Zealand.

Jane Gravelle, Congressional Research Service, Washington, USA.

Michelle Harding, The Treasury, Wellington, New Zealand.

Christopher Heady, Department of Economics, University of Kent, UK.

David Holland, Inland Revenue, Wellington, New Zealand.

Åsa Johansson, OECD Paris, France.

Steven Johnston, Ministry of Social Development, Wellington, New Zealand.

Guyonne Kalb, Melbourne Institute of Applied Economic and Social Research, University of Melbourne, Melbourne, Australia.

Suzi Kerr, Motu Economic and Public Policy Research, Wellington, New Zealand.

Kelly Lock, Motu Economic and Public Policy Research, Wellington, New Zealand.

Greg Smith, Australian Catholic University, Canberra, Australia, and Review Panel 'Australia's Future Tax System'.

Peter Birch Sørensen, University of Copenhagen, Copenhagen, Denmark and Danish Council of Economic Advisers.

Philip Spier, Ministry of Social Development, Wellington, New Zealand.

Laura Vartia, OECD Paris, France.

David White, Centre for Accounting, Governance, and Taxation Research, Victoria University of Wellington, New Zealand.

George R. Zodrow, Economics Department, Rice University, Houston, USA.

Acknowledgements

This volume is the product of a lot of work by many people. The editors would like to thank in particular the other members of the organizing committee of the Victoria University of Wellington (VUW) tax conference; especially Matt Benge, Vanessa Borg, Sarah Dunstan, Erin Kilgour, Lisa Marriott and Tony van Zijl. The conference, and hence the contributed chapters of this volume, would not have been possible without the generous support of a number of institutions and individuals. We thank Bob Buckle and Neil Quigley at VUW and Bill Moran and Robin Oliver (New Zealand Treasury and Inland Revenue respectively) for having the foresight to bid for and commit resources to what turned out to be a hugely successful enterprise.

We are especially grateful to the contributors to this volume, who took time out of their busy schedules to prepare and present papers at the Wellington conference, and to prepare their chapters speedily for this volume. The generous sponsorship of individual papers, conference sessions and the conference as a whole by a number of organizations was also invaluable to this enterprise. In particular we thank Victoria University of Wellington (Centre for Accounting, Governance and Taxation Research, and the Institute for the Study of Competition and Regulation); four New Zealand government departments – Treasury, Inland Revenue, Department of Labour and Ministry of Economic Development; the accounting firms PricewaterhouseCoopers and Ernst & Young and especially their New Zealand chairmen John Shewan and Rob McLeod respectively; the New Zealand Institute of Chartered Accountants; Motu Economic and Public Policy Research; and CPA Australia.

Lastly, to the numerous conference participants – whether as part of the contributed panel sessions, as paper discussants or as session chairs, asking questions and challenging speakers, or simply attending – we would like to express our gratitude. Their various contributions may not be included in this volume, but they undoubtedly helped to improve the quality of the chapters included here.

1. Introduction

Iris Claus, Norman Gemmell, Michelle Harding and David White

1.1 BACKGROUND

The idea for this book arose in conjunction with a conference organized by Victoria University of Wellington with support from the New Zealand Treasury and from Inland Revenue in February 2009. Over the years, New Zealand governments have frequently been praised for their commitment to tax reform, for developing a tax system that displays many desirable features, and for avoiding many of the pitfalls of numerous other OECD countries' tax systems. It is perhaps no coincidence, therefore, at a time when the late-2000s global economic crisis is generating increasing fiscal pressures in many countries, that Wellington was the scene for a major gathering of some of the world's leading experts on tax policy. The overarching question that the conference sought to address was: 'what can tax policy makers in open economies learn about beneficial directions for medium-term tax reform in the light of global developments and lessons from the latest taxation research?' That is also the underlying theme of this book, and in this introduction we bring together some of the lessons learned from the international and country perspectives presented in later chapters.

The book covers a range of tax reform issues from general assessments of different countries' tax systems to key aspects of taxes on labour, capital, individuals and corporations. The chapters included in this volume cannot resolve many of the issues currently challenging tax policy makers around the world, faced with an increasingly integrated world economy, and the aftermath of the ongoing global recession. However, they do provide some of the latest thinking by some of the world's most respected contributors to tax debates in the United States, Europe, Australia and New Zealand. In many cases, further work will be required to yield definitive answers to some important tax policy questions – such as the role of global 'taxes' to deal with climate change externalities. For many current tax policy questions, however, a number of tentative, and some more robust, answers are possible.

As might be expected from the assembled contributors and conference location, a number of chapters focus on New Zealand, or use the New Zealand context to illustrate arguments or provide evidence. New Zealand is a small island economy in the South Pacific. However, current tax policy reform issues in New Zealand are surprisingly representative of many of those facing other small open economies. In addition, New Zealand has historically provided an interesting 'test case' for a number of major tax policy interventions, and it remains one of few countries where governments are prepared to at least look at some of the more radical options for reform.

1.2 SOME TAX POLICY LESSONS

This section summarises the lessons to emerge from the subsequent chapters by first considering 'general issues' related to tax structure and design (sub-section 1.2.1) and then considering lessons specific to particular taxes: corporate/capital taxes in sub-section 1.2.2 and personal/labour taxes in sub-section 1.2.3.

1.2.1 General Issues

Three general tax design questions are prominent in current tax policy debates. (1) Is 'broad base, low rate' (BBLR) still a useful barometer of tax system efficiency, or should tax rates on capital income be set lower than the (top) rate on labour income? (2) How important is alignment of corporate and top personal tax rates? (3) How far does tax structure design and the mix of different taxes affect economic performance such as gross domestic product (GDP) growth rates?

Broad base, low rate?

A clear message from this book is the importance of adopting a consistent framework between BBLR or tax systems that set different capital/labour tax rates or different corporate/(top) personal tax rates. For a given revenue requirement, taxing all forms of income defined as broadly as possible, at as low a rate as possible, is still widely respected internationally as a useful guiding principle. However, (a) it is often undermined in a number of countries by *ad hoc* policy interventions designed to deal with specific revenue-raising or social policy concerns; and (b) increased globalisation is making its achievement more difficult, at least in terms of a common low rate for all sources of income. For a given tax base, the general principle of broadening bases in association with rate reductions remains a good rule of thumb for efficient taxation. International evidence for both corporate and personal taxes point to trends in this direction over the last several decades; see Peter et al. (2008) and Devereux (2008) respectively. Nevertheless, the Nordic countries have demonstrated that a dual tax system that taxes capital and labour income at differential rates can be made to work, if applied consistently, and where it is desired to keep top rates of tax on labour income particularly high (generally 50 per cent or more), and international migration of labour/human capital is not a serious concern.

Rate alignment

On the second question – is rate alignment a good idea? – clearly taxing similar forms of income similarly makes sense to avoid unnecessary distortions and tax arbitrage. However, the global drive towards lower corporate tax rates as capital becomes more mobile, while governments appear to want to maintain progressive personal income taxation, makes achieving alignment more difficult. Where labour is also highly mobile, as in countries like Ireland, Luxembourg and New Zealand, the case for alignment is stronger, alongside a case for moving the tax mix towards less mobile tax bases such as land or immovable property. The alternative is rigorous, enforceable anti-avoidance legislation that prevents tax-motivated incorporation and other undesirable responses to the tax rate differential. This is not easily achieved, however, as recent UK experience suggests (with a small company rate below 20 per cent and a top personal rate of 40 per cent); see Crawford and Freedman (2009).

Taxes and growth

Common questions asked by policy makers are whether higher tax rates are bad for economic growth and, if so, are some taxes more harmful than others? Is globalisation affecting this relationship as capital becomes more mobile? Answering these questions has been difficult with plenty of micro-level evidence of individuals or businesses changing their behaviour in response to various tax settings, but mixed evidence at the macro level that such responses matter for aggregate growth of GDP or productivity. However, recent OECD and other aggregate-level evidence has been complemented by new evidence at the firm and sector levels, and both seem increasingly to tell a consistent story (see Chapter 2).

This points to a tentative 'tax and growth' ranking of (from most to least harmful): corporate, personal income, consumption and 'recurrent taxes on immovable property'. However, as noted above, allowing a wedge to develop between personal and corporate tax rates can create avoidance opportunities, leading the OECD to more circumspect advice:

that moving the revenue mix from the first two to the last two should be growth enhancing via improvements to productivity and investment. OECD evidence also suggests a number of other features of 'pro-growth' tax systems – such as less progressive rate structures (but at some cost to equity considerations); levying consumption taxes at a single rate with as few exemptions as possible; and reducing high marginal and average tax rates on low-wage workers in countries where these act as a disincentive to work.

The aftermath of the global recession

At the time of writing (March 2009) it is unclear how deep or long the recession will be that was initiated by the global financial crisis of 2008–09. However, it is already clear that governments in many major economies are engaging in very large fiscal stimulus packages, involving unprecedented deficits, with ongoing public debt burdens for decades to come. This will put pressure on many OECD governments to raise additional tax revenues over the next decade at least, raising questions regarding how governments will, and should, attempt to achieve this. A number of responses can be made.

First, given the need to raise average tax burdens – tax revenues to GDP – the global decline in corporate tax rates may slow, together with a slowing or even reversal of recent trends towards lower and less progressive personal income tax rates. Second, however, tax rate rises are likely to be least harmful to efficiency if levied on relatively immobile factors, and rate rises can be kept lower to the extent that countries can extend the relevant tax bases. Third, countries that have managed to maintain relatively low post-crisis public debt levels will be better able to compete more effectively for mobile tax bases via lower tax rates on capital and/or corporations. Hence the desire by more indebted governments to raise their corporate tax revenues may be thwarted both by the need to stimulate business investment after the crisis and by international competition over corporate tax rates from less-indebted governments. In this context, general OECD governments' hostility towards multinationals' use of tax havens can also be expected to intensify.

Finally, one benefit of the financial crisis and subsequent recession is that governments may become willing post-crisis to undertake, and persuade voters to accept, major tax system reform as the imperative of raising additional revenue as efficiently as possible becomes more acceptable. Understanding better which taxes have most/least impact on both static and dynamic efficiency is an important objective for tax research.

1.2.2 Corporate and Capital Taxes

Given historical trends, an obvious question for tax reformers in small open economies is: will international downward pressures persist, and force further corporate tax rate reductions? Most researchers working in this area conclude that the long-term trend towards lower corporate tax rates looks set to continue (perhaps after a short-term interruption following the financial crisis as described above). The trend may, however, be slower in future with fewer base broadening options left to exploit. But, with further opportunities for increased capital mobility (as larger fractions of economies become more open to international competition), a continuing downward trend could be expected.

Of course, not all economic activities are equally vulnerable to foreign competition – there are 'location-specific' advantages to some industries and some foreign firms may need to locate in host countries in order to serve these markets or access their natural resources. Across the world, these aspects are likely to stop the corporate tax 'race to the bottom' reaching a zero tax rate. However, within a country, if a common corporate tax rate has to be applied to both mobile and immobile corporations, and both types compete for similar resources (labour, financial capital and so on) it will be more difficult to maintain a relatively high corporate tax rate to exploit location-specific factors. Perhaps for this reason, the review of Australia's tax system is considering recommending different tax regimes for these two types of corporation – in Australia's case by granting foreign and domestic firms differential access to imputation credits.

As noted earlier, how far rates of tax on capital or company profits fall will depend on how responsive firms are to tax rates and on the ease of 'profit-shifting' across countries. A growing body of research is producing clear evidence that both real and intangible (patents/trademarks) capital and multinational firms' profits are becoming increasingly internationally mobile over time, and governments are increasingly competing over corporate tax rates to attract/retain that capital and profit. US multinationals seem to be especially tax sensitive. However, specific incentives targeted at investment may not be very effective. As Jane Gravelle argues in Chapter 3, even if they are effective in stimulating investment, their impact on aggregate output and consumption would still be limited. This largely reflects the fact that capital is only one factor of production, and diverting resources to investment involves immediate consumption sacrifices for modestly higher levels later on.

Given all of this, and expected future trends towards greater globalisation, a sensible corporate tax policy would be to aim to broaden the base as much as possible to allow a lower rate.

1.2.3 Personal/Labour Taxes and Transfers

Labour supply responses

A great deal of research over the years has examined how far levels of, or changes in, effective tax rates and social welfare payments affect labour force participation. Some tendency towards greater consistency of results has emerged as, for example, single men and secondary earners appear in most countries to be at opposite ends of the spectrum of labour supply responses (lower and higher respectively). However, the chapters in this book point to two important caveats.

First, labour supply responses for any particular group are not independent of the institutional context in which these labour supply decisions are made. As a result, some groups (for example single men) may be more responsive in some countries (New Zealand seems to be an example) than in others. Careful attention to country-specifics and the heterogeneity of different taxpayer sub-groups may therefore be important, as tax micro-simulation models generally confirm. Second, failing to observe large changes in employment numbers, for example, when tax rates change does not necessarily imply low tax responsiveness – it may simply reflect a tendency for income and substitution effects to cancel. Third, countries such as the UK and New Zealand, which have introduced family-related and work-related tax credits designed to encourage increased labour force participation appear to have had some success, but the opportunity costs in terms of the (foregone) tax revenue cost per job created can be substantial.

Fourth, population ageing will affect all mature economies to varying degrees in coming decades. This throws up an array of policy choices relating to both tax and pension systems. Perhaps surprisingly, relatively little is known about labour supply responses of the over-65s such that it is hard to predict the impact of demographic ageing on participation. Whatever the responsiveness of older age groups now (with relatively generous pensions typically in place), the responsiveness of older taxpayers in future could be quite different when faced with a new institutional setting (for example changed pension entitlements) and increased longevity.

Tax progressivity

Progressive rate structures are a common feature of personal income taxes in many countries though, as John Creedy points out in Chapter 7, it was not always so. In particular progression is not a necessary characteristic of a 'fair' personal tax structure. In fact, optimal tax theory does not give unambiguous guidance on how personal income tax rates should be structured. Much depends on value judgments such as how individuals' 'welfare' should be measured (for example consumption, sense of well-being, and so on), how averse society is to supporting the less well-off, and which/how far individuals change their behaviour in response to changes in tax rates.

Of course, different groups of taxpayers are often affected quite differently by alternative tax policy changes so that assessing the merits of these changes requires a disaggregated approach. Simple unambiguous statements about preferred tax changes are rarely possible on efficiency or equity grounds. Nevertheless, Creedy shows that for the New Zealand structure of personal income tax rates and thresholds (which, apart from the absence of an initial tax-free zone, is fairly representative of many countries' systems), the distributional gains from a higher top personal rate could well be small and would be achieved at a significant cost in terms of distortions created.

A related issue is whether distributional concerns are best dealt with via social welfare systems. Again, answers here are likely to differ by country and tax/transfer regime – for example a well-designed tax may be more effective than a badly-designed transfer system. Nevertheless, distributional measures often appear more sensitive to changes in social welfare payments suggesting that these may better target poverty and inequality aspects. This, of course, involves an additional trade-off. More targeting of social welfare payments often implies high withdrawal (abatement) rates that damage efficiency, whilst low targeting can be both fiscally costly and less redistributive. Countries like Australia, New Zealand and the UK that rely more on income-tested tax credits, payable across a wide range of income levels, face this challenge more acutely with high effective marginal tax rates facing many lower and middle income earners.

1.3 OUTLINE OF THE BOOK

The various chapters of the book have been organised into five parts. The two chapters in Part I explore the impacts of taxes (and subsidies) on productivity and investment. Part II examines recent thinking and evidence on corporate and capital taxation, paying particular attention to international dimensions, while Part III focuses on personal income taxation and the welfare systems that often operate in conjunction with them. Part IV turns to a particularly prominent issue in recent international tax debates – the use of tax and other instruments to deal with environmental externalities, both national and global. Finally, Part V reports some tax reform experience – for Australia and New Zealand – where tax policy debates are currently very much alive and are seeking to learn from past reform, and non-reform, episodes.

In a major series of papers, economists at the OECD have studied the effects of various types of taxes on the economic growth of developed nations within the OECD. In their overview in Chapter 2, Chris Heady and his co-authors note that both the level of taxes and design of tax instruments affect the decisions of households to save, supply labour and invest in human capital; the decisions of firms to produce, create jobs, invest and innovate, as well as the choice of savings channels and assets by investors. Their chapter focuses on the effects of changes in tax structures on GDP per capita and its main determinants. It finds that, in general terms, corporate taxes are most harmful for growth, followed by personal income taxes, consumption taxes and then recurrent taxes on immovable property. It does not, however, set out a policy prescription for individual countries, noting that taxes depend on country-specific factors and that tax shifts require a non-trivial trade-off between tax policies that increase GDP per capita and equity concerns, which are likely to be evaluated differently by different countries.

In Chapter 3, Jane Gravelle addresses two issues on the impact of taxes and subsidies on investment. The first is the potential magnitude of effects on the economy from investment subsidies, including the enhancement of long-run standards of living in closed and open capital-importing economies. She finds that in a closed economy model, an investment tax incentive is likely to yield a very small benefit for a large welfare cost in terms of increases in sustainable consumption. For an open economy that imports capital, the economy can even suffer a welfare loss, depending on the elasticity of supply of imported capital, by increasing the return to non-resident suppliers of capital.

The second set of issues involve the pitfalls in the design of investment subsidies, including the difficulty of designing and enacting neutral subsidies that will not lead to welfare losses. Of the different forms of incentives, Gravelle argues that 'investment subsidies have generally favoured equipment investment, and arguments advanced for favouring these assets are difficult to justify. Large investment subsidies for debt-financed investment can lead to very low or negative tax burdens, which are difficult to justify on any grounds'.

Part II consists of three chapters. In Chapter 4, Rosanne Altshuler appraises the evidence on the impact of globalisation on corporate behaviour in the United States, and the implications for tax policy. She proposes several key lessons from recent experience and evidence, associated with US multinationals. First, both real and intangible (for example patents) capital and corporate profits are becoming increasingly internationally mobile and more responsive to international differences in tax rates. At the same time, governments are increasingly competing with each other to attract and retain these mobile resources. Altshuler's conclusion is that the taxation of international capital income cannot be isolated from the rest of the tax system. That system needs to be made simpler, with lower tax rates across broader tax bases in order to limit the extent of tax planning and protect domestic tax revenues.

Chapter 5, by Peter Sørensen, looks at one solution to the problem of taxing mobile capital while avoiding the need to sacrifice revenues from taxes on immobile tax bases – the 'dual income tax' system adopted by a number of Nordic countries in the early 1990s. This combines progressive taxation of labour income with a low flat uniform tax on all income from capital. Sørensen explains the historical background for the ambitious Nordic tax reforms and discusses the rationale for dual income taxation, and its implementation in Finland, Norway and Sweden. A central issue raised by the dual income tax is how to separate labour income from capital income and how to prevent taxpayers such as small businesses from shifting income from one tax base to the other to reduce their total tax liability. The chapter discusses alternative ways of achieving this split and describes the principles and methods adopted by the Nordic countries.

In Chapter 6, George Zodrow examines the impact of increasing globalisation for company income tax policy in small open economies, focusing on the implications of international capital (and labour) mobility and international tax competition. The chapter considers how robust the arguments are for setting zero or negative tax rates on capital income. This analysis pays particular attention to the implications of the existence of firm-specific and location-specific economic rents and the issues raised by various forms of international tax avoidance. Zodrow's conclusion is that 'setting company tax in a small open economy is an exceedingly difficult task, and no single tax structure will simultaneously deal with all the issues'. However, he argues that international tax considerations generally strengthen traditional closed-economy 'broad base, low rate' arguments.

Part III turns to labour taxation. In Chapter 7, John Creedy considers how far the large and complex literature on optimal income taxation can guide the practical design of income tax structures. He begins by showing that maximising welfare for even the simplest linear tax structure produces complex results unless highly restrictive assumptions are made. A more general consideration of optimal tax structures can lead to quite different results depending on the nature of the social welfare function being maximised. Creedy then considers marginal income tax reforms using a behavioural tax microsimulation model to illustrate such reforms in the context of the widely-used multi-step income tax function (calibrated to approximate the New Zealand income tax and transfer structure). Creedy shows that changes to the top marginal tax rate have little effect on progressivity and redistributive measures, and are dependent on the income distribution. He also shows that the labour supply decisions and welfare of individuals, even with similar preferences, can vary widely on introduction of a top marginal tax rate.

In Chapter 8, Guyonne Kalb shows how behavioural tax microsimulation models, which incorporate a large amount of detail on the relevant tax/transfer systems, can be used to model discrete labour supply choices in response to tax structure changes. Models for Australia and New Zealand are described, with separate models for each country estimated for single men, single women, single parents and couple families. Kalb derives average wage elasticities and compares these for a range of different subgroups. Comparing the results across the two countries, she finds that the magnitude of the elasticities are generally similar. However, whereas Australia conforms to the familiar pattern observed internationally, that single parents and married/de facto women are the most responsive demographic groups, in New Zealand these appear to be single men and women.

Finally, in Part III, Chapter 9 by Jacinta Dalgety and co-authors present evidence for New Zealand on the impact of a series of changes in financial incentives and support for working, including subsidised childcare, on sole parents' labour market behaviour. The chapter examines both the additional employment generated by these work incentives and the effects on the duration of benefit receipt. Separating policy impacts from wider economic changes is not straightforward; hence this chapter adopts a number of methods. A key finding from this exercise is that the introduction of in-work tax credits appeared to result in an estimated additional 8000 sole parents engaged in some form of paid employment. The number of sole parents working 20 hours or more per week (who qualified for the in-work tax credit) also appeared to increase, with numbers on benefits for sole parents falling by 12 per cent over four years.

Part IV examines the use of tax, and tax-related policies to address environmental externality issues. In Chapter 10, John Freebairn compares the differing effects of a carbon or emissions tax versus a tradable permit scheme aimed at reducing greenhouse gas emissions. He shows that within a conventional environmental economics framework (of public and private costs) the two interventions are equivalent in a world of perfect information and perfect global implementation. He then explores the consequences of introducing more realistic assumptions including imperfect information, technological innovation and information revelation over time. Freebairn concludes that, once these real-world considerations are allowed for, whether a carbon tax is superior to emissions permits depends on whether greater certainty regarding the 'cost increment' (price change) or greater certainty of emissions adjustment (quantity change) from the policy is preferred. Freebairn argues in favour of the greater price certainty associated with the carbon tax. He also concludes that a carbon *consumption* tax base is superior to a carbon *production* tax base; that is the tax should apply to domestic production plus imports, but exclude exports.

In Chapter 11, Suzi Kerr and Kelly Lock turn to a rather different environmental issue, that is, how public policy should respond to allocating the social costs of abating water pollution – in this case, Lake Rotorua, one of New Zealand's largest lakes. At issue here is a long and continuing episode of artificial nutrients being applied to farmland in Lake Rotorua's catchment area which are leaking into, and polluting, the lake. This chapter examines how the social benefits and costs of water quality improvements in Lake Rotorua are likely to be shared in the absence of a nutrient trading system and presents different perspectives on, and principles for, deciding how costs should be allocated. Kerr and Lock then show how different options for allocating nutrient allowances and achieving pollution reductions over time conform with those cost-sharing principles. They argue that, unlike typical textbook examples, there is no single 'correct' answer to the question of who should pay, but will depend on what the community thinks is fair and what will be politically feasible.

In a final Part V, two chapters examine lessons to be learned from past tax reform exercises in Australia and New Zealand. This is especially relevant for both these countries as they each consider significant medium-term reform to their tax and transfer systems. In Chapter 12, Greg Smith, an external member of the recent Australian Tax Review conducted by the Australian Treasury, examines the Australian case. Smith begins by detailing the extensive tax and transfer reform agenda pursued in Australia since 1983, broadly in pursuit of a 'broad base, low rate' system. At the same time tax and transfer arrangements continued to be based heavily on income, and on delivering relatively steep progressivity. As Smith puts it: '[t]he intrinsic complexities and idiosyncrasies of the income base and progressive rates provide ongoing fertile ground for reform-minded policy attention'. As a result future tax policy review must address 'high marginal tax rates, relatively high taxes on capital and saving relative to labour and current consumption, and ever-increasing complexity and compliance cost'. On a positive note, Smith suggests that a defining feature of Australian (and New Zealand) political economy over much of the last 25 years is the strong track record of reform in the aftermath of adverse economic times. Perhaps there will be a 'silver lining' to the global recession of the late-2000s.

Finally, in Chapter 13, Matt Benge and David Holland assess the case for reform of company taxation in New Zealand. Steering away from radical reform options, such as 'Allowance for Corporate Equity' (ACE) or cash-flow taxation, they concentrate on possible reforms to tax rates and structures within OECD norms. A cornerstone of New Zealand's tax paradigm, they argue, has been the alignment of the company and top personal tax rates. The chapter outlines the problems that have arisen from the divergence of these rates in recent years and examines a number of possible approaches, drawn from international experience, for resolving these problems in New Zealand. The conclusion the authors come to is that the preferred option would be to align the company and top personal tax rates and apply this to a broad tax base.

REFERENCES

Crawford, C. and J. Freedman (2009), 'Small business taxation', in Institute for Fiscal Studies (ed.), *Dimensions of Tax Design: The Mirrlees Review*, Oxford: Oxford University Press for the Institute for Fiscal Studies.

Devereux, M.P. (2008), 'Business taxation in a globalising world', *Oxford Review of Economic Policy*, **24**, 625–38.

Peter, K.S., S. Buttrick and D. Duncan (2008), *Global reform of personal income taxation 1981–2005: evidence from 189 countries*, Georgia State University, Andrew Young School of Policy Studies, Andrew Young School of Policy Studies Research Paper Series No. 08–08.

PART I

The impact of taxes on investment and productivity

2. Taxes and firm performance: evidence from the OECD

Åsa Johansson, Christopher Heady, Jens Arnold, Bert Brys and Laura Vartia*

2.1 INTRODUCTION

This chapter analyses the effects of changes in tax structures (the ways in which different tax instruments are designed and combined to generate revenues) on the performance of firms, and thus on the level and growth of GDP per capita. It draws on the results of a recent OECD study on tax and economic growth, described in Johansson et al. (2008).[1] Since practical tax policy has many objectives, the results presented here do not constitute policy recommendations, as the single-minded pursuit of GDP growth could compromise other policy objectives. In particular, the chapter draws attention to a number of instances in which there is a trade-off between growth and equity.

Focusing on tax structures rather than levels (as measured, for example, by the overall tax–GDP ratio) is desirable because cross-country differences in tax levels largely reflect societal choices as to the appropriate level of public spending, an issue that is beyond the scope of tax policy analysis. In addition, the focus on tax structures allows a consideration of revenue-neutral tax policy changes, and thus avoids the difficulty of taking account of how any changes in aggregate revenue might be reflected in changes in public expenditure. The importance of this second point can be seen by comparing (i) a tax revenue increase that finances increased infrastructure investment with (ii) a similar increase to finance increased social benefits. Policy (i) can be expected to have a better growth outcome than policy (ii), and therefore neither policy could be said to represent *the* effect of tax revenue on economic growth.

In practice, it is difficult to distinguish between the effects of tax policy on levels and on growth rates of GDP. Indeed, any policy that raises the level of GDP will increase the growth rate of GDP because changes in GDP levels take time. Also, transitional growth may be long-lasting, and so it has not proved possible to distinguish effects on long-run growth from transitional growth effects, although some elements of the tax system are likely to influence long-run growth. For instance, it is possible that tax changes that encourage innovation and entrepreneurship may have persistent long-run growth effects, while those that affect investment also can have long-lasting effects on growth that fade out in the long run. In contrast, tax changes affecting labour supply will have only a transitory effect on growth. This chapter looks at consequences of taxes for both GDP per capita levels and their transitional growth rates but concentrates on the effects of taxation on the behaviour of firms in terms of investment and total factor productivity growth, as these are the most likely to produce long-term changes in growth rates. Despite this focus on firm behaviour, both the macroeconomic results in section 2.2 and the policy discussion in section 2.4 also reflect household responses to taxation in the form of labour supply and savings decisions.

The remainder of the chapter is organised as follows. Section 2.2 reports on the effects of changes in the tax mix between major categories of taxes at the macroeconomic level, showing that income taxes are more harmful to growth than consumption or property taxes. In view of these results, section 2.3 examines the effects of both corporate and personal income taxes on investment and productivity growth, at both the industry level and the firm level. Section 2.4 discusses the policy implications from these results, and section 2.5 provides a brief conclusion.

2.2 THE OVERALL TAX MIX

All OECD countries rely on a mix of taxes on consumption, property, personal income (defined in this chapter to include employee and employer social security contributions and payroll taxes) and corporate income. Setting the right mix is important, because the growth effects of collecting revenue from different sources can be very different. For example, Kneller et al. (1999) find that taxes on income have a negative effect on growth while taxes on consumption have no effect.

In order to analyse the effect of the tax mix in detail and over as long a period as possible, estimates at the macro level were obtained by introducing a set of tax structure indicators into a panel regression of GDP per capita covering 21 OECD countries over the period 1970–2005 (for details see Arnold, 2008). The setup also takes into account the fact that more use of a given tax instrument reduces the amount of revenues that need to be raised from other taxes, when considering revenue-neutral tax changes. This is achieved by always omitting one element of the tax mix in each regression (indicated in the bottom line of Table 2.1) and this component

Table 2.1 Estimated cross-country effects of the tax mix on long-run GDP per capita[a]

The estimated empirical model is:

$$\Delta \ln y_{it} = \Phi_i (\ln y_{it-1} - \theta_1 \ln s^k_{it} - \theta_2 \ln h_{it} + \theta_3 n_{it} + \Sigma \theta_j V^j_{it} - a_{it})$$

$$+ b_{1i} \Delta \ln s^k_{it} + b_{2i} \Delta \ln h_{it} + b_{3i} \Delta n_{it} + \Sigma b_{ji} \Delta V^j_{it} + \varepsilon_{it}$$

Dependent Variable: Log GDP p.c.	(1)	(2)	(3)	(4)	(5)
Baseline model					
Physical capital	0.18***	0.25***	0.18***	0.16***	0.21
	(0.05)	(0.05)	(0.05)	(0.05)	(0.45)
Human capital	1.19***	1.30***	1.18***	1.40***	1.57***
	(0.13)	(0.12)	(0.13)	(0.11)	(0.11)
Population growth	−0.08***	−0.08***	−0.07***	−0.07***	−0.07***
	(0.01)	(0.01)	(0.01)	(0.01)	(0.01)
Control variable					
Overall tax burden (Total revenues / GDP)	−0.27***	−0.24***	−0.26***	−0.22***	−0.14***
	(0.05)	(0.05)	(0.05)	(0.04)	(0.04)
Tax structure variables					
Total taxes	−0.98***				
	(0.20)				
Personal income taxes		−1.13***			
		(0.19)			
Corporate income taxes		−2.01***			
		(0.32)			
Consumption and property taxes			0.93***		
			(0.20)		
Consumption taxes (excl. property taxes)				0.74***	0.72***
				(0.18)	(0.19)
Property taxes				1.45***	
				(0.43)	
Property taxes: recurrent taxes on immovable property					2.47***
					(0.84)

Table 2.1 (continued)

Dependent Variable: Log GDP p.c.	(1)	(2)	(3)	(4)	(5)
Property taxes: other property taxes					−0.34 (0.51)
Observations	696	675	696	696	698
Revenue-neutrality achieved by adjusting	Cons. & Prop. Taxes	Cons. & Prop. Taxes	Income Taxes	Income Taxes	Income Taxes

Note:

[a] In the estimated model, y refers to output per capita, s^k to the investment rate into physical capital, h to human capital, n to the population growth rate, respectively. The vector V contains a set of policy variables. All equations include short-run dynamics, country-specific intercepts and country-specific time controls. Standard errors are in brackets. *: significant at 10% level; ** at 5% level; *** at 1% level.

is assumed to be absorbing changes in the other taxes that are included in the regression, to maintain revenue neutrality.

The interpretation of the results needs to take account of three important aspects of the estimation procedure. First, the estimated equation does not simply look across countries and examine whether those with one sort of tax mix have higher GDP than others, which carries the risk of mistakenly attributing some of the differences between countries to taxes when they are really caused by something else. Instead, it is looking at changes in these variables and examining how each country's GDP changes when its tax mix changes. This minimises the risks associated with simple cross-country analysis and has the added advantage of capturing the effect that is of interest to policy makers: how will GDP respond if they change the tax mix? Second, as the estimates are based on the changes in the tax mix that have been observed in OECD countries, they show the effects of fairly modest changes in the tax mix and do not necessarily apply to more substantial changes. Finally, to aid the interpretation of the results, they are presented in terms of their effects on the long-run level of GDP, making the conservative assumption that tax mix changes do not alter the long-run growth rate of GDP. As mentioned in the introduction, there are not sufficient data available to test whether this assumption is correct.

Table 2.1 reports the long-run effects of various revenue neutral tax shifts, based on the estimated dynamic equation, which also includes other basic growth determinants from a 'baseline model' as well as the overall tax burden as a control variable.[2] Column (1) shows a negative coefficient on the share of (personal and corporate) income taxes, indicating that an increase in the share of these taxes that is balanced by an decreased share of consumption and property taxes will reduce long-run GDP per capita and thus reduce growth. Column (2) looks at the different effects of personal and corporate taxes and shows that an increase in corporate income taxes (financed by an increase in consumption and property taxes) has a stronger negative effect on GDP per capita than a similar increase in personal income taxation.

Columns (3)–(5) report on a shift in the opposite direction: increasing consumption and property taxes while reducing income taxes. Column (3) shows a positive effect that is similarly-sized to the negative effect reported in column (1). Results reported in column (4) break up the effect of an increase in consumption and property taxes, allowing a reduction in income taxation. While both of them are associated with higher GDP per capita than relying on income taxes, the effect is significantly larger for property taxes. Column (5) separates recurrent taxes on immovable property from all other property taxes and the positive effect on GDP is significantly larger for recurrent taxes on immovable property than for all other property taxes and consumption taxes. Further analysis (not reported in Table 2.1) of the countries that separate data for recurrent taxes on immovable property into those levied on households from those levied on corporations suggests that taxes levied on households have the least adverse effect on GDP per capita. However, it should be noted that this result is based on about half the number of countries represented in the results reported in Table 2.1.

In summary, these results suggest a 'tax and growth ranking' with recurrent taxes on immovable property being the least harmful (or most beneficial) tax instrument in terms of its effect on long-run GDP per capita, followed by consumption taxes (and other property taxes), personal income taxes and corporate income taxes. An idea of the possible magnitude of these differences is given by the estimates of the effect on GDP per capita of a shift of 1 per cent of tax revenues from income taxes to consumption and property taxes. These suggest that such a revenue-neutral shift would increase GDP per capita by between a quarter of a percentage point and one percentage point in the long run depending on the empirical specification.

2.3 THE EFFECTS OF PERSONAL AND CORPORATE INCOME TAXES ON FIRM PERFORMANCE

2.3.1 Personal Income Taxes

This chapter includes social security contributions and payroll taxes in its definition of personal income taxes, and these taxes can affect the relative price of capital and labour and so could lead to a reallocation of inputs within and between firms and/or industries that could have transitional growth effects. For instance, a change in the relative factor price could lead to less usage of one or more of the production inputs in a firm and/or industry. It is possible that all inputs not used in this firm/industry are either reallocated to other less productive firms/industries or not used at all, thereby lowering the efficiency in the use of production inputs, that is, total factor productivity (TFP) growth.

It is also possible that labour taxes influence foreign direct investment adversely by increasing labour cost in the host country. For instance, Hajkova et al. (2006) found that the impact on FDI of labour taxes is generally substantially larger than that of cross-border effective corporate tax rates.[3] This can hinder technology transfers and spill-overs of best practices from multinationals to domestic firms, thereby reducing TFP.

Also, top marginal income tax rates have a theoretically ambiguous impact on TFP via entrepreneurship by affecting risk-taking by individuals. On the one hand, high taxes reduce the post-tax income of a successful entrepreneur relative to an unsuccessful one and can reduce entrepreneurial activity and TFP growth. On the other hand, high tax rates provide for increased risk-sharing with the government if potential losses can be written off against other income, which may encourage entrepreneurial activity (Myles, 2009). However, Gentry and Hubbard (2000) suggest that the higher is the difference between the marginal tax rates when successful and unsuccessful (a measure of tax progressivity) the lower is risk-taking as the extra tax that applies to high profits is greater than the tax saving that is produced by losses, effectively reducing the strength of the risk-sharing effect.

Estimating the effect of taxation on TFP based on industry-level data is difficult as available tax indicators are not differentiated by industries, although their impact may vary across industries. As discussed in Vartia (2008), an indirect way to test for these tax effects is to identify industry-specific characteristics relevant for different tax policies, and examine the interaction between these characteristics and the appropriate taxes. For example, the estimation assumes that one industry characteristic that affects the sensitivity of TFP to social security contributions is labour intensity. If the results of the econometric analysis support the hypothesis that the negative impact of taxes on TFP is stronger in certain industries due to these salient characteristics, then the estimated coefficient of the interaction term should be negative whereas if tax incentives have a stronger positive effect on TFP in industries with certain characteristics, the coefficient should be positive. One important caveat to this approach is that the estimated effect only captures the effect of a tax that is related to industry characteristics. Any direct effect of the tax on TFP (unrelated to the industry characteristics) is captured in the fixed effects.

TFP at the industry level is calculated as the 'Solow-residual' from a production function where the factor shares in the production function are proxied by the cost shares in value-added. The empirical results draw on a specification that captures two empirical regularities, namely technological catch-up with the leading firms/industries and persistence of TFP levels over time (Scarpetta and Tressel, 2002; Griffith et al., 2006). The same empirical approach is used in assessing the effects of corporate taxes on TFP below.

The main empirical results of the effect of personal income taxes on TFP are shown in Table 2.2. As suggested above, it seems reasonable to assume that the impact of social security contributions (SSCs) on firms' behaviour should depend on their labour intensity. Thus, column (1) reports on the effect of introducing an interaction term between labour intensity and SSCs. The coefficient on this term is negative and significant at the 5 per cent level, indicating that SSCs have a negative influence on TFP and that this effect is larger in labour-intensive industries. Column (2) shows a similar result when only employers' SSCs are considered. However, the magnitude of the effect of SSCs on the long-run level of TFP is estimated to be relatively small.

When considering the effects of top marginal income tax rates on TFP growth, it is reasonable to suppose that any effect will be stronger in industries with a high rate of new firm entry. This is partly because new firms are more risky and partly because new firms are more likely to be either unincorporated or closely held corporations, and so more likely to take account of the personal tax treatment of profits than is a publicly traded corporation. The results in column (3) support this supposition by showing that top marginal personal income tax rates have a more negative effect on TFP in industries characterised by high firm entry rates.

In order to obtain an approximate idea of the implications of this result for long-run growth, a simulation experiment was conducted and indicated that the effect of a reduction of the top marginal tax rate from

Table 2.2 Estimated effects of income taxes on TFP: industry level[a]

The estimated empirical model is:

$$\Delta \ln TFP_{i,j,t} = \delta_1 \Delta \ln TFP_{F,j,t} + \delta_2 \ln(TFP_{i,j,t-1}/TFP_{F,j,t-1}) + \delta_3 HK_{i,j,t} + \beta INDcharac_j{*}TAX_{i,t-1} + \varphi X_{i,j,t1} + \Sigma_i \Sigma_t D_{i,t} + \Sigma_j D_j + \varepsilon_{i,j,t}$$

Dependent variable: TFP growth	(1)	(2)	(3)	(4)
Basic model				
Leader TFP growth	0.06 (0.02)***	0.06 (0.02)***	0.05 (0.02)**	0.06 (0.02)***
TFP relative to leader TFP ($t-1$)	−0.01 (0.00)***	−0.01 (0.00)***	−0.01 (0.00)***	−0.01 (0.00)***
Human capital ($t-1$)	0.01 (0.00)**	0.01 (0.00)**	0.01 (0.00)**	0.01 (0.00)**
Interaction between industry characteristics and tax				
Labour intensity and social security contributions ($t-1$)	−0.01 (0.00)**			
Labour intensity and employer's social security contributions ($t-1$)		−0.01 (0.00)**		
Labour intensity and social security contributions ($t-1$) with low adm. extension				−0.01 (0.01)
Labour intensity and social security contributions ($t-1$) with high adm. extension				−0.01 (0.00)**
Entry rate and top personal income tax ($t-1$)			−0.04 (0.01)***	
Other policy variables				
Anti-competitive regulation impact ($t-1$)	−0.03 (0.01)***	−0.03 (0.01)***	−0.01 (0.01)	−0.03 (0.01)***
Job turnover and employment protection legislation			−0.00 (0.00)	

Dependent variable: TFP growth	(1)	(2)	(3)	(4)
Observations	2802	2802	2910	2802
Fixed effects:				
Country*year	yes	yes	yes	yes
Industry	yes	yes	yes	yes

Note:

[a] In the estimated empirical model $\Delta \ln TFP_{i,j,t}$, $\Delta \ln TFP_{F,j,t}$, $\ln(TFP_{i,j,t-1}/TFP_{F,j,t-1})$, $HK_{i,j,t}$, $INDcharac_j{*}TAX_{i,t-1}$, $X_{i,j,t-1}$, $\Sigma_i\Sigma_t D_{i,t} + \Sigma_j D_j$ refer respectively to (i) TFP growth in a country i, industry j and year t; (ii) TFP growth in an industry in the best practice country; (iii) the relative difference between TFP in an industry and in that industry in the best practice country; (iv) a human capital measure; (v) the interaction term between industry characteristics and the relevant tax; (vi) other policy variables and (vii) fixed effects. The level of TFP is measured as the 'Solow-residual' from a production function. The anti-competitive regulation impact is an industry-specific measure of the degree to which each industry in the economy is exposed to anti-competitive regulation in non-manufacturing sectors. In column (4) the coefficients of the interaction term between social security contributions and labour intensity are distinguished by the degree of administrative extension of collective wage agreements. In columns (1)–(2) and (4) the interaction term between job turnover and employment protection legislation is dropped as there may be some collinearity problems related to job turnover and labour intensity. The estimation sample includes 13 OECD countries and 21 industries over the 1981–2001 period. The results are robust to introducing other interaction terms with other tax variables. Robust standard errors are reported in the parentheses. * denotes significance at 10%; ** at 5%; *** at 1%.

55 per cent to 50 per cent on the average yearly TFP growth rate (over 10 years) would be 0.05 percentage points larger for industries with the median firm entry rate than for industries with the lowest level of firm entry. Under the assumption that the effect of top marginal rates are close to zero in industries with the lowest level of firm entry (that is, that the top marginal rate has no direct effect, unrelated to the rate of firm entry), this may be interpreted as a median effect. The effect of this tax reduction on TFP depends on the industry structure and this tax cut would increase the average annual productivity growth rate by 0.06 percentage points more in an industry at the 75th percentile of firm entry than in an industry at the 25th percentile of the distribution of firm entry.

Column (4) shows weak evidence that the negative effect of SSCs tends to be stronger in countries with a sizeable administrative extension of collective wage agreements to non-unionised firms. The extension of wage agreements may magnify the effects of SSC increases on labour cost by making it more difficult to shift the burden of this increase onto workers' wages and more so in industries that are more labour-intensive.

2.3.2 Corporate Income Taxes

Corporate taxes can be expected to reduce investment by firms as they increase the user cost of capital. In addition, they can be expected to reduce TFP growth for a number of reasons. First, as with labour taxes, corporate taxes can distort relative factor prices resulting in a reallocation of resources towards possibly less productive sectors (for example the non-corporate sector) which may lower total factor productivity (Boersch-Supan, 1998). Second, complex corporate tax codes can cause high tax compliance costs for firms and high administrative burdens for governments, which absorb resources that could be used for productive activities, causing productivity and efficiency losses. Third, high corporate taxes may reduce incentives to invest in innovative activities by reducing their after-tax return. Fourth, to the extent that corporate taxes reduce FDI and the presence of foreign multinational enterprises they can hinder technology transfers and knowledge spillovers to domestic firms.

In order to test the impact on investment and TFP, empirical evidence was obtained from both firm-level data covering a sample of 14 European OECD countries and industry-level data covering 21 industries in 16 OECD countries.

Investment

The empirical results, both at firm and industry level, assessing the effect of taxes on investment were obtained by introducing the tax-adjusted user cost in a standard investment equation with adjustment costs of capital (see Schwellnus and Arnold, 2008 and Vartia, 2008 for details). In addition to the standard user cost components (the required rate of return to the investment, the economic depreciation rate and anticipated capital gain/loss due to a change in before-tax price of the asset) the tax-adjusted user cost takes into account taxes on profits and the present value of the tax savings from depreciation allowances. The industry-specific user cost is constructed as a weighted average of the asset-specific user cost where the weights are the share of each asset in total industry investment.

The main empirical findings at the firm level are summarised in Table 2.3 (see Schwellnus and Arnold, 2008, for details). Column (1) shows that increases in the tax-adjusted user cost of capital are found to reduce investment at the firm level, while column (2) shows that this effect is larger for more profitable firms. A simulation experiment suggests that a reduction of the statutory corporate tax rate from 35 per cent to 30 per cent reduces the user cost by approximately 2.8 per cent. Applying the estimated long-run tax adjusted user cost elasticity (from column (1)), this implies a long-run increase of the investment-to-capital ratio of approximately 1.9 per cent.

Table 2.3 Estimated effects of corporate taxes on investment: firm level[a]

The estimated empirical model is:

$$(I/K)_{icst} = \beta_1(I/K)_{ics,t-1} + \beta_2(I/K)^2_{ics,t-1} + \beta_3(Y/K)_{ics,t-1} + \beta_4(CF/K)_{ics,t-1} + \beta_5 UCtax_{cs,t-1} + \gamma_s + \gamma_{ct} + \theta_{icst}$$

Dependent variable: investment-to-capital ratio	(1)	(2)	(3)
Basic model			
Investment-to-capital ratio ($t-1$)	0.532***	0.531***	0.534***
	(0.026)	(0.026)	(0.026)
Investment-to-capital ratio squared ($t-1$)	−0.415***	−0.414***	−0.418***
	(0.025)	(0.025)	(0.025)
Output-to-capital ratio ($t-1$)	0.000***	0.000***	0.000
	(0.000)	(0.000)	(0.000)
Cashflow-to-capital ratio ($t-1$)	0.048***	0.048***	0.047***
	(0.003)	(0.003)	(0.003)
Tax adjusted user cost ($t-1$)	−0.829**	0.147	
	(0.410)	(0.689)	
Interactions between firm and sector characteristics and tax			
Profitability and tax adjusted user cost		−0.723**	
		(0.351)	
Tax adjusted user cost (Age < 6&Empl < 30)			−0.339
			(0.497)
Tax adjusted user cost (Age < 6&Empl > = 30)			0.401
			(0.476)
Tax adjusted user cost (Age > = 6&Empl < 30)			−0.832*
			(0.437)
Tax adjusted user cost (Age > = 6&Empl > = 30)			−1.039**
			(0.430)
Long-run tax adjusted user cost elasticity	−0.69		
Observations	211 599	211 599	211 599
Fixed effects:			
Sector	yes	yes	yes
Size–age	no	no	yes
Country–year	yes	yes	yes
R^2	0.12	0.12	0.12

Notes:

[a] In the estimated empirical model (i) $(I/K)_{ics,t}$ denotes the investment-to-capital ratio; (ii) $(I/K)_{ics,t-1}$ its lag; (iii) $(I/K)^2_{ics,t-1}$ its squared lag; (iv) $(Y/K)_{ics,t-1}$ the lag of the output-to-capital ratio; (v) $(CF/K)_{ics,t-1}$ the lag of the cashflow-to-capital ratio; (vi) $UCtax_{cs,t-1}$ the lag of the tax adjusted user cost; and (vii) γ_s and γ_{ct} sector and country-year fixed effects, respectively. The estimation sample contains 12 European OECD countries and only observations with investment ratios between 0 and 1. Robust standard errors corrected for clustering at the country-sector level in parentheses. * denotes significant at 10%; ** at 5%; *** at 1%.

Column (3) shows that the size of the negative tax effect on investment appears to be similar for small and large firms (measured by the number of employees). In contrast, older firms' investment appears to be more negatively affected by increases in the tax-adjusted user cost than young firms, to the extent that it is only the effect on older firms that is statistically significant. One possible explanation is that young firms are generally less profitable than older firms and therefore less affected by corporate taxation. The other explanation may be that among young firms there is a disproportionately high share of small firms that benefit from exemptions or reduced rates.

The main results obtained at the industry level are summarised in Table 2.4 (see Vartia, 2008, for details). Columns (1) and (2) report the results of using two different estimation techniques. Investment is clearly negatively affected by increases in corporate taxation but the long-run user cost elasticity is estimated to vary between −0.4 and −1, depending on the empirical specification. A simulation experiment indicates that a cut in the statutory corporate tax rate from 35 per cent to 30 per cent would increase the long-run investment–capital ratio by 1.0 per cent or 2.6 per cent, depending on the specification. These two estimates at the industry level lie either side of the firm-level estimate.

Productivity

Turning to the empirical findings for TFP, the approach was based on identifying industry-specific characteristics that are expected to cause a differential effect of corporate taxes on industry TFP in the same way as in the analysis of personal income taxes (above). In particular, the estimation approach (both at firm and industry level) assumes that corporate taxes affect TFP more in firms and industries with higher profitability. Also, to assess the effect of tax incentives for R&D expenditures on TFP, it is assumed that the effect is greater in industries with higher R&D intensity.

Table 2.5 summarises the main empirical results concerning the influence of corporate taxes, measured by the main statutory corporate tax rate, on TFP at the firm level (see Schwellnus and Arnold, 2008, for details). Column (1) shows that lowering corporate taxes is estimated to boost firm-level TFP in profitable industries.

As with the results in Table 2.2, related to the effect of income taxes on TFP, a simulation experiment was carried out using the results shown in column (1) of Table 2.5. This suggests that the effect of a reduction of the corporate tax rate from 35 per cent to 30 per cent on the average yearly TFP growth rate (over 10 years) would be 0.4 percentage points higher for firms in industries with median profitability than for firms in industries with the lowest level of profitability. Under the assumption that the effects

Table 2.4 Estimated effects of corporate taxes on investment: industry level[a]

The estimated empirical model is:

$$\ln(I/K)_{i,j,t} = \beta_1 \ln(I/K)_{i,j,t-1} + \beta_2 UCtax_{i,j,t-1} + \beta_3 D\ln Y_{i,j,t-1} + \beta_4 PMR_{i,j,t-1} + \varepsilon_{i,j,t}$$

Dependent variable: log of investment-to-capital	(1) OLS	(2) System GMM
Log of investment-to-capital ratio ($t-1$)	0.66	0.73
	(0.02)***	(0.05)***
Log of tax adjusted user cost ($t-1$)	−0.12	−0.26
	(0.03)***	(0.11)***
Log difference in value added ($t-1$)	0.35	0.65
	(0.10)***	(0.07)***
Anti-competitive regulation impact ($t-1$)	−0.21	0.33
	(0.08)***	(0.39)
Long-run adjusted user cost elasticity	−0.35	−0.98
Observations	3818	3818
Hansen J test		
Prob > chi2		0.334
Fixed effects		
Country*industry	yes	
Year	yes	yes

Note:

[a] In the estimated empirical model $(I/K)_{i,j,t}$, $UCtax_{i,j,t-1}$, $Dln Y_{i,j,t-1}$ and $PMR_{i,j,t-1}$ refer respectively to (i) investment-to-capital ratio in country i, industry j and year t; (ii) the tax-adjusted user cost; (iii) the relative change in value added; and (iv) the impact of anti-competitive regulation. The anti-competitive regulation impact is an industry-specific measure of the degree to which each industry in the economy is exposed to anti-competitive regulation in non-manufacturing sectors. The long-run elasticity is computed as $\beta_2/(1-\beta_1)$. The effects are similar when a non-log version of the investment equation is estimated. The estimation sample includes 16 OECD countries and 21 industries for the period 1983–2001. Robust standard errors are reported in the parentheses. * denotes significance at 10%; ** at 5%; *** at 1%.

of corporate taxation are close to zero for firms with the lowest tax base (that is, assuming that there is no direct effect of the tax, independently of firm profitability), this may be interpreted as a median effect. The effect of this tax cut on TFP depends on the industry structure and this reduction would increase the average annual productivity growth rate by 0.4 percentage points more in an industry at the 75th percentile of profitability than in an industry at the 25th percentile of profitability.

Column (2) shows that the negative effect of corporate taxes is uniform

Table 2.5 Estimated effects of corporate taxes on TFP: firm level[a]

The estimated empirical model is

$$\Delta \ln TFP_{icst} = d_1 D\ln TFP_{Fcst} + d_2 \ln(TFP_{isc,t-1}/TFP_{Fcs,t-1}) + d_3 Profit_s^* TAX_{c,t-1} + \gamma_s + \gamma_{ct} + \theta_{icst}$$

Dependent variable: TFP growth	(1)	(2)	(3)
Basic model			
Leader TFP growth	0.173***	0.173***	0.501***
	(0.019)	(0.019)	(0.022)
TFP relative to leader ($t-1$)	−0.190***	−0.190***	−0.115***
	(0.015)	(0.015)	(0.010)
Interactions between firm and sector characteristics and tax			
Profitability and tax	−0.307**		
	(0.128)		
Profitability and tax		−0.145	
(Age < 6&Empl < 30)		(0.176)	
Profitability and tax		−0.275**	
(Age < = 6&Empl > = 30)		(0.130)	
Profitability and tax		−0.285**	
(Age > 6&Empl < 30)		(0.127)	
Profitability and tax		−0.357***	
(Age > = 6&Empl > = 30)		(0.134)	
Declining and profitability			−0.038
and tax			(0.088)
Rising and profitability and			−0.251***
tax			(0.090)
Observations	287727	287727	287727
Fixed effects:			
Sector	yes	no	no
Sector–size–age	no	yes	no
Sector–catchup	no	no	yes
Country–year	yes	yes	yes
R^2	0.10	0.10	0.44

Note:

[a] In the estimated empirical model (i) $\Delta\ln TFP_{icst}$ denotes TFP growth in firm i, country c, sector s and year t; (ii) $D\ln TFP_{Fcst}$ denotes TFP growth in the technological leader firm; (iii) $(TFP_{ics,t-1}/TFP_{Fcs,t-1})$ denotes the inverse of distance to the leader; (iv) $Profit_s{*}TAX_{c,t}$ the interaction between profitability and the corporate tax; and (v) γ_s and γ_{ct} sector and country-year fixed effects, respectively. The estimation sample contains 12 European OECD countries over the period 1998–2004. TFP is the residual of a Cobb–Douglas production function estimated at the country-sector level. Robust standard errors corrected for clustering at the country-sector level in parentheses. * denotes significant at 10%; ** at 5%; *** at 1%.

across firms of different size and age classes, except for firms that are both small and young (where the effect is smaller and statistically insignificant). This may be due to some countries' exemptions or reduced rates targeted at start-up firms, which would reduce the amount of their corporate tax payments. Column (3) shows that 'rising' firms[4] that are in the process of catching up with the technological frontier are particularly affected by corporate taxes. This could be because such firms rely heavily on retained earnings to finance their growth. Even in sectors with low average profitability there is a subset of highly profitable firms that catch up with the technological frontier.

Table 2.6 reports the main empirical results obtained at the industry level, again using the main statutory corporate tax rate as the measure of corporate taxation (see Vartia, 2008, for details). Column (1) shows that lowering corporate taxes is estimated to boost TFP in profitable industries. A similar simulation experiment to that carried out on the results presented in Table 2.5 suggests that the effect (over 10 years) of a reduction of the corporate tax rate from 35 per cent to 30 per cent on the average yearly TFP growth rate would be 0.08 percentage points higher for industries with the median profitability than for an industry with the lowest level of profitability. As mentioned above, this may be interpreted as a median effect if one is prepared to assume that there is no direct effect of the tax (independent of profitability). The effect of this tax cut on TFP depends on the industry structure and this reduction would increase the average annual productivity growth rate by 0.08 percentage points more in an industry at the 75th percentile of profitability than in an industry at the 25th percentile of profitability. This estimate is considerably smaller than that obtained from the analysis of firm-level data.

Column (2) reports the effect of tax incentives for R&D spending, which is obtained by using the B index. This index measures the minimum value of before-tax income that a firm needs to cover the cost of R&D investment where the cost is standardised to one dollar. R&D tax incentives are measured as one minus the B index as a proxy of the generosity of R&D tax incentives. This shows that R&D tax incentives are estimated to raise TFP and that this effect is larger in R&D-intensive industries. However, the average effect of tax incentives on the level of TFP is rather small. A simulation experiment indicates that the effect on the annual TFP growth rate of an increase of the tax incentives from 10 per cent to 15 per cent (equivalent to a 5 cents increase in tax subsidy per dollar invested in R&D) would be 0.01 percentage points larger for an industry having the median R&D intensity than for an industry with the lowest level of R&D intensity. Again, this may be interpreted as a median effect if it is

Table 2.6 Estimated effects of corporate taxes on TFP: industry level[a]

The estimated empirical model is:

$$\Delta \ln TFP_{i,j,t} = \delta_1 \Delta \ln TFP_{F,j,t} + \delta_2 \ln(TFP_{i,j,t-1}/TFP_{F,j,t-1}) + \delta_3 HK_{i,j,t} + \beta INDcharac_j{*}TAX_{i,t-1} + \varphi X_{i,j,t-1} + \Sigma_i \Sigma_t D_{i,t} + \Sigma_j D_j + \varepsilon_{i,j,t}$$

Dependent variable: TFP growth	(1)	(2)
Basic model		
Leader TFP growth	0.04	0.05
	(0.02)*	(0.02)**
TFP relative to leader TFP ($t-1$)	−0.01	−0.01
	(0.00)***	(0.00)***
Human capital ($t-1$)	0.01	0.01
	(0.00)**	(0.00)**
Interactions between industry characteristics and tax		
Profitability and corporate tax ($t-1$)	−0.04	
	(0.01)***	
R&D intensity and R&D tax incentives ($t-1$)		0.003
		(0.001)**
Other policy variables		
Anti-competitive regulation impact ($t-1$)	−0.01	−0.01
	(0.01)**	(0.01)**
Job turnover and employment protection legislation	−0.00	−0.00
	(0.00)	(0.00)
Observations	2910	2767
Fixed effects:		
Country*year	yes	yes
Industry	yes	yes

Note:

[a] In the estimated empirical model $\Delta \ln TFP_{i,j,t}$, $\Delta \ln TFP_{F,j,t}$, $\ln(TFP_{i,j,t-1}/TFP_{F,j,t-1})$, $HK_{i,j,t}$, $INDcharac_j{*}TAX_{i,t-1}$, $X_{i,j,t-1}$, $\Sigma_i \Sigma_t D_{i,t} + \Sigma_j D_j$ refer respectively to (i) TFP growth in a country i, industry j and year t; (ii) TFP growth in an industry in the best practice country; (iii) the relative difference between TFP in an industry and in that industry in the best practice country; (iv) a human capital measure; (v) the interaction term between industry characteristics and the relevant tax; (vi) other policy variables; and (vii) fixed effects. TFP is measured as the 'Solow-residual' from a production function. The anti-competitive regulation impact is an industry-specific measure of the degree to which each industry in the economy is exposed to anti-competitive regulation in non-manufacturing sectors. The estimation sample includes 13 OECD countries and 21 industries over the 1981–2001 period. The results are robust to introducing other interaction terms with other tax variables. Robust standard errors are reported in the parentheses. * denotes significance at 10%; ** at 5%; *** at 1%.

assumed that the effect of tax subsidies is close to zero in industries with very low R&D intensity. The effect of R&D incentives could potentially be larger in R&D-intensive industries. Indeed, this increase in tax incentives is estimated to raise the average annual productivity growth rate by 0.09 percentage points more in an industry at the 75th percentile of the distribution of R&D intensity than in a sector at the 25th percentile of R&D intensity.

This result should not be taken as necessarily supporting the use of R&D incentives to promote growth. This is because these incentives can cost considerable amounts of foregone revenue and, to achieve revenue-neutrality, would need to be compensated by tax increases elsewhere. One obvious source of compensating revenue would be from an increase in the corporate tax rate, but we have just seen that this would reduce TFP growth and investment. Unfortunately, the estimates presented here are not sufficiently precise to say whether or not increased R&D incentives financed by increased corporate tax rates would increase growth, and so no firm conclusion is possible from these results.

An alternative to using the main statutory corporate tax rate in the estimation of the effect of corporate taxes on TFP would have been to use effective corporate tax rates, which take account of the definition of the tax base as well as the tax rate. Effective tax rates are derived from theoretical investment models. Depending on the assumptions of the model the effective rates can refer to a marginal effective tax rate (METR) which is applied to incremental investment projects earning just their minimum required return or to an average effective tax rate (AETR) which is applied to discrete investment projects earning some economic rent.

To test the difference that this would make, empirical analysis was undertaken using data on the effective tax rates computed by the Institute for Fiscal Studies (IFS) based on the methodology of Devereux and Griffith (2003). The focus is on two important elements of corporate tax codes: the depreciation allowances and statutory corporate tax rates.

The empirical results using industry-level data on a panel of 12 OECD countries covering 21 industries over the 1981–2001 period suggest that the average effective corporate tax (AETR) has a negative effect on TFP. A simulation experiment indicates that the effect of a reduction of the effective tax rate from 35 per cent to 30 per cent on the average yearly TFP growth rate (over 10 years) would be 0.1 percentage points larger for an industry with the median profitability than for an industry with the lowest level of profitability. This is slightly larger than the results derived from the estimates reported in Table 2.6.

2.4 POLICY IMPLICATIONS

The estimates presented in sections 2.2 and 2.3 can be seen as some sort of average effect for the countries whose data are included. This means that they cannot be used directly to predict what will happen in any particular country. The tax policy changes that are most likely to increase growth in any country will depend on its starting point, in terms of both its current tax system and the areas (such as employment, investment or productivity growth) in which its current economic performance is relatively poor. In addition, the estimates are based on the relatively small tax policy changes that most OECD countries have undertaken and cannot be used to estimate the impact of larger changes. Nonetheless, the estimates do provide a basis for the serious consideration of a number of directions for tax reform.

In examining these directions, governments will need to take account of other factors apart from the growth of GDP. Issues of revenue sufficiency, equity, simplicity and compliance costs are just some examples of the factors that are often considered. Thus the suggestion that reducing corporate taxes can increase the level and, possibly, the rate of growth of GDP is not sufficient on its own to recommend the policy. It is not possible to discuss all the relevant policy concerns here but attention will be given to the key issue of equity.

2.4.1 Growth Promoting Tax Policies

The results presented in section 2.2 suggest a 'tax and growth ranking' with recurrent taxes on immovable property being the preferred tax instrument in terms of long-run GDP per capita, followed by consumption taxes (and other property taxes), personal income taxes and corporate income taxes. This ranking is consistent with earlier empirical results (for example Kneller et al., 1999) and is readily explained in theoretical terms. The growth effects of each type of tax are considered in turn below (see Johansson et al., 2008, for a more detailed discussion).

- *Recurrent taxes on immovable property* (especially residential property) are relatively good for growth because most OECD countries provide various tax preferences for owner-occupied housing (such as tax deductibility of interest on house loans and exemption from capital gains tax), which result in a misallocation of capital towards housing, away from other investments. In this situation, the pre-tax rate of return on housing investment is below the pre-tax rate of return on investment elsewhere in the economy. This implies that increasing recurrent taxes on immovable property will shift some investment out of housing into higher return investments and so increase the rate of growth.

- *Taxes on property transactions* – another major form of property tax – also have the benefit of shifting investment out of housing into higher-return activities. However, they have the disadvantage of discouraging housing transactions and thus the reallocation of housing to its most productive use, thus reducing growth. Other property taxes – on financial transactions, inheritance and net wealth – can also distort the allocation of capital and/or the incentive to save. Thus, property taxes in general are likely to be more harmful to growth than recurrent taxes on immovable property.
- *Consumption taxes* can affect labour supply by reducing the real value of wages but are otherwise seen as neutral. For example, they do not discourage savings and investment. Also, they are normally applied on a destination basis – applied to imports and refunded/exempted on export – and so do not affect the behaviour of firms that produce internationally traded goods. They can distort the behaviour of firms producing non-traded goods if applied at non-uniform rates, but the spread of general consumption taxes, such as VAT, means that consumption taxes are more uniform now than they used to be in most OECD countries, although reduced VAT rates are still common. Thus, consumption taxes can be expected to have little negative effect on growth, although they do not have the advantages of recurrent taxes on immovable property.
- *Personal income taxes* are seen as more harmful to growth than consumption taxes for two reasons. First, they are generally progressive, with marginal tax rates (which discourage growth) that are higher than their average rates (which generate government revenues). This means that they discourage growth more per unit of tax revenue than consumption taxes, which are generally flat rate and not (or not very) progressive. Second, they typically tax the return to savings (interest or dividends) in addition to taxing the income from which savings are made, thus discouraging savings. While this second effect may not harm the growth of publicly quoted companies that can raise funds overseas, it can reduce the growth financing for small and medium-sized companies. These negative effects on growth are illustrated by the results in sub-section 2.3.1, relating to the effects of personal income tax on total factor productivity growth.
- *Corporate income taxes* can be expected to be the most harmful for growth as they discourage the activities of firms that are most important for growth: investment in capital and in productivity

improvements. These effects are illustrated by the results presented in sub-section 2.3.2. Also, in practice, complex corporate tax codes cause high tax compliance costs for firms and reduce FDI. In addition, most corporate tax systems have a large number of provisions that create tax advantages for specific activities, typically drawing resources away from the sectors in which they can make the greatest contribution to growth.

This 'tax and growth ranking' means that growth could be increased, at least temporarily, without reducing tax revenue by a partial shift from income taxes to consumption and property taxes. Taxes on residential property are likely to be best for growth. However, few countries manage to raise substantial revenues from property taxes, with housing generally taxed more lightly than other assets. In practical policy terms, therefore, a greater revenue shift could probably be achieved into consumption taxes.

While recurrent taxes on immovable property are the best taxes to increase – from a growth point of view – corporate taxes appear to be the taxes that should be reduced most. However, lowering the corporate tax rate substantially below the top personal income tax rate can jeopardize the integrity of the tax system as high-income individuals will attempt to shelter their savings within corporations. This means that it often makes sense to think about reducing income taxes in a co-ordinated way.

Of course, changing the balance between different tax sources should not been seen as the only way in which tax structure can influence economic growth. Improving the design of individual taxes can also be important. For example, the results of sub-section 2.3.1 suggest that flattening the personal income tax schedule could be beneficial for GDP per capita, notably by favouring entrepreneurship. Indeed, the reform of individual taxes can complement a revenue shift. For example, broadening the base of consumption taxes is a better way of increasing their revenues than rate increases, because a broad base improves efficiency while a high rate encourages the growth of the shadow economy. More generally, most taxes would benefit from a combination of base broadening and rate reduction.

2.4.2 Equity Considerations

From a practical policy point of view, the main difficulty with these pro-growth tax policies is that they are likely to increase inequality. In most OECD countries, it is the personal income tax that accounts for almost all of the progressivity in the tax system. So, a move away from personal income tax towards consumption and property taxes, neither of which are seen as progressive, is very likely to increase inequality. This is particularly true if the personal income tax is reduced in the way suggested by the results in sub-section 2.3.1: reducing the top marginal rate of income tax.

In addition, corporate tax is generally perceived as a tax on the rich, and so any move away from it would also be seen as regressive. However, there are two reasons why this perception may be too strong. First, in many countries, a large proportion of company shares are owned by pension funds, so after-tax profits go to benefit a fairly broad range of workers when they retire. Second, to the extent that cuts in corporate taxes increase investment (as demonstrated in sub-section 2.3.2), they will lead to an increase in demand for labour and thus result in an increase in the wage. So, in principle, cuts in corporate taxes could benefit workers. Unfortunately, there is no clear consensus on the extent to which these two effects reduce the regressive nature of corporate tax cuts in practice.

A further difficulty is that both consumption taxes and recurrent taxes on residential immovable property are widely seen as inequitable. In the case of consumption taxes, the argument is based on the observation that poorer people spend a higher proportion of their disposable income[5] than richer people. But much low income observed at a point in time is temporary and need not reflect low lifetime living standards: while some people are persistently poor, many have volatile earnings. Over a lifetime, income and expenditure must be equal (apart from inheritances, which are generally small), and indeed annual expenditure is arguably better than annual income as a guide to lifetime living standards. If we were to look at the effect of taxes on lifetime income inequality, the contrast between 'progressive' direct taxes and 'regressive' indirect taxes would be much smaller. However, it would still be the case that personal income taxes are more progressive than consumption taxes.

The case of recurrent taxes on residential property is more complex. There is no reason in principle why these taxes could not be mildly progressive, either by applying a tax-free allowance that would effectively exempt low-income housing or applying a progressive rate structure.[6] However, most countries have not done this and, in fact, some have property valuation systems that reduce the effective tax rate paid on expensive dwellings. In addition, many countries have not kept their property valuations up to date, with the result that some households are paying taxes that are wildly out of line with the present value of their home. If these faults were corrected, recurrent taxes on residential property would probably become less unpopular than they are currently, but one problem would remain: the tax is levied on some measure of the value of the property and thus may not reflect the owner's ability to pay. The classic example is that of an elderly widow who is living in the house where she raised her children, which is now both too large for her and has a value that is out of proportion to her current income. Many countries have measures which attempt to ameliorate this problem, but it is still one that is raised in most countries when the level of property taxation is discussed.

2.5 CONCLUSIONS

This chapter has presented empirical analysis that suggests that growth can be increased, at least in the short–medium term, by shifting the balance of taxation away from income taxes and towards a mixture of consumption taxes and taxes on immovable property (particularly on residential property). This confirms the expectations of theoretical analysis and shows that tax structure – and not just the overall tax–GDP ratio – is an important element in promoting economic growth.

The chapter has also shown that it is not only the tax structure that matters. The design of individual taxes – such as the top marginal rate of income tax – can also be important to growth. Indeed, improving the design of individual taxes will increase the benefit of shifting the tax mix away from income taxation.

The main drawback of these policies is that they are likely to lead to increased inequality, which implies that countries need to consider the trade-off between equity and growth carefully. However, the trade-off could be made more favourable by improving the design and implementation of residential property taxes. There is also uncertainty about the extent to which lowering corporate taxes would increase inequality in practice.

NOTES

* The authors are at the OECD except for Christopher Heady, who was at the OECD and is now at the University of Kent. The project on which this chapter draws benefited greatly from important contributions from Stefano Scarpetta. The authors would also like to thank Jørgen Elmeskov, Giuseppe Nicoletti, Jeffrey Owens, Jean-Luc Schneider, Cyrille Schwellnus and Ana Cebreiro-Gomez but remain responsible for all errors. The views expressed in this chapter are those of the authors and do not necessarily reflect those of the OECD or the governments of its member countries.

1. The details of the empirical results, based on data from OECD countries, are presented in Arnold (2008) for the macro results, Vartia (2008) for the industry-level results and Schwellnus and Arnold (2008) for the firm-level results.
2. This control variable is used to remove the bias that could result from a correlation between the tax mix and the overall tax burden. However, the value of the coefficient on this variable does not represent an accurate estimate of the effect of the overall tax

burden on GDP because, as discussed in the introduction, it takes no account of how any additional tax revenue might be spent.
3. The effect on FDI of a one standard deviation change in the tax wedge on labour income is around 10 times larger than the effect of a similar change in the marginal and average cross-border effective tax rate.
4. Rising firms are defined as those for which the gap between their TFP and that of the technological leader firm is falling. Declining firms are those for which the TFP gap with the leader firm is increasing.
5. It is important to compare expenditure to disposable income in this context because income tax (and benefit) systems are generally progressive, and so poorer people will automatically have a higher proportion of their pre-tax income available to spend. It is the progressivity of consumption taxes with respect to disposable income that determines whether consumption taxes increase or reduce measured inequality.
6. Even a proportional property tax could be progressive with respect to income if richer people's property holdings increase more than in proportion to their income.

REFERENCES

Arnold, J. (2008), *Do tax structures affect aggregate economic growth? Empirical evidence from a panel of OECD countries*, OECD Economics Department, Working Paper No. 643.

Boersch-Supan, A. (1998), 'Capital productivity and the nature of competition', *Brookings Papers on Economic Activity, Microeconomics*, 205–44.

Devereux, M.P. and R. Griffith (2003), 'Evaluating tax policy for location decisions', *International Tax and Public Finance*, **10**, 107–26.

Gentry, W. and R.G. Hubbard (2000), 'Tax policy and entrepreneurial entry', *American Economic Association Papers and Proceedings*, **90**(2) (May), 283–7.

Griffith, R., S. Redding and H. Simpson (2004) *Foreign ownership and productivity: New evidence from the services sector and the R&D lab*, London School of Economics, Centre for Economic Performance, Discussion Paper No. 649.

Hajkova, D., G. Nicoletti, L. Vartia and K.Y. Yoo (2006), 'Taxation and business environment as drivers of foreign direct investment in OECD countries', *OECD Economic Studies*, **43**(2), 8–38.

Johansson, Å., C. Heady, J. Arnold, B. Brys and L. Vartia (2008), *Tax and economic growth*, OECD Economics Department, Working Paper No. 620.

Kneller, R., M.F. Bleaney and N. Gemmell (1999), 'Fiscal policy and growth: Evidence from OECD countries', *Journal of Public Economics*, **74**, 171–190.

Myles, G. (2009), *Economic growth and the role of taxation*, OECD Economics Department, Working Paper, Nos 713, 714, 715.

Scarpetta, S. and T. Tressel (2002), *Productivity and convergence in a panel of OECD industries: Do regulations and institutions matter?*, OECD Economics Department, Working Paper No. 342.

Schwellnus, C. and J. Arnold (2008), *Do corporate taxes reduce productivity and investment at the firm-level? Cross-country evidence from the Amadeus dataset*, OECD Economics Department, Working Paper No. 641.

Vartia, L. (2008), *How do taxes affect investment and productivity? Industry level analysis of OECD countries*, OECD Economics Department, Working Paper No. 656.

3. Economic effects of investment subsidies

Jane Gravelle*

3.1 INTRODUCTION

Explicit investment subsides in the United States can be dated back to the early 1960s when the investment tax credit was introduced, although the accelerated depreciation methods adopted in 1954 and 1962 were also justified on the basis of economic stimulus; see Gravelle (1994) for a history. While the investment credit was initially considered as a permanent part of the tax system, the credit was subsequently used as a short-term stimulus, and then returned to being a permanent tax feature. In 1986, however, the United States repealed the investment credit and created a system with the present value of tax depreciation close to economic depreciation. Depreciation was accelerated but designed to offset inflation, although a subsequent decline in inflation reduced effective tax rates, especially for shorter-lived assets that are more sensitive to inflation, as discussed in Gravelle (2001). The revenue gains from the repeal of the investment credit were used to reduce the corporate tax rate.

According to Pechman's (1987) study of comparative tax systems, every country studied (Sweden, the Netherlands, France, Italy, Germany, the United Kingdom, Canada, and Japan) had experimented with tax incentives for investment. Pechman noted a growing disenchantment almost everywhere with investment incentives because of their distortions and inequities. Investment subsidies have tended to favor certain types of assets – plant and equipment – and have been provided in a form that is distorting even among the class of assets covered. Indeed, despite the move towards lower statutory tax rates rather than investment subsidies, plant and equipment continues to be favored over structures, as shown in Table 3.1 where effective marginal tax rates (EMTRs) are reported for Australia and the G-7.

The EMTR reports the tax on a marginal unit of investment, and reflects both the statutory tax rate and any investment subsidies. If the statutory and effective marginal tax rates are the same, there are no

Table 3.1 Statutory and effective marginal tax rates: G-7 and Australia, 1982 and 2005

	Tax rates 1982			Tax rates 2005		
	Statutory	EMTR: plant and equipment	EMTR: Industrial buildings	Statutory	EMTR: Plant and equipment	EMTR: Industrial buildings
Australia	50	32	52	30	24	29
Canada	44	9	42	36	25	36
France	50	26	46	34	20	30
Great Britain	52	0	9	30	20	29
Germany	62	47	60	38	29	39
Italy	39	18	22	37	19	33
Japan	55	42	54	40	28	43
United States	50	22	37	39	24	41

Source: Data developed in Devereux et al. (2002), provided by the Institute for Fiscal Studies; available at: http://www.ifs.org.uk/publications.php?publication_id=3210. Assumes constant interest and inflation rates.

investment subsidies. In 1982, when tax rates were around 50 percent, only three countries (Great Britain, Italy, and the United States) had any significant subsidy for buildings, while all eight countries had subsidies for equipment; in every country, the effective tax rates were lower for plant and equipment than for industrial buildings. By 2005, statutory tax rates were around 35 percent. No country had a significant subsidy for buildings, but most had EMTRs for plant and equipment below the statutory rates and, while the relative reduction was smaller than in 1982, in most cases it was still significant.

An investment subsidy differs from the two potential alternative methods of reducing tax burdens on marginal investments – reducing tax rates and substituting a consumption or cash-flow tax for capital income taxes – in several major ways. Investment subsidies are more focused on the margin than are rate cuts, but unlike a cash-flow tax they retain existing depreciation deductions and deductions for interest. Thus, while an investment subsidy has more 'bang for the buck' in reducing marginal tax rates at a given revenue cost than rate reductions, it does not go so far as a cash-flow tax. In a revenue-neutral world, of course, all revenues must be made up by some other tax and the three approaches to reducing capital income taxes differ in the degree to which they impose lump sum taxes on the old versus increasing labour income taxes, assuming that labour income is the major alternative tax base. Cash-flow taxes still yield substantial revenues and thus require less in the way of additional taxes from other sources when substituted for an income tax; asset values, however, fall. Reducing tax rates directly reduces revenue and requires, for the same effective tax rate on new investment, more additional taxes. Investment subsidies occupy an intermediate position.

Both rate cuts and true cash-flow taxes are neutral with respect to assets of different durabilities and neither provides additional benefits to debt-financed investment. When inflation is present, debt finance is typically subsidised in an income tax, so that reducing the corporate tax rate or replacing it with a cash-flow tax reduces that subsidy. Investment subsidies, while they can be designed to be neutral typically have not been and, as noted above, have mainly favored equipment; they apply to debt-financed as well as equity-financed investments.

Considering an investment subsidy, therefore, leads to two issues for investigation. The first is: how effective the subsidy (or a rate cut) is in increasing future well-being in a society; that is, what might a country expect to gain from a subsidy? The second is: if a reduction in marginal tax rates is desired, what are the benefits and costs of choosing an investment subsidy over other alternatives, such as rate reductions or partial substitution with a cash-flow tax? And, how might investment subsidies be designed to be most efficient?

3.2 AGGREGATE EFFECTS OF AN INVESTMENT SUBSIDY ON THE ECONOMY

What are the potential gains to a society from reducing the tax burden at the margin for an investment subsidy? One important aspect to considering these welfare effects is to recognise that it is not the overall effect on *output* that matters, but rather on the level of *sustainable consumption.*

3.2.1 A Simple Base Case

To explore the potential effects of a general investment subsidy on steady-state welfare, consider a simple profit maximizing problem with price as the numeraire:

$$\pi = Q(K, L) - cK - wL \tag{3.1}$$

where π is profit, Q is output, K is capital, L is labour, c is the user cost of capital, and w is the wage rate. In this simple case, assume a Cobb–Douglas production function of the form $Q = AK^{\alpha}L^{(1-\alpha)}$. The cost of capital is the sum of the pretax return r and the depreciation rate δ, that is $c = r + \delta$. In the presence of taxes the cost of capital is:

$$c = r + \delta = (R + \delta)\,(1 - uz - k)/(1 - u) \tag{3.2}$$

where R is the required after-tax rate of return, u is the statutory tax rate, z is the present value of depreciation deductions, and k is an investment credit without a basis adjustment (that is, an investment credit that does not reduce the basis for depreciation). We assume initially that z is equal to economic depreciation $[\delta/(R + \delta)]$ and set values typical of a modern economy, with $R = 0.05$, $\delta = 0.07$, and $u = 0.3$. To reduce the cost of capital by 10 percent without a basis adjustment requires an investment tax credit rate of 8.25 percent; that is, 10 percent times $(1 - u\delta/(r + \delta))$. Note that this is a very large investment subsidy given the 30 percent tax rate and the depreciation rate; the effective tax rate $(r - R)/r$ falls by more than half, from 30 percent to 12.7 percent, a 57.7 percent reduction.

We assume domestic labour supply and the after-tax required return, R, to be fixed (and thus the change in the cost of capital is exogenous). A fixed R corresponds to a perfectly elastic supply of capital. We calibrate the model with price as the numeraire, and with $\alpha = 0.3$ (the share of output accruing to capital in either pre-tax return or depreciation). With these values, the capital stock is 2.12 times output (since $cK = \alpha Q$), a reasonable value for business capital. In order to estimate the effect of changing c to $0.9c$, we take the first order conditions from equation (3.1) with respect to K to find the relationship between K and c, which, after some rearrangement and dividing new values (denoted with an asterisk) by the old values, gives:

$$(K^*/K) = (0.9)^{1/(\alpha-1)} \tag{3.3}$$

This yields an increase in the capital stock of 16.2 percent.

Although this appears to be a large increase in the capital stock, because capital is only one of the inputs and, to a lesser degree, because of the declining marginal factor productivity, the gain in output is much smaller:

$$(Q^*/Q) = (K^*/K)^{\alpha} \tag{3.4}$$

or an increase in output of 4.2 percent.

Measuring a gain in gross output, however, does not allow for the need to use some of the additional output to replace the larger capital stock.

Given the values used in our example, the capital stock in the economy is 2.12 times the output. Net output, after accounting for depreciation, is about 85 percent of gross output. Out of the 4.2 percent increase in output, more than half, 2.4 percent, must be diverted to replacing the increment of depreciating capital stock. As a result, the percentage increase in net output is 2.2 percent. But even this rate of increase is not sustainable. To sustain a higher level of output the new increment of capital stock must also grow. That is, net steady state investment must be subtracted to determine the steady state sustainable consumption. Assuming a steady state growth rate of 3 percent, the combination of net and replacement investment accounts for a 3.4 percent increase in output. This leaves only a 1.5 percent increase in sustainable consumption – equivalent to six months of ordinary growth. Incidentally, this analysis could also be applied to a rate cut that yielded the same reduction in the cost of capital: the revenue cost would be different but not the economic effects.

The effects for an open capital-importing country are even smaller. In this case, not only must part of the output be used to replace and grow the higher capital stock, but investors must ultimately realize their after-tax rate of return on the new increment of investment. If the rate of return is 5 percent and the growth rate is 3 percent, an additional 2 percent of the capital stock is required to compensate foreign investors in the steady state; the increased output used for replacement investment, net investment, and payments to foreign investors accounts for 4.1 percent, or 90 percent of the increase in output. As a result, domestic consumption increases by only 0.6 percent, equivalent to slightly over two months' normal growth.

This illustration, using reasonable values for mature economies, indicates that capital deepening through even significant reductions in the effective tax rate via investment subsidies can only produce limited effects on output. Part of this effect occurs because as capital is added, the added productivity of that capital declines, while the amounts needed to sustain the capital stock grow linearly with the capital stock. Indeed, it is well known in growth theory that it is possible for the capital stock to become too large so that more capital, even in a closed economy, can reduce steady-state consumption. This barrier to gain is even more pronounced in an open economy case where the return paid to foreign investors also grows linearly. Despite these limited effects, however, the scenario just described is likely to be overly optimistic for several reasons: consumption is further reduced due to debt finance; the unitary elasticity implied by the Cobb–Douglas production function is too high; and the supply of capital is not perfectly elastic.

There are some other effects that are not considered. First, the possibility of imperfect product substitution was found by Gravelle and Smetters (2006) to reduce capital mobility in the same way as imperfect portfolio substitution and thus could play a role in reducing the effectiveness of any subsidy. Second, in a capital-importing country, if the foreign investors are from countries that use a credit system, which include important investing countries such as the US, the UK, and Japan, the investment subsidies may have less effect as additional home country taxes may offset part of the incentive. Finally, the analysis does not consider any effects from measures taken to offset the revenue losses from investment subsidies. If labor supply declines as a result of increased taxes on labor income, this decline could offset any output effects (although most empirical evidence suggests labor is relatively inelastically supplied). Revenue losses made up by incurring additional debt would compete with capital used for investments that contribute to future well-being.

3.2.2 Debt Finance

Debt finance reduces the steady-state consumption in the open capital-importing country because foreign investors with debt finance receive the pre-tax nominal interest rate, while the discount rate of the firm allows for a tax deduction. As an illustration, suppose the nominal interest rate is 8 percent and the share debt financed is a third. The payment to foreign investors is increased by 8 percent times the tax rate times the share debt financed, in this case by about 0.2 percent of consumption, reducing the steady-state gain to consumption by about a third, from 0.6 percent to 0.4 percent.

3.2.3 The Factor Substitution Elasticity

Turning to the next issue, the Cobb–Douglas production function's unitary elasticity, while often used in simple models, is probably high, based on recent evidence. (These elasticities are negative but are reported in absolute values). The development of this literature is surveyed in Hassett and Hubbard (2002) and Chirinko (2002) and is largely related to the United States. In early empirical work, investment studies examined the flow, not the stock, of capital. Initial studies used an adjustment process between actual and desired capital stock, but this could capture accelerator effects, and when critics isolated user cost, they found negligible effects, with investment elasticities ranging from 0 to 0.3.

Models incorporating adjustment costs and using q (the ratio of market value to replacement cost) also did not do well and produced implausible adjustment parameters. In general, most studies using aggregate investment data found very small effects of permanent changes in tax variables. The problem with these studies was the tendency of many variables to move together over the business cycle. Subsequent studies used panel investment data and in some cases found elasticities of around 0.6, although other studies found estimates of 0.18 to 0.35. Some other studies used data on the capital stock, with results ranging from zero to slightly over 1, although most of these studies fell in the neighborhood of 0.3 to 0.7.

Subsequent to these reviews some additional research has been done. Chirinko et al. (2004) used a long panel data set on firms and estimated an elasticity of 0.4. Barnes et al. (2008) found the same value for the UK using a similar approach. Chatelain et al. (2002) found an elasticity of 0.63 for Germany, 0.38 for France, 0.32 for Italy, and a statistically insignificant 0.09 for Spain. An earlier study by Caballaro (1994) using capital stock data had found a unit elasticity and a similar value was found for Canadian data by Schaller (2006), while Smith (2008) found a value of 0.4 for the UK using Caballaro's approach as well as an industry level data set. (Caballaro and Schaller excluded structures which, in earlier studies, were found to be less responsive than equipment.) Finally, in a study of a small open economy, Coulibaly and Millar (2007) estimated an elasticity of 0.8 for South Africa. They also suggested that the insignificant elasticity they obtained for the embargo period may reflect the difference between a closed and open economy. An earlier study by de Wet and Koch (2004), however, using firm level data, found an elasticity of 0.18.

The institution in the United States of a temporary bonus depreciation for 2002–04 provided an opportunity to examine the effect of a temporary provision which should have relatively powerful effects in theory. These studies exploited the differential effects in the cost of capital of allowing 50 percent of the cost of equipment to be expensed, across asset type. Cohen and Cummins (2006) found little evidence for a significant effect. They suggest several potential reasons for a small effect. One possibility is that firms without taxable income could not benefit from the timing advantage.

In a Treasury study, Knittel (2007) confirmed that firms did not elect bonus depreciation for about 40 percent of eligible investment, and speculated that the existence of losses and loss carry-overs may have made the investment subsidy ineffective for many firms, although there were clearly some firms that were profitable that did not use the provision. Cohen and Cummins also suggested that the incentive effect was quite small (largely because depreciation already occurs relatively quickly for most equipment), reducing the user cost of capital by only about 3 percent, that planning periods may be too long to adjust investment across time, and that adjustment costs outweighed the effect of bonus depreciation.

Knittel (2007) suggests that firms may have found the provision costly to comply with, particularly because most states did not allow bonus depreciation. A study by House and Shapiro (2006) found a more pronounced response to bonus depreciation, given the magnitude of the incentive, but found the overall effect on the economy was small, which in part is due to the limited category of investment affected and the small size of the incentive. Their differences with the Cohen and Cummins study reflect in part uncertainties about when expectations are formed and when the incentive effects occur. Cohen and Cummins also report the results of several surveys of firms, where from two-thirds to over 90 percent of respondents indicated bonus depreciation had no effect on the timing of investment spending.

It is not clear what the implications of the studies of bonus depreciation are for the factor substitution elasticity, but this provision was one that was expected, because of its 'fire-sale' nature, to have a large effect. Yet the results do not support a great deal of responsiveness. While the research has produced a range of estimates of the factor substitution elasticity, most of the studies suggest a value of less than unity, perhaps considerably less than unity.

Columns 2 and 3 of Table 3.2 compare the estimates of the effects for the Cobb–Douglas unitary elasticity case with a case (Sigma = 1.0) of a constant elasticity of substitution (Sigma = 0.5) as embodied in the following production function:

$$Q = A[aK^{(1-1/\sigma)} + (1-a)L^{(1-1/\sigma)}]^{[1/(1-1/\sigma)]} \tag{3.5}$$

The derivation of capital demand is somewhat more complicated and is presented in the Appendix. The results, for a substitution elasticity of 0.5, show that a lower factor substitution elasticity can significantly reduce the long-term gains to standards of living, cutting them approximately in half. Thus, in a closed economy, the long-run percentage increase in consumption is only 0.7 percent; for the open economy, the gain is only 0.3 percent. With debt finance, the gain in an open economy is 0.2 percent.

3.2.4 Savings Responses

In the cases considered thus far, the after-tax rate of return, R, is fixed, which assumes that the supply of capital is infinitely elastic. This assumption is probably unrealistic in either a closed or an open economy. By introducing imperfectly elastic savings response into the model, we

Table 3.2 Percentage change in output and consumption (from reducing the cost of capital by 10%)*

Factor substitution elasticity: σ Savings supply elasticity: ε	$\sigma = 1$ $\varepsilon = \infty$	$\sigma = 0.5$ $\varepsilon = \infty$	$\sigma = 1.0$ $\varepsilon = 3$	$\sigma = 0.5$ $\varepsilon = 3$	$\varepsilon = 0$
Capital stock	16.2	7.7	12.3	6.9	0.0
Gross output	4.6	2.2	3.7	2.0	0.0
Net output	2.2	1.2	2.1	1.1	0.0
Sustainable consumption: closed economy	1.5	0.7	1.2	0.6	0.0
Sustainable consumption: open economy**	0.6	0.3	−0.1	0.0	−3.1

Note:
* Equivalent to a 57.7 percent reduction in effective tax rate. ** Estimates assume all equity finance. With an 8 percent interest rate and 1/3 debt finance, the gain would be smaller, for example 0.4 percent of consumption in the case with σ = 1and $\varepsilon = \infty$ and 0.2 percent of consumption for $\sigma = 0.5$ and $\varepsilon = \infty$. Similar adjustments would be made for other cases.

Source: Author's calculations, see text.

introduce a new equation and a new unknown, R, the required after-tax return. The equation is for the supply of capital is:

$$K = BR^{\varepsilon} \tag{3.6}$$

The demand for capital from the first-order condition of the production function is equated to the supply to solve for R, which in turn determines c. In the cases already considered, ε is infinity. The issues differ between a closed and an open capital-importing economy.

A closed economy

In a closed economy, the supply of capital depends on the saving behavior of individuals in that economy. As investment subsidies increase demand for capital in a fixed supply world, the after-tax return to savers rises. Only if that rise induces additional savings can the aggregate capital stock expand. Capital can also be diverted from other sectors, such as owner-occupied housing, but then the gain in the business sector is offset by the loss in the remaining sector. (A small efficiency gain is possible, but not necessarily the case, as discussed below.)

In theory, even the direction of an effect on savings of an increase in the rate of return is unclear. An increase in the rate of return can lead to more savings or less savings depending on income and substitution effects. The outcome depends on a number of important issues and model assumptions. In addition, it is not clear that individuals behave as predicted by current inter-temporal savings models, which require very complex decisions; they may use rules of thumb such as a fixed share of income (with no effect on savings) or a target future accumulation (where increases in the rate of return allow one to save less to achieve a target). This view of savings is consistent with empirical evidence over time in the United States that suggests savings rate are relatively steady for long periods rather than reflecting the dramatic shifts that would be expected from tax policy and other changes.

Some formal growth models predict a substantial effect on savings. The earliest model of economic growth, the Solow model, simply took the savings rate to be fixed. The Solow model with its fixed savings rate was consistent with both a steady-state growth in output per capita in the US economy, as well as a savings rate that seemed to show no trend; see Gravelle (1994, chapter 1) for a discussion of time-series savings estimates. Economists, however, subsequently developed inter-temporal growth models. There are essentially two forms: the infinite horizon or Ramsey model, and the overlapping generations life-cycle model (OLG) model. These models, along with bounded rationality models that rely on rules of thumb, are reviewed in Bernheim (2002).

While these models are used in academia, they are not used by forecasters, whose cyclical models begin with sticky prices and which eventually exhibit, in most cases, Solow model characteristics. In the infinite horizon model, by contrast, the long-run supply of savings is perfectly elastic. The infinite horizon model is a special case of the OLG model, where agents take into account the utility of their descendents, while the OLG model has either no bequests or bequests motivated by other considerations. Both models assume a degree of knowledge, sophistication, and foresight that most ordinary savers are unlikely to have. It is not clear how the Ramsey model, intended by both its originator and those who refined it as a social planner's guide, came to be considered a realistic description of individual behavior. It does not account for marriage, and so cannot capture the possibility that one's descendents will receive bequests from others. More importantly, it reaches corner solutions in any economy where there are many jurisdictions with different types of tax rates (such as the states in the US or countries around the world). Since we do not observe one country or one state owning all of the capital, the model appears at odds with reality.

The overlapping generations model does not create the corner solutions, although it still assumes an extraordinary degree of sophistication and knowledge. Unlike the infinite horizon model, income effects can occur, and the extent to which capital income taxes affect savings and output depend on how the revenue is being made up and on numerous features of the models (see Gravelle 2002). As shown by Auerbach and Kotlikoff (1967), Gravelle (1991), and Engen et al. (1997), while the replacement of a capital income tax with a consumption tax tends to produce a large savings response, the replacement of capital income taxes with wage taxes does not, and can cause it to decline. Hence, the effects of investment subsidies in this model depend on how closely investment subsidies reflect a consumption type approach compared to a rate reduction approach.

This closeness depends in part on the form of the investment subsidy. For example, a partial expensing in the long run is similar to a consumption tax (except that it continues to allow interest deductions) and in an all-equity world would be equivalent to partial replacement of an income tax with a cash-flow tax. The investment credit is quite different, however, because rather than moving tax liability into the future, it adds a layer of tax subsidy. Gravelle (2009) shows that much of the effect of a shift to a consumption tax on saving in a life-cycle model is simply due to the need to increase savings to account for the lump sum loss in value imposed by a consumption tax as the government effectively becomes a partner in the investment. Since the consumption tax offers a deduction up front and imposes taxes on the total net flow (the return of the investment and the earnings on the investment), an increase in savings is required simply to restore the asset value. The value of assets falls by the tax rate (if the tax rate is 30 percent, asset values fall by 30 percent) and savings should eventually increase from the current level to $1/(1-t)$ times the current level.

In our example, the investment credit rate is 8.25 percent, and thus asset values would fall by that amount. Suppose the same subsidy were achieved by partial expensing. To determine the level of partial expensing necessary to achieve the same result as the investment credit we equate the cost of capital with a share, x, expensed to the cost with an investment credit, k:

$$(R+\delta)\{1-u[x+(1-x)z]\}/(1-u)=(R+\delta)(1-uz-k)/(1-u) \quad (3.7)$$

The results indicate that the share expensed would be 68 percent. Since the tax rate is 30 percent, the fall in asset value should be 0.3 times 0.68, or 20.4 percent. Savings would rise by 9 percent due to the timing effect with the investment credit and by 26 percent for the expensing provision. Thus, an investment credit has an effect through this route of a third of the expensing approach, suggesting that the results from a life-cycle model would exhibit savings responses that are much smaller than those for a consumption tax.

One could also make a case that savings responses in a closed economy are much less because the life-cycle model is an unrealistic depiction of behavior that is at odds with empirical evidence and that rule-of-thumb models are more appropriate. This view is supported not only by the evidence on the relative constancy of the savings rate in the United States over many years, but also by Madrian and Shea (2001) who found that participation in employer savings plans was strongly affected by the default (opt in or opt out); behavior that is entirely inconsistent with the optimizing behavior assumed in the life-cycle model. In that case, a savings elasticity closer to zero would be expected.

An open, capital-importing economy

In an open economy, the supply of capital depends on international capital mobility. Although models often assume capital to be perfectly mobile, there is considerable empirical evidence and theoretical reason to doubt such perfect substitutability. Foreign jurisdictions may appear more risky since investors are less certain about the risk environment in other countries. There may also be some exchange rate risk. Individuals and firms have strong home biases. Finally studies of the mobility of equity capital have suggested that these capital flows are elastic, but far below infinity. Gravelle and Smetters (2006), based on a review of evidence, choose a portfolio substitution elasticity of three that they considered somewhat high. A study by de Mooij and Ederveen (2003) presents a meta-analysis of 25 research studies and concludes with a central semi-elasticity of –2.4 with respect to a change in the tax rate. In equation (3.7), if the after-tax return were $r(1 - t)$, where r is the pre-tax return and is fixed, taking logs and differentiating with respect to the tax rate would indicate that the percentage change in the supply of capital is equal to ε times the $dt/(1 - t)$. Thus, to convert this elasticity to the form used in the model, the 2.4 percent elasticity would have to be multiplied by $(1 - t)$ or, in this case 2.4 times 0.7 or an elasticity of 1.7. It is possible, however, that this elasticity has increased over time.

Table 3.2 considers two elasticity values: an elasticity of three and an elasticity of zero. For the closed economy, the higher elasticity lowers the gain in both the Cobb–Douglas case and the CES of 0.5 case. The elasticity of zero eliminates any gain. For the open economy, however, the elasticity of three causes a steady state loss in consumption. This outcome is not surprising as the optimal tax rates are higher when inbound capital flows are less than perfectly elastic: for a simple tax rate change, the economy begins to lose when tax rates fall below $1/(1 + \varepsilon)$, or in this case 25 percent. Maximizing $F(K) - r(1 - t)K$ with respect to t, and recognising that r and K are functions of t, where r is the marginal product of capital, yields this result. When inbound capital is very elastic the optimal tax rate for maximizing consumption is close to zero, whereas when it becomes very inelastic, the tax rate rises towards 100 percent.

If inbound investment is perfectly inelastic, the tax cut simply increases the after-tax return to foreign investors, in this example, by up to 3 percent of consumption.

Conclusion

This analysis is highly suggestive that attempting to improve welfare through investment subsidies is unlikely to be very successful. In a closed economy, results are likely to be quite small because so much of the output gain must be devoted to steady state investment, and some of the tax reduction (perhaps most of it) will only increase after-tax returns to savings. If the gains appear limited in a closed economy, they are even more limited in an open capital-importing economy. At best they are likely to be negligible, and there is a strong likelihood that welfare will decline as the benefits of the lower tax rates are captured by foreign suppliers of capital in higher rates of return. Most countries are in an intermediate position, and that position can also be affected by reductions of outbound investment, as most outbound investment is probably not effectively taxed in the home country. To the extent that capital growth is financed by reductions in outbound investments rather than domestic savings, output gained domestically is lost abroad (there may be some welfare gains, however).

These results are affected by the assumptions. Let us consider, for example, a country with a smaller capital–output ratio. If we reduce that ratio by slightly over 15 percent by raising the after-tax return to 7 percent, the sustainable consumption in a closed economy under the most optimistic case (unitary factor substitution elasticity; infinite supply elasticity) rises to 2.1 percent, although it rises to only 0.8 percent in the open economy case because of the higher rate of return. If we reduce it by dropping the capital income coefficient to 25 percent, the effect on consumption in the steady state in the most optimistic case is only 1.1 percent in the closed economy and 0.5 percent in the open economy. Thus, these results seem robust to significant variations in the assumptions, and that is particularly the case for the capital-importing country. Note that these effects are for the optimistic case and would be reduced similarly to the base case with reductions in factor substitution and savings elasticities.

3.3 THE CHOICE AND DESIGN OF INVESTMENT SUBSIDIES

Investment subsidies can be contrasted with two alternative ways of reducing the cost of capital: a rate reduction and a shift to a cash-flow consumption tax. Investment subsidies occupy an intermediate position between the two. They focus, for the amount of revenue loss, more at the margin than corporate rate cuts, but less than consumption taxes. More incentives can be obtained per dollar of revenue loss with an investment subsidy (an issue referred to as 'bang for the buck') than with a rate cut. Both corporate rate cuts and consumption tax shifts differ from investment subsidies in two important and presumably desirable ways: they are neutral across assets and they do not create or add to negative effective tax rates for debt financed investment. As noted above, the consequences for savings in the closed economy environment in the steady state can differ as well, depending on the design of the investment subsidy.

Before turning to these issues, it is important to consider that a shift to a consumption tax entails extremely challenging transition and design issues that are far less serious with investment subsidies and rate cuts. In particular, if the objective is to achieve a revenue base that is not significantly smaller than the capital income tax it is replacing, depreciation deductions for existing capital assets, as well as interest deductions and deductions for existing inventories, must be denied. The latter is a particularly serious barrier; see Gravelle (2006) for a discussion of these issues. Thus the remainder of this discussion, where comparison is appropriate, will largely focus on the alternative of a rate reduction.

3.3.1 Role of the Corporate Tax in the Tax Structure

There is one important aspect in which rate cuts are different from investment subsidies: investment subsidies apply to all businesses, while corporate rate reductions apply only to incorporated businesses. For reasonable reductions in the corporate rate, this difference can be advantageous, because corporate equity tends to bear the heavier taxes. For very large rate reductions, however, problems can develop in the use of the corporate tax as a shelter, an issue that is particularly important in the United States where the restrictions regarding which classification a business is in are relatively lax. Thus, if there is a significant individual tax meant to apply to capital income, lowering the corporate rate too far can induce tax sheltering activity (which increases administrative burdens) and cause individual income tax revenue losses.

3.3.2 Bang for the Buck

Although investment subsidies are often perceived as providing more 'bang for the buck' Gravelle (2008) finds an investment credit to be almost as costly per dollar as a rate reduction. This effect can be explored by examining an investment tax credit. From equation (3.2), the cost of capital is:

$$c = (R + \delta)(1 - uz - k)/(1 - u) \tag{3.8}$$

The percentage change in c with a change in k is equal to $-dk/(1-uz)$, and if e is the elasticity of investment, I, with respect to c, then $dI = -eIk/(1-uz)$. Since the revenue loss is Ik, the ratio of stimulus to revenue loss is $e/(1-uz)$.

With a rate cut we obtain, using the same method, $dI = -eI\, du(1-z)/[(1-u)\,(1-uz)]$. The revenue loss, with economic depreciation is $rdu/(1-u)\,K$, where K is the capital stock. Since I is equal to $(g + \delta)\,K$, the ratio of stimulus to revenue loss (given that $z = \delta/r + \delta$), is $e(g + \delta)/[(R + \delta)(1-uz)]$. Thus, the ratio of the cost, beginning with a system with economic depreciation, is $(g + \delta)/(r + \delta)$. In our illustration, for example, this bang for the buck would be 0.83. One reason that investment subsidies tend to lose so much revenue is that they are not confined to new investment; they are also granted for replacement investment. Hence they do not really have a powerful 'bang for the buck' compared to a rate reduction. In fact, for equipment, which is the most typical target of investment subsidies, if the average depreciation rate is 15 percent the ratio of cost is 0.9.

3.3.3 Neutrality

One of the problems that occurs with investment incentives historically is that they are not neutral across assets, partly because they have tended to be restricted to equipment, and partly because they have often been granted in the form of an investment credit. Investment credits have some significant timing benefits compared to accelerated depreciation and thus tend to be attractive as investment subsidies. They tend to produce, for a permanent subsidy, a smooth pattern of revenue loss over time. Depreciation tends to have a very uneven pattern. At the extreme, partial expensing involves a very large short-run revenue cost that then declines over time as future depreciation deductions are foregone. Accelerated depreciation also has a very uneven pattern, which rises and then declines.

Investment credits are not neutral, however, even if they are uniformly applied. For neutrality, the cost of capital should change independent of the depreciation rate. But as can be seen from differentiating equation (3.8), the change in cost of capital is $-(R + \delta)k/(1 - u)$. This effect was recognised in the US investment credit, which limited the treatment for very short-lived assets.

This treatment is somewhat moderated if the credit has a basis adjustment – that is, depreciation is not allowed for the amount of the investment financed by the credit. In this case:

$$c = (R + \delta)(1 - uz)(1 - k)/(1 - u) \tag{3.9}$$

and the change in c is $dc = -[R/(1-u) + \delta]$k. The influence of the depreciation rate is lessened, but remains.

There are neutral investment subsidies, however. One, as noted earlier, is partial expensing where a fraction x is deducted immediately and the remainder is depreciated. In this case:

$$c = (R + \delta)\{1 - u[x+(1-x)z]\} \tag{3.10}$$

In this case, the change in c, with z equal to economic depreciation, is $dc = -xuR/(1-u)$.

Partial expensing has the advantage of being neutral but it is often not practical from a budgetary standpoint as a permanent provision, outside of a formal cash-flow tax, since its short-run revenue cost is so large. In a cash-flow tax, this revenue cost is offset by the loss of existing depreciation and interest deductions.

It is possible to structure an investment credit as a neutral policy (given existing economic depreciation) by restricting the credit only to investment in excess of depreciation. This produces a smooth revenue pattern (although the credit rate would have to be much larger to achieve the same overall reduction in cost of capital). It is neutral because an additional dollar of investment will lead to additional depreciation deductions, z in present value, that will reduce the credit. Thus, the cost of capital is:

$$c = (R + \delta)[1 - uz - k(1 - z)]/(1 - u) \tag{3.11}$$

and the change in the cost of capital is $-kR/(1-u)$.

Because of this anticipation of future depreciation effects, this approach does not gain in 'bang for the buck' as might initially be imagined, but it will create a smoother revenue pattern. Firms may, however, reorganise to reduce the depreciation floor, so this approach does have some avoidance problems.

The investment credit could also be made neutral by varying the rate across assets, with lower rates for shorter-lived assets. This approach would require estimates of the components of the cost of capital, unlike approaches such as expensing or allowing credits for investment in excess of depreciation, which have an automatic tendency to move towards neutrality.

While one could design an investment subsidy that is neutral most subsidies, as indicated in this chapter, favour equipment, and the form most commonly used, the investment credit, favors short-lived assets within equipment. (No subsidy approach is without some type of flaw, however.) No arguments have been advanced to justify the favoring of shorter-lived assets within the equipment category, but there have been discussions of rationales for favoring equipment over structures. Gravelle (2001) reviews a number of the arguments. Some of those, such as that equipment is more 'productive', are dismissed by standard economic analysis. Arguments were also made in the United States that buildings were favored because they used more debt and benefited from other characteristics, which should be dismissed on factual grounds according to Gravelle (2001). Another argument, that asset tax-lives may be too short due to technological obsolescence, should justify more accurate measures of depreciation and not explicit subsidies. Moreover, short-lived assets that become obsolete do have a safety mechanism in that the remainder of the cost of equipment that is scrapped can be deducted.

One argument that did, however, receive some attention in the economics literature was the argument that equipment investment produces some externalities, such as increasing labor skill through 'learning by doing'. De Long and Summers (1991) presented a study that indicated that investment in equipment as a share of output was correlated with economic growth; this study was, in this author's view, successfully challenged by Auerbach et al. (1994). One other argument, made by Judd (1997), suggested that equipment-producing firms are imperfectly competitive. Such a view would seem to be less easily justified in the global economy, and it almost certainly would not apply with equal force to all assets. To identify goods, measure the effects of imperfect competition, and develop reasonable subsidy offsets is probably beyond the ability of government interventions.

3.3.4 Negative Tax Rates and Debt Finance

Reducing the corporate tax rate benefits equity investment that is heavily taxed. It also reduces an existing subsidy for debt, which arises when inflation is present due to the deduction of the inflation premium (or the failure to tax the gain from repaying debt in cheaper dollars). An investment subsidy, on the other hand, can reduce the tax burden on equity below zero and will reduce the burden on debt (at the firm level) to become negative.

With respect to equity investments, while some forms of subsidy (such as accelerated depreciation or partial expensing), can never reduce tax below zero, an investment credit can, particularly when tax rates are low and particularly for less durable assets. In our earlier example, the investment credit of 8.25 percent reduced the overall tax rate to 12.7 percent, but if applied only to equipment, with a depreciation rate of 7 percent, the tax rate would be −4.5 percent. If applied to a shorter-lived asset with a depreciation rate of 33 percent, the tax would be −87.8 percent. There are increased possibilities of negative tax rates when depreciation is already accelerated, since negative tax rates occur when the present value of tax depreciation deductions plus the investment subsidy reach the equivalent of expensing (that is, $uz + k = u$). For example, the present value of the most common asset class in the United States tax system (a 7-year class with accelerated depreciation) is 87 cents on the dollar. At a 35 percent tax rate, the value of depreciation is 30.5 percent, leaving room for only a 4.5 percent investment credit before tax rates become negative.

These effects are more pronounced for debt. Any investment subsidy will produce a negative tax rate. Suppose that the asset being considered is debt financed and that the interest rate produces an after-tax cost of capital of 5 percent – that is, the interest rate is $0.05/(1 - t)$, or 7.14 percent. In this case, the tax rate at the firm level before the subsidy is zero, but the effective tax rate with an 8.25 percent credit is −24 percent. If applied only to equipment assets with a depreciation rate of 15 percent, the tax rate would be −49 percent.

These outcomes are even more pronounced in the presence of inflation. For example, consider a fairly low inflation rate of 2 percent. In order for a firm to have a real discount rate of 5 percent with this inflation rate, the interest rate must be 10 percent, so that the after-tax nominal rate is 7 percent (after allowing for deduction at a 30 percent rate) and the real rate is 5 percent. However, the real interest rate is actually 8 percent (10 percent minus 2 percent). Without any subsidy, this inflation effect produces a negative tax rate of −12 percent rather than the zero tax rate that would be expected for debt finance. With the 9.25 percent investment credit, there is a negative tax rate of –40 percent. If applied only to equipment, the rate is −67 percent.

In a closed economy, if interest is taxed when paid to the individual, some of this tax may be recouped on the individual side, although if the corporate and individual tax rates differ, negative tax rates can remain. For an open capital-importing country, however, the corporate level is the only level at which the tax applies for that country.

3.4 CONCLUSIONS

Two important conclusions emerge from this analysis. First, modeling the effects of subsidies, whether granted via rate reductions or investment subsidies, suggests that little gain in long-run welfare can be expected. Indeed, for a small open economy, a country can easily make itself worse off. Second, there are many difficulties to be encountered in designing investment subsidies, which can maintain existing distortions (such as those favoring debt finance) and can introduce distortions across assets.

NOTE

* The views in this chapter do not reflect the views of the Congressional Research Service.

REFERENCES

Auerbach, A.J. and L.J. Kotlikoff (1987), *Dynamic Fiscal Policy*, New York: Cambridge University Press.

Auerbach, A.J., K.A. Hassett and S.D. Oliner (1994), 'Reassessing the social returns to equipment investment. *Quarterly Journal of Economics*, **109**, 789–802.

Barnes, S., Price, S. and M.S. Barriel (2008), *The Elasticity of Substitution: Evidence from a UK Firm-Level Data Set*, London: Bank of England.

Bernheim, B.D. (2002), 'Taxation and saving', in A.J. Auerbach and M. Feldstein (eds), *Handbook of Public Economics, Volume 3*, New York: Elsevier.

Caballaro, R.J. (1994) Small sample bias and adjustment costs. *The Review of Economics and Statistics*, 76, 53–8.

Chatelain, J.B., A. Generale, I. Hernando, U. von Kalckreuth and P. Vermeulen (2002) *Firm investment and monetary policy transmission in the Euro area*. Mimeo (January).

Chirinko, R.S. (2002) 'Corporate taxation, capital formation, and the substitution elasticity between labor and capital', *National Tax Journal*, **55**, 339–55.

Chirinko, R.S., S.M. Fazzari and A.P. Meyer (2004) *That elusive elasticity: A long panel approach to estimating the price sensitivity of business capital*, CESifo Working Paper No. 1240.

Cohen, D. and J. Cummins (2006), *A retrospective evaluation of the effects of temporary partial expensing*, Federal Reserve Board, Finance and Economics Discussion No. 2006-19, Washington, DC.

Coulibaly, B. and, J. Millar (2007) *Estimating the long run user cost elasticity for a small open economy: Evidence using data from South Africa*, Federal Reserve Board, Finance and Economics Discussion Paper No. 2007–25, Washington, DC.

De Long, J.B. and, L. Summers (1991), 'Equipment investment and economic growth' *Quarterly Journal of Economics*, **106**, 445–502.

de Mooij R. and S. Elderveen (2003), 'Taxation and foreign direct investment: A synthesis of empirical research,' *International Tax and Public Finance*, **10**, 673–94.

de Wet, A. and S.F. Koch (2004) *How responsive is capital formation to its user cost? An exploration of corporate tax effects*, African Development and Poverty Reduction: The Macro–Micro Linkage, Forum Paper.

Devereux, M.P., R. Griffith and A. Klemm (2002), 'Corporate income tax reforms and international tax competition, *Economic Policy*, **35**, 451–95.

Engen E., J.G. Gravelle and K.A. Smetters (1997), 'Dynamic tax models: Why they do the things they do, *National Tax Journal*, **50**, 657–82.
Gravelle, J.G. (1991), 'Income, consumption, and wage taxation in a life-cycle model: Separating efficiency from distribution', *American Economic Review*, **81**, 985–95.
Gravelle, J.G. (1994) *The Economic Effects of Taxing Capital Income*, Cambridge, MA: The MIT Press.
Gravelle, J.G. (2001), 'Whither tax depreciation?', *National Tax Journal*, **54**, 513–26.
Gravelle, J.G. (2002), 'Behavioral responses to a consumption tax', in G.W. Zodrow and P. Mieszkowski (eds), *United States Tax Policy in the 21st Century*, New York: Cambridge University Press.
Gravelle, J.G. (2006), *The advisory panel's tax reform proposal*, Congressional Research Service Report RL33545, Washington, DC: Library of Congress.
Gravelle, J.G. (2009) 'Consumption taxes and risk revised', in J.G. Head and R. Krever (eds), *Tax Reform in the 21st Century: A Volume in Memory of Richard Musgrave*', The Netherlands: Kluwer Law International.
Gravelle, J.G. and, K.A. Smetters (2006), 'Does the open economy assumption really mean that labor bears the burden of a capital income tax?' *Advances in Economic Policy and Analysis*, **6**(1), 1–42.
Hassett, K. and R.G. Hubbard (2002), 'Tax policy and business investment,' in A. Auerbach and M. Feldstein (eds), *Handbook of Public Economics, Volume 3*, New York: Elsevier.
House, C. and M. Shapiro (2006) *Temporary investment tax incentives: Theory with evidence from bonus depreciation*, National Bureau of Economic Research, Working Paper No. 12514.
Judd, K. (1997), *The optimal tax rate for capital income is negative*, National Bureau of Economic Research, Working Paper No. 6004.
Knittel, M. (2007) *Corporate response to bonus depreciation: Bonus depreciation for tax years 2002–2004*, US Department of Treasury, Office of Tax Analysis, Working Paper No. 98.
Madrian, B.C. and D.F. Shea (2001), 'The power of suggestion: Inertia in 401(k) savings behavior', *Quarterly Journal of Economics*, **118**, 1149–87.
Pechman, J.A. (1987), *Comparative Tax Systems: Europe, Canada and Japan*, Arlington, VA: Tax Analysts.
Schaller, H. (2006), 'Estimating the long run user cost elasticity', *Journal of Monetary Economics*, **53**, 725–36.
Smith, J. (2008), *That elusive elasticity and the ubiquitous bias: Is panel data a panacea*?, Bank of England, Working Paper No. 342.

APPENDIX 3A: A CES PRODUCTION FUNCTION AND SAVINGS

To solve the model for a CES production function, it is necessary to calibrate the values of A and a in equation (3.5) to fit the same share of capital income for the Cobb–Douglas case (that is, to generate the same capital stock relative to output).

To calibrate a, we take the first-order conditions for capital and labour from equation (3.5) and dividing, obtain the capital–labor ratio:

$$K/L = [aw/(1-a)c]^{\sigma} \tag{3A.1}$$

K is known through the factor share formula ($cK = \alpha Q$), with Q normalised to 1, and setting the wage rate initially to 1, the value of labour is 0.7. Thus equation (3A.1) has one unknown, a. Once the value of a is determined, equation (3.5) can be used to solve for A, since Q, K, L, and a are known. Once calibrated, take the first-order condition for capital from equation (3.5) which, after some manipulation is:

$$K = \{[(Aa/c)^{(\sigma-1)} - a]/(1-a)\}^{/(\sigma-1)} \tag{3A.2}$$

Then solve for Q based on the production function.

In the imperfectly elastic savings model, R becomes a variable. B must be calibrated by equating capital demand (which is equal to the initial value of K) with capital supply, where all the other values are known. To solve the model, these values are equated, producing one equation with one unknown, R. Once R is determined, capital stock and output can then be determined.

PART II

International, corporate and capital taxation

4. Lessons from the study of taxes and the behavior of US multinational corporations

Rosanne Altshuler*

4.1 INTRODUCTION

Until recently, the richest datasets available for the study of how taxes affect the behavior of multinational corporations were those that provided information on the activities of US corporations. Both public and confidential data sources have allowed researchers to investigate how corporate taxes impact where US corporations invest, how that investment if financed, and how countries compete to attract US foreign direct investment among other topics. The availability of comprehensive data over a relatively long period of time has also allowed researchers to observe how the behavior of US firms has changed as globalization has intensified. This chapter reviews recent research on how the global activities of US multinational corporations respond to taxation. While the typical review tends to focus on contributions to the academic literature, the goal of this chapter is to focus on how the evidence gleaned from US data sources can help guide corporate tax reform.[1]

I draw seven lessons from the study of the activities of US multinational corporations. First, the real assets of US corporations are internationally mobile and the location of these assets has become more sensitive to differences in tax rates over time. Second, the evidence suggests that the same phenomena hold for intangible capital which is typically the source of a multinational's competitive advantage abroad. Third, tax avoidance through income shifting seems to have gotten worse in recent years, at least for US multinationals. Fourth, host country governments engage in tax competition to attract US investment and this competition has intensified over time. But host country governments are not the only players in the tax competition game: the fifth lesson is that home countries and multinationals themselves are also important players in the 'race to the bottom'. US multinationals have successfully used new 'self-help' techniques made possible by recent US legislative changes to lower their effective tax burdens abroad.

The last two lessons more directly address issues of tax reform. The sixth lesson is that the efficiency standards that have been proposed for evaluating the international tax systems are not particularly useful for guiding policy. This is because standards in the literature such as capital export or capital import neutrality make very special assumptions and do not take into account all of the decision margins facing corporations engaged in cross-border investments. The seventh and final lesson concerns the evaluation of tax reforms: any analysis of how different tax policies will impact home country multinationals must take the details of the current tax system and the new system into account. For example, careful studies suggest that moving from the current US tax system which taxes the worldwide profits of US corporations to a territorial tax system which taxes only profits earned in the US could actually raise revenues relative to the current system and make investment abroad in low-tax countries less attractive to US multinationals.

The chapter is organized around these seven lessons. However, before turning to the lessons, the chapter begins (section 4.2) with a short review of the current US system for taxing the international income of US corporations. The remainder of the chapter discusses policy lessons that can be drawn from recent research on the behavior of US multinational corporations. The final section concludes.

4.2 A BRIEF REVIEW OF THE US SYSTEM FOR TAXING INTERNATIONAL INCOME

It is necessary to review the basic rules of the US tax system towards international income before turning to findings from studies that have investigated how multinational behavior responds to these rules. The current US tax system subjects both the domestic and foreign earnings of US corporations to US taxation. If foreign operations are organized as subsidiaries (that is, they are separately incorporated in the foreign country), then active business profits are not generally taxed at home until they are remitted to the US parent corporation. All repatriated foreign income is taxed, including not only dividends but also royalties, interest, and other foreign payments.

To alleviate the double taxation of foreign source income, the US allows firms to claim credits for income taxes paid to foreign governments against US tax liability on foreign source income. A limitation on the credit prevents American firms from using foreign tax credits to reduce

US tax liabilities on income earned at home. If a firm's foreign tax payments exceed the limitation on the credit, the firm pays no residual US taxes on income repatriations from low-tax countries (those countries with statutory corporate tax rates above the US rate). A firm in this situation is said to have 'excess credits'. If a firm's foreign tax payments are less than the credit, the firm pays a residual US tax on income repatriations from low-tax countries equal to the difference between the US corporate rate and the foreign rate. A firm in this situation is said to have 'excess limitation'.

Two steps are important in the foreign tax credit limitation calculation. First, the foreign income is separated into baskets to restrict cross-crediting, that is, credits flowing from highly taxed income to shield income that has been lightly taxed. Before the 2004 American Jobs Creation Act (AJCA), the three significant income baskets were general nonfinancial active income, financial services income, and passive income. The AJCA effectively collapsed the baskets into two, active income and passive income. Within any basket, excess credits generated by one type of income (for example, dividends) can flow over to other income in the basket (for example, royalties) and shield that income from any residual US tax.

In the second step of the foreign tax credit limitation calculation, parent overhead expenses such as interest are allocated to each basket to calculate the net foreign income on which the credit can be claimed. This only affects companies if they cannot credit all the foreign taxes they have paid. If a company has excess credits, allocation of expenses to foreign income increases US tax by reducing allowable credits. If the company does not have excess credits, or is currently not repatriating income, the allocations have no effect on current US tax liability. Allocations of overhead expenses can be very large and can play an important role in tax reforms.

Under the current system, certain types of foreign income do not qualify for deferral and are instead taxed upon accrual under what are generally referred to as Controlled Foreign Corporation (CFC) rules. (A CFC is a foreign corporation that is at least 50 percent owned by a group of US shareholders each of whom have at least a 10 percent interest in the company.) The CFC rules are designed to hamper the ability of firms to avoid US taxes on foreign income by retaining it abroad in low-tax jurisdictions. In general, these 'anti-tax avoidance' provisions deny deferred taxation on passive portfolio income and the payment of interest, dividends and royalties from one CFC to a CFC in another jurisdiction. Under the CFC rules, this highly mobile income is taxed currently as if it had been repatriated to the US parent.

In 1997, regulations introduced 'hybrid entities' which allowed US companies to avoid the current tax under the CFC rules on intercompany payments like interest and royalties. These regulations are sometimes referred to as 'check-the-box' because they gave companies the freedom to either identify an entity as a separate corporation or to 'disregard' it as the unincorporated branch of another corporation by simply checking the box on a tax form. Hybrid entities are business operations that are regarded as corporations by one country while being an unincorporated branch to another.

Check-the-box allows US multinationals to lower their taxes in high-tax countries by shifting income from affiliates in high-tax countries to affiliates in tax havens. Consider a parent company that plans to invest in Germany. Check the-box lets the firm cut its tax bill by routing capital used to finance the investment through a tax haven affiliate using the following strategy. The parent company first injects equity (the investment funds) into a wholly-owned Cayman Islands affiliate. That affiliate then lends the money to another wholly-owned affiliate, this one in Germany. The German firm uses the loan for an investment project and pays interest to the Cayman affiliate. The parent 'checks the box' on the German affiliate, making it an unincorporated branch of the Cayman subsidiary for US tax purposes, a 'tax nothing'. But the German government considers it to be a separate corporation.

The interest payment from the German firm to the Cayman subsidiary is not taxed anywhere. The interest payment is deductible in Germany and not taxed in the US because under check the box the combined German/Cayman operation is regarded as a single corporation. And the interest is untaxed in the Caymans, which has a zero tax rate. The interest payment will not be taxed until it is paid back to the US parent. This strategy for capitalizing a high-tax affiliate was not tax advantaged prior to 1997 since the interest payment would have been taxed at the US rate when paid to the tax haven under the CFC rules.

Why would a home country like the United States allow this kind of method of shifting (or 'stripping') income out of a high-tax location to a tax haven? It depends on its judgment on the consequences of lowering the tax burden on US companies in the high-tax location. If its home-based companies move capital to the high-tax location from foreign low-tax locations – from Ireland to Germany for example – both the world and the home country are better off. Capital has moved to a location with a higher pre-tax return relative to where it would be employed if check-the-box were not in place.[2]

What about the policy responses of the high-tax country? The high-tax host country could resist the income stripping strategy made possible by check-the-box by enforcing 'thin capitalization' rules which limit the extent to which a company can leverage itself up, particularly when the interest is paid to related parties offshore. But it may not choose to do so as a way of attracting inward foreign direct investment by discriminating in favor of internationally mobile companies that can take advantage of these income-shifting strategies. Tax competition can operate along many dimensions, not just by lowering statutory corporate tax rates or granting investment credits.

Hybrid entities can also be used to route dividends to a holding company in a country with a favorable tax regime, one that operates a dividend exemption system and has an extensive tax treaty network assuring low withholding taxes on dividends. Multinationals frequently find it convenient to organize their foreign investments through such holding companies. Without the use of a hybrid entity, the intercompany dividends would generally be subject to current US tax.

Hybrids may also be used to shift income from intellectual property like patents to tax havens by making the intercompany royalty payments invisible. The tax haven entity can engage in a cost-sharing agreement whereby it pays for part of the parent's R&D project. This gives it the right to license the resulting technology to other foreign subsidiaries in exchange for royalty payments. Because the appropriate cost-sharing payments and royalties are very uncertain, the multinational can attempt to underprice the former and overprice the latter, leaving a large amount of income in the tax haven. The royalty payments by the high-tax affiliate are not subject to the CFC rules because the tax haven entity and the high-tax affiliate can be declared as one consolidated incorporated subsidiary.

Hybrid securities are another planning device that can sometimes achieve the same results as hybrid entities. These instruments are regarded as debt by the host country and equity by the country to which income payments are made. They exploit the difficulties that tax authorities have in determining the distinction between tax deductible debt and taxable equity. These hybrid securities are particularly effective in saving taxes when the receiving country employs a dividend exemption system. Examples are the Netherlands, France and Canada which exempt dividends paid from an active direct investment abroad. Thus a Canadian company can capitalize an operating subsidiary in the United States with a hybrid security and receive payments that are deductible in the United States but exempt at home. Once again the income completely escapes taxation at the corporate level. Hybrid securities can be combined with hybrid entities to ensure a deduction in the paying host country, no tax in the receiving foreign country and no tax by the United States.

I turn next to the seven lessons.

4.3 LESSON 1: REAL CAPITAL IS MOBILE AND HAS BECOME MORE SENSITIVE TO DIFFERENCES IN HOST COUNTRY TAX RATES

An important concern for policy analysts is how any change to the system of taxing cross-border income will affect the global allocation of capital. To address this question it is necessary to know the degree to which international capital flows respond to changes in the after-tax rates of return at home and abroad. Work on this question using data from the 1980s suggests that the location decisions of US multinationals are responsive to tax differences (see Grubert and Mutti, 1991; Hines and Rice, 1994).[3]

Grubert and Mutti (1997) were the first to suggest that the sensitivity of US investment abroad to after-tax rates of return abroad may have increased in the 1990s. To investigate this question, Altshuler et al. (2001), hereafter AGN, examined whether the distribution of US foreign direct investment became more sensitive to inter-country differences in tax rates between 1984 and 1992. Interest in this question stems from two factors. First, production appears to have become more globally integrated over this time period. In addition, starting in the 1980s, corporate taxes fell in several countries including Canada, the United States, the United Kingdom, France, Belgium and the Netherlands.

To estimate the sensitivity of foreign direct investment to differences in after-tax returns across countries, AGN examine data from US Treasury tax files on real capital (inventory, plant and equipment) of foreign manufacturing affiliates of US multinationals for 1984 and 1992. There are two advantages to studying data that span more than a single year. First, researchers can control for unobservable time-invariant characteristics, such as risk and political instability, which influence investment and are specific to individual countries. In addition, using more than one year of data allows for an econometric test of whether the responsiveness of investment to taxes changed over the time period spanned by the data.

To measure the sensitivity of location decisions to host country tax rates, AGN regress a measure of real capital held in each of their sample countries on tax and non-tax characteristics of countries. These regressions yield an elasticity that measures the sensitivity of the demand for capital in a country to changes in after-tax returns. The resulting elasticity estimates indicate that a 1 percent increase in after-tax returns led to an almost 3 percent increase in the real capital stock of manufacturing affiliates in 1992 and a 1.5 percent increase in 1984. This significant increase in elasticities suggests that the allocation of real capital abroad became more sensitive to differences in host country taxes between 1984 and 1992. While this research does not identify what factors are responsible for these results, they are certainly consistent with the view that technological advances along with the loosening of trade restrictions and capital controls have increased the ease with which capital can cross national borders. According to this view, different locations have become closer substitutes for the location of production.

Altshuler and Grubert (2004) extend this work using data from 1992, 1998 and 2000 to explore whether firms have become even more sensitive to differences in tax burdens abroad. While their results from the econometric work are not conclusive, they suggest that in recent years local taxes have become a more significant factor for explaining differences in the distribution of real assets abroad. Altshuler and Grubert report that the capital demand elasticity increases from about three in 1992 to four in 2000. Statistical tests, however, reject that these elasticities are significantly different from each other. Work with more recent data may show a statistically different and larger estimate of the capital demand elasticity. While policy makers do seem cognizant that real capital is mobile, these estimates contribute important parameters to the debate.

4.4 LESSON 2: THE MOBILITY OF INTANGIBLE CAPITAL SEEMS TO HAVE INCREASED OVER TIME

US direct investment abroad is strongly motivated by the exploitation of intangible assets like patents and trademarks which are typically developed in the United States. The ability to shield US taxes on royalties under the US foreign tax credit system along with income shifting opportunities creates incentives to exploit intangible assets abroad which have been developed by the parent corporation at home. While part of the return on intangibles abroad is paid out in royalties to the parent, the evidence suggests that the foreign subsidiary retains a significant portion.

There is little empirical evidence on the impact of taxes on the location of intangible capital. Although royalties do not fully capture the returns to intangible assets, they do indicate where intangible assets are being invested. Data in the Bureau of Economic Analysis (BEA) Benchmark Surveys of US Investment Abroad suggest that low-tax countries are becoming much more important destinations for US-produced intangible assets. Specifically, Altshuler and Grubert (2004) find that the share of total affiliate royalties from Ireland and Singapore doubled between 1994 and 1999. The share of total royalties paid by subsidiaries in these locations increased from about 9 percent to 21 percent, and the share of royalties paid to the US parent increased from about 8 percent to 20 percent. In

1999, royalties paid by Irish affiliates exceeded royalties paid by German or United Kingdom affiliates, and total royalties paid by Singapore affiliates were only 25 percent lower than royalties paid by Japanese affiliates.[4]

Recent work by Mutti and Grubert (2007) using information from the US Treasury tax files suggests that there has been substantial movement of intangible assets from the United States to foreign countries. The new tax planning techniques discussed above seem to play an important role in this story. The 'check-the-box' regulations have made it easier for US firms to set up hybrid entities in low-tax locations like Ireland and the 'pure' tax havens of Bermuda, the Cayman Islands and Luxembourg. Once a low-tax hybrid is established, the US parent can set up a favorable cost sharing agreement. The low-tax hybrid 'buys in' to the parent R&D project. The low-tax hybrid can eventually license the resulting technology to a high-tax affiliate in return for royalty payments.

Mutti and Grubert (2007) find that the importance of cost-sharing payments increased between 1996 and 2002, relative to both royalties and earnings and profits. They report that 'cost sharing payments from affiliates in Ireland and from tax havens are particularly significant, both economically and statistically' (p. 28). This is the first evidence that US parents are able to relocate intangible assets abroad without actually carrying out research and development in affiliates. The migration of intellectual property is a hot topic today in the United States and likely to generate lively debate when the country begins to focus on international tax reform.

4.5 LESSON 3: INCOME SHIFTING IS GETTING WORSE

Opportunities for cross-border shifting are an important feature of both worldwide and territorial tax systems. The observation that the reported profitability of US multinationals is much higher in low-tax countries than high-tax countries, suggesting tax induced income shifting, goes back a long way, at least to Grubert and Mutti (1991). Differences in profitability could be generated by the shifting of debt (and therefore interest deductions) to high-tax jurisdictions, the manipulation of transfer prices for goods and services, or the failure to pay adequate royalties for intellectual property contributed by the parent company. Grubert (2003) suggests that the location of intangible income and the allocation of debt among high- and low-tax countries seem to account for all of the observed differences in profitability across high- and low-statutory tax countries.

Interest stripping is likely the easiest way for firms to minimize worldwide tax payments. Altshuler and Grubert (2002) present evidence from the US Treasury tax files that suggests that the financial structure of multinationals is influenced by local tax rates. In a regression with debt–asset ratios as a dependent variable, they show that affiliate leverage is a highly significant negative function of local statutory tax rates.

Again, while there are no direct measures of income shifting, there is suggestive evidence that it is getting worse. Altshuler and Grubert (2005), on the basis of a comparison of Treasury data for manufacturing subsidiaries in 1996 and 2000, find that the negative correlation between corporate statutory rates and pre-tax earnings and profits has intensified. Their results indicate that by 2000, the profit ratio in a country with a 10 percent tax rate was almost twice as large as one with a 40 percent statutory tax rate. McDonald (2008) finds that the negative correlation between profit margins and the statutory tax rate in the Treasury tax files became even stronger in 2002.

It is important to note that this evidence only pertains to profitability differences among foreign countries. We do not know whether the high profits in low-tax countries constitute income shifted from another foreign country or income shifted from the United States.

4.6 LESSON 4: GOVERNMENTS ARE ENGAGED IN TAX COMPETITION AND IT HAS LIKELY INTENSIFIED OVER TIME

Table 4.1 presents the global average effective tax rates faced by US manufacturing subsidiaries of US parent corporations calculated from the US Treasury tax files. The global average effective tax rate faced by US manufacturing parents fell by about 12 percentage points between 1980 and 2000. Furthermore, the distribution of worldwide tax rates became tighter in the last decade (the standard deviation fell and decreased relative to the mean) indicating some convergence in effective tax rates.

As mentioned above, Altshuler et al. (2001) used these data from the Treasury tax files to show that the location of capital invested abroad by manufacturing affiliates of US multinationals became more sensitive to differences in host country effective tax rates between 1984 and 1992. In research using the same Treasury tax return data for 1984 through 1992, Grubert (2001a) looked for changes in the behavior of both taxpayers and governments. Among other questions, he asked whether the behavior of governments during this period suggests more tax competition. Grubert found that smaller, poorer, and more open countries lowered their effective tax rates the most between 1984 and 1992. This is consistent with tax

Table 4.1 Average effective tax rates for US manufacturing corporations

Year	Average effective tax rate	Standard deviation
1980	0.33	0.85
1982	0.34	0.98
1984	0.34	1.03
1986	0.32	1.05
1988	0.31	1.09
1990	0.26	0.89
1992	0.25	0.86
1994	0.22	0.72
1996	0.23	0.79
1998	0.24	0.77
2000	0.21	0.67

Note:
Host country average effective tax rates are calculated by dividing the total income taxes paid by US CFCs in the manufacturing sector by their total earnings and profits (only CFCs with positive earnings and profits are included in the totals). Data is from 58 countries. The global means for each year presented in the table are an average of the effective tax rates in all 58 countries weighted by the number of CFCs in each country in 1990. The data come from the Treasury tax files.

competition since one would expect that these countries would be most affected by the increased mobility of capital.

Altshuler and Grubert (2004) use the same tax return data to focus more closely on the period from 1992 to 2000. While tax competition between countries may be responsible for part of the drop in effective tax rates since the 1990s, the growth of hybrids (and thus company responses) may play an important role in explaining the most recent decreases in effective tax rates. For this reason, Altshuler and Grubert study the changes in country effective tax rates between 1992 and 1998 separately from the changes between 1998 and 2000 (after the check-the-box regulations came into effect).

Altshuler and Grubert's results suggest that tax competition was the driving force behind the decrease in country effective tax rates between 1992 and 1998. Countries that lost shares of US manufacturing real capital prior to 1992 cut their rates the most over the subsequent six years. Further, smaller countries and those with high initial average effective tax rates experienced above average declines in effective tax rates.

The decrease in effective tax rates between 1998 and 2000 does not seem to be driven by the same tax competition dynamic. However, Altshuler and Grubert report changes in the country's capital share, the initial level of the country's effective tax rate, and whether the country is small do not explain differences in declines in effective tax rates over this period. A different phenomenon seems to be at work which brings us to the next lesson.

4.7 LESSON 5: HOST COUNTRY GOVERNMENTS, HOME COUNTRY GOVERNMENTS AND MULTINATIONAL CORPORATIONS ARE ALL PLAYERS IN THE TAX COMPETITION GAME

Most studies of tax competition and the 'race to the bottom' focus on potential host countries competing for mobile capital, neglecting the role of corporate tax planning and of the home governments that facilitate this planning. This neglect reflects the narrow view frequently taken of the policy instruments that countries have available in tax competition – statutory corporate tax rates, tax holidays and tax credits, for example. But high-tax host governments can, for instance, permit income to be shifted out to tax havens as a way of attracting mobile companies. Home countries will cooperate in this shift if their companies' gain is greater than any reduction in the domestic tax base. Altshuler and Grubert (2005) use various types of US data to identify the role of the three parties (host governments, home governments and multinationals) in the evolution of tax burdens on US companies abroad from 1992 to 2002.

Evidence from the Treasury tax files seems to confirm the role of the companies and the cooperation, or non-resistance, of home and host countries in lowering the cost of investment abroad. Altshuler and Grubert find that controlled foreign corporation effective tax rates after 1997 were much less closely correlated with the local statutory corporate tax rate than prior to 1997, suggesting that some profitable companies in high-tax locations were able to take advantage of the new tax planning opportunities. Furthermore, as mentioned above in section 4.5, the disparity of CFC profitability between high-tax and low-tax countries widened substantially after 1997. This might have happened, for example, if parents use one of the new tax planning strategies in which a highly profitable operation formerly incorporated in a high-tax location 'disappears' into a low-tax sibling that has stripped income out of it. In fact, the tangible capital reported by CFCs incorporated in tax haven locations such as Bermuda and the Cayman Islands grew very rapidly after 1996.

The surveys of direct investors by the Bureau of Economic Analysis (BEA) in the US Commerce Department show a very large increase in intercompany payments and in the income of holding companies abroad after 1997. This presumably resulted from the new planning structures facilitated by the 1997 Treasury regulations. In interpreting this growth in intercompany income it is important to distinguish between deductible payments like interest and nondeductible payments like dividends paid out of after-tax income. Using two different BEA series, Altshuler and Grubert (2005) conclude that approximately 40 percent of the growth of intercompany income was in the form of payments deductible in the host country (and presumably not taxable in the receiving country). This suggests that corporations saved about $7 billion in taxes in 2002 compared to what they would have paid if they continued to behave the same way as in 1997. This is about 4 percent of foreign direct investment income, a substantial reduction in such a short period. This work provides evidence of the empirical significance of tax planning strategies involving the use of tax havens. Home governments and multinationals themselves have joined host governments in the tax competition game.

4.8 LESSON 6: THE EFFICIENCY CRITERIA THAT HAVE BEEN PROPOSED TO EVALUATE INTERNATIONAL TAX SYSTEMS ARE NOT PARTICULARLY USEFUL FOR GUIDING POLICY

Several standards have been proposed for optimal worldwide efficiency such as Capital Export Neutrality (CEN), Capital Import Neutrality (CIN) and Capital Ownership Neutrality (CON).[5] Grubert and Altshuler (2008) point out that these criteria take only a partial view of all the decision margins facing companies making cross-border investments.[6] For example, all focus on investment of tangible capital without considering the critical role of the location of intangible capital. Also, none of them takes the opportunities for income shifting into account. As a result, there is frequently not a very good mapping between efficiency criteria such as CEN or CIN that have been proposed and a particular reform alternative.

The usual standards that have been proposed such as CEN or CIN explicitly or implicitly make very special assumptions for which there is very little empirical evidence. One issue is the supply of capital available to US multinational companies. For example, CEN assumes that all investment by US companies comes from domestic saving, more correctly from a fixed pool of capital available to the US corporate sector. CIN and CON seem to assume that capital is supplied at a fixed rate by the integrated world capital market, but that is only the start of the story. As mentioned above, all three ignore the presence of intangible assets and how they affect the relationship between investments in different locations, or how opportunities for income shifting under one system or another alter effective tax rates in different locations.

Therefore, even if policy makers accept an integrated worldwide capital market that offers financing to companies on the same terms irrespective of where they are based, that is not sufficient to choose the optimal policy. Consider a potential investment in a low-tax location. The question is what other investments in that or other locations it competes with. For example, consider a locational intangible like a fast food trademark that requires that the company produce locally in order to supply its customers. In that case, all competitors compete in the same location and should bear the same (presumably local) tax burden. Now consider a mobile intangible like the design of a computer chip that can be produced in various locations for the worldwide market. In that case, the competitors for the potential low-tax investment may be in high-tax locations including the United States.[7] CIN and CON implicitly assume the first case and CEN seems to lean toward the second where all foreign affiliate production substitutes for domestic US production. None of the standards proposed fits all cases and tax policy cannot feasibly be calibrated to have different rules for different cases.

Furthermore, even if one assumes that the low-tax investment only has local competitors, CIN or CON may not be optimal because opportunities for income shifting can magnify the benefit of a low-tax location. The tax planning itself also wastes resources. For example, the investment might be financed by borrowing by a related party in a high-tax location, or the subsidiary may pay low royalties for a very valuable patent, creating very low or negative effective tax burdens. Being part of a multinational company may offer the subsidiary substantially lower tax burdens than purely local competitors.

Accordingly, Grubert and Altshuler (2008) conclude that the goal of reform within an income tax should be to eliminate unnecessary waste and the possibility of extremely high or low tax burdens that are not justified under any standard. With this goal in mind, policy makers can ensure that the system is moving toward the optimum without overshooting it and running the risk of making things worse.

4.9 LESSON 7: THE STARTING POINT FOR TAX REFORM IS THE CURRENT SYSTEM

The current system must be the starting point for the analysis of any tax policy change. Further, when considering tax reform the details of the new system must be specified to understand the welfare gains or losses of any change. While this seems like an obvious point, discussions of reform often focus on comparing idealized tax systems and, as a result, are not informative to policy makers.

Consider, for example, the current US system for taxing international income. At first glance, one might predict that the worldwide or 'residence' tax system would dampen the tax incentive to invest abroad in low-tax countries. This contrasts with the tax incentives of firms subject to dividend exemption or 'territorial' tax systems. These firms face the local tax rate when investing abroad, of course, but owe no residual home country taxes on foreign investment. As a result, one might expect that switching from a residence to a territorial system would lead to a substantial reallocation of US investment worldwide.

Altshuler and Grubert (2001) study how the location decisions of US multinationals may change if the US were to adopt a system that exempts foreign dividends from home taxation and find some surprising results. They start by comparing the US allocation of foreign direct investment (FDI) in manufacturing across low-tax versus high-tax jurisdictions with that of two major dividend exemption countries, Canada and Germany, to investigate whether the distribution of Canadian and German FDI is more skewed toward low-tax countries. Although they find that US investment in Asia is more skewed towards the low-tax countries, the picture that emerges for Europe is mixed. Compared to the US, Canadian investment in the European Union is heavily weighted towards Ireland (a low-tax country). Whether US firms would shift towards a similar regional distribution in Europe under a territorial tax system is an open question.

Altshuler and Grubert calculate effective marginal tax rates to quantify the burden of US taxes on the typical investment in a low-tax affiliate under the current system and under dividend exemption. The calculations show that effective tax rates in low-tax countries may actually increase under dividend exemption. Whether the incentive to invest in low-tax countries increases depends on how (and whether) expenses incurred at home are allocated to foreign source income under the new system, as well as individual characteristics of multinationals. For example, under dividend exemption there would be no foreign tax credits to shield royalty payments. This would increase the tax burden of investing abroad for firms with a high proportion of intangible relative to tangible assets.

Finally, Altshuler and Grubert use US Treasury data from the tax returns of multinationals to gauge how location decisions will be affected by a move towards dividend exemption. Taken together, the paper presents no consistent or definitive evidence that location decisions would be significantly changed if the US were to adopt a dividend exemption system. Grubert (2001b) looks at a related question: how would US tax revenues change if the US were to adopt a dividend exemption system? Again the results are surprising and depend on both the allocation rules enacted with dividend exemption and how firms respond to the new system. Exempting dividends from US taxation would likely raise revenue if expense allocation rules are imposed. In the absence of expense allocation rules, dividend exemption loses revenue.

The lesson is that it is fundamental to understand both the starting point for reform and the form that reform will take. Without information on the burdens firms face under the current system and the details on the new system, it is impossible to make judgments on whether a different system is better than the current system.

4.10 CONCLUSIONS

Recent studies of how US multinationals respond to home and host country tax systems paint a picture of increasing responsiveness to tax policy. Real and intangible capital has become more mobile, income shifting has gotten worse, tax planning has become more sophisticated and tax competition has intensified. Recent evidence suggests that tax policies that affect corporate decisions can also influence portfolio decisions of resident investors. As globalization has spread and global operations become more connected, the taxation of international income has become increasingly complex.

The policy question, of course, is how to reform corporate tax systems. Given the increased sophistication of tax planners, the mobility of capital and even corporate headquarters, a reasonable question is whether there should even be a separate corporate tax. Putting aside options for eliminating the corporate tax, the lessons from the research on US multinationals suggest that a simple tax system with low tax rates and a broad base may best fit the world economy. Lower tax rates generate fewer distortions and decrease the gains to tax planning. Broadening the base by including all income regardless of source and taxing it currently is one possibility. Grubert and Altshuler (2008) propose such a system for the United States. However, much more work needs to be done to understand all of the implications of moving to a system with a lower corporate tax rate. This type of reform, however, may be exactly what the lessons discussed in this chapter suggest.

NOTES

* I thank Howard Gleckman, Roberton Williams, Tony Booth, and participants from the 'New Zealand Tax Reform – Where to Next?' conference held at Victoria University of Wellington in Wellington, New Zealand on February 11–12, 2009 for helpful comments. Much of this chapter reviews joint work with Harry Grubert to whom I owe an enormous intellectual debt.

1. Hines (1997, 1999) and Gordon and Hines (2002) review the literature on the impact of taxation on the activities of multinational companies. I review some of the more recent literature in this chapter and, as noted, focus on empirical work with data from US multinational corporations.
2. Another way in which home countries increase the competitiveness of their companies is by not requiring them to allocate overhead expenses to foreign income. Thus a company can borrow at home and invest equity in a low-tax jurisdiction, thereby receiving a tax deduction for the interest while paying little or no tax on its earnings. Among the OECD countries, only the United States makes a serious effort to require interest allocations, and that is incomplete because it operates only through the foreign tax credit limitation.
3. See also Grubert and Mutti (2000), Altshuler et al. (2001), and most recently, Altshuler and Grubert (2004).
4. Detailed data on royalty payments by subsidiaries from the 2004 BEA Benchmark Survey are not yet available. The US Direct Investment data published annually in the Survey of Current Business, however, does contain information on royalty payments from US affiliates to US parents. The story has not changed. Ireland and Singapore account for almost 20 percent of total royalties. Royalties from Irish affiliates remain larger than those from German and United Kingdom affiliates, and royalties from Singapore affiliates are still significant relative to those from Japanese affiliates (royalties paid from Singapore affiliates are about two-thirds as large as those paid by Japanese affiliates).
5. The concepts of CEN and CIN, introduced by Richman (1963), have been widely discussed in the literature. The CON efficiency benchmark is introduced in Desai and Hines (2003). We concentrate on these standards which take worldwide efficiency as the goal. Some have proposed national welfare under the assumption that home governments can not obtain reciprocal concessions necessary to approximate worldwide efficiency.
6. This section of the chapter borrows heavily from Grubert and Altshuler (2008).
7. See Grubert and Mutti (1995) for a discussion of the general second-best rule.

REFERENCES

Altshuler, R. and H. Grubert (2001), 'Where will they go if we go territorial? Dividend exemption and the foreign location decisions of U.S. multinational corporations', *National Tax Journal,* **54**, 787–809.

Altshuler, R. and Grubert, H. (2002), 'Repatriation taxes, repatriation strategies, and multinational financial policy', *Journal of Public Economics*, **87**(1), 73–107.

Altshuler, R. and H. Grubert (2004), 'Taxpayer responses to competitive tax policies and tax policy responses to competitive taxpayers: Recent evidence', *Tax Notes International*, **34**, 1349–62.

Altshuler, R. and H. Grubert (2005), 'The three parties in the race to the bottom: Host governments, home governments and multinational corporations', *Florida Tax Review*, **7**, 154–83.

Altshuler, R., H. Grubert and T.S. Newlon (2001), 'Has U.S. investment become more sensitive to tax rates?', in J.R. Hines (ed.), *International Taxation and Multinational Activity*, Chicago: University of Chicago Press, pp. 9–32.

Desai, M.A. and J.R. Hines (2003), 'Evaluating international tax reform', *National Tax Journal*, **56**, 487–502.

Gordon, R.H. and J.R. Hines (2002), 'International taxation', in A.J. Auerbach and M. Feldstein (eds), *Handbook of Public Economics, Vol. 4*, Amsterdam: North-Holland, pp. 1935–95.

Grubert, H. (2001a), 'Tax planning by companies and tax competition by governments: Is there evidence of changes in behavior?', in J.R. Hines (ed.), *International Taxation and Multinational Activity*, Chicago: University of Chicago Press, pp. 113–39.

Grubert, H. (2001b), 'Enacting dividend exemption and tax revenue', *National Tax Journal*, **54**, 811–27.

Grubert, H. (2003), 'Intangible income, intercompany transactions, income shifting and the choice of location', *National Tax Journal*, **56**, 221–42.

Grubert, H. and R. Altshuler (2008), 'Corporate taxes in the world economy: Reforming the taxation of cross-border income', in J. Diamond and G. Zodrow (eds), *Fundamental Tax Reform: Issues, Choices and Implications*, Cambridge, MA: MIT Press, 319–54.

Grubert, H. and J. Mutti (1991), 'Taxes, tariffs and transfer pricing in multinational corporation decision making', *Review of Economics and Statistics*, **33**, 285–93.

Grubert, H. and J. Mutti (1995), 'Taxing multinationals in a world with portfolio flows and R&D: Is capital export neutrality obsolete?, *International Tax and Public Finance*, **2**, 439–57.

Grubert, H. and J. Mutti (1997), *Do taxes influence where U.S. corporations invest?*, mimeo.

Grubert, H. and J. Mutti (2000), 'Do taxes influence where U.S. corporations invest?', *National Tax Journal*, **53**(4), 825–39.

Hines, J.R. (1997), 'Tax policy and the activities of multinational corporations', in A.J. Auerbach (ed.), *Fiscal Policy: Lessons from Economic Research*, Cambridge, MA: MIT Press, pp. 401–45.

Hines, J. R. (1999), 'Lessons from behavioral responses to international taxation', *National Tax Journal*, **52**, 305–22.

Hines, J.R. and E. Rice (1994), 'Fiscal paradise: Foreign tax havens and American business', *Quarterly Journal of Economics*, **109**, 149–82.

McDonald, M. (2008), *Income Shifting from Transfer Pricing: Further Evidence from Tax Return Data*, Office of Tax Analysis Technical Working Paper No. 2, Washington, DC: U.S. Treasury Department.

Mutti, J. and H. Grubert (2007), *The effect of taxes on royalties and the migration of intangible assets abroad*, NBER Working Paper Number No. 13248, Cambridge, MA: NBER.

Richman, P.B. (1963), *Taxation of Foreign Investment Income: An Economic Analysis*, Baltimore, MD: Johns Hopkins Press.

5. Dual income taxes: a Nordic tax system

Peter Birch Sørensen

5.1 PRINCIPLES OF DUAL INCOME TAXATION

5.1.1 What is a Dual Income Tax?

The Nordic dual income tax (henceforth termed the DIT) is a particular form of schedular income tax which combines progressive taxation of labour and transfer income with a low flat tax on all capital income. In the pure version of the system the flat tax rate on capital income is aligned with the corporate income tax rate and with the marginal tax rate on labour income in the first bracket. In this case the DIT may be described as a system that combines a flat tax on total income with a progressive surtax on labour and transfer income.

An important part of the philosophy underlying the DIT is that the capital income tax base should be broad, to ensure the greatest possible degree of tax neutrality. Under a consistent DIT, the personal capital income tax base would thus include the following components:

- interest
- dividends
- capital gains
- rental income
- royalties
- imputed returns on owner-occupied housing
- imputed returns on capital invested in non-corporate firms

In case the sum of these components is negative, the taxpayer is entitled to a tax credit equal to the capital income tax rate times the negative balance.

The quest for tax neutrality was well reflected in the Norwegian DIT introduced in 1992 which aimed to tax all capital income once but only once. Hence the Norwegian tax reform involved full alleviation of the double taxation of corporate income. For distributed corporate profits, this was achieved by aligning the corporate income tax rate with the personal capital income tax rate and by offering a full imputation credit for the underlying corporation tax against the personal capital income tax on dividends. For retained corporate profits, double taxation was avoided by allowing shareholders to add (their proportionate share of) the company's retained taxable profits to the basis of their shares when calculating the taxable capital gain on shares. Further, to achieve rough neutrality in the tax treatment of wage earners and entrepreneurs, the Norwegian DIT split the income from self-employment and from small companies into an imputed return to capital, taxable as capital income, and a residual income subject to labour income tax. Under the Norwegian DIT the capital income tax base also included an imputed return to owner-occupied housing, albeit based on assessed property values that were typically well below market values.

Before discussing the rationale for the dual tax system outlined above, it may be useful to consider how it relates to various other 'grand designs' for the personal tax system.

5.1.2 The Dual Income Tax versus Other Blueprints for the Personal Tax System

Historically the personal tax systems of most OECD countries have been inspired by the philosophy of the progressive comprehensive income tax. Under this tax system the taxpayer's net incomes from all sources are added together, and this sum total is then subject to a progressive tax schedule with rising marginal tax rates. Ideally, comprehensive income in the sense of Schanz-Haig-Simons is defined as the increase in the taxpayer's purchasing power over the tax period. Hence income should be measured in real terms, with appropriate inflation adjustment of nominal returns to capital, and all accrued real capital gains (losses) should be taxed (deducted), whether they have been realised or not.

Apart from its consistency with a particular notion of equity in taxation – that all those with the same purchasing power, however they derive it, should pay the same amount of tax – the comprehensive income tax has the appeal of eliminating any incentive to artificially transform one kind of income into another, since the taxpayer faces the same marginal tax rate on all types of income. Yet, in practice governments have been reluctant to tax unrealised capital gains and other forms of accrued income such as returns to institutional saving, because such income may be hard to measure and/or because the taxpayer may lack the liquidity needed to pay tax on unrealised income. Hence, to the extent that capital gains are taxed at all, the tax is typically deferred until the time of realisation, giving rise to the well-known lock-in effect and implying a tax preference for capital gains, due to the benefit from tax deferral. Moreover, in practice the returns to nominal assets are rarely subject to systematic adjustment for inflation before being subject to tax, so the effective tax rate on real income may deviate substantially from the statutory tax rate.

Because of these and other problems with (the practical implementation of) the comprehensive income tax, many academics have favoured the expenditure tax under which all savings would be deductible from the tax base whereas all dissavings would be added to the base so that tax would be levied on taxpayers' consumption rather than on their income. A key feature of the expenditure tax is that the after-tax return to savings is the same as the before-tax return on the underlying asset, provided the marginal tax rate is constant over time. Thus the expenditure tax is broadly equivalent to a tax system that exempts the normal return to saving from tax. Because it taxes the taxpayer's observed net cash inflow rather than the accounting income, the expenditure tax tends to avoid the practical problems involved in implementing a comprehensive income tax on accrued capital income. However, while economic theory provides good reasons why capital income should not necessarily be taxed at the same rate as labour income, it also provides several reasons why a positive tax rate on capital income should be part of an optimal tax system (see Sørensen, 2007a). Moreover, because of the perceived transition problems and international complications involved in the switch to an expenditure tax, no OECD government has yet implemented such a tax system.

Recent years have witnessed an increased interest in the so-called flat tax which imposes a constant marginal tax rate on income or consumption above the personal exemption level (see Keen et al., 2006). The flat tax advocated by Hall and Rabushka (1995) is essentially a linear consumption tax and hence equivalent to a linear expenditure tax, since the Hall–Rabuska tax exempts capital income and allows full expensing of all business investment. However, the flat taxes that have recently spread throughout Eastern Europe typically include some or all capital income in the tax base. In these cases the flat tax is just a linear variant of the comprehensive income tax.

The Nordic DIT combines a flat tax on capital income with a progressive labour income tax schedule where the marginal tax rate rises with the level of labour income. The DIT may be seen as a compromise between the comprehensive income tax and the expenditure tax. Whereas the expenditure tax completely exempts the normal return to capital from tax, the DIT imposes a positive tax on income from capital, but at a low flat rate below the top marginal tax rate on labour income.

Like the DIT, the so-called comprehensive business income tax (CBIT) proposed by the US Treasury Department (1992) also combines a flat tax on capital income with a progressive labour income tax. Under the CBIT, interest expenses would no longer be deductible from taxable profits, and business income would be subject to a flat (corporate) tax rate (roughly) equal to the top marginal personal income tax rate. In this way interest, dividends and capital gains would be taxed at source and would therefore be exempt at the individual investor level, since the business income tax would serve as a final withholding tax on capital income. Labour income would continue to be taxed according to a progressive tax schedule, so the marginal rates applying at low levels of income would fall below the business income tax rate. Being source-based, the CBIT would apply equally to foreign and domestic investors supplying capital to the domestic economy.

Thus, while the CBIT aligns the flat capital income tax rate with the top marginal personal tax rate, the pure version of the DIT aligns the capital income tax rate and the corporate income tax rate with the marginal personal tax rate in the first bracket. Moreover, although the DIT could be implemented as a pure source-based tax, as proposed by Cnossen (2000), the tax treaties signed by the Nordic countries typically imply that no withholding taxes are levied on interest and dividends paid out to non-resident investors, so in practice the DIT is a residence-based tax.

5.1.3 The Case for the Dual Income Tax[1]

Compared to a traditional income tax, the unconventional feature of the DIT is that it combines a flat tax on capital income with progressive taxation of labour income. At the theoretical level, it can be argued that such a system is desirable because it serves to equalize the tax treatment of non human and human capital investment (see Nielsen and Sørensen, 1997). If the labour income tax were purely proportional, it would tend to exempt the return to human capital investment from tax. To illustrate, suppose taxpayers with a potential income of \$100 000 in period 1 decide to enrol in an education programme which raises their potential income in period 2 to \$210 000. By sacrificing an income of \$100 000 in the first period, they can thus raise their income in period 2 by \$110 000, implying a 10 per cent pre-tax rate of return to their human capital investment. If labour income is taxed at a flat rate of 50 per cent, the net income foregone in year 1 is \$50 000, while the increase in after-tax income obtainable in year 2 is \$55 000 (= 0.5 × 110 000), so measured in after-tax terms the return to human capital investment is still equal to the 10 per cent pre-tax rate of return. By contrast, the income tax reduces the net return obtainable on physical and financial investments. Thus a purely proportional income tax will tend to favour human over non-human capital investments. But if the labour income tax were progressive, with higher levels of income being subject to higher marginal tax rates, the returns to human capital investments would likewise be curbed by the tax system, thereby tending to eliminate the tax distortion in favour of such investments.

While the above theoretical argument has played a certain role in academic discussions of the DIT, policy makers have been rather more persuaded by a number of practical and pragmatic considerations that speak in favour of setting a relatively low and flat tax rate on capital income. The case for a *low* marginal tax rate on income from capital rests on the following arguments:

- *Inflation*: Income tax is typically levied on the full nominal return to capital, including the inflation premium that compensates for the erosion of the real value of nominal assets. Thus many forms of capital income are overtaxed if charged at the top marginal tax rate applying to labour income.
- *Capital mobility*: As the international mobility of capital increases, there is a growing risk that a high domestic capital income tax rate will induce taxpayers to move their wealth abroad, particularly to foreign low-tax jurisdictions, making it difficult to bring that income into the domestic tax net. Setting a low domestic capital income tax rate reduces the risk of capital flight.
- *Tax neutrality*: Capital income accrues in many forms, some of which are hard to tax (for practical or political reasons). Lowering the tax rate on those types of capital income that *can* be taxed reduces the distortions arising when certain types of capital income cannot be included in the tax base. A low tax rate also makes it easier to broaden the tax base, for instance by including capital gains without causing severe lock-in effects.

In addition, proponents of the DIT offer the following arguments in favour of a flat rather than a progressive tax on capital income:

- *Lock-in effects*: Capital gains taxation based on the realisation principle generates a lock-in effect which hampers the reallocation of capital towards more productive uses. Progressive taxation of realised gains exacerbates this lock-in effect because the taxpayer may be pushed into a higher tax bracket in the year of realisation. A low flat tax on capital income avoids this additional distortion.

- *Tax arbitrage*: Aligning the corporate with the personal tax rate on capital income, and equalizing marginal capital income tax rates across taxpayers, eliminates the scope for tax arbitrage activities that seek to exploit such differences in tax rates.
- *Clientele effects*: Under a progressive capital income tax investors in high-income brackets may choose to specialize in holding assets whose returns accrue in tax-favoured form (for example in the form of capital gains benefiting from tax deferral). Since the productivity of assets may depend on who owns them, such tax distortions to ownership patterns may be undesirable. A switch to proportional capital income taxation will reduce such distortions.
- *Tax administration*: A flat tax rate on capital income simplifies tax administration by allowing the tax on interest and dividends to be collected as a final withholding tax.

The argument that the lack of inflation adjustment under a conventional income tax implies over-taxation of nominal capital income played an important role in persuading Nordic policy makers of the fairness of the DIT. Even at low rates of inflation this argument still has considerable force, since a low inflation rate tends to go hand in hand with low nominal interest rates. For example, suppose the rate of inflation is 2 per cent, while the nominal interest rate is 4 per cent, implying a 2 per cent real interest rate. If the tax rate levied on nominal interest income is 50 per cent, the capital income tax would then confiscate all of the 2 per cent real rate of return, that is, the effective tax rate on the real interest income would be a punitive 100 per cent!

Nordic policy makers also recognised that, in an economy where a large proportion of private savings is channelled into tax-favoured assets like owner-occupied housing and retirement savings accounts or assets yielding low-taxed or tax-exempt capital gains, a high marginal tax rate on other forms of capital income is not a very effective means of redistributing income from the rich to the poor. In such an environment, even high marginal tax rates on the returns to the non-favoured assets are likely to generate little revenue while causing large distortions to the pattern of saving and investment. Indeed, in countries like Norway and Sweden with liberal rules for the deductibility of interest expenses, the personal capital income tax actually caused a huge revenue loss in the late 1980s because of extensive debt-financed household investments in tax-favoured assets. In particular, many taxpayers in high-income brackets took advantage of tax asymmetries to reduce their tax liability. When the marginal tax rate on capital income was lowered through the transition to the DIT, the revenue loss from interest deductibility and the scope for tax arbitrage was reduced considerably. Paradoxically, the sharp reduction of capital income tax rates thus generated a significant revenue gain which enabled the Nordic governments to lower the tax burden on labour income.

The Nordic experience also suggests that, by lowering the capital income tax rate through the transition to a DIT, it becomes easier (economically and politically) to reduce tax non-neutralities through a broadening of the capital income tax base. In particular, a low flat tax capital income tax rate facilitates the taxation of realised capital gains by reducing the familiar lock-in effects. When switching to the DIT, Norway and Sweden did in fact tighten their capital gains tax rules quite considerably.

In summary, the Nordic governments abandoned high progressive taxes on capital income, not because they gave up their traditional distributional policy goals, but because they realised that a high progressive tax on (some forms of) capital income is an inefficient means of redistributing income compared to a progressive labour income tax. After all, much capital income derives from savings out of labour income, and inequalities stemming from large inherited stocks of wealth may be better addressed through instruments such as an inheritance tax. Moreover, when the capital income tax rate is not too high, it becomes easier to move towards a comprehensive capital income tax base which in turn tends to improve horizontal as well as vertical equity among taxpayers.

5.1.4 The Critique of the Dual Income Tax

A balanced assessment of the DIT must of course acknowledge the weaknesses as well as the strengths of the system. In particular, while the switch to a low uniform tax on all capital income reduces the scope for many tax arbitrage activities, it also opens up new possibilities for income shifting by taxpayers who are able to transform high-taxed labour income into low-taxed capital income. The special provisions needed to contain such income shifting may be seen as the Achilles heel of the DIT; they are the subject of section 5.2 below.

In the eyes of many observers, the growing international mobility of capital has tended to strengthen the case for the DIT, since a low capital income tax rate reduces the risk of capital flight. However, some participants in the Nordic tax policy debate have challenged this viewpoint, arguing that the capital flight problem mainly relates to a source-based capital income tax like the corporation tax, whereas the problem is much smaller under a residence-based tax like the personal income tax, since individuals are much less mobile than capital. According to this view, the marginal personal tax rate on capital income should be kept in line with the marginal personal tax rate on labour income to preserve horizontal equity and eliminate possibilities for income shifting, while the capital flight problem should be addressed by setting the corporate income tax rate well below the top marginal personal tax rate.

While influential among Nordic tax lawyers, this view has met with opposition from tax economists who point out that as long as capital gains on shares cannot be taxed at the time of accrual, a corporate tax rate well below the personal capital income tax rate would generate a strong incentive to accumulate income within existing corporations even if the capital could be invested more productively elsewhere. Indeed, the evidence from OECD countries suggests that, on average, a one percentage point cut in the corporate tax rate (keeping the personal tax rate on interest income constant) generates a 2.6 percentage point increase in the fraction of private savings channelled through the corporate sector (see Fuest and Weichenrieder, 2002). A large positive gap between the marginal personal capital income tax rate and the corporate tax rate is thus likely to have a strong distortionary lock-in effect on capital invested in existing corporations. Even though the capital flight argument may seem most relevant in the context of corporate income taxation, it is therefore desirable to keep the personal capital income tax rate roughly in line with the corporate tax rate to avoid lock-in effects hampering the free flow of capital towards its most productive uses.[2] Moreover, because of the well-known practical difficulties of monitoring foreign source capital income, a high personal capital income tax rate may in fact induce some capital flight even if investors maintain domestic residence.

5.1.5 Alternative Visions for the Dual Income Tax and Current Nordic Practices

An important policy choice in the design of a DIT is whether the low flat tax rate on capital income should apply to the full return to capital or only to a 'normal' rate of return. When the DIT was first introduced in the Nordic countries, the flat capital income tax was intended to fall on the full return to capital. In particular, the imputed returns to capital invested in small businesses included a generous risk premium, and the flat tax rate on corporate source income was levied on the 'equity premium' as well as on the normal risk-free return.

However, from 2006 Norway switched to an alternative version of the DIT in which the flat capital income tax rate applies only to the 'normal' rate of return on shares. Under the new Norwegian tax system shareholder income (dividends plus capital gains on shares) exceeding an imputed normal return carries a combined corporate and personal tax burden very close to the top marginal tax rate on labour income. As explained below, the attraction of imposing an additional layer of tax on above-normal returns is that this will eliminate the incentive for income shifting under the DIT in a manner that does not distort investment incentives.

Table 5.1 provides an overview of current tax practices in Finland, Norway and Sweden.[3] In these countries, the flat capital income tax rate ranges between 28 and 30 per cent. This is roughly in line with both the corporate tax rate and the lowest marginal rate in the labour income tax schedule, but far below the top marginal tax rate on labour income. Because of the 'flatness' of the capital income tax, it can in many cases conveniently be collected by final withholding. However, for symmetry and neutrality, the Nordic countries offer a tax credit for negative net capital income, or allow it to be offset against positive income in the first tax bracket. Though it was originally part of the DIT philosophy to avoid double taxation of corporate source income, the Nordic countries have not fully done so, although Norway comes close by exempting an imputed normal return to all shares from taxes on dividends and capital gains. The next section of the chapter will include a discussion of corporate-personal tax integration under the DIT.

5.2 TAXING BUSINESS INCOME UNDER THE INCOME TAX[4]

The key distinction under the DIT is that between capital income and other income. Implementing this distinction is mainly a challenge in the area of business income taxation. This section considers alternative options for the taxation of business income under the DIT and describes the Nordic practices in this area.

5.2.1 Taxing Income from Self-Employment under the Dual Income Tax

Design issues

The self-employed work in their own businesses, so part of their business income must be seen as labour income. At the same time, the self-employed have also invested (part of) their wealth in their businesses, so another part of their income is a return to their business assets which is clearly a form of income from capital. If all of the business income of the self-employed were taxed as labour income at progressive rates, their capital income would be overtaxed relative to other types of capital income under a DIT. On the other hand, if all income from self-employment were taxed at the low flat rate applying to capital and corporate income, the self-employed would escape tax progressivity altogether, even though part of their income stems from their work effort.

Table 5.1 *Dual income taxation in the Nordic countries (2008, tax rates, %)*

	Finland	Norway	Sweden
Personal tax rate on:			
capital income	28	28	30
labour income	27–50	28–48	31.5–56.5
offset of negative capital income	Deductible against positive capital income	Deductible against other income in the first tax bracket	Tax credit
Corporate income tax rate	26	28	28
Integration of corporate and personal income tax	*Quoted companies:* 70 per cent of dividends are taxed (as capital income) *Unquoted companies:* Dividends below an imputed return on shares are exempt from personal tax; 70 per cent of dividends above that limit are taxed (as labour income)[1]	Dividends and capital gains in excess of an imputed rate of return on shares are taxed (as capital income)	*Quoted companies:* No integration *Unquoted companies:* Dividends and capital gains on unquoted shares are taxed at reduced rates[3, 5]
Personal tax rate on:			
dividends	19.6 (= 0.7 × 28)	28[2]	30[3]
capital gains on shares	28	28[4]	30[5]
Withholding tax rate[6] on:			
interest	28	28	30
dividends	19	0	30

Table 5.1 (continued)

Notes:
[1] 70 per cent of dividends exceeding €90 000 but falling below the imputed return are taxed as capital income.
[2] Applies only to dividends in excess of an imputed rate of return on the shares.
[3] For active owners of closely held companies, dividends below an imputed return are taxed at a reduced rate of 20 per cent while dividends above the imputed return are taxed as labour income. Dividends received by 'passive' owners of unquoted companies are taxed at a reduced rate of 25 per cent.
[4] Applies to capital gains in excess of an imputed rate of return on the shares.
[5] For active owners of closely held companies, capital gains below an imputed return are taxed at a reduced rate of 20 per cent while gains above the imputed return are taxed as labour income. Gains realised by 'passive' owners of unquoted companies are taxed at a reduced rate of 25 per cent.
[6] For domestic residents.

Source: Author's compilation of information from the International Bureau of Fiscal Documentation.

To avoid such unequal tax treatment, it is necessary to split the income of the self-employed into a labour income component and a capital income component. Since the working hours and effort of the self-employed cannot be observed by the tax authorities, whereas the stock of business assets can in principle be observed, it is natural to split the income of the self-employed by first imputing a rate of return to their business assets, which is categorised as capital income, and then treat the residual business profit as labour income.

The imputed rate of return to business assets may be computed on a 'gross assets' or on a 'net assets' basis. Under the 'gross assets' method, the net financial liabilities of the firm are not deducted from the asset base. The labour income of the entrepreneur is thus calculated by deducting an imputed return to 'gross' business assets (the assets recorded in the firm's balance sheet) from the 'gross' profits of the firm (defined as profits before interest), and taxable net capital income is calculated by deducting interest expenses from the imputed return to the gross assets. To illustrate, let Y denote business income before deduction for interest, let A indicate the stock of business assets recorded in the firm's balance sheet, and let D denote the stock of business debt. If r is the rate of return imputed to business assets, and i is the actual interest rate paid on business debt, the imputed capital income (C_G) and the imputed labour income (W_G) under the gross assets method is calculated as follows:

Income splitting under the gross assets method

$$C_G = rA - iD \tag{5.1}$$

$$W_G = Y - rA \tag{5.2}$$

By contrast, under the 'net assets' method capital income is determined by imputing a return to the net assets of the firm (business assets minus business debt), and labour income is found by deducting this imputed return from net profits (profits after deduction for interest). If C_N and W_N denote the imputed capital income and labour income under the net assets method, we thus have:

Income splitting under the net assets method

$$C_N = r(A - D) \tag{5.3}$$

$$W_N = Y - iD - C_N = Y - iD - r(A - D) \tag{5.4}$$

From these equations it follows that

$$C_G - C_N = (r - i)D \tag{5.5}$$

$$W_G - W_N = (i - r)D \tag{5.6}$$

If the imputed rate of return equals the rate of interest paid on business debt ($r = i$), the two methods will thus be equivalent, generating exactly the same split of total business income into capital income and labour income. But if the imputed return exceeds the interest rate, a larger fraction of business income will be categorised as capital income (and a correspondingly lower fraction will be taxed as labour income) under the gross assets method than under the net assets method. The opposite will hold if the imputed return is lower than the interest rate.

Moreover, deviations between the imputed return and the interest rate on debt will tend to distort business investment under the gross assets method. To see this, let t denote the flat capital income tax rate, and let the function $T(W)$ indicate the progressive tax schedule for labour income. From (5.1) and (5.2), we then find that the entrepreneur's total tax bill under the gross assets method (T_G) will be

$$T_G = tC_G + T(W_G) = t(rA - iD) + T(Y - rA) \tag{5.7}$$

Now suppose the entrepreneur undertakes an additional debt-financed investment of \$1. Suppose further that this additional investment raises business income by the amount $\Delta Y = i$. In the absence of tax, the investment would thus barely be worth undertaking since it generates a pre-tax return which is just sufficient to cover the interest on the additional debt. With $m \equiv T'(W)$ denoting the marginal tax rate on labour income, and with A and D both increasing by one unit, we see from (5.7) that the change in the entrepreneur's total tax bill (ΔT_G) will be equal to

$$\Delta T_G = t(r - i) + m(i - r) = (t - m)(r - i) \tag{5.8}$$

If the imputed rate of return exceeds the rate of interest ($r > i$) and if the marginal labour income tax rate exceeds the capital income tax rate ($m > t$), we see from (5.8) that the extra investment reduces the entrepreneur's tax bill. The reason is that a larger share of total profit gets taxed at the low capital income tax rate rather than at the high marginal labour income tax rate. Hence an investment that would not yield any net profit in the absence of tax actually becomes profitable in the presence of tax. Thus taxation under the gross assets method artificially stimulates investment when the imputed return exceeds the interest rate. On the other hand, if the imputed return falls short of the interest rate at which the entrepreneur can borrow, the gross assets method of taxation artificially discourages investment.

By contrast, under the net assets method of income splitting, the entrepreneur's total tax bill (T_N) is given as

$$T_N = tC_N + T(W_N) = tr(A - D) + T[Y - iD - r(A - D)] \tag{5.9}$$

Since the recorded net assets of the firm ($A - D$) are unaffected by an additional unit of debt-financed investment, and since profits net of interest are likewise unaffected in our example where $\Delta Y = i$, we see from (5.9) that the entrepreneur's total tax bill is unchanged, since neither the imputed capital income nor the imputed labour income will change. Hence the net assets method of income-splitting ensures that the DIT remains neutral towards marginal investment decisions.

This analysis would seem to imply a preference for the net assets method on tax neutrality grounds, but unfortunately this method also allows greater scope for tax arbitrage. To see how, note from (5.9) that under the net assets method interest expenses become deductible against the high marginal tax rate on labour income, because they reduce the residual net profit which is taxed as labour income. This provides an incentive for entrepreneurs with high earnings to record private debt (debt incurred for non-business purposes, say, to finance the purchase of a consumer durable or a piece of real estate) as business debt in order to benefit from interest deductibility.

To limit the scope for such transactions, the self-declared business income should be adjusted in cases where the declared net assets of the firm become negative, since negative net business assets indicate that private debt has been transferred to the business sphere. Specifically, taxable business income should be raised by the imputed return times the recorded negative net worth of the firm to (roughly) offset the fact that reported business income has been artificially lowered by allocating non-business interest expenses to the firm. To the extent that the tax law allows deduction for non-business interest expenses, the upward adjustment of taxable business income should of course be accompanied by a corresponding downward adjustment of the entrepreneur's non-business capital income (which might well be negative, in which case the entrepreneur would receive a tax credit equal to the capital income tax rate times the negative capital income).

The net assets method may also require a similar adjustment of taxable business income in certain other cases in order to prevent tax arbitrage, as explained in Sørensen (2007b). Thus the choice between the gross and the net assets method involves a trade-off between the superior neutrality properties of the net assets method and the greater simplicity and lower vulnerability to tax arbitrage offered by the gross assets method.

Another avoidance problem arising under both methods of income-splitting is that entrepreneurs may gain by transferring low-yielding non-business assets (for example, a piece of real estate or a motor vehicle used for private consumption) from the private sphere to the business sphere. By adding to the recorded stock of business assets an asset with little or zero (taxable) yield, the entrepreneur will have a higher proportion of business income taxed as capital income, since the base for calculating the imputed return goes up, while total business income stays (almost) unchanged. To prevent such transformation of labour income into capital income, the tax law must include clauses limiting the scope for transferring non-business assets to businesses.

When determining the rate of return imputed to business assets, policy makers must decide whether to include a risk premium in the imputed return. The case for doing so depends critically on the tax treatment of losses. If the tax code allows full loss offsets[5] and the marginal tax rate on business income is constant over time, it is not necessary to include a risk premium in the imputed return to avoid discouraging investment and risk-taking, as shown by Sørensen (2007b). Indeed, in this case the DIT will actually stimulate risk-taking even when the imputed return contains no risk premium. The reason is that, with full loss offsets, the high labour income tax rate imposed on residual business income works as an insurance device which reduces the variability (and hence the riskiness) of after-tax business income.

However, because of the risk of abuse, the tax code rarely allows full loss offset. Moreover, if marginal business income is taxed progressively as labour income, losses incurred in bad years will often be deducted against a lower tax rate than the marginal tax imposed on profits accruing in good years. If these tax asymmetries are strong, the tax system will tend to discourage risk-taking. In that situation there is a case for including a risk premium in the imputed return on business assets which is taxed as capital income. Ideally, the imputed risk premium should vary with the risk characteristics of each individual investment project, but since tax authorities lack the information and the administrative capacity to undertake a detailed differentiation of risk premia, they may choose to apply the same risk premium across the board. Inevitably, this premium will be too high for some investment projects and too low for others, implying some distortion to the pattern of risk-taking.

Nordic practices

The Nordic DIT countries all provide an option for the self-employed to have their income split into a capital income component and a labour income component. Norway uses a variant of the gross assets method, while Finland and Sweden practice variants of the net assets method. Apart from distinguishing between labour and capital income, the Swedish scheme also allows imputed labour income retained in the firm to be taxed at the low corporate income tax rate, postponing imposition of the progressive labour income tax until the time when profits are distributed.

Although Denmark does not apply a pure DIT, having maintained some amount of progressivity in the taxation of capital income, the country does tax labour income more heavily at the margin. Denmark therefore allows the self-employed to opt for a splitting of their business income into capital income and labour income. Entrepreneurs opting for income splitting may choose between the simpler gross assets method and a more complicated net assets method similar to the Swedish scheme.

Final observations on income tax design for the self-employed

In designing tax rules for the self-employed under the DIT, the following considerations should be kept in mind:

1. If the tax rate in the lowest bracket of the labour income tax schedule is aligned with the tax rate on capital income, entrepreneurs whose business income falls within the lowest tax bracket will have no need for income splitting, since they face the same marginal tax rate on capital income and labour income. If the upper threshold for the lowest tax bracket is set at a fairly high income level, many proprietors

would never need to have their income split, allowing a considerable administrative simplification.

2. Income-splitting should be an option but not a requirement for the taxpayer, since it offers an opportunity for entrepreneurs to avoid over-taxation of the capital income component of their business income. If entrepreneurs do not opt for income-splitting, their business income will automatically be taxed as labour income. Income-splitting requires that taxpayers keep proper accounts of their assets and liabilities, so taxpayers wishing to benefit from the low tax rate on capital income will have an incentive to keep proper books rather than relying on simplified accounting. Switching to a dual income tax may therefore help to promote modern business record-keeping in small enterprises, which may be desirable in itself.
3. In part because it requires fewer anti-avoidance measures, the gross assets method is administratively simpler than the net assets method, for the revenue authorities as well as for taxpayers. If priority is given to simplicity and low compliance costs, there is a case for choosing the gross assets method of income-splitting.

5.2.2 Taxation of Closely-Held Corporations Under the Dual Income Tax

The income shifting problem

The taxation of small corporations with active owners working in their own business raises a similar issue as the taxation of the self-employed: part of the income from the company must be seen as a return to the capital invested in the firm, whereas another part is the reward for the work effort and skills of the owner(s). In the absence of special rules for these companies, the dividends and capital gains on shares realised by the owner would be treated as capital income under the DIT (perhaps with some form of relief for the underlying corporation tax), while the management salaries paid to the owner(s) would be treated as labour income. If the sum of the corporation tax and the personal tax on dividends and/or capital gains is less than the marginal tax rate on labour income, owners have an obvious incentive to pay themselves dividends or to realise a capital gain on (part of) their shares rather than paying themselves a realistic salary.

Taxing active shareholders like proprietors

A possible solution to this problem would be to tax the income from small companies accruing to active, controlling shareholders in the same way as income from self-employment. This would imply that a fraction of corporate profits equal to the fraction of shares owned by 'active' shareholders working in their own company would be split into an imputed return on corporate assets, which would be taxed as capital income, and a residual profit that would be taxed as labour income. This income splitting would apply regardless of the actual amount of dividends or capital gains realised by the owners, so the owners would be unable to transform labour income into capital income by paying themselves lower salaries and instead taking out higher dividends or capital gains. The corporation tax would serve as a withholding tax on corporate profits, but it would be credited against the shareholder's personal tax bill to prevent double taxation of corporate equity income.

The main problem with this scheme is the difficulty of identifying the 'active' controlling shareholders who should be subject to mandatory income-splitting. It would seem natural to require mandatory income-splitting only in cases where shareholders carry out a certain minimum amount of work in the company and have a certain minimum (controlling) ownership share in the firm, possibly in conjunction with close relatives. If both these conditions are met, shareholders will most likely be able to transform management salary or other labour income from the firm into dividends or capital gains to reduce their tax bill.

However, such rules can easily be circumvented. For example, controlling shareholders might invite relatives or friends to step in as minority shareholders so that they are no longer subject to the income-splitting rules even if they maintain effective control over the firm's dividend policy. Alternatively, dominant shareholders might exchange shares in each other's companies to avoid mandatory income-splitting without giving up control of their respective companies.

The Norwegian experience suggests that such tax avoidance is not just a theoretical possibility. As part of the transition to the DIT in 1992, Norway introduced mandatory income-splitting rules for 'active' shareholders along the lines described above. Yet, between 1992 and 2000 the proportion of corporations subject to income splitting fell from 55 per cent to 32 per cent, indicating that a growing number of taxpayers were able to change status from 'active' to 'passive' shareholders.

More fundamentally, the dividing line between 'active' and 'passive' shareholders is essentially arbitrary and may lead to unequal tax treatment of shareholders who are for practical purposes in equal positions.

An alternative solution: a shareholder income tax with a rate-of-return allowance

Because of these difficulties, it seems desirable to avoid having to distinguish between active and passive shareholders. This section describes an alternative scheme which does not require this distinction. A version of this scheme has been implemented in Norway from the start of 2006, following recommendations from an expert committee.[6]

The basic principle of the scheme is simple: shareholder income below an imputed 'normal' return is tax exempt at the shareholder level, since such income has already been subject to corporation tax at a rate corresponding to the capital income tax rate, but dividends and capital gains in excess of the imputed normal return is subject to a personal shareholder income tax. By an appropriate choice of tax rates, the sum of the corporation tax and the personal shareholder income tax corresponds to the top marginal tax rate on labour income. Hence controlling shareholders can gain nothing by transforming labour income into shareholder income, thus obviating the need to split the income of 'active' shareholders.

The shareholder income tax is imposed only when income from the firm is distributed as a dividend or is realised as a capital gain on shares. In other words, the tax base is the realised income from the shares minus a rate of return allowance (RRA). The realised income is the sum of dividends and any realised net capital gain on the shares in the company. Dividends and capital gains are thus treated symmetrically. If the realised income falls short of the RRA, the unutilised RRA may be carried forward and deducted in a later year.

The RRA is calculated as an imputed rate of return times the basis of the share. The basis for the current year is the sum of the original basis and all unutilised RRAs from previous years, that is, the original basis is stepped up year by year by any unutilised RRAs. This step-up is necessary to ensure that only capital gains in excess of the normal return are subject to shareholder income tax.

The imputed rate of return should correspond to a normal after-tax rate of return from investment in the capital market, since this is the taxpayer's opportunity cost of investing in shares rather than, say, bonds. At the same time, since the corporate tax rate corresponds to the capital income tax rate under a pure dual income tax, shareholder income not exceeding the imputed return should be left free of personal income tax to avoid double taxation of the normal return to investment.[7]

The simple numerical example below illustrates how the base for the shareholder income tax is calculated. We consider a shareholder who injects equity into a company at the start of year 1, receives a dividend at the end of year 1, and a dividend *or* a capital gain on the share at the end of year 2. The imputed return on shares, the after-tax interest rate, and the return to the company's investment after corporation tax are all assumed to be 5 per cent. Plausibly, we also assume that one dollar of retained profit will generate a one dollar increase in the market value of shares in the company, as long as the retained profit does not exceed the shareholder's tax-free imputed return.

Year 1		
a.	Injection of equity at the start of the year	1000
b.	Profit after corporation tax (5 per cent of a)	50
c.	Dividend	30
d.	Retained profit (a − b)	20
e.	RRA (5 per cent of a)	50
f.	Unutilised RRA (e − c)	20
Year 2		
g.	Stepped-up basis of share (a + f)	1020
h.	Profit after corporation tax (5 per cent of (a + d))	51
i.	RRA (5 per cent of g)	51
Scenario 1: shares are realised at the end of year 2		
j.	Revenue from sale of shares at the end of year 2 (a + d + h)	1071
k.	Stepped-up basis of share at the start of year 2 (= g)	1020
l.	RRA for year 2 (= i)	51
m.	Taxable capital gain (j − k − l)	0
Scenario 2: all profits are distributed at the end of year 2		
n.	Dividend at the end of year 2 (d + h)	71
o.	Total RRA (f + i)	71
p.	Taxable dividend (n − o)	0

On these assumptions we see that whether the shareholder's return takes the form of dividends or capital gains, taxable income is zero in both scenarios. This illustrates the important point that the shareholder income tax is neutral with respect to investment and financing decisions. In the absence of the shareholder income tax, the investment considered in our example is just barely worth undertaking for the company since it yields a return that only just matches the market interest rate. The example shows that the shareholder income tax will not affect the profitability of such a 'marginal' investment, regardless of whether profits are distributed or retained in the company.

The neutrality of the shareholder income tax reflects its equivalence to a cash-flow tax which is known to be neutral. This equivalence result (which assumes full loss offsets) is demonstrated formally in Sørensen (2005), and it may be explained intuitively as follows. A cash-flow tax is neutral because it effectively makes the government a silent partner in all investment projects, sharing symmetrically in all gains and losses. Thus a cash-flow tax allows full expensing of investment, generating an immediate tax reduction equal to the tax rate t times the investment outlay K. Alternatively one might allow investors to deduct in all future periods an RRA on the initial investment outlay, as the shareholder income tax actually does. When the future tax savings from the RRAs are discounted at the market interest rate i, their net present value will be $NPV = t \cdot RRA \cdot K/i$. If we set $RRA = i$, as in our numerical example, we get $NPV = t \cdot K$, indicating that a shareholder income tax with a rate-of-return allowance equal to the market interest rate will ensure equivalence with the neutral cash flow tax, generating exactly the same tax liability in present value terms.

One attractive aspect of the neutrality of the shareholder income tax is that it does not induce shareholders to postpone realisation of their shares in order to defer capital gains tax, even though the tax is levied only upon realisation (see Sørensen, 2005).[8] The intuition for this result is that if investors realise an accrued capital gain in order to reinvest the after-tax gain, they will not be taxed on the normal return to the reinvested gain under the shareholder income tax. By contrast, a conventional income tax discourages the realisation of gains because it taxes the normal return to reinvested gains.

In a setting with uncertainty and risk, the neutrality of the shareholder income tax relies on the symmetry of the tax: whenever the realised rate of return r falls short of the RRA, the shareholder should ideally be granted a tax reduction equal to $t \cdot (RRA - r)$ in present value terms, where t is the (marginal) shareholder income tax rate. This may be achieved by allowing the taxpayer to offset any realised loss on a share against any taxable income from other shares during the same year, and by allowing any remaining loss to be carried forward indefinitely with interest to be offset against future shareholder income. As long as taxpayers earn sufficient taxable shareholder income in the future, such a carry-forward rule will ensure full loss offset in present value terms. In cases where taxpayers do not receive (sufficient) future income from shares, full neutrality would require that they be granted a tax credit equal to the shareholder income tax rate times their remaining loss, to be offset against their tax liability on other income. Note that to preserve symmetry and neutrality, the 'loss' on a share must be defined as $RRA - r$, that is, it must include the rate of return allowance. In other words, for tax purposes taxpayers are deemed to incur a loss whenever their realised capital gains fall short of their RRA for the current year plus any unutilised RRAs carried over from previous years.

With such fully symmetric tax rules, one can show that the imputed rate of return allowance does *not* have to include a risk premium to ensure neutrality of the shareholder income tax (see Sørensen, 2005). To understand this, note that if the future tax reductions due to the RRA accrue with certainty, as will in principle be the case with full loss offsets, the future tax breaks should be discounted at the risk-free (after-tax) interest rate i, even if the other cash flows associated with the equity investment are uncertain. Hence the present value of the tax savings from an extra dollar of equity investment will be $NPV = t \cdot RRA/i$ (recall that t is the shareholder income tax rate). If the RRA is set equal to the risk-free interest rate i, we therefore get $NPV = t$, showing that the government effectively finances a fraction of the investment outlay corresponding to the fraction of the cash receipts from the investment that must be paid in tax. Essentially the government just participates in the investment as a silent partner, and adding another partner sharing symmetrically in gains and losses cannot be distortionary.

Note that when the RRA does not include a risk premium, the shareholder income tax becomes a tax on the equity premium; that is, a tax on the difference between the return on shares and the risk-free interest rate. Since the equity premium is on average positive and quite substantial, this means that the shareholder income tax will on average collect a non-negligible amount of revenue even with full loss offsets.[9]

In Norway where a version of the shareholder income tax was introduced from 1 January, 2006, the imputed rate of return is in fact set equal to the (after-tax) interest rate on 3-month government bonds. These are practically risk free, but despite the fact that the RRA does not include a risk premium, Norwegian policy makers decided to impose certain limitations on loss offsets in order to prevent abuse. Specifically, an unutilised RRA for one share cannot be used to reduce taxable capital gains on other shares or to reduce other taxable income. The concern was that unless such a limitation was introduced, taxpayers would engage in so-called year-end transactions simply with the purpose of reducing tax liability.

In the Norwegian context this potential tax avoidance problem arises because the RRA on a share is assigned to the taxpayer who owns the share at the end of the year. If an unutilised RRA from a share were fully deductible against other income, a Norwegian personal taxpayer could purchase a share from a tax exempt corporate or institutional investor or from a foreign investor (for whom the RRA has no value) right before New Year and sell it again right after New Year. This would leave the taxpayer with an unutilised RRA that could be used to shield other taxable income.

The problem with year-end trades could be avoided if the RRA for any given year only corresponds to the fraction of the year in which the taxpayer has owned the share. Indeed, this would seem the most accurate and consistent way of calculating the RRA, but it would also increase the burden of administering the shareholder income tax, by requiring the authorities to keep track of trades in shares occurring during the fiscal year.[10] For administrative reasons, the Norwegian authorities therefore decided to assign the RRAs to the taxpayers owning the shares at the end of the year, relying instead on limitations on loss offsets to deal with the problem of tax-motivated year-end transactions.

As indicated by these observations, the rules for loss offsets and for the assignment of RRAs under a shareholder income tax require careful consideration and may involve difficult trade-offs between the goals of tax neutrality and administrative simplicity.

The tax treatment of dividends and capital gains exceeding the RRA also requires some consideration. To ensure that 'active' shareholders cannot transform labour income into lightly taxed capital income, tax rates must be chosen such that

$$(1 - \tau)(1 - t^s) = 1 - m \quad \Rightarrow \quad \tau + t^s(1 - \tau) = m \qquad (5.10)$$

where τ is the corporate income tax rate (assumed to equal the capital income tax rate), t^s is the shareholder income tax rate, and m is the top marginal tax rate on labour income. The term $(1 - \tau)(1 - t^s)$ is the after-tax income left in the hand of the shareholders if they realise a unit of labour income as a dividend or capital gain, while $1 - m$ is the after-tax income earned when the income is paid out as a management wage or salary (which is deductible from the corporate tax base).

The corporate tax rate would be chosen with a view to the international mobility of capital, while the choice of the top marginal labour income tax rate would involve considerations of equity, revenue and the potential international mobility of high-paid labour. The shareholder income tax rate t^s would then have to be adjusted to roughly satisfy equation (5.10). Note that the value of t^s implied by (5.10) would not necessarily correspond to the capital income tax rate, so in general shareholder income would be subject to a separate schedular tax rather than being included in the capital income tax base.[11]

It might be objected that choosing the shareholder income tax rate on the basis of the top marginal labour income tax rate could imply over-taxation of the labour income of active shareholders relative to the labour income of proprietors and wage earners, since the two latter groups will face a lower average tax rate on labour income under a progressive tax schedule. However, if controlling active shareholders wish to take advantage of the low marginal tax rates at the bottom of the labour income tax schedule, they can usually do so by paying themselves wages or salaries rather than dividends or capital gains, so the potential horizontal inequity mentioned is hardly a serious one.

In principle, the shareholder income tax utilises the very same information on dividends, acquisition prices and realised sales prices which is needed to implement a conventional income tax on dividends and on realised capital gains on shares. However, under a conventional capital gains tax the tax authorities do not need to verify the basis value of the share until the time it is realised. Since many unquoted shares are never traded, this reduces the need for checking the basis value of shares. Under the shareholder income tax the basis value of the share must be determined already when it is acquired, and the basis must be stepped up every year in case of unutilised RRAs. In practice tax administrators will therefore have to process more information under the shareholder income tax than under a conventional capital gains tax. On the other hand, it will often be easier to document and verify the acquisition price of a share at the time of purchase than when it is subsequently realised.

Another alternative: a dual income tax with an allowance for corporate equity

The shareholder income tax described above is a residence-based personal tax on the worldwide income from shares. Through the RRA, the shareholder income tax offers relief for the double taxation of corporate income.

As an alternative to alleviating the double taxation of corporate income at the individual shareholder level, relief could be granted at the corporate level. For example, in line with the so-called ACE proposal by the Institute for Fiscal Studies (1991), companies could be allowed to deduct an imputed normal return on their equity (or on new equity formed after the reform), just as they are currently allowed to deduct interest on debt. Under a DIT with an ACE system, a separate shareholder income tax would no longer be needed to prevent income shifting, provided the flat capital income tax rate t applying to dividends and capital gains (as well as to other forms of capital income) were chosen such that

$$(1 - \tau)(1 - t) = 1 - m, \tag{5.11}$$

since the total corporate and personal tax burden on labour income realised as dividends or capital gains would then equal the marginal tax burden on wage income. Further, the ACE allowance granted at the corporate level would ensure that dividends and capital gains would only be taxed at the shareholder level at the capital income tax rate *t* as long as they do not exceed the imputed normal return to the company's equity.[12]

At least two arguments can be given in favour of double tax relief at the company level rather than at the shareholder level. First, for companies with access to the international equity market, tax relief at the level of domestic shareholders may not be very effective in reducing the cost of capital, since the cost of equity finance for these companies tends to be determined by the returns required by international investors who are not affected by domestic personal tax rules. By contrast, relief at the level of domestic (resident) companies would significantly strengthen the incentive for domestic investment, including inward direct investment by foreign multinational enterprises. Second, double tax relief at the corporate level would presumably be simpler to administer than a shareholder income tax with an RRA, since the latter tax involves large numbers of taxpayers and transactions.

A further attraction of the ACE system is that it offsets the investment distortions caused by deviations between true economic depreciation and depreciation for tax purposes. If firms write down their assets at an accelerated pace, the current tax saving from accelerated depreciation will be offset by a fall in future RRAs of equal present value, since accelerated depreciation reduces the book value of the assets (and hence the equity base) to which future rates of return are imputed. In fact, regardless of the rate at which firms write down their assets in the tax accounts, the present value of the sum of the capital allowance and the ACE allowance will always equal the initial investment outlay, so the ACE system is equivalent to the immediate expensing of investment allowed under a neutral cash flow tax, as explained by Griffith et al. (2008).

One potential drawback of combining a DIT with an ACE system is that the capital gains on shares generated by retained earnings benefit from the deferral of tax until the time of realisation. Hence normal returns retained within companies might be undertaxed since they would not bear corporation tax, due to the ACE allowance. Corporate-source labour income and rents realised as capital gains on shares would also be undertaxed, for although these incomes would be subject to corporation tax as they accrued (since by assumption they would exceed the ACE allowance), they should ideally be taxed at the same total marginal rate as labour income at the time of accrual. Thus there would be a tax incentive to accumulate income within the corporate sector, generating an undesirable lock-in effect.

However, to approximately offset the compound interest gain from tax deferral, policy makers could make a schematic upward adjustment of realised taxable gains that would increase systematically with the length of the holding period, in line with the proposal by Vickrey (1939). This would tend to eliminate the tax advantage to corporate-source income and rents which are realised in the form of capital gains (for example as stock compensation). Moreover, since holdings of listed shares are recorded in the computer registers of financial intermediaries and stock exchanges, it should be possible to tax the gains on listed shares already at the time of accrual, since this would not seem to involve any serious valuation and liquidity problems. In that case the adjustment for the length of the holding period would only have to be applied when taxing gains on non-listed shares which are rarely traded.

While an ACE system would generally provide a stronger stimulus to domestic investment than a shareholder income tax with an RRA, it would also cause a larger fall in tax revenues, since the RRAs under the shareholder income tax are only granted to domestic personal shareholders, whereas ACE relief at the corporate level benefits all shareholders of domestic companies, including foreign investors and tax-exempt institutional investors. Hence tax relief would be given even in cases where no domestic tax is paid on the imputed return. Moreover, in cases where the home countries of foreign investors would have granted a foreign tax credit for the corporation tax paid to the domestic source country, exempting the imputed normal return from domestic company tax is simply a give-away to the foreign fiscal authority that does not improve the incentive to invest in the domestic economy.

The revenue loss from an ACE system could be limited by granting the allowance only for additions to the equity base undertaken after the time of reform. This would fully preserve the incentive to undertake new investment without bestowing a windfall gain on the owners of 'old' capital already installed. Presumably such a system would have to be supplemented by certain anti-avoidance rules to prevent existing companies from liquidating and then starting up as new companies in order to qualify for an ACE allowance for all of their equity.

5.2.3 The Taxation of Small Companies in the Nordic Countries

The previous sections discussed alternative ways of taxing income from closely held corporations under a dual income tax, assuming that policy makers give high priority to the goal of tax neutrality. The present section briefly summarises actual tax practices in the Nordic countries.

Finland and Sweden both have special tax rules for the owners of closely-held companies.[13] Until 2005, Finnish tax law required that the 'grossed-up' dividends from shares in non-listed companies exceeding an imputed return to the company's net assets be taxed as labour income, with a credit being granted for the underlying corporation tax. Dividends below the imputed return were effectively exempt from tax at the shareholder level, as a consequence of the Finnish imputation system and the correspondence between the tax rates on corporate and capital income. Realised capital gains on shares were fully taxed as capital income. To reduce the tax incentive for owners of small companies to transform labour income into capital gains, Finland has thus accepted double taxation of retained corporate earnings.

From 2005 Finland has abolished its imputation system. To maintain some alleviation of double taxation, only 70 per cent of dividends from quoted companies are included in the shareholder's capital income. For unquoted companies any dividend below the imputed return is tax exempt in so far as it does not exceed €90 000 for individual shareholders. Seventy per cent of any dividend above this limit is included in taxable capital income for dividends below the imputed return, while 70 per cent of any dividend above the imputed return is included in taxable labour income. Essentially Finnish tax law thus includes a schematic version of the shareholder income tax for unquoted companies, combined with partial double tax relief for quoted companies.

Until recently Sweden also allowed an imputed return to be deducted from the taxable income from shares in unquoted companies. However, from 2006 this RRA was replaced by a reduced tax rate on dividends and capital gains on unquoted shares (see notes 3 and 5 in Table 5.1). To address the income shifting problem, Swedish tax law imposes progressive labour income tax on dividends and realised capital gains above an imputed return to the basis value of shares in closely held companies. However, this is only done for shareholder income realised by 'active' shareholders carrying out a certain amount of work in their own companies. If the dividend or realised capital gain falls short of the imputed return in any year, the residual amount is carried forward with interest and added to the amount of shareholder income that may be taxed as capital income in the future.

From the introduction of the DIT in 1992 until the end of 2005, Norway treated 'active' shareholders in much the same manner as the self-employed, applying a (complex) version of the income-splitting scheme described in section 5.2. However, because of the difficulties of distinguishing between active and passive shareholders, Norway abolished the special tax rules for active shareholders from 1 January 2006, replacing them by a shareholder income tax which applies to all individual resident shareholders. Various aspects of this new Norwegian tax regime were analysed above.

5.3 WOULD A DUAL INCOME TAX BE RELEVANT FOR NEW ZEALAND?

New Zealand is currently considering the longer term needs for adjustment or reform of its personal and corporate income tax system. This section therefore offers some brief observations on the possible relevance of the DIT as a blueprint for a future tax reform in a small open economy such as New Zealand.

The DIT was developed in the Nordic countries which have large public sectors, relying on total tax revenues in the range 45–50 per cent of GDP, and which have historically had rather ambitious goals regarding the redistribution of income. As a consequence, the Nordic welfare states necessarily impose high tax burdens on labour income in the form of personal income taxes and social security contributions.[14] Historically, the Nordic personal tax systems have been based on the philosophy of comprehensive income taxation, although in practice many forms of capital income have enjoyed favourable tax treatment. The DIT system emerged as the Nordic governments gradually came to acknowledge that taxing (some forms of) nominal capital income at the high marginal tax rates applied to (high levels of) labour income created intolerable distortions and horizontal inequities in an environment where capital was becoming increasingly mobile relative to labour and where some forms of capital income could not be subject to (full) tax, for practical or political reasons.

The current situation in New Zealand differs from that in the Nordic countries in some important respects. First, at around 38 per cent of GDP, the total revenue collected by the New Zealand government is somewhat smaller. Second, the international mobility of labour in New Zealand is among the highest in the world, and much higher than in the Nordic countries. In particular, the labour markets of New Zealand and Australia are highly integrated. Both of these characteristics of the New Zealand economy suggest that the case for the DIT may be weaker in this country than in the Nordic countries.

In principle, the current personal tax system in New Zealand is based on the idea of comprehensive income taxation, although important items such as capital gains and imputed rents on owner-occupied housing are excluded from the tax base. Marginal personal tax rates are modest by Nordic standards, with a top rate of 39 per cent. However, for families with children, the abatement of family tax credits means that the effective marginal tax rate often increases by 20 percentage points or more, adding considerably to the progressivity of the tax-transfer system and raising the effective marginal tax rate to 59 per cent for many taxpayers.

According to New Zealand Treasury (2008), this effective top marginal tax rate applies to some, but far from all forms of capital income. Apart from the tax exemption for capital gains and imputed rents, the tax code also allows favourable tax treatment of investments channelled through a number of special vehicles.

The corporate income tax rate in New Zealand currently stands at 30 per cent. The double taxation of dividends is alleviated through an imputation system granting individual shareholders a full credit for the underlying corporation tax against the personal tax on dividends. Double taxation of retained earnings is avoided through the exemption of capital gains from personal income tax.

To reduce distortions to the pattern of saving and investment, it seems that New Zealand could benefit from moving towards a more uniform taxation of the various forms of capital income. At the same time the high mobility of the labour force and the competition for high-skilled labour across the Tasman Sea suggests the desirability of taking down the high effective marginal tax rates on labour in New Zealand.

Against this background, one option for personal tax reform might be to maintain and indeed strengthen the philosophy of comprehensive income taxation by broadening the capital income tax base (and perhaps the tax base more generally) while reducing marginal tax rates so as to align the top marginal personal tax rate with the current corporate tax rate of 30 per cent. Assuming that the imputation system for dividend taxation is preserved, the corporation tax would continue to serve as a withholding tax. If capital gains on shares were included in the personal tax base, the double taxation of retained corporate profits could be alleviated by allowing shareholders to add (their proportionate share of) retained taxable profits to the basis of their shares when calculating the taxable capital gain on shares, in line with previous Norwegian practice (see subsection 5.1.1).

However, a reform along the lines suggested above would still leave several potential problems. First, if the abatement of benefits and tax credits like the Working for Families (WfF) credit were based on comprehensive income, the effective top marginal tax rate – including the top marginal rate on capital income – would still be quite high, at around 50 per cent given current abatement rules. Levying such a high effective marginal tax rate on realised nominal capital gains would undoubtedly create serious and potentially unacceptable lock-in effects. On the other hand, if capital gains were left out of the base for calculating eligibility for the various tax credits, they would still benefit from favourable tax treatment relative to other forms of capital income, thus compromising the goal of tax neutrality underlying the reform. In response to this problem, policy makers might decide to grant tax credits like the WfF only on the basis of the taxpayer's labour income, but in that case they would face the same problems of separating capital income from labour income as those arising under a DIT.

Second, even abstracting from the complications arising from the abatement of the WfF and other benefits, the so-called inflation argument in favour of the DIT would still apply: taxing returns to nominal assets at the same marginal rate as labour income implies that the real asset returns are overtaxed, due to the lack of inflation adjustment.

Third, the current corporate tax rate of 30 per cent is relatively high compared to the corporate tax rates in other small OECD economies, so the forces of tax competition will most likely call for a lowering of the corporate tax rate in New Zealand in the medium and long term. This would open a gap between the personal capital income tax rate and the corporate rate if the principle of comprehensive personal income taxation were maintained. Given the benefits from tax deferral under a realisations-based capital gains tax, such a gap could generate an undesirable lock-in of capital in existing corporations. To fix this problem, it would be necessary to adjust for the length of the holding period when levying capital gains tax, as discussed in section 5.2. In addition to this complication, the tax system would be complicated by the mechanisms needed to alleviate the double taxation of distributed as well as retained profits, as mentioned above. It is not obvious that such a tax system would be easier to administer than, say, a DIT with a shareholder income tax along the current Norwegian lines or a DIT with an ACE.

Against this background, despite the structural differences between the Nordic economies and the New Zealand economy, there may still be a case for considering the introduction of some version of the dual income tax in New Zealand.

NOTES

1. This section draws on Sørensen (1994) where the reader may find a more detailed account of the background for the introduction of the DIT in the Nordic countries.
2. I shall return to the issue whether a serious lock-in effect can in fact be avoided in cases where the corporate tax rate is significantly lower than the personal capital income tax rate.
3. Denmark was the first country to introduce the DIT, in 1987, but has subsequently moved to a hybrid between the comprehensive income tax and DIT. It is therefore not included in Table 5.1.
4. This part of the chapter draws on Hagen and Sørensen (1998) and particularly on Sørensen (2007b). These articles provide further details on the design of business income taxation under a DIT.
5. This would involve unlimited carry-forward of losses with interest to preserve the present value of the deduction.

6. The present author was a member of that committee. The scheme described below is analysed more formally in Sørensen (2005).
7. Companies could be required to keep a taxed profits account to ensure that only 'normal' dividends paid out of taxed profits are exempt from personal tax.
8. The shareholder income tax is in fact a special case of the generalised cash-flow tax described in Auerbach and Bradford (2004). The Auerbach–Bradford scheme ensures holding-period neutrality even though tax is due only when assets are realised.
9. Of course, the fact that the shareholder income tax only exempts the risk-free *after-tax* return also adds to its revenue-raising capacity.
10. Since non-listed shares are rarely traded, the problem would mainly relate to listed shares. Because trades in such shares are computerised, it should be possible to require financial intermediaries and professional traders to report investor holding periods to the tax authorities.
11. In Norway shareholder income is treated as capital income and the capital income tax rate is set equal to the corporate tax rate. These choices have pedagogical advantages, but they also mean that equation (5.10) leaves less flexibility in the choice of the top marginal labour income tax rate.
12. Note that when tax rates are set in accordance with (5.11), the capital income tax rate will generally differ from the corporate tax rate.
13. Denmark does not have special tax rules for closely-held companies. Instead, the country relies on a separate schedular progressive tax on dividends and capital gains on shares to ensure that the total corporate and personal tax burden on corporate equity income is roughly in line with the marginal tax rate on labour income.
14. Denmark stands out from the other Nordic countries by having virtually no social security taxes, relying instead on the personal income tax, much like New Zealand.

REFERENCES

Auerbach, A.J. and D. Bradford (2004), 'Generalized cash flow taxation', *Journal of Public Economics*, **88**, 957–80.

Cnossen, S. (2000), 'Taxing capital income in the Nordic countries: A model for the European Union?', in S. Cnossen (ed.), *Taxing Capital Income in the European Union – Issues and Options for Reform*, Oxford: Oxford University Press.

Fuest, C. and A.J.Weichenrieder (2002), 'Tax competition and profit shifting: On the relationship between personal and corporate tax rates', *IFO-Studien*, **48**, 611–32.

Griffith, R., J.R. Hines and P.B. Sørensen (2008), 'International capital taxation', forthcoming as Chapter 10 in *The Mirrlees Review: Reforming the Tax System for the 21st Century*, to be published by the Institute for Fiscal Studies, London.

Hagen, K.P. and P.B. Sørensen (1998), 'Taxation of income from small businesses: Taxation principles and tax reforms in the Nordic countries', Chapter 2 in P.B. Sørensen (ed.), *Tax Policy in the Nordic Countries*, London: Macmillan Press.

Hall, R.E. and A. Rabushka (1995) *The Flat Tax*, Second Edition, Stanford: Hoover Institution Press.

Institute for Fiscal Studies (1991) *Equity for companies: a corporation tax for the 1990s*, A Report of the IFS Capital Taxes Group, London: The Institute for Fiscal Studies, Commentary 26.

Keen, M., Kim, Y. and R. Varsano (2006), *The flat tax(es): principles and*

evidence, IMF Working Paper No. WP/06/218, Washington, DC: International Monetary Fund.
New Zealand Treasury (2008), *Medium Term Tax Policy Challenges and Opportunities* (November), Wellington, New Zealand.
Nielsen, S.B. and P.B. Sørensen (1997), 'On the optimality of the Nordic system of dual income taxation', *Journal of Public Economics*, **63**, 311–29.
Sørensen, P.B. (1994), 'From the global income tax to the dual income tax: Recent tax reforms in the Nordic countries', *International Tax and Public Finance*, **1**, 57–80.
Sørensen, P.B. (2005), 'Neutral taxation of shareholder income', *International Tax and Public Finance*, **12**, 777–801.
Sørensen, P.B. (2007a), 'Can capital income taxes survive? And should they?' *CESifo Economic Studies*, **53**, 1–57.
Sørensen, P.B. (2007b), 'The Nordic dual income tax: Principles, practices, and relevance for Canada', *Canadian Tax Journal*, **55**, 557–602.
US Treasury Department (1992), *Taxing Business Income Once – Integration of the Individual and Corporate Tax Systems*, Washington, DC: US Treasury.
Vickrey, W. (1939), 'Averaging of income for income tax purposes', *Journal of Political Economy*, **47**, 379–97.

6. International taxation and company tax policy in small open economies

George R. Zodrow*

6.1 INTRODUCTION

Company tax policies around the world are in a state of flux, as many countries have reformed their corporate income tax systems in response to the ongoing process of globalisation, in an environment characterised by highly mobile international capital, international tax competition, and aggressive international tax avoidance by many multinational corporations (MNCs).[1] This environment is especially difficult for countries that can approximately be characterised as small open economies, that is, countries that face a perfectly elastic supply of capital at a rate of return that is determined in international capital markets as well as fixed prices for internationally traded goods; New Zealand is often characterised as an especially open economy (New Zealand Treasury, 2008). Tax competition for highly mobile capital has placed downward pressure on company tax rates, as countries strive to be competitive in attracting highly prized and highly mobile capital investments, especially those that promote the transfer of technology and have the potential of increasing productivity and growth rates, and New Zealand is no exception (New Zealand Inland Revenue Department, 2008). At the same time, however, such pressure is countered by a variety of factors, including arguments for taxing relatively immobile investments that generate economic rents at high rates and for aligning tax rates under the corporate and personal income tax systems to limit opportunities for domestic tax avoidance. In addition, increasingly aggressive efforts at tax avoidance, especially by large multinational corporations, further complicate the issue.

This chapter examines company income tax policy from the perspective of a small open economy operating in an environment characterised by international capital mobility, tax competition and tax avoidance, focusing on issues related to the company taxation of inbound foreign direct investment (FDI).[2] It begins by briefly considering various positions regarding company income tax policy in a small open economy that have appeared in the literature, focusing first on arguments for tax exemption of capital income and then on the many qualifications to these arguments that in practice have lead to significant, if arguably declining, levels of taxation of capital income. This analysis pays particular attention to the implications of the existence of firm-specific and location-specific economic rents and the issues raised by various forms of international tax avoidance. The chapter then traces out the implications of the analysis for evaluating various potential company income tax reforms, including brief discussions of applications of the analysis to the case of New Zealand – a topic that is covered in depth in the chapter by Benge and Holland in this volume.

6.2 GENERAL DISCUSSION OF COMPANY TAX POLICY IN A SMALL OPEN ECONOMY

This section of the chapter begins with a discussion of the standard argument that a small open economy should not apply a source-based (production-based) tax on internationally mobile capital, and then considers the many qualifications to that argument.

6.2.1 The Standard 'Zero Tax' Argument

A now well-known argument is that a small open economy should not apply a source-based tax to internationally mobile capital (Zodrow and Mieszkowski, 1983; Gordon, 1986; Razin and Sadka, 1991).[3] The intuition is the imposition of such a tax on perfectly mobile capital will simply cause it to migrate to other jurisdictions until its after-tax return increases to the internationally determined rate of return. This emigration of capital lowers the productivity of the fixed factors in the taxing country – land and labour (or at least relatively immobile labour), so that local factors of production ultimately bear the entire burden of the capital income tax, including both the revenue raised and the efficiency costs of the tax. These efficiency costs include suboptimal capital intensities, a tax bias favouring labour-intensive goods (Gordon and Hines, 2002), and a tendency toward underprovision of public services in the presence of international tax competition (Zodrow and Mieszkowski, 1986; Wilson, 1986). Indeed, Harberger (1995, 2008) argues that in a small open economy, immobile labour and land may bear more than 100 per cent of a corporate income tax, once general equilibrium effects across business sectors are considered.

6.2.2 Extensions of the 'Zero Tax' Argument

The discussion thus far has implicitly considered a marginal effective tax rate applied to capital investments in the absence of tax avoidance. However, much of the recent research on international taxation has focused on the role played by investments that earn economic rents and the implications of tax avoidance activity, especially by multinational corporations, for statutory corporate income tax rates.

The role of firm-specific economic rents

Another key element of setting tax policy in a world characterised by increasing globalisation is its effects on investment by multinationals. The economic theories underlying the formation of MNCs stress their potential to earn significant firm-specific economic rents, attributable to factors unique to the firm such as specialised technological knowledge, superior managerial skills or production techniques, or valuable product brands, trademarks, reputations and other intangible assets (Dunning, 1981). Moreover, there is some indirect empirical evidence suggesting that the relative importance of such rents is increasing over time, as Auerbach (2006) shows that the dispersion of relative profitability for US corporations has increased significantly in recent years, suggesting an increase in the importance of investments that generate above-normal returns made by a relatively small number of highly profitable firms.

Economic analyses have stressed that multinational decisions regarding the location of investments expected to generate significant economic rents are typically made among numerous mutually exclusive discrete choices; for example, a firm may want to take advantage of significant economies of scale due to large fixed costs by choosing a single location to serve multiple national markets. Under the circumstances, Devereux and Griffith (2003) argue that the average effective tax rate, which is a function of the statutory rate as well as the effective marginal tax rate, is the key determinant of MNC investment location decisions. Because investments generating firm-specific economic rents are also highly mobile (and indeed may be especially highly prized by national governments as they are most likely to be associated with high levels of technology transfer, access to skilled labour and the generation of other external benefits, including a competitive environment that fosters invention and innovation), the logic underlying the standard tax competition model implies that the statutory tax rate applied to such investments should also equal zero (Gordon and Hines, 2002).

The role of income shifting

The pervasive phenomenon of income shifting by multinationals through various financial accounting manipulations accentuates the downward pressure on statutory tax rates attributable to international tax competition for investments that earn firm-specific economic rents. In particular, it is corporate statutory tax rates that are relevant for income shifting as they determine the value of deductions and the tax cost of incremental revenues; that is, in the presence of income shifting, any country with a relatively high tax rate will receive a disproportionately large share of worldwide deductions while losing its fair share of worldwide revenues. Furthermore, a low statutory rate may make a country attractive for investment by MNCs simply because it creates the potential for additional income shifting (Slemrod, 1997). Serious concerns about income shifting have been expressed in New Zealand, including concerns that tax avoidance is encouraged by relatively high effective tax rates on labour income and will create the perception that the tax system is unfair and reduce compliance (New Zealand Inland Revenue Department, 2008; New Zealand Treasury, 2008).

6.2.3 Qualifications to Arguments for Low Corporate Income Taxes

It is clear that, notwithstanding the arguments made thus far, corporate income tax rates have not converged to zero and that the corporate income tax is still an important source of revenues in most developed and developing countries. A wide variety of arguments have been offered in support of company taxation, all of which qualify the argument that a small open economy should exempt capital income from tax. Although it is difficult to judge the relative importance of each of these qualifications, the pervasiveness of corporate income taxation around the world suggests together they have been taken seriously by policymakers.

Questioning the basic assumptions of the small open economy model

Gravelle and Smetters (2006) argue that, at least in the US context, both the assumptions of perfect capital mobility and perfect substitutability between imports and domestically produced goods that underlie the zero tax result may be inappropriate. In this case, domestic labour does not bear the full burden of a corporate income tax, which is to a perhaps significant extent borne by capital, including foreign capital owners. Moreover, Gravelle and Smetters stress that even if a perfectly elastic supply of capital is a reasonable approximation for a small open economy, these same incidence results obtain if the substitution elasticity between domestic traded goods and imports is sufficiently low. These results, however, have been questioned by Randolph (2006) who argues that results similar to those in the standard model are obtained if the Gravelle–Smetters model is extended by allowing the corporate sector to produce both a good that is imperfectly substitutable with imports and a second good that is perfectly substitutable. In addition, several recent studies have obtained relatively high estimates of import substitution elasticities, consistent with the conjectures of Harberger (2008) and others. Thus the relative importance of the Gravelle–Smetters argument is a subject of ongoing debate.

The role of location-specific economic rents

Perhaps the most important argument in support of a relatively high level of company income taxation is that it allows the government to obtain significant revenues from the taxation of location specific economic rents. Such rents, which may accrue to both domestic and foreign firms, can reflect resource rents as well as economic rents that arise because of factors such as local economies of agglomeration, productive government infrastructure, easier access to consumers, lower transport costs, and inexpensive but relatively productive local factors of production including skilled labour, in addition to the ability to avoid trade barriers such as tariffs and quotas.

The taxation of location-specific economic rents provides an efficient and thus highly desirable source of revenue. Moreover, such taxes are especially attractive from the standpoint of domestic residents and thus from a political perspective if the rents accrue to foreigners (Mintz, 1995), and empirical evidence suggests that a higher share of foreign ownership in a country results in a higher average corporate income tax rate (Huizinga and Nicodème, 2006).

The potential for taxing location-specific economic rents may be particularly important in an island economy such as that of New Zealand where access to local markets is especially critical. Indeed, a significant fraction of FDI in New Zealand seems to service the domestic market, including banking and finance, communications and media, automotive, insurance, retail wholesale distributors, industry and community services, construction and trade services; or to access New Zealand's natural resources (primary food production, food processing, oil, gas, minerals and electricity). Combined with a desire to tax rents earned by relatively immobile domestic capital and empirical evidence that rates of return to capital in New Zealand are relatively high (Hall and Scobie, 2005), the opportunity to tax location-specific rents provides an important qualification to arguments for low source-based taxes on capital income.

The personal income tax backstop argument

The traditional rationale for a corporate income tax – independent of international considerations – is that it is essential to limit avoidance of the personal income tax; that is, in the absence of a corporate income tax, individuals could incorporate and defer personal income tax on labour income by retaining the earnings in corporate form while financing consumption with loans from their companies. Although commonly provided as a rationale for corporate taxation of domestic companies, this argument extends to foreign companies to the extent that domestic individuals or firms can establish corporations that are nominally 'foreign' (for example, in a tax haven) and thus largely avoid domestic tax liability on their sheltered income (Gordon and MacKie-Mason, 1995; Gordon and Slemrod, 2000). In New Zealand, a top individual marginal tax rate of 39 per cent,[4] relative to a 30 per cent tax rate on corporations (as well as on portfolio investment entities) and a 33 per cent tax rate on trusts, creates clear incentives for income shifting, and concern about increased income shifting due to the deviation from the traditional policy of rate alignment naturally permeates discussion of reducing the corporate statutory rate (New Zealand Inland Revenue Department, 2008).

A key factor in determining the importance of this argument is whether the sheltered labour earnings are likely to be exempt from individual level tax or taxed eventually when distributed to the owners of the corporation. In the latter case, the central issue is whether the combined tax burden due to current taxation at the statutory corporate income tax rate and eventual individual level taxation of capital income falls significantly below the tax rate applied to individual labour income. Retention in corporate form implies that tax will be deferred, but given the widespread availability of tax-deferred savings in most nominally 'income tax' countries, this may not be a serious problem. For example, Griffith et al. (2009) argue that rough neutrality between the taxation of labour income and capital income is achieved if the pattern of tax rates satisfies $(1 - t_c)(1 - t_r) = (1 - t_L)$ where t_c is the statutory corporate tax rate, t_r is the individual level tax on capital income, and t_L is the top individual tax rate on labour income.[5] Of course, earnings retained in the corporate sector that are ultimately taxed as realised capital gains will benefit from deferral. If deemed desirable, this advantage could be negated by adjusting the taxation of realised capital gains on shares of closely-held corporations to reflect the benefit of deferral (Auerbach, 1991), although such taxation of capital gains effectively on an accrual basis would be perceived as unusually harsh. Alternatively, income shifting can be reduced by placing limits on the extent to which investment income earned by closely-held corporations is subject to reduced tax rates (New Zealand Inland Revenue Department, 2008).

On the other hand, if the labour earnings are effectively exempt from taxation – for example, because capital gains are never taxed, even at death – then incorporation is an effective tax sheltering tool to the extent that the statutory corporate tax rate falls below the individual's personal income tax rate. For example, in New Zealand capital gains are not taxed and corporate income earned by trusts is exempt from further taxation; a recent dramatic increase in the amount of imputation credits held by closely-held companies suggests a sizable increase in sheltering activities by these companies (New Zealand Inland Revenue Department, 2008).

More generally, in the presence of a corporate income tax, the effectiveness of incorporation as a sheltering device depends on the differential between the corporate and individual income tax rates and the extent to which the two tax systems are integrated. Specifically, more effective integration increases the attractiveness of incorporation as a tax shelter because it reduces the incorporation tax penalty that must be paid in the form of a separate corporate income tax. In addition, even with a fully integrated system, a corporate tax is likely to facilitate tax administration by serving as an effective tax withholding device.

Several factors limit the relevance of the backstop argument for a corporate income tax. First, the scope of the argument is limited as it applies only to self-employed individuals or the owners of closely-held corporations. Second, the extent to which the corporate tax serves as an effective backstop to the personal income tax is unclear, given the relatively low income tax compliance of sole proprietors and small businesses in most countries.

Nevertheless, in the absence of a corporate income tax or the presence of a significant tax rate differential favouring the corporate tax, the potential for tax avoidance and evasion could be significant, implying serious equity and perception problems, and empirical evidence suggests that the extent of such income shifting may be significant (Gordon and Slemrod, 2000; de Mooij and Nicodème, 2008). It is clear that the backstop argument provides a potentially important rationale for a company tax in New Zealand, and underlies its long tradition of rate alignment.[6]

The role of tax avoidance revisited

As discussed above, the relative ease with which multinational corporations can use financial accounting manipulations to shift income across jurisdictions provides a powerful additional argument for lower statutory corporate income tax rates. However, this argument must be qualified to the extent that possibilities for such tax avoidance by MNCs mitigate the otherwise negative effects on FDI of relatively high statutory and effective tax rates. Indeed, to the extent that such tax avoidance opportunities are available primarily to MNCs and such firms are more mobile than domestic companies, a relatively high statutory rate may be desirable as an 'optimal capital income tax' strategy that attracts FDI at minimal revenue cost by imposing a high tax burden on relatively immobile domestic capital but a low effective tax burden, taking into account tax avoidance activities, on relatively mobile international capital (Gugl and Zodrow, 2006). An aggressive version of this strategy would include lax enforcement of rules designed to limit tax avoidance by MNCs or even explicit regulations that facilitate such tax avoidance – the 'new' variation of international tax competition stressed by Altshuler and Grubert (2006).[7] Of course, the pursuance of such a strategy will understandably be viewed as highly inequitable by domestic firms and may be difficult to maintain politically.

The treasury transfer effect

An often-invoked rationale for imposing a relatively high tax burden on FDI in countries that import capital from capital-exporting countries that tax their MNCs on a residence basis but allow credits for foreign taxes paid, including the US, the UK and Japan, is the 'treasury transfer' effect. The essence of this argument is that, under certain circumstances, a host country that imports capital primarily from countries that grant foreign tax credits (FTCs) should raise its tax rate approximately equal to the rate utilised by those countries, since such a rate increase will essentially transfer revenues from the treasury of the home country to the treasury of the host country without having any deleterious effects on FDI. This result obtains because the rate increase in the host country is offset by foreign tax credits which reduce the final domestic tax liability of the MNC.

The prospect of such a 'free' source of tax revenue is naturally appealing. However, in practice, the treasury transfer effect is often of limited relevance. Most obviously in the case of New Zealand, the US and UK are by a considerable margin secondary to Australia as a source of FDI. Australia operates a territorial corporate income tax system and thus does not grant any foreign tax credits to its multinationals.[8] But even apart from this consideration, several arguments suggest a limited role in practice for the treasury transfer effect. First, because of various limitations placed on the use of foreign tax credits, many US multinationals are in an 'excess foreign tax credit' position – that is, they already have more credits than they can use currently, so that additional credits are of limited value.[9] Second, the treasury transfer effect may be illusory in many cases because host country taxes are assessed currently but foreign tax credits in the home country are not granted until the funds are repatriated to the parent firm; as a result, the home country repatriation tax may have little or no effect on investment financed with the retained earnings of the subsidiary

(Hartman, 1985; Sinn, 1987). Under this view, investments financed with retained earnings are affected only by host country taxes.[10] Together, these arguments suggest that the treasury transfer effect should play little if any role in the determination of company tax policy in New Zealand.

The political desirability of business taxation

Political realities may make some form of corporate income taxation inevitable, given popular demands to tax 'rich' corporations owned by wealthy investors. In particular, the long history of company taxation in most countries suggests that taxing both domestic and foreign corporations may be indispensable from a political viewpoint, regardless of how compelling the arguments against such taxation may be to economists (Bird, 1996). In addition, source countries often assert a sovereign 'right' to tax the income generated within their boundaries, beyond any royalties that are imposed on the extraction of natural resource (Musgrave, 2000). Finally, the corporate income tax is an excellent example of a 'hidden tax', one whose burden is not readily apparent and is thus attractive from a political, if not a public choice, standpoint.

Nevertheless, in New Zealand as elsewhere around the globe, the political arguments favouring relatively high corporate income taxation are increasingly offset in public discussion of tax policy by the spectre of increasing globalisation and international tax competition. Accordingly, it is far from clear that political considerations present an insurmountable obstacle to reductions in corporate income taxation, although they are likely to preclude the elimination of the company tax.

6.3 EVALUATION OF SPECIFIC COMPANY TAX REFORM OPTIONS

The discussion thus far demonstrates clearly that setting company tax policy in a small open economy is an exceedingly difficult task, and that no single tax structure will simultaneously deal with all the issues discussed above. Accordingly, it is not surprising that countries attempt to strike a balance between the various competing forces described above, that the balance struck differs across countries depending on their individual circumstances, and that this balance is continually being reconsidered especially in light of the economic forces associated with increasing globalisation and a more highly integrated global economy. For example, while noting that numerous arguments suggest that corporate tax rates will not follow a 'race to the bottom' of a zero rate, the New Zealand Treasury (2008) argues that competition for mobile capital is likely to put downward pressure on corporate tax rates – and that the tax rate in Australia, currently under review by the government, is naturally a critical benchmark. Within the context of striking such a balance between exemption and full taxation of mobile international capital, a wide variety of company tax reform options might be considered in any small open economy. The following discussion focuses on several of these options, beginning with several revenue-neutral base-broadening approaches and then turning to options that would reduce the overall amount of revenue obtained from capital income taxation.

6.3.1 Revenue-Neutral Base-Broadening and Rate-Reducing Income Tax Reform

The traditional arguments supporting income tax reform in the direction of broadening the base by eliminating tax preferences and other deviations from the accurate measurement of real economic income and using the resulting revenues to reduce statutory tax rates for both domestic and foreign firms are largely strengthened by the international taxation considerations discussed above. Base-broadening, rate-reducing corporate income tax reforms are in general desirable because they reduce the efficiency costs associated with tax distortions across assets and business sectors (unless such 'distortions' are desirable to offset important externalities) as well as distortions of the choice of organisational form, method of finance, and payout policies; they simplify tax administration and compliance, and eliminate both the perception and the reality of inequitable government favouritism toward certain industries. Although New Zealand has historically been known for its extremely broad tax bases (with the exception of the exemption of capital gains at the individual level), some tax preferences have been creeping into the system implying some limited scope for a base-broadening, rate-reducing reform (New Zealand Inland Revenue Department, 2008; New Zealand Treasury, 2008).

These standard arguments are significantly reinforced if one considers the possibilities for international tax avoidance, as a lower statutory rate reduces incentives for multinationals to shift revenues out of, and deductions into, a taxing jurisdiction. Lower statutory corporate income tax rates are also likely to be effective in attracting foreign direct investments that generate firm-specific economic rents by lowering the average effective tax rate applied to such rents. The combination of lower rates and eliminating tax preferences, however, is not likely to reduce effective marginal tax rates on average to any significant extent, and thus will not increase the equilibrium level of investment at the margin.

Several objections are commonly raised to the base-broadening, rate-reducing approach to company income tax reform. A standard criticism is that reductions in statutory rates are very costly in terms of revenue relative to the additional investment incentives they generate because lower rates apply to the income earned by existing capital. A closely related point is that reductions in statutory rates financed with base-broadening reduce the taxation of both domestic and foreign investments that earn location-specific rents or are otherwise immobile. Finally, to the extent that a lower statutory corporate income tax rate creates or increases a rate differential between personal and corporate income tax rates, it exacerbates incentives for tax avoidance in the form of shifting income from the personal tax base to the corporate tax base.

Although these arguments have some validity, each must be qualified. There is no question that a corporate tax rate reduction benefits existing investments and results in lower taxation of location-specific economic rents. However, as suggested above, the 'bang for the buck' from rate reduction may not be as small as is sometimes envisioned, because it may stimulate investments that generate firm-specific economic rents. In addition, in some cases increases in alternative revenue instruments, such as production-based taxes in the case of resource rents, can be used to maintain the taxation of location-specific rents. Assuming that base-broadening efforts are designed to result in a tax base that measures real economic income as closely as possible,[11] the base-broadening, rate-reducing approach has the important advantage of creating a tax system that is based on solid economic principles and is hopefully more stable than one based on granting tax preferences that are often as much or more politically than economically motivated. Finally, if rate reduction is perceived to result in an unacceptable level of benefit to existing investments, that tax reform-induced benefit could be eliminated with appropriately designed transitional taxes, such as the 'windfall recapture tax' that was proposed, but ultimately not enacted, to deal with this issue under the large rate reductions enacted in the US Tax Reform Act of 1986.[12]

A corporate tax rate reduction that widens the differential between the top personal tax rate and the corporate rate does encourage income shifting from the personal tax base to the corporate tax base, and recent empirical work suggests that the magnitude of this effect may be significant. However, as argued above, the importance of this effect depends on the extent to which tax administration and enforcement are effective in limiting opportunities for such income shifting, and on the extent to which it results only in deferral, rather than complete exemption, of individual level taxation on the shifted income.

On balance, the traditional base-broadening, rate-reducing approach to company tax reform has considerable appeal. Note that the same logic applies to the personal income tax. In particular, given the relatively high mobility of labour in New Zealand, including highly skilled labour,[13] low marginal tax rates on labour income are highly desirable as well, and a substitution of labour taxes for capital taxes is less desirable than it would be if labour mobility were lower (New Zealand Inland Revenue Department, 2008; New Zealand Treasury, 2008).

6.3.2 Further Rate Reductions under an Income Tax Reform

If the corporate income tax rate reduction that can be achieved with (politically feasible) base broadening is deemed to be insufficient, several other approaches can be utilised within the context of an income tax.

The comprehensive business income tax

The Comprehensive Business Income Tax (CBIT) was proposed by the US Department of the Treasury (1992) as a means of integrating the corporate and personal income taxes in the US.[14] The CBIT further broadens the base of the corporate income tax – beyond the extent typically associated with a traditional classical income tax – by disallowing deductions for interest expense. In addition, under a fully integrated system, individual level taxation of capital income is needed only to the extent of differences in corporate and individual tax rates (the rate under the CBIT as proposed in the US would have approximated the top individual tax rate), and the extent to which the taxation of capital gains in excess of those attributable to retained earnings is deemed desirable. Thus, for debt-financed investment, the CBIT effectively shifts the locus of taxation from the holder of the debt to the corporation. Since much interest income typically escapes taxation at the level of the bondholder, a CBIT would likely raise revenue and allow further rate reduction – estimated to be roughly three percentage points in the case of the US – although in general this depends on whether the revenue increase due to the elimination of interest deductibility is offset by the revenue decline due to reduced taxation of capital income at the individual level (and any changes in the taxation of foreign shareholders). Since both interest and dividends are treated uniformly – that is, they are not deductible and are thus taxed at the corporate level – the tax bias favouring debt finance under the typical income tax is eliminated.

The effect of a revenue-neutral CBIT on effective marginal tax rates would depend on the net effect of a reduction in the tax burden on equity-financed investment (assuming that the statutory rate declines) and the increase in the tax burden on debt-financed investment, which would now all be assessed at the business level, raising the source-based tax on debt-financed foreign direct investment. Such relatively harsh treatment of debt would likely reduce the level of debt-financed investment, especially by multinationals – unless multinationals responded by keeping their investment level largely unchanged while reallocating their debt to other countries where full interest deductibility was allowed. The statutory rate reduction obtained under a CBIT would moderately reduce incentives for income shifting, as well as the level of taxation of economic rents. The CBIT is thus more attractive to countries attempting to attract multinationals with investments that generate firm-specific rents, than to countries focused on taxing location-specific rents earned by both domestic firms and multinationals.

In addition, note that since the CBIT disallows deductions for interest expense, it would raise the same foreign tax creditability issues that plague cash-flow taxes (for example, the Flat Tax and the X-Tax) with the same feature. The combination of an increase in the effective marginal tax rate applied at the business level to debt-financed foreign direct investment (and the transition problems that this would cause for highly leveraged firms) plus the lack of foreign tax creditability would seem to make the CBIT an unattractive option for most small open economies.

Increasing the individual-level share of the taxation of capital income

From the perspective of attracting foreign direct investment that earns either normal returns or firm specific rents, the CBIT has the disadvantage of increasing the share of the tax burden on capital income that is borne at the corporate rather than the individual level.[15] Altshuler and Grubert (2008) stress that shifting the mix of capital income taxation from the corporation to the individual level, while largely irrelevant in a closed economy (apart from administrative considerations), is desirable as globalisation and capital mobility increase. For example, additional corporate income tax rate reduction could be effected by shifting the point at which the tax burden is imposed from the company level to the individual level in the form of a higher rate or more comprehensive taxation of dividends, capital gains (discussed further below) and interest income at the individual level for domestic investors. Such an approach could keep the combined capital income tax burden on domestic investors roughly constant, especially if the company and personal tax systems are largely integrated,[16] while applying a lower statutory rate to the income (including firm-specific economic rents) earned by highly mobile international capital, while reducing incentives for international tax avoidance.

6.3.3 Corporate Rate Reduction with Increases in Labour or Consumption Taxation

Although such base-broadening, rate-reducing approaches to corporate income tax reform can be used to lower the statutory company tax rate somewhat, that rate would still likely be relatively high after such a reform, and the associated effects on effective marginal tax rates applied to capital income would be relatively small (under the reasonable assumption that any tax preferences eliminated had some impact in terms of reducing the cost of capital for the preferred investments). Accordingly, further reductions in the corporate statutory rate, financed with increases in the taxation of labour income or consumption rather than tax changes that increase the burden on capital income, may be desirable, especially for countries that are focused on attracting foreign direct investment, including investments that generate firm-specific economic rents, and concerned about revenue losses due to income shifting by foreign multinationals. Indeed, both the New Zealand Inland Revenue Department (2008) and the New Zealand Treasury (2008) suggest that moving toward increased reliance on consumption-based taxes may be desirable – partly on the grounds that corporate income taxes are more harmful than consumption-based taxes to economic growth (see Johansson, et al., Chapter 2 in this volume); in addition, the Treasury stresses that limited use of payroll taxes in New Zealand implies that the tax burden on capital income is relatively high in comparison to other OECD countries.

Such an approach could be implemented simply by decreasing income tax rates and increasing tax rates applied to consumption; for example, under a value-added tax. Such a tax substitution, however, is often deemed to be undesirable on distributional grounds. In this case, an alternative approach is to reduce the taxation of capital income relative to the taxation of labour income. Such an approach clearly deviates from traditional arguments for comprehensive income taxation of all capital and labour income at the same rate. However, as discussed above, the application of a lower rate to capital income than that applied to labour income may be desirable for a wide variety of reasons, especially in an environment characterised by increasing international capital mobility, international tax competition, and international tax avoidance. That is, in general there is no particular reason to believe that the optimal balance between labour and capital income taxation necessarily prescribes equal tax rates for both types of income, and the arguments for relatively lower rates on capital income typically found in the optimal income taxation literature are augmented by international taxation considerations (Sørensen, 2005; Auerbach, 2008a).

However, applying lower income tax rates to capital income naturally creates incentives for the conversion of labour income into capital income. As discussed above, lower rates for capital income may simply be accompanied by a variety of administrative measures designed to limit the conversion of labour income to more lightly taxed capital income. An alternative and more systematic approach, which attempts to limit the conversion of labour income into capital income through the use of special imputation rules, is the 'dual income tax' (DIT) pioneered in the late 1980s and early 1990s by the Nordic countries, and adopted more recently in numerous other settings (Genser and Reutter, 2007).

Since the dual income tax is addressed at length by Sørensen (Chapter 5 in this book), the following discussion will be brief. Under a 'pure' dual income tax,[17] all capital income is taxed at a single proportional rate at either the business or individual levels (equal to the minimum non-zero tax rate applied to labour income), while labour income is taxed at progressive rates under the individual income tax. Dividends are excluded from the individual capital income tax base, while capital gains are taxed at the individual level on a realisation basis but with shareholders allowed to write up their basis by net retained earnings. Capital income taxes are collected via withholding at source, which in the simplest version of the tax (which does not allow capital loss offsets against labour income or apply personal exemptions or standard deductions against capital income) represents a final tax. In principle, full tax withholding could be extended to foreigners, but in practice this is very limited, for the same reasons as noted above in the discussion of the CBIT. Profits of proprietorships and closely-held companies are split into a capital income component, typically calculated by applying a presumptive rate of return to the firm's capital, which is taxed at the proportional rate on capital income, and a labour income component, which equals the residual profit and is taxed at progressive rates under the personal income tax.

The structure of the dual income tax is clearly designed to strike a balance between the standard small open economy argument for low tax rates on capital income, including firm-specific rents, supplemented by concerns regarding the implications of international tax avoidance, and the opposing arguments for taxing capital income at relatively high rates to capture location-specific economic rents earned by both multinationals and relatively immobile domestic firms, while maintaining a backstop to the personal income tax.

The primary problem with the dual income tax approach – its 'Achilles heel' according to Sørensen (2005) – is that despite the imputation method used to split capital income described above, in practice considerable income shifting by the owners of closely-held companies still occurs.[18] In addition, as mentioned above, in response to intense tax competition with respect to the taxation of interest income, in practice DIT countries impose at most partial withholding taxes at source on interest payments. Note, however, that to the extent interest income is taxed at source under a DIT, its treatment of debt is relatively harsh (compared to the typical treatment of full deductibility and limited if any withholding), discouraging multinationals from allocating debt to any country that has adopted a DIT.

In summary, by largely separating the taxation of capital income from the progressive income taxation of labour income, the dual income tax approach provides a mechanism for dealing with the many tensions faced by tax policy makers in a small open economy described above. It thus represents a reasonable approach to balancing the offsetting tensions that characterise today's fiscal landscape, and deserves serious consideration by governments who are attempting to design company tax policy in the face of increasing international capital mobility, international tax competition and international tax avoidance.

6.3.4 Consumption-Based Business Taxes and Consumption Tax Reforms

As discussed above, one response to the forces of increasing globalisation has been to reduce business level taxes as much as possible in order to attract foreign direct investment (including investments earning firm specific rents) and minimise business income shifting opportunities, and concentrate the taxation of capital income at the individual level.[19] Implementation of a dual income tax would reduce the taxation of capital income at the individual level as well. A natural question, especially in light of the desire to stimulate domestic saving in New Zealand to reduce persistent current account deficits and reliance on potentially unstable mobile foreign capital, is whether it would be desirable to eliminate the taxation of the normal returns to capital by adopting a more radical and certainly more controversial reform – implementing direct taxation on the basis of consumption rather than income.

Many consumption-based direct taxes have been proposed in recent years.[20] In general terms, under a consumption-based approach, a business level tax would apply an effective tax rate of zero to the normal returns earned by marginal investments while taxing above normal returns or economic rents at the statutory tax. Under most plans, this would be achieved by subjecting businesses to a cash-flow tax that would allow immediate expensing of all investment purchases and either disallow deductions for interest expense or tax loans on a cash-flow basis (with loan proceeds taxed and both interest and principal repayments deductible). However, under the alternative 'Allowance for Corporate Equity' (ACE) approach, firms would continue to get deductions for depreciation and interest expense, and would be allowed an additional deduction for equity-financed investment – equal to the product of the book value of equity capital and a fixed rate of return – analogous to the deductions for interest expense allowed for debt-financed investment under the income tax. Capital income at the individual level would either be exempt or subject to consumption-based cash-flow taxation as well – in the latter case with deductions for saving and taxation of all withdrawals (that is, the same treatment provided to much retirement savings under many tax systems that are nominally described as income taxes).

There is of course a huge literature on the relative advantages of income and consumption taxation, developed largely in the context of closed economies.[21] In brief, proponents of consumption-based taxes argue that they are preferable to income taxes because they are: (1) relatively efficient, primarily because they eliminate the income tax distortion of consumption-saving decisions as well as a wide variety of investment distortions; (2) fairer than the income tax because they do not discriminate against individuals who save and earn capital income while still utilising multiple rates to achieve progressivity; and (3) simpler in terms of administration and compliance.

From the perspective of a small open economy, a consumption-based tax has the advantage of applying an effective marginal tax rate of zero to the normal returns earned by both foreign and domestic investment while taxing location-specific economic rents at the statutory rate – which under most plans would be set equal to the maximum individual tax rate on labour income. In addition, alignment of the business level tax rate and the top individual rate implies that a consumption tax acts as an effective backstop to individual level taxation of labour income. The business tax under a consumption tax also satisfies at least partially the political need for such a tax.

At the same time, however, several factors suggest that implementing a consumption-based tax may not be appropriate for a small open economy attempting to attract investment in the world economy. A consumption-based tax naturally also taxes firm-specific economic rents at the statutory rate, and thus may discourage relatively mobile investments that generate such rents, especially if the statutory rate is kept high in order to collect significant revenues from both domestic and international investments that earn location-specific economic rents and to make up for the loss of revenue that occurs with the tax exemption of normal returns to investment. Similarly, a relatively high statutory tax rate under the business component of a consumption tax will create incentives for tax avoidance in the form of income shifting by multinationals, resulting in a potentially significant negative effect on tax revenues. It should also be noted, however, that under certain forms of consumption-based taxation interest deductions are not allowed, in which case businesses would face a large incentive to allocate debt to income tax jurisdictions where interest was deductible, thus mitigating the effect of a relatively high cash-flow tax rate.

Several other issues associated with implementing a consumption tax are problematical. Since normal returns are not subject to the business tax, some (probably relatively small) amount of revenues that might be obtained via the treasury transfer effect would be foregone. Moreover, it seems clear that the US, and perhaps other countries that grant foreign tax credits, would not allow creditability for a cash-flow business tax, despite arguments that creditability would be appropriate (McLure and Zodrow, 1988).[22] Consumption-based taxes are not immune to tax avoidance manipulations, especially in a world where one's trading partners continue to use the income tax (Bankman and Schler, 2007). Finally, the transition problems associated with implementing a consumption tax – including the need to renegotiate existing treaties with income tax countries – would be formidable (Gravelle, 2002), although a variety of factors act to mitigate some of these problems (Zodrow, 2002).

This discussion suggests that, although consumption-based direct taxation has many advantages, there are also a number of reasons why caution would be advisable, and why the desirability of such reform in a given country would depend on its specific circumstances. Moreover, if a country is seriously contemplating a move towards consumption-based direct taxation, the discussion above also suggests that serious consideration should be given to the ACE approach to such a tax. Because the ACE approach is closer to an income tax in structure than any of the cash-flow tax options – it basically adds a generous investment incentive to an income tax in the form of the additional deduction for corporate equity, while continuing to allow deductions for depreciation and interest expense – it would involve fewer transitional issues and would not be perceived as a radical departure from income tax, as would any of the cash-flow-based consumption tax options. Moreover, for essentially the same reasons, the US has not questioned the credibility of the ACE tax, for example when it was enacted briefly in Croatia (Rose and Wiswesser, 1998; Zodrow, 2003). The investment stimulus and efficiency gains associated with adopting an ACE would of course be enhanced if the equity deduction were not granted to existing capital; indeed, Griffith et al. (2009) propose such an approach, and show that the potential problem of firms liquidating and reforming to take advantage of the new equity deduction is limited as long as asset sales are treated as fully taxable.

The ACE approach does not have the apparent simplicity advantages of allowing expensing rather than deductions for economic depreciation.

However, the practical benefits of allowing expensing for tax purposes are limited, given that firms will still have to determine depreciation deductions for financial accounting purposes. A related point is that the ACE approach also avoids some problems peculiar to allowing expensing under the cash-flow approach, including increasing the gains to various tax avoidance schemes and creating new avoidance opportunities (especially in the international arena), and increasing the likelihood of negative business tax bases and the problems they engender (McLure and Zodrow, 1996b). Moreover, in a variant of his X-Tax, Bradford (2003) argues that an approach similar to that under an ACE tax is in fact a highly desirable way to implement a consumption tax, as it reduces transition problems and eliminates the potential distortions of investment timing decisions that arise under strict cash-flow accounting when future tax rate changes are anticipated. The ACE approach – like the cash-flow options but in contrast to the income tax – has the advantage that inflation adjustment of depreciation allowances is unnecessary as any understatement of such allowances is exactly offset in present value terms by a higher value for the equity deduction. Indeed, this argument applies to all mismeasurement of depreciation allowances since, as with the expensing option under the cash-flow approaches, the present value of the deductions allowed – for depreciation and the equity deduction – equals the purchase price of the asset.

The determination of the imputed rate of return on equity would of course be difficult under the ACE tax, and its neutrality properties would not obtain unless that rate were determined accurately. (The same issue arises in the determination of the carry-forward interest rate for negative cash flows under the various cash flow options.) Griffith et al. (2009) conclude that the appropriate rate would be the risk-free rate plus an 'average' risk premium to reflect the possibility that any losses might not be recovered in full. Since the appropriate risk premium will differ across firms, but administrative realities imply that a single rate will be used, some distortions of investment decisions will arise. In addition, because the statutory tax rate under an ACE tax would likely be relatively high, it cannot avoid the problems of taxing firm-specific economic rents, creating incentives for income shifting by multinationals, and perhaps losing some revenue by forgoing the treasury transfer effect. But no tax is perfect, and the ACE tax achieves all the benefits of consumption-based taxation outlined above. In particular, it might be an attractive business tax reform option in a country – like New Zealand – that can be characterised as a relatively small open economy, has a significant fraction of investments that earn location-specific economic rents, and wishes to increase domestic saving by eliminating income taxation of the normal return to saving.

Finally, the argument made by Altshuler and Grubert (2008) discussed above – that concerns regarding globalisation and international capital mobility suggest that the taxation of capital income should be concentrated at the individual rather than the corporate level – can be applied in this case as well, with the same advantages and disadvantages. Specifically, if some taxation of capital income were deemed desirable, consumption-based taxation could be applied at the business level, coupled with individual level taxation of capital income. Such an approach results in a hybrid system that has the advantages of consumption-based taxation of the business level, while retaining some taxation of capital income, to satisfy distributional concerns or to reflect a policy response to arguments implying that the optimal tax rate on capital income, while lower than that applied to labour income, is nevertheless not zero (Auerbach, 2008a, b; Zodrow, 2007). Indeed, the 'Growth and Investment Tax' proposed by the President's Advisory Panel on Federal Tax Reform (2005) in the US consisted of a consumption-based business level tax that allowed immediate expensing of all business-related purchases (while ignoring loans), coupled with taxation of dividends and capital gains at a flat rate of 15 per cent. Similarly, the reform proposed for the UK by Griffith et al. (2009) consisted of an ACE tax at the business level, similarly coupled with individual level capital income taxation.

6.4 CONCLUSION

This chapter argues that any moderately small open economy operates in an environment characterised by increasing international capital mobility, international tax competition and international tax avoidance. Although one can construct theoretical arguments with policy prescriptions that range from zero taxation of capital income to full taxation of capital income and a rate equal to the top individual rate applied to labour income, in practice neither of these extreme solutions is likely to be desirable. Instead, policies on the taxation of capital income will depend on specific circumstances – with the primary factors being the extent to which the supply of international capital is highly elastic, the relative importance of firm-specific and location-specific economic rents, and the extent to which income shifting, including by multinational corporations and between the personal and company tax bases, is a problem that cannot be resolved with regulations designed to limit such shifting. In general, the traditional arguments for base broadening and rate reduction are strengthened by international considerations, which also imply that taxation of capital income at rates lower than those applied to labour income is likely to be desirable, with the dual income tax being one potential way to achieve such differentiation. Finally, although there are many advantages to direct taxation on the basis of consumption, there are also many problems associated with implementing such a reform. On balance, in the current environment, if a consumption-based approach is deemed desirable, the ACE approach is the most feasible of the many available consumption-based business tax options. Moreover, it could in principle be accompanied by individual level income taxation of dividends and capital gains, if a full implementation of a consumption tax were deemed undesirable.

NOTES

* I have benefited from the comments of Iris Claus and the participants at a conference on 'New Zealand Tax Reform – Where To Next?' sponsored by the New Zealand Treasury, Inland Revenue and Victoria University of Wellington, and held at Victoria University Wellington, February 11–13, 2009.

1. See Zodrow (2008a, b) for discussions of recent evidence on the extent of international capital mobility, international tax competition and international tax avoidance.
2. See Devereux and Sørensen (2006), Altshuler and Grubert (2008) and Griffith et al. (2009) for discussions of company income taxation that include excellent treatments of outbound FDI, including the choices between territorial and residence (both accrual and deferred) tax systems, and destination-based and residence-based taxes; see Head (2009) for a recent discussion of the integration of corporate and individual tax systems.
3. These arguments of course supplement the traditional efficiency case against the corporate tax, especially when applied to multinational corporations (Nicodème, 2008).
4. The top statutory individual marginal tax rate is scheduled to decline to 37 per cent in 2011. Effective tax rates at relatively low incomes can also be quite high due to the phase out of various credits (New Zealand Treasury, 2008).
5. Of course, in the case of New Zealand, this argument would apply for retained earnings only if capital gains were made subject to tax as part of base broadening of the personal income tax (New Zealand Treasury, 2008), although the calculation of tax on such gains should in principle reflect adjustments for corporate taxes paid and inflation.
6. Note, however, that the backstop function could be served with a corporate cash-flow tax assessed at the top individual rate (Hubbard, 2002; Zodrow and McLure, 1991; Zodrow, 2006).
7. Indeed, Hong and Smart (2007) argue that tax havens should be 'praised' for allowing this flexibility, which implies that FDI will be less sensitive to cross-country tax rate differentials, thus allowing higher corporate tax rates in host countries to be welfare-increasing for their citizens. In contrast, Slemrod and Wilson (2006) note that this is not the case when tax havens also facilitate sheltering of domestic labour income.
8. Australia accounts for roughly half of FDI in New Zealand, with the shares of the US, the Netherlands and the UK ranging from 6 to 12 per cent.
9. Moreover, the likelihood that a US firm is in an excess foreign tax credit position has been increased by (1) the use of tax avoidance techniques that effectively separate foreign taxes paid, that can be credited currently from the associated foreign source income which can then be deferred – perhaps indefinitely provided that the multinational does not need to repatriate the funds back to the US – from US tax liability; (2) the rules used by the US to allocate expenses to foreign source income (see Zodrow (2008b) for further discussion).
10. This argument applies the logic of the 'new view' of dividend taxation in an international context and is subject to the same criticisms; in particular, Grubert (1998) finds that

repatriation flows are negatively related to repatriation taxes, a result that is consistent with the 'traditional view' that such taxes do have an effect on investment behaviour.

11. A separate issue is whether the measurement of income should be adjusted for inflation, as described in Thuronyi (2000). As long as the inflation rates are relatively low and fairly stable, the complexity of a comprehensive system of inflation adjustment can be avoided (although at the cost of some additional complexity in the treatment of asset sales) with ad hoc adjustments such as appropriately accelerated depreciation allowances (or partial expensing) and LIFO inventory accounting.
12. The proposed windfall recapture tax would have calculated the deferred income due to accelerated depreciation deductions (defined as those in excess of the deductions allowed under the 'earnings and profits' accounting method) taken prior to the enactment of reform and effectively taxed that income at the pre-reform tax rate; see Zodrow (1988).
13. Indeed, the New Zealand Treasury (2008) argues that New Zealand probably has the most mobile labour force of all the countries in the OECD, noting that approximately one-quarter of skilled New Zealanders live abroad, with trans-Tasman migration a particularly important phenomenon.
14. The proposed CBIT would have also applied to unincorporated businesses.
15. Of course, this is an advantage from the perspective of effectively collecting revenue on domestic investment.
16. See US Department of the Treasury (1992), Hubbard (2005) and Head (2009) for discussions of alternative means of achieving corporate–individual tax integration.
17. This definition follows Cnossen (2000); see also Sørensen (1994) and Nielsen and Sørensen (1997). Of course, in practice, actual dual income taxes differ to varying degrees from this ideal version.
18. Devereux and Sørensen (2006) note that Norway has attempted to remedy this problem (for 'active' shareholders in a closely-held company) by replacing the income-splitting approach with a shareholder tax that results in taxation of returns in excess of a normal rate of return (termed the rate-of-return allowance) at individual rates.
19. The same reasoning played a role in the development of the recent Norwegian reform, noted above, that provides a rate-of-return allowance at the personal level to shareholders rather than at the business level as under the conventional 'allowance for corporate equity' (ACE) tax discussed below (Sørensen, 2005).
20. These include the Flat Tax proposed by Hall and Rabushka (1995) and its X-Tax variant as designed by Bradford (1986, 2003), the 'cash-flow income tax' proposed by Aaron and Galper (1985) and its close relative the 'Unlimited Savings Allowance' or USA Tax (see Weidenbaum, 1995), the 'hybrid consumption tax' proposed by McLure and Zodrow (1996a, b), the 'allowance for corporate equity' or ACE tax adopted temporarily in Croatia (Institute for Fiscal Studies, 1991; Rose and Wiswesser, 1998; Keen and King, 2002), and a tax on net corporate distributions, adopted in Estonia.
21. For recent discussions see Auerbach (2008a), Zodrow (2007) and Banks and Diamond (2008), as well as the articles in Zodrow and Mieszkowski (2002), Aaron et al. (2007) and Diamond and Zodrow (2008).
22. Note, however, that the US has agreed to allow creditability for a portion of the Italian IRAP (Imposta Regionale sulle Attivita Produttive), a type of origin-based value-added tax that is quite similar to a cash-flow business tax with no deductions for labour compensation; roughly speaking, the creditable portion is the value-added tax base less compensation and interest payments (Adelchi Rossi, 2002).

REFERENCES

Aaron, H.J. and H. Galper (1985), *Assessing Tax Reform*, Washington, DC: Brookings Institution.

Aaron, H.J., L.E. Burman and Steuerle C.E. (eds) (2007), *Taxing Capital Income*, Washington, DC: Urban Institute Press.

Adelchi, R. (2002), 'Relief from double taxation under the new U.S.–Italy tax treaty', *Tax Notes International*, **28**, 487–502.

Altshuler, R. and H. Grubert (2006), 'Governments and multinational corporations in the race to the bottom', *Tax Notes* (February 6), **110**, 459–74.

Altshuler, R. and H. Grubert (2008), 'Corporate taxes in the world economy: Reforming the taxation of cross-border income', in J.W. Diamond and G.R. Zodrow (eds), *Fundamental Tax Reform: Issues, Choices, and Implications*, Cambridge, MA: MIT Press.

Auerbach, A.J. (1991), 'Retrospective capital gains taxation', *American Economic Review*, **81**, 167–78.

Auerbach, A.J. (2006), *The future of capital income taxation*, Berkeley Program in Law and Economics Working Paper No. 217, Berkeley: Berkeley Program in Law and Economics.

Auerbach, A.J. (2008a), 'Tax reform in the 21st century', in J.W. Diamond and G.R. Zodrow (eds), *Fundamental Tax Reform: Issues, Choices and Implications*, Cambridge, MA: MIT Press.

Auerbach, A.J. (2008b), 'Income or consumption taxes?', Paper presented at a conference in Honour of Richard Musgrave, Sydney, Australia, 2–4 June, 2008.

Bankman, J. and M. Schler (2007), 'Tax planning under the flat tax', in H.J. Aaron, L.E. Burman and C.E. Steuerle (eds), *Taxing Capital Income*, Washington, DC: Urban Institute Press, pp. 245–84.

Banks, J.W. and P.A. Diamond (2008), 'The base for direct taxation', Chapter prepared for *Reforming the Tax System for the 21st Century: The Mirrlees Review*.

Bird, R.M. (1996), *Why Tax Corporations?* Department of Finance, Technical Committee on Business Taxation, Working Paper No. 96-2.

Bradford, D.F. (1986), *Untangling the Income Tax*, Cambridge, MA: Harvard University Press.

Bradford, D.F. (2003), 'Addressing the transfer-pricing problem in an origin-basis X-tax', *International Tax and Public Finance*, **10**, 591–610.

Cnossen, S. (2000), 'Taxing capital income in the Nordic countries: A model for the European Union?', in S. Cnossen (ed.), *Taxing Capital in the European Union*. Oxford: Oxford University Press.

de Mooij, R. and G. Nicodème (2008), 'Corporate tax policy and incorporation in the EU', *International Tax and Public Finance*, **15**, 478–98.

Devereux, M.P. and R. Griffith (2003), 'Evaluating tax policy for location decisions', *International Tax and Public Finance*, **10**, 107–26.

Devereux, M.P. and P.B. Sørensen (2006), 'The corporate income tax: International trends and options for functional reform', *European Economy*, European Commission Economics Papers No. 264.

Diamond, J.W. and G.R. Zodrow (2008), 'Consumption tax reform: Changes in business equity and housing prices', in J.W. Diamond and G.R. Zodrow (eds), *Fundamental Tax Reform: Issues, Choices and Implications*, Cambridge, MA: MIT Press.

Dunning, J.H. (1981), *International Production and the Multinational Enterprise*, London: Allen and Unwin.

Genser, B. and A. Reutter (2007), 'Moving towards dual income taxation in Europe', *FinanzArchiv*, **63**, 436–56.

Gordon, R.H. (1986), 'Taxation of investment and savings in the world economy', *American Economic Review*, **76**, 1086–102.
Gordon, R.H. and J.R., Jr. Hines (2002), 'International taxation', in A.J. Auerbach and M. Feldstein (eds), *Handbook of Public Economics, Volume 4*, Amsterdam: North Holland/Elsevier.
Gordon, R.H. and J.K. MacKie-Mason (1995), 'Why is there corporate taxation in a small open economy? The role of transfer pricing and income shifting', in M. Feldstein, J.R. Hines, Jr. and R.G. Hubbard (eds), *The Effects of Taxation on Multinational Corporations*, Chicago: University of Chicago Press.
Gordon, R.H. and J. Slemrod (2000), 'Are "real" responses to taxes simply income shifting between corporate and personal income tax bases?', in J. Slemrod (ed.), *Does Atlas Shrug? The Economic Consequences of Taxing the Rich*, New York and Cambridge, MA: Russell Sage Foundation and Harvard University Press.
Gravelle, J.G. (2002), 'Behavioral responses to a consumption tax', in G.R. Zodrow and P. Mieszkowski (eds), *United States Tax Reform in the 21st Century*, Cambridge, MA: Cambridge University Press.
Gravelle, J.G. and K.A. Smetters (2006), 'Does the open economy assumption really mean that labour bears the burden of a capital income tax?', *Advances in Economic Analysis and Policy*, **6**, 1–42.
Griffith, R., J.R. Hines, Jr. and P.B. Sørensen (2009), 'International capital taxation', in The Institute for Fiscal Studies (ed.), *Dimensions of Tax Design: The Mirrlees Review*, Oxford: Oxford University Press for the Institute for Fiscal Studies.
Grubert, H. (1998), 'Taxes and the division of foreign operating income among royalties, interest, dividends and retained earnings', *Journal of Public Economics*, **68**, 269–90.
Gugl, E. and G.R. Zodrow (2006), 'International tax competition and tax incentives for developing countries', in J. Alm, J. Martinez-Vasquez and M. Rider (eds), *The Challenges of Tax Reform in a Global Economy*, New York: Springer.
Hall, R.E. and A. Rabushka (1995), *The Flat Tax*, Stanford: Hoover Institution Press.
Hall, J. and G. Scobie (2005), *Capital shallowness: A problem for New Zealand?*, New Zealand Treasury Working Paper No. 05/05.
Harberger, A.C. (1995), 'The ABCs of corporate tax incidence: Insights into the open-economy case', in *Tax Policy and Economic Growth*, Washington, DC: American Council for Capital Formation Center for Policy Research.
Harberger, A.C. (2008), 'Corporate tax incidence: Reflections on what is known, unknown, and unknowable', in J.W. Diamond and G.R. Zodrow (eds), *Fundamental Tax Reform: Issues, Choices and Implications*, Cambridge, MA: MIT Press.
Hartman, D.G. (1985), 'Tax policy and foreign direct investment', *Journal of Public Economics*, **26**, 107–21.
Head, J. (2009), *Australian business income tax reform in retrospect: An analytical perspective*, Paper prepared for presentation at the Conference on Australian Business Tax Reform in Retrospect and Prospect, Sydney, 23–25 February, 2009.
Hong, Q. and M. Smart (2007), *In praise of tax havens: international tax planning and foreign direct investment*, CES-ifo Working Paper No. 1942 (March).
Hubbard, R.G. (2002), 'Capital income taxation in tax reform: Implications for

analysis of distribution and efficiency,' in G.R. Zodrow and P. Mieszkowski (eds), *United States Tax Reform in the 21st Century*, Cambridge: Cambridge University University Press.
Hubbard, R. G. (2005), 'Economic effects of the 2003 partial integration proposal in the United States', *International Tax and Public Finance*, **12**, 97–108.
Huizinga, H. and G. Nicodème (2006), 'Foreign ownership and corporate income taxation: An empirical evaluation', *European Economic Review*, **50**, 1223–44.
Institute for Fiscal Studies, Capital Taxes Group (1991), *Equity for Companies: A Corporate Tax for the 1990s, Commentary No. 26*, London: Institute for Fiscal Studies.
Keen, M. and J. King (2002), 'The Croatian profit tax: An ACE in practice', *Fiscal Studies,* **23**, 401–18.
McLure, C.E., Jr. and G.R. Zodrow (1988), *Implementing direct consumption taxes in developing countries*, World Bank Policy Research Working Paper Series No. 131.
McLure, C.E., Jr. and G.R. Zodrow (1996a), 'A hybrid consumption-based direct tax proposed for Bolivia', *International Tax and Public Finance*, **3**, 97–112.
McLure, C.E., Jr. and G.R. Zodrow (1996b), 'A hybrid approach to the direct taxation of consumption', in M. Boskin (ed.), *Frontiers of Tax Reform*. Palo Alto: Hoover Institution Press.
Mintz, J.M. (1995), 'The corporation tax: A survey', *Fiscal Studies*, **16**, 23–68.
Musgrave, P.B. (2000), 'Interjurisdictional equity in company taxation: Principles and applications to the European Union', in S. Cnossen (ed.), *Taxing Capital in the European Union*. Oxford: Oxford University Press.
New Zealand Inland Revenue Department (2008), *Briefing for the Incoming Minister of Revenue, 2008* (November), available at http://www.taxpolicy.ird.govt.nz/publications/files/IRBIM2008.pdf, accessed on January 5, 2009.
New Zealand Treasury (2008), *Medium Term Tax Policy Challenges and Opportunities*, (November), available at http://www.treasury.govt.nz/publications/informationreleases/taxconference, accessed on January 5, 2009.
Nicodème, G. (2008), *Corporate income tax and economic distortions*, Centre Emile Berneheim Working Paper No. 08-033, Bruxelles: Université Libre de Bruxelles, Solvay Business School.
Nielsen, S.B. and P.B. Sørensen (1997), 'On the optimality of the Nordic system of dual income taxation', *Journal of Public Economics*, **63**, 211–29.
President's Advisory Panel on Federal Tax Reform (2005), *Simple, Fair and Pro-Growth. Proposals to Fix America's Tax System*, Report of the President's Advisory Panel on Federal Tax Reform (1 November 2005), available at http://www.taxreformpanel.gov.
Randolph, W.C. (2006), *International burdens of the corporate income tax*, CBO Working Paper. Washington, DC: Congressional Budget Office.
Razin, A. and E. Sadka (1991), 'International tax competition and gains from tax harmonization', *Economics Letters*, **37**, 69–76.
Rose, M. and R. Wiswesser (1998), 'Tax reform in transition economies: Experiences from the Croatian tax reform process of the 1990s', in P.B. Sørensen (ed.), *Public Finance in a Changing World*, London: MacMillan Press.
Sinn, H.W. (1987), *Capital Income Taxation and Resource Allocation*, Amsterdam: North Holland.
Slemrod, J. (1997), 'The taxation of foreign direct investment: Operational policy perspectives', in J.M. Poterba (ed.), *Borderline Case: International Tax*

Policy, Corporate Research and Development, and Investment, Washington, DC: National Academy Press.
Slemrod, J. and Wilson, J.D. (2006), *Tax competition with parasitic tax havens*, National Bureau of Economic Research Working Papers 12225.
Sørensen, P.B. (1994), 'From a global income tax to the dual income tax: Recent reforms in the Nordic countries', *International Tax and Public Finance*, **1**, 57–79.
Sørensen, P.B. (2005), 'Neutral taxation of shareholder income', *International Tax and Public Finance*, **12**, 777–801.
Thuronyi, V. (2000), 'Adjusting taxes for inflation', in V. Thuronyi (ed.), *Tax Law Design and Drafting*, The Hague: Kluwer.
US Department of the Treasury (1992), *Integration of the Individual and Corporate Tax Systems: Taxing Business Income Once*, Washington, DC: US Government Printing Office.
Weidenbaum, M. (1995), 'Tax reform tour guide: The Nunn-Domenici "USA tax" proposal', *American Enterprise*, **6**, 67–8.
Wilson, J.D. (1986), 'A theory of interregional tax competition', *Journal of Urban Economics*, **19**, 296–315.
Zodrow, G.R. (1988), 'The windfall recapture tax: Issues of theory and design', *Public Finance Quarterly*, **16**, 387–424.
Zodrow, G.R. (2002), 'Transitional issues in the implementation of a flat tax or a national retail sales tax', in G.R. Zodrow and P. Mieskowski (eds), *United States Tax Reform in the 21st Century*, Cambridge, UK: Cambridge University Press.
Zodrow, G.R. (2003), 'Alternative forms of direct consumption taxes: The Croatian approach', in M. Ahlheim, H.-D. Wenzel and W. Wiegard (eds), *Tax Policy: Theoretical Foundations and Practical Applications*, Heidelberg: Springer.
Zodrow, G.R. (2006), 'Capital mobility and source-based taxation of capital income in small open economies', *International Tax and Public Finance*, **13**, 269–94.
Zodrow, G.R. (2007), 'Should capital income be subject to consumption-based taxation?', in H. Aaron, L. Burman and C.E. Steuerle (eds), *Taxing Capital Income*, Washington, DC: The Urban Institute.
Zodrow, G.R. (2008), 'Corporate income taxation in Canada', *Canadian Tax Journal*, **56**, 392–468.
Zodrow, G.R. (forthcoming), 'International capital mobility and international tax competition', *National Tax Journal*.
Zodrow, G.R. and C.E. McLure Jr. (1991), 'Implementing direct consumption taxes in developing countries', *Tax Law Review*, **46**, 405–87.
Zodrow, G.R. and P. Mieszkowski (1983), 'The incidence of the property tax: The benefit view versus the new view', in G.R. Zodrow (ed.), *Local Provision of Public Services: The Tiebout Model after Twenty-Five Years*, New York: Academic Press.
Zodrow, G.R. and P. Mieszkowski (1986), 'Pigou, Tiebout, property taxation, and the underprovision of local public goods', *Journal of Urban Economics*, **19**, 356–70.
Zodrow, G.R. and P. Mieszkowski (eds) (2002), *United States Tax Reform in the 21st Century*, Cambridge, UK: Cambridge University Press.

PART III

Personal tax and welfare systems

7. Personal income tax structure: theory and policy

John Creedy*

7.1 INTRODUCTION

If asked for practical advice about taxation, economists for many years would have referred to Adam Smith's (1776) famous four maxims (contribution according to ability to pay,[1] certainty, convenience, and 'efficiency' – the latter including administrative costs, distortions to activity, and the 'vexation and oppression' involved). While the list of such criteria was extended and clarified,[2] in the discussion of ability to pay it is clear that there was no acceptance of a redistributive role.[3] An explicit preference for equality of treatment via proportional taxation was made most clear in the often-quoted remark by McCulloch, the author of the most extensive and systematic treatment of public finance in the classical literature. McCulloch (1845, p. 142) argued that 'The moment you abandon the cardinal principle of exacting from all individuals the same proportion of their income or of their property, you are at sea without rudder or compass, and there is no amount of injustice and folly you may not commit'. The appropriate tax rate is thus determined by the independently given revenue requirement.[4]

The main change in the approach to taxation came from the later integration of public finance into the general area of welfare economics, which was itself a major concomitant of the successful introduction of a utility maximising approach to exchange in the 1870s. However, the most systematic early developments came from Cohen-Stuart (1889) and Edgeworth (1897) in investigating the broad implications for progressivity of the utility maximising principle, in the context of the minimisation of the total disutility from taxation – ignoring any possible benefits. With the criterion of minimising total sacrifice, progression arises from decreasing marginal utility, but with equal absolute sacrifice it depends on the precise behaviour of the marginal utility of income. Even here, taking a 'classical utilitarian' perspective, there was no explicit independent role for redistribution: the maximand was strictly considered to be *total* utility.

This movement reached its ultimate conclusion in the 'optimal tax' literature, beginning virtually a century after the initial introduction of a utility analysis into economics,[5] whereby the mathematical analyses of Edgeworth were extended by allowing, in particular, for labour supply incentive effects of taxes and transfers, and including a range of specifications of the objectives of taxation, thus introducing an explicit redistributive role. In this final development, most of the important criteria suggested by Smith and others were quietly ignored. The relevant branch of welfare economics into which optimal tax theory falls is the theory of the 'second best', in view of the fact that the government is unable to tax individuals' ability 'endowments' and instead taxes their incomes. Sometimes stress is placed on asymmetric information aspects, in that the government cannot observe ability levels.[6]

In drawing on this branch of modern economic theory to provide policy advice regarding tax structures, a number of serious difficulties immediately arise. Tax models have a way of getting very complicated very quickly. For example, for the simplest possible tax-transfer structure – the linear income tax – with individuals differing only by productivity, the government budget constraint is non-linear in the tax parameters if there are some non-workers. Many interdependencies are usually involved and while economists are specially trained to identify such inter-relations, clear views can only be obtained by abstracting from many realistic features. Indeed, many of the strong results from tax analyses (for example certain equivalence results concerning uniform direct and indirect taxes in general equilibrium models) are best interpreted as demonstrating that in fact they are most unlikely to apply in practice.[7] Furthermore, value judgments are inevitably involved because virtually every tax and transfer has distributional implications, and ultimately what matters is not the equity effect of a single tax considered in isolation, but the overall impact of a wide range of taxes and transfer payments (the latter being a relatively modern development). Many economic analyses are specially designed to give insights into the nature of the interdependencies involved.

The possible effects of taxes are often expressed in terms of measures for which it is extremely difficult to obtain empirical counterparts. Insofar as these models provide policy advice, this is often expressed in broad terms and is of a negative nature. As Edgeworth suggested when discussing income taxation and the concept of minimum sacrifice:

> Yet the premises, however inadequate to the deduction of a definite formula, may suffice for a certain negative conclusion. The ground which will not serve as the foundation of the elaborate edifice designed may yet be solid enough to support a battering-ram capable of being directed against simpler edifices in the neighbourhood. (1925, ii, p. 261)

It is important to understand why clear results may not be achieved, or why intuitively appealing results may not be reliable. But patience in the face of such limited results requires a taxonomic turn of mind that is more congenial to economists than those who need to provide direct policy advice or support. The more realistic the model, the more it has to be restricted to highly specific questions. For a general discussion of types of tax model, see Creedy (2001a).

The theory of optimal income taxation provides an interesting case study. It can be argued that analyses in this tradition have generated valuable insights into the highly complex relationships involved. They have clarified what early investigators referred to as 'the grammar of arguments' and there was no pretence that they were designed as guidance for practical policy advice. The results are largely – as in so many other cases – of a negative nature. Nevertheless, it is possible that the substantial changes in the personal income tax structures of many countries over the last 30 years – in particular, reductions in the number of marginal tax rates and the degree of rate progression – have been influenced by the optimal tax literature.[8] Care must be taken in making such statements. Establishing a clear rationale for each policy action is of course far from straightforward, and the social welfare functions which play a fundamental role in optimal tax theory seldom represent the varied objectives of politicians.[9]

In view of these problems, the aims of this chapter are extremely modest. It begins in section 7.2 by briefly discussing the role of 'rules of thumb' in policy advice, in particular the rule concerning broad bases and low rates, and the adherence to it in New Zealand. Section 7.3 then considers the simplest possible tax and transfer system, the linear income tax, as a way of illustrating why optimal tax models quickly become intractable. Insights regarding the tax rate schedule from optimal tax modelling are then discussed briefly in section 7.4. Optimal tax modelling typically relies on small simulation models in which there is negligible population heterogeneity. However, practical policy advice regarding the effects of alternative tax structures can be provided with the use of behavioural microsimulation models in which the full extent of population heterogeneity is represented along with all the details of highly complex tax and transfer systems (compared with the simple stylised forms used in optimal tax analyses).

Nevertheless, when using such models it is important to be aware of their limitations. In particular, they deal only with the supply side of the labour market and, despite modelling labour supply, have no genuine dynamic element. Furthermore, they deal only with financial incentive effects rather than administrative behaviour and monitoring features designed to reduce moral hazard.[10] While it does not seem practicable to use such models to produce optimal non-linear structures, a method of examining marginal reforms is proposed and illustrated using a simple model in section 7.5.

In the absence of direct policy advice from economic theory, more partial arguments are discussed in subsequent sections. These regard things to keep in mind with nonlinear personal tax structures. In view of the importance of changes in the top marginal tax rate in many countries (including recently in New Zealand and the UK), special attention is given to the role and effectiveness of a top marginal tax rate at higher income levels, in revenue raising and generating redistribution and progressivity. Section 7.6 examines the effect of a top rate on selected progressivity measures. The complications relating to potential labour supply effects, caused by increasing marginal income tax rates and means-tested transfer payments, are then considered in section 7.7. Examples are given of the variety of welfare effects arising from the introduction of a top marginal tax rate. Brief conclusions are in section 7.8.

7.2 A RULE OF THUMB

There are some basic principles which are worth keeping in mind in thinking about tax structures. These include points such that: there is a difference between legal and economic incidence and taxes can be shifted in various ways (including tax capitalisation); large efficiency costs (in the form of excess burdens) can arise even when taxes appear to have little effect on behaviour; incentives matter. These points differ from the kind of maxim proposed by Smith (1776), in that here the emphasis is on the link from theoretical insights to specific policy advice. This list could easily be extended, but still does not provide strong positive advice. However, many economists (particularly those working in treasury departments) take as a starting point the basic principle that the best taxes are those having a broad base and low tax rate.

As a simple 'rule of thumb', this is not a statement derived from a set of fundamental or universal principles, or axioms. It is meant only as a guiding aim which, though not precise, does have valuable content. Departures from the rule require a special case to be made. A broad base, which is obtained by allowing few exemptions and deductions, is of course required in order to achieve a low tax rate, for a given revenue objective. In turn, the need for low rates is generally seen in terms of the efficiency costs of taxation, where appeal is made to the long-established result that the excess burden of a tax is approximately proportional to the square of the tax rate.[11]

Of course, it is not straightforward to explain concepts such as excess burden to politicians, or to persuade them of the importance of the principle of tax capitalisation or of incentive effects. These latter effects influence another term in the excess burden approximation, the compensated demand elasticity – whether of consumption goods or leisure. The confusion between Marshallian and Hicksian (compensated) responses is also common in this context. Nevertheless it is important to continue to stress these concepts and to argue that particular policies require a trade-off to be made in terms of a balance of the perceived benefits of a tax policy against the estimated efficiency costs. It is necessary to make explicit the value judgments involved and the nature of the trade-off between gains and losses. This leads to the concept of the social welfare function which is central to optimal tax theory.

The New Zealand tax system typically scores relatively well when applying the basic 'broad base-low rate' rule of thumb. For example, the goods and services tax, GST, has few exemptions and a single rate, whereas many other countries exempt (or zero rate) goods such as food, and apply a higher rate to 'luxury' goods. Attempts to justify exemptions are usually made on equity grounds: household budget shares for those goods are typically higher for households with low total expenditure. But this kind of selectivity has poor 'target efficiency' qualities, the rich after all do spend more on the same goods, and there are also good administrative arguments for uniformity. These administrative arguments have less force in the context of developing economies. The spurious argument is often used that indirect taxes are 'regressive' because high-income households save more, but this is easily dismissed.[12] Furthermore, the information needed for the imposition of an optimal non-uniform indirect structure is unlikely to be available and equity objectives can be achieved using direct taxes and transfers (which relate directly to the characteristics of the individuals involved). Exceptions are of course made in the case of excises, such as those imposed on tobacco, alcohol and petrol, which are imposed for a variety of paternalistic and externality arguments (along with revenue raising qualities). These appear to have little overall redistributive effect, but excess burdens on some household types can be quite large; on excise taxes in New Zealand, see Creedy and Sleeman (2006).

Regarding the income tax, New Zealand has no tax-free threshold and has not (for the employed) a wide range of deductions relating to various expenses, as in many countries, such as Australia where base erosion seems endemic. This all produces a higher tax base in New Zealand and helps to keep income tax rates lower than otherwise. When making comparisons it is necessary to keep in mind that there are no separate social insurance contributions in New Zealand, as in many other countries. However, in viewing the base, New Zealand cannot be said to have a 'comprehensive' income tax: in particular, most capital gains are not taxed.

The broad base–low rate rule of thumb suggests, through the excess burden relationship with the tax rate, a preference for a flattish income tax rate structure, although of course this does not allow for redistribution objectives and associated trade-offs which may lead to modifications. In New Zealand there are means-tested transfer payments which produce very high effective marginal tax rates for lower-income earners. Furthermore, the abatement (that is, taper, or benefit withdrawal) range for some transfers extends far up the income range, so that effective tax rates are significantly above the marginal income tax rates. Furthermore, a higher 'top' marginal income tax rate was reintroduced, after being eliminated in the 1980s reforms which had substantially flattened the income tax rate structure.

A top marginal tax rate is typically introduced on the grounds that it is needed for reducing inequality. However, it is well-known that tax rate progression is not needed for progressivity – indeed a linear tax (basic income–flat tax, or BI–FT) is highly redistributive, such that many individuals face a negative average rate, and the average rate is increasing over the whole income range. Furthermore, the top rate may in practice produce little extra revenue: section 7.6 discusses this aspect further. The argument is also sometimes made that 'the labour supply elasticity', especially for higher-income 'prime-age' males, is low so that the incentive effects of a top rate are negligible. However, labour supply behaviour is much too complicated to be described by a single elasticity. Further, even if the observed elasticity were low or zero, this could still coexist with large welfare costs and high excess burdens because it is the Hicksian elasticity that matters. Section 7.7 below returns to this issue.

7.3 THE LINEAR INCOME TAX

It seems useful, though at first sight perhaps perverse, to begin by ignoring the fundamental question of the 'optimal' form of an income tax and transfer system, and to concentrate instead on the narrower question of determining the optimal tax rate in the simplest possible kind of modelling framework, namely a linear (or basic income–flat tax) structure. There is thus only one policy variable, the tax rate, that can be chosen independently, while the other decision variable, the universal or basic income, is determined via the government's budget constraint (discussed in more detail below). Indeed, this type of system is the 'basic workhorse' of optimal tax analysis, on which a number of variants have been built. It serves to demonstrate that the simplest system – it would indeed be impossible to imagine a simpler redistributive tax and economic environment to examine – is very far from being straightforward.

The framework is entirely static, involving a single period partial equilibrium model. Individuals can vary their hours of work continuously, at a fixed gross wage rate. Each individual's ability level, which determines the wage rate, is fixed and there are no other sources of income other than the untaxed transfer payment and earnings. Apart from the exogenous endowment of ability, there is an endowment of time (normalised to unity) which is divided between work and leisure. Individuals are considered to maximise utility, which depends only on an index of the consumption of marketed goods and services (where the price index is normalised to unity) and the proportion of time spent working. Apart from differences in abilities, individuals are assumed to be identical: they have the same utility functions and have no non-income characteristics which influence judgements regarding, for example, special 'needs' (hence the basic income can be the same for all individuals). Of course, population heterogeneity is a fundamental feature of the 'real world' and plays a crucial role in actual tax policy design (and is discussed further below). As mentioned earlier, the aim here is to demonstrate how awkward even the simplest unrealistic model is. The introduction of taste differences raises the potential for 'incentive compatibility' problems.

The framework is thus designed to be the simplest possible model for considering the elements involved in the trade-off between equity and efficiency considerations in setting the parameters of the simplest possible tax and transfer system. It is indeed trivially simple – and yet it turns out to give rise to substantial complexities. One simplification – the concentration on one form of government expenditure – is worth stressing here, particularly in view of the fact that one important lesson from a welfare economics perspective is that what matters is the overall effect of a multi-tax, multi-expenditure system, rather than the effects of each component taken in isolation. Any revenue collected for non-transfer purposes is considered simply to disappear into a 'black hole', rather than being devoted to activities such as the production of public goods, or education and health services, which would in principle affect individuals' utilities. Furthermore, such expenditure would be expected to affect indivduals' productivities and thus their wage rates. The extension of an optimal tax approach to the analysis of the composition of government expenditure, as well as its magnitude, in this framework presents further complexities which cannot be discussed here, but which of course cannot be ignored in practical discussions.

The cornerstone of the analysis is the government's budget constraint,

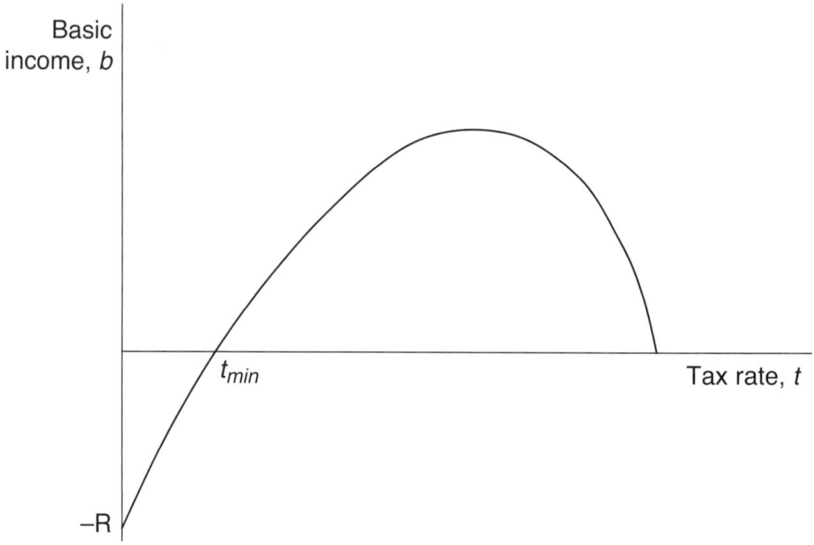

Figure 7.1 The government's budget constraint

showing the relationship between the basic income, b, and the tax rate, t, needed to finance it. This is illustrated in Figure 7.1, where a minimum tax rate, t_{min}, is needed to finance the non-transfer expenditure. If the tax is below this rate, the system requires the use of a negative basic income, that is a poll tax, to raise the non-transfer revenue. The constraint reflects a 'battle' between 'rate' and 'base' effects of an increase in t: an increase in the rate produces a higher revenue with an unchanged total income (the base), but the base falls because of adverse incentive effects. This supposes that the substitution effect – arising from the cheaper price of leisure – outweighs the income effect of the change in the net wage. Initially the 'tax rate' effect dominates the 'tax base' effect, but at some point, where the percentage increase in the tax rate is exactly matched by the percentage reduction in total income, total revenue (and thus b) reaches a maximum. If $\overline{y}$ denotes average income and R is non-transfer revenue per head, the budget constraint is:

$$b = t\overline{y} - R \tag{7.1}$$

Hence, $[d(b + R)/dt] = \overline{y} + t(d\overline{y}/dt)$, and:

$$\frac{t}{(b + R)} \frac{d(b + R)}{dt} = 1 + \frac{t}{\overline{y}} \frac{d\overline{y}}{dt} \tag{7.2}$$

Thus the budget constraint becomes flat when the elasticity, $\left(\frac{td\bar{y}}{\bar{y}dt}\right) = -1$. This point is clearly reached before t reaches unity.

Although the equation of the budget constraint looks superficially simple, to move from (7.1) to a relationship between b and t is not simple because $\bar{y}$ is a function of the tax parameters, the preferences of individuals and the form of the distribution of wage rates, w. Unless strong assumptions are made regarding utility functions and the wage rate distribution, (7.1) is non-linear.[13]

The choice of t (and consequently of b) must obviously be somewhere along the government's constraint. The issue thus arises of the choice of decision mechanism. The crucial point about the optimal tax framework is that tax choices are considered to be made by a single individual – variously referred to as a policy maker or decision-maker or independent judge – who is entirely disinterested; that is, does not have a personal interest in the outcome. Hence a social welfare, or social evaluation, function is maximised, representing the value judgments of the decision maker. The welfare function is *not* regarded as representing any kind of aggregation of the views of members of the population.

The role of optimal tax analysis is therefore, from the very outset, to examine the implications of adopting particular value judgments. Even if the model were not so unrealistic, no professional economist could state, on the basis of an optimal tax analysis, that, for example, 'the tax rate should be set at $t = x$'. Furthermore, the addition of the words 'in order to maximise the welfare of society' at the end of that sentence would be meaningless, given the concept of the welfare function used. The approach can say only, for example, that 'for the value judgements made explicit in the evaluation function used, the optimal rate turns out to be $t = x$'.

Clearly, a vast range of welfare functions could potentially be examined. In the majority of analyses, the implications of adopting a 'welfarist' evaluation function are examined: this means that welfare, W, is considered (where it is also individualistic) to depend on the variables that are of importance for the individuals themselves; that is, their utility levels. Hence, with n individuals $W = W(U_1, \ldots U_n)$.[14] Each individual is maximising utility, subject to the tax parameters chosen, so indirect utility for each person, V_i, can be written as $V_i(t, b)$ where the other parameters (such as those of the direct utility function) have been suppressed. Hence, in principle, it is possible to think of the welfare function being abbreviated into an expression in terms of the decision variables t and b, and this in turn gives rise to social indifference curves.

These can be represented in Figure 7.1 as upward sloping convex indifference curves the nature of which depend on, among other things, the judge's attitude towards inequality.[15] If the judge has extreme aversion to inequality, concern is only to maximise the welfare of the poorest person and indifference curves are horizontal. Such a judge would select the tax rate at which the budget constraint reaches a peak, that is for which the elasticity, $\left(\frac{td\bar{y}}{\bar{y}dt}\right) = -1$. The downward sloping section of the constraint is thus irrelevant. As inequality aversion falls, and the judge places relatively greater emphasis on efficiency considerations, the indifference curves become steeper (a given increase in t must be accompanied by a higher increase in b to compensate) and the optimal tax rate falls. However, an indifference to inequality – as in the case of classical utilitarian judges – does not necessarily produce vertical indifference curves. The optimal rate is likely to produce a positive b and may also involve the existence of some non-workers.

Any information that an increase in an existing tax rate is likely to produce a reduction in total revenue clearly suggests that, whatever the inequality aversion of the judge, the rate is too high. Non-transfer government revenue also plays a role. With zero net revenue, the optimal linear rate is expected to fall as the elasticity of substitution between net income (consumption) and leisure rises, because the substitution effect of a tax rise is likely to be larger (so the budget constraint is flatter). But with positive net revenue, the fall in the optimal rate is eventually reversed as the elasticity of substitution rises. This is because the minimum rate needed to finance the non-transfer revenue increases as the elasticity rises.

So far, the results are quite general. Anyone asking for specific advice about the optimal rate to impose in a linear tax structure would not welcome the information simply that the first-order conditions imply a tangency between the budget constraint and the highest social indifference curve. More structure must be imposed, but even with simple forms for the social welfare function (such as the widely used iso-elastic case of constant relative inequality aversion), the common utility functions, and the wage rate distribution, closed-form solutions are not available.[16] Numerical simulation results, involving iterative methods to solve for the basic income which can be financed with any given tax rate, are therefore ubiquitous in the optimal tax literature.

The tangency solution view of first-order conditions for social welfare maximisation therefore provides limited insights. Starting from the same conditions, an alternative approach, which exploits duality theory, can be used to show that the optimal linear tax must satisfy the following condition, first given by Tuomala (1985):

$$1 - \frac{\overline{\tilde{y}}}{\bar{y}} = |\eta_{\bar{y},t}| \tag{7.3}$$

where $|(\downarrow(\bar{y}, t)|$ represents the absolute value of the elasticity of average earnings with respect to the tax rate, and has already been discussed in the context of the shape of the government budget constraint. The term $\bar{y}$ is a welfare-weighted average of earnings, where the weights are equal to $(\nu_i/\Sigma_{i=1}^{n}\nu_i)$ with $\nu_i = (\partial W/\partial V_i)/(\partial V_i/\partial b)$. The latter is the weight attached by the social welfare function to an addition to person i's income (from an increase in the basic income).

The left-hand side represents the proportional difference between the welfare-weighted mean of earnings and the arithmetic mean, which can be interpreted as a measure of the inequality of gross earnings. For example, extreme inequality aversion on the part of the judge would attach the highest value of 1 to this inequality measure, whatever the statistical earnings differences, and as seen above $|\eta_{\bar{y},t}| = 1$ represents the highest point of the government budget constraint. This might be thought to provide further insights in view of the fact that both sides of the equality in (7.3) deal with earnings, which are clear 'empirically relevant counterparts', unlike some other components of the model. Discussion can proceed in term of a diagram showing the profiles of each side of the equation as t varies, and the way in which they, and hence their point of intersection, are likely to shift as basic assumptions are changed. However, this expression does not provide a closed-form solution. Even the welfare weights, v_i, depend in general on the tax parameters.

The optimal policy perspective of choice by an independent decision-maker clearly differs from public choice models which consider particular aggregation mechanisms, such as majority voting. The first problem in considering voting schemes is that indivduals' preferences over t are not in general single peaked. However, some interesting comparisons can be made between the different approaches. For example, in the simple majority voting framework, a voting equilibrium is known to exist, despite the existence of double-peaked preferences regarding the tax rate, if there is 'hierarchical adherence', such that the ordering of individuals by their income is independent of the tax rate. In this case the median voter theorem can be invoked and the median here is the person with median wage. Equation (7.3) applies also in this case, except that the welfare-weighted mean, $\bar{y}$, is replaced by the median. In the case of stochastic voting, the voting equilibrium is generated by maximisation of a function that may appear to look something like a social welfare function, involving the weighted arithmetic mean of utilities, or the weighted geometric mean, depending on the precise details. Again, unless special assumptions are made, interior solutions are not available.

The absence of closed-form solutions for this, the simplest possible model of a population group and a tax structure, is not of course the property that limits its value in providing policy advice. A wide range of simulation analyses can easily be carried out. The problem is that it is so far removed from reality, in order to illustrate as simply as possible the nature of the trade-offs involved and the underlying structure of such models, as to be useless as a practical tool. It was never intended to provide such a tool. However, its very simplicity serves to demonstrate that more realistic models are likely to be completely intractable, which raises the question of how to proceed. Before considering this question, the following section turns to the initial question raised and ignored in starting from a linear tax – that of the form of optimal tax function.

7.4 OPTIMAL TAX STRUCTURES

In view of the difficulties of examining even the simplest structure, it cannot be expected that a more general analysis of the optimal rate structure would generate clear results. The optimal tax problem, which in general asks what tax structure maximises a specified evaluation, or social welfare function, is known from the work of Mirrlees (1971) to give rise to a problem in the calculus of variations. In view of the non-linearities involved, solutions generally require numerical simulation methods, unless strong simplifying assumptions are made. Explicit solutions include Atkinson and Stiglitz (1980), Deaton (1983) and examples given in Hindriks and Myles (2006). Unfortunately, it turns out that there are few general results available – the optimal structure depends on the nature of the social welfare function examined as well as the wage rate distribution and the nature of preferences.

Earlier work suggested that, for a range of assumptions, the optimal structure is approximately linear. But in fact it is not difficult to produce models in which different tax structures are optimal. A small selection of examples includes those discussed by Diamond (1988), Chang (1994), Hashimzade and Myles (2004), Myles (1999), Saez (2001) and Tuomala (2006). A basic issue relates to the social welfare function itself. Much of the literature is 'welfarist' in that the welfare function is specified as some function of (indirect) utilities, that is, terms which matter to individuals. But since the fundamental aim is to consider the implications of adopting alternative value judgements, other 'non-welfarist' forms cannot be ruled out. For example, social welfare may be based solely on an income-based measure of poverty. These can give quite different results. For further discussion see Kanbur et al. (1994) and for a broader treatment of non-welfarist objectives, see Kanbur et al. (2004). Non-welfarist objects may go further than simply attaching no value to leisure, in that they may prefer

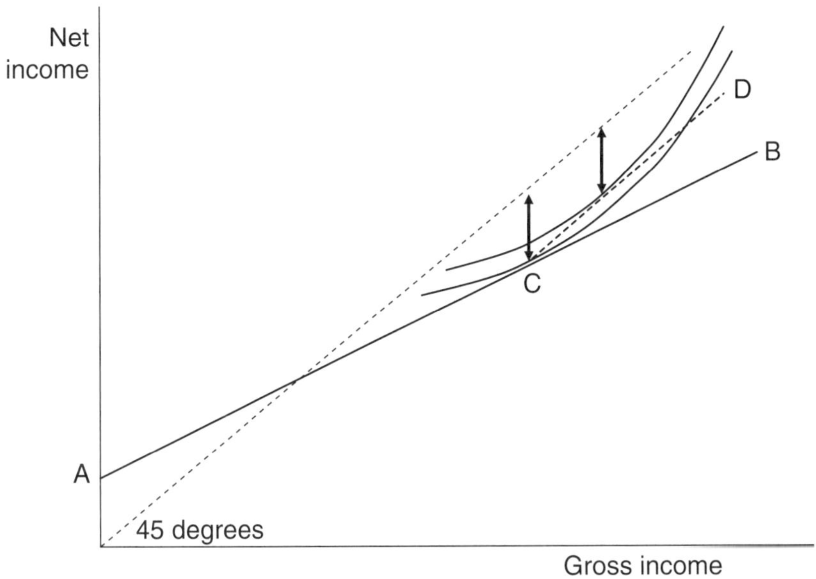

Figure 7.2 *Tax rate on top income*

to encourage labour supply (whereas in a welfarist approach the existence of non-workers is acceptable in an optimal structure); see, for example, Besley and Coate (1992).

Hence the general treatment of optimal tax structures yields very few clear results.[17] The most unambiguous results can in fact easily be established. First, any range where the marginal tax rate is greater than 100 per cent is clearly irrelevant. It can also be shown that negative marginal tax rates (in contrast with average tax rates) can be ruled out: however, this is not true of a social welfare function based on income-poverty, where a negative marginal rate can result for the lowest earners.

A further result states that the marginal tax rate on the highest income should be zero. In Figure 7.2 consider the tax function AB, where the person with the highest wage rate reaches a tangency position at C. If the tax function is changed to ACD, where CD is parallel to the 45 degree line, the individual then faces a zero marginal rate on any extra income earned. This induces a movement to a new tangency on a higher indifference curve. The total tax revenue is unchanged and no one else is affected: hence the richest person is better off and the non-zero top marginal rate cannot have been optimal, for any Paretian welfare function. However, this result is of no practical relevance as there is no way to determine just where the rate should become zero.

One approach has been to consider piecewise-linear tax functions with just two or three rates. This allows for consideration of the question of whether marginal tax rates should be higher for those with relatively low earnings. Such higher marginal rates arise from the means-testing of transfer payments. The resulting non-convexity of budget sets facing individuals can give rise to complex labour supply behaviour. Means-testing is preferred by those who advocate 'target efficiency' as the criterion by which schemes should be judged. Numerical analyses using 'welfarist' social welfare functions show that in a very wide range of situations, the evaluation function is increased by a shift to lower taper rates and a flatter rate schedule.[18] Results inevitably involve special cases in highly simplified models with little of the considerable population heterogeneity that is observed in practice. They therefore cannot provide a strong basis for policy advice. Indeed, assumptions giving rise to means-testing in an optimal structure are given in Diamond (1998). An emphasis on 'workfare', designed largely to encourage positive labour supply, rather than 'welfare', can also lead to high marginal rates imposed on low earners, as shown by Besley and Coate (1992).

Despite the dearth of general results, the optimal tax literature does support a broad argument for relatively low rates (the second part of the broad base, low rate rule of thumb), even with high inequality aversion, especially compared with the top rates operating in many countries in the 1970s. A small degree of substitution between leisure and net income imposes strong constraints on the government's ability to redistribute income. In the linear tax case, non-transfer government revenue also plays a role. With zero net revenue, the optimal linear rate falls as the elasticity of substitution (between consumption and leisure) rises. With positive net revenue, the optimal rate falls and then rises as the elasticity rises (because the minimum rate needed to finance the non-transfer revenue rises as the elasticity rises). As suggested earlier, the finding that, even in simplified models, optimal rates are not high may perhaps have had some influence on policy since the late 1970s when the very high top marginal rates existing in some countries started to be reduced.

A behavioural tax microsimulation model, which encapsulates the actual degree of population heterogeneity and most of the detail of actual tax and transfer systems, does not provide a convenient vehicle for producing an optimal tax structure. However, its advantage of providing information about changes in taxes may be exploited to examine the optimal direction of reforms. That is, such a model may be used to explore the directions of small changes in tax parameters which improve a specified social welfare function. An illustration of the kind of analysis which would be possible, but using a much simpler model, is provided in the following section.

7.5 MARGINAL INCOME TAX REFORM

Consider the more realistic problem of how to move towards an optimal structure by a process of marginal tax reform. This has previously been examined in the context of indirect taxation, involving fixed incomes but differential taxation on a range of goods, where x_{ji} is the consumption of the ith taxable good by the jth household, and t_i is the unit tax on good i.[19] A standard result shows that an increase in social welfare, W, resulting from a change in the ith tax rate is:

$$\frac{\partial W}{\partial t_i} = \sum_{j=1}^{n} v_j x_{ji} \tag{7.4}$$

where v_j is the social value of additional consumption by household j. Furthermore, aggregate tax revenue, R, from indirect taxes on K goods is given by:

$$R = \sum_{j=1}^{n} \sum_{k=1}^{K} t_k x_{jk} \tag{7.5}$$

and $(\partial R/\partial t_i)$ can be expressed in terms of (Marshallian) demand elasticities, at observed consumption levels, and expenditures. It is then possible to obtain values of the ratio, $(\partial W/\partial t_i)/(\partial R/\partial t_i)$, the marginal welfare cost of raising tax rate i, for each good and thus to determine the required direction of changes, since an optimal system is characterised by an equimarginal condition.

In considering income tax structures, a similar type of approach could be adopted to examine marginal adjustments to a piecewise linear system. The social welfare function W is in this case a function of a set of marginal income tax rates and income thresholds (as well as summarising the value judgments involved). Similarly, total net revenue, R, is a function of the same set of tax parameters. It can be shown that if t_i now represents the ith marginal rate, and y_j is person j's earnings, a similar result to that given above holds, whereby $(\partial W/\partial t_i) = -\Sigma_{j=1}^{n} v_j y_j$ For any piecewise linear tax function, the tax paid by household j, $T(y_j)$, can be expressed as:

$$T(y_i) = t_k(y_j - a'_k) \tag{7.6}$$

where y_j falls in to the kth tax bracket and a'_k is a function of all the thresholds (denoted $a_1, \ldots, a_K$) and marginal rates. The total tax revenue raised by those in the kth bracket, T_k, is thus:

$$T_k = t_k \sum_{j=1}^{n} (y_j - a'_k) \tag{7.7}$$

It would be possible to combine this kind of approach with a number of simplifying assumptions regarding elasticities of earnings with respect to tax rates and the proportions of earnings and people above a top rate, to consider, say, whether (for a given set of tax thresholds) a top marginal rate should be reduced or increased. For an extensive discussion on the use of elasticities to derive optimal tax rates, with emphasis on the choice of a top tax rate, and references to earlier literature, see Saez (2001). This appears to be an attractive route because, unlike the usual approach to optimal tax modelling, the conditions can be expressed in terms of (what appear to be) empirically observable counterparts such as elasticities. However, given the considerable complexities introduced by nonlinear budget constraints – unlike the consumption tax case where linear pricing is a reasonable assumption – any clear results need strong assumptions and could only be regarded as illustrative rather than of practical relevance. Nonlinear budget sets make it difficult to generalise regarding labour supply responses and welfare changes even for workers with similar preferences and with relatively simple tax structures. In practice, populations display considerable heterogeneity in preferences and household circumstances, and tax and transfer structures are extremely complex.

However, given a behavioural tax microsimulation model, there is no need to make simplifying assumptions about elasticities of earnings with respect to tax rates. The full extent of heterogeneity can be captured in behavioural microsimulation models. Such models could not realistically be used to produce an optimal tax structure, even for a clearly specified social welfare function. But for marginal reforms, the required changes, from an initial actual tax structure, could be obtained numerically. Starting from the actual tax structure, and considering small changes in a range of tax parameters, it is possible to use a microsimulation model to obtain values of welfare and revenue changes, denoted ΔW and ΔR respectively, for each tax parameter in turn. The marginal welfare costs, that is the change in welfare per dollar of extra revenue, $\Delta W/\Delta R$, should be similar for all tax parameters in an optimal system and so the direction of an optimal reform is indicated by relative orders of magnitude of these ratios.

In the absence of a New Zealand behavioural microsimulation model, the present section illustrates – nevertheless using a very simple model – the way in which such a model could be used to examine optimal marginal income tax reforms. The first stage in illustrating the approach is to specify a hypothetical population. Two sets of populations were examined, single individuals with no dependents and workers in couple households with children (each couple is in fact modelled as if there is just one potential

Table 7.1 Hypothetical tax structure

	Singles			Couples with children		
	Threshold	t_i	μ_i	Threshold	t_i	μ_i
1	0	0.15	150	0	0.15	300
2	200	0.25	170	200	0.85	440
3	650	0.35	235	450	0.25	170
4	1000	0.40	285	650	0.55	365
5	–	–		1000	0.6	415
6	–	–		1400	0.4	135

worker). The tax and transfer structure for each group is fully specified by a set of income thresholds and marginal rates, t_i, which apply above those thresholds, giving rise to a piecewise-linear budget line that relates net income and hours of work. Each linear section, *i*, has a slope that is equal to the net wage $w = w_g(1 - t_i)$, where w_g is the gross wage rate, and when extended to the intercept where hours of work are zero, a non-wage virtual income of μ_i.

Each group is considered to face the tax and transfer structures shown in Table 7.1. In the table, the tax rates and income thresholds (expressed in terms of weekly income) are given, along with the μ_i. Only μ_1 is in fact specified and the other information is used to produce the other virtual incomes; for example, it can be shown that, for $i = 2, \ldots n$, $\mu_i = \mu_{i-1} + y_i(t_i - t_{i-1})$. These effective tax schedules are chosen to be similar to those in New Zealand, although the marginal rate of 0.85 applied above $200 is less than the very high rate of almost 100 per cent which actually applies as a result of means-testing. The extension of means-tested benefits to higher-income ranges means that for couples with children, the marginal tax rate actually drops from 0.60 to 0.40 at a weekly income of $1400. Calculation of labour supply must allow for the possibility of multiple local optima.

The population heterogeneity in each case is such that the joint distribution of wage rates and preference parameters (α, the coefficient on net income) in Cobb–Douglas utility functions is jointly lognormal, with a correlation of −0.75. The arithmetic mean of α is set at 0.75 for the case of both singles and couple workers, while the mean of log-wages is 2.7 and 3.0 for singles and couples respectively. The variance of logarithms of α is 0.10 for singles and 0.15 for couple workers. These values were chosen following experimentation in which the distributions of earnings (for simulated populations of 10000 in each case) were similar to those for New Zealand in terms of the pattern of modes and antimodes. Suppose that the social welfare function, *W*, for each group takes the familiar additive individualistic Paretean form and is expressed as a function of utilities, U_j, with an inequality aversion coefficient of $\varepsilon = 0.5$:

$$W = \frac{1}{1-\varepsilon}\sum_{j=1}^{n} U_j^{1-\varepsilon} \tag{7.8}$$

A feature of optimal tax models is that results depend on the cardinalisaton of utility functions used. The use of money metric utility, with current 'prices' as reference prices, was suggested by Creedy et al. (1998b). The calculation of a social welfare function using money metric utility in a behavioural microsimulation model based on discrete hours random utility modelling of labour supply is examined by Creedy et al. (2008b).

Tables 7.2 and 7.3 show marginal changes for each marginal tax rate, for single individuals and workers in couple households. The change in each marginal tax rate involved a reduction of 0.02, that is, two percentage points, with thresholds unchanged. Each table shows the welfare and revenue changes, along with the ratios $\Delta W/\Delta R$, and the elasticities of welfare with respect to revenue, $\eta_{W,R}$. In the case of couples, it can be seen that a reduction in the 5th marginal rate of two percentage points actually leads to an increase in tax revenue: this marginal rate is in practice affected by both means testing of transfers and the top marginal income tax rate. In these illustrative examples, the optimal reform is clear: a reduction in the top income tax rate produces the greatest 'payoff' in terms of social welfare. Such illustrative exercises cannot be used as a basis for policy advice in practice, but they do highlight the way in which a behavioural microsimulation model could be exploited.

7.6 REDISTRIBUTION AND PROGRESSIVITY

It has been mentioned that a common argument for applying a higher marginal tax rate to 'top incomes' is that it is needed for redistribution and progressivity. But the effects of a tax structure cannot be evaluated by looking at the marginal rate structure alone, as they depend fundamentally on the nature of the income distribution. This section provides some illustrative calculations of the effects of income tax structures under different income distributions. It is therefore concerned more with statistical issues than economic theory insights.

Consider the effect of income taxation alone. Table 7.4 shows thresholds and rates in New Zealand for the years 2006–07 and 2008–09. The rate structures are similar (except for the lowest rate) but thresholds are higher in 2008–09, reflecting the growth of incomes. On the assumption that pre-tax incomes are normally distributed as Λ (μ, σ^2) where μ and σ^2

Table 7.2 Marginal tax reforms: singles

k	ΔW	ΔR	$\Delta W/\Delta R$	$\eta_{W,R}$
1	1.1974	−4.5569	−0.2628	−0.0646
2	1.9103	−7.9664	−0.2398	−0.0589
3	0.5746	−2.4185	−0.2376	−0.0584
4	0.356	−0.6511	−0.5467	−0.1343

Table 7.3 Marginal tax reforms: couples

k	ΔW	ΔR	$\Delta W/\Delta R$	$\eta_{W,R}$
1	1.1489	−5.6348	−0.2039	−0.0930
2	0.9349	−2.6391	−0.3543	−0.1616
3	0.7277	−2.3056	−0.3156	−0.1440
4	0.7248	−1.7888	−0.4052	−0.1848
5	0.3486	0.2484	1.4032	0.6400
6	0.3950	−0.6345	−0.6225	−0.2839

Table 7.4 New Zealand income tax structures

2006–07		2008–09	
Threshold	Tax rate	Threshold	Tax rate
0	0.15	0	0.125
9500	0.21	14000	0.21
38000	0.33	40000	0.33
60000	0.39	70000	0.39

are the mean and variance of logarithms, suppose $\sigma^2 = 0.8$.[20] This gives a Gini inequality measure of 0.459, and an Atkinson inequality measure (with inequality aversion of 0.5) of 0.178.[21]

Tables 7.5 and 7.6 report, for alternative values of μ, summary measures of the distribution of pre-and post-tax income. The upper part of each table shows the results for the actual structure and the lower part gives results obtained without the top marginal rate. The variable $\bar{x}$ the arithmetic mean pre-tax income, while G, K, L and g measure respectively the Gini inequality of post-tax income, the Kakwani measure of tax progressivity, the reduction in the Gini measure when moving from pre- to post-tax incomes (that is, the Reynolds–Smolensky measure of redistribution), and the overall effective tax ratio; on these measures see, for example, Creedy (1996).

Table 7.5 2006–07 tax structure

	Income tax only					Income tax with MIG			
						$y_m = 12k$		$y_m = 15k$	
μ	$\bar{x}$	G	K	L	g	G	g	G	g
With top marginal tax rate									
9.8	26903	0.4389	0.1031	0.0300	0.226	0.3373	0.152	0.2875	0.101
10.0	32860	0.4351	0.1079	0.0338	0.239	0.3669	0.194	0.3269	0.160
10.2	40134	0.4318	0.1101	0.0372	0.252	0.3885	0.226	0.3582	0.204
10.3	44356	0.4304	0.1101	0.0386	0.259	0.3966	0.240	0.3710	0.222
Without top marginal tax rate									
9.8	26903	0.4436	0.0906	0.0253	0.218	0.3425	0.145	0.2927	0.094
10.0	32860	0.4415	0.0924	0.0274	0.229	0.3737	0.184	0.3340	0.150
10.2	40134	0.4400	0.0919	0.0289	0.239	0.3971	0.213	0.3672	0.191
10.3	44356	0.4395	0.0908	0.0294	0.245	0.4062	0.225	0.3809	0.207

Table 7.6 2008–09 tax structure

	Income tax only					Income tax with MIG			
						$y_m = 12k$		$y_m = 15k$	
μ	$\bar{x}$	G	K	L	g	G	g	G	g
With top marginal tax rate									
9.8	26 903	0.4355	0.1302	0.0334	0.204	0.3402	0.134	0.2923	0.086
10.0	32 860	0.4316	0.1332	0.0373	0.219	0.3682	0.177	0.3303	0.145
10.2	40 134	0.4281	0.1333	0.0408	0.234	0.3884	0.210	0.3600	0.189
10.3	44 356	0.4267	0.1321	0.0422	0.242	0.3958	0.224	0.3721	0.207
Without top marginal tax rate									
9.8	26 903	0.4391	0.1201	0.0298	0.199	0.3441	0.129	0.2963	0.081
10.0	32 860	0.4367	0.1204	0.0322	0.212	0.3736	0.169	0.3358	0.137
10.2	40 134	0.4350	0.1177	0.0339	0.224	0.3955	0.199	0.3673	0.179
10.3	44 356	0.4345	0.1153	0.0344	0.230	0.4039	0.212	0.3803	0.195

As expected, the tax structure (with or without a top rate) is more progressive and more redistributive as $\bar{x}$ increases, since more people are in the higher marginal rate ranges (though clearly this effect is reduced when the top rate of 0.39 is eliminated). However, for any given value of $\bar{x}$, the changes resulting from the elimination of the top marginal rate are very small. For example, considering the changes in the Gini measures of post-tax income, these are only affected at the third decimal place. The progressivity measures change by less than 0.01, and the effects on revenue, measured by g, involve reductions of less than one percentage point.

For comparison, the right-hand side of each table shows the effect on the Gini inequality measure of post-tax income and the overall average tax rate of introducing a minimum income guarantee (MIG), whereby those with after tax income below y_m have their income brought up to y_m. Such transfer payments clearly have a much larger effect than marginal rate progression applied to the higher income ranges.

7.7 WELFARE CHANGES AND A TOP MARGINAL RATE

This section illustrates the variety of welfare changes arising from the introduction of a top marginal tax rate. It demonstrates that, even for individuals with similar tastes, welfare effects can vary substantially. Welfare changes are defined in terms of the individual's expenditure function, which is usually written as $E(w, U)$, representing the minimum income needed to achieve a specified utility level, U, at a net wage, w. The approach used here is the standard method of obtaining welfare changes, which is sufficient for illustrative purposes.[22] The income involved in the expenditure function is in this context a 'full income' measure, M, defined as follows. If T is the maximum number of hours available for work, $M = wT + \mu$, where μ is virtual non-wage income, that is the value of net income for zero hours of work (for the relevant section of the budget constraint). The expenditure function is thus written as $M(w, U)$ rather than $E(w, U)$ and is obtained by inverting the indirect utility function.

A change to the tax and transfer system may arise from changes in the effective marginal rates, the number of thresholds (and therefore non-linear segments of the budget constraint), or the gross income thresholds. This may (but need not necessarily) change the individual's optimal labour supply and produce a change in the endogenous net or virtual wage rate and virtual income. The welfare effect of such a tax change is complicated by the fact that a change in either the net or virtual wage affects both the

Table 7.7 Examples of single individuals

Initial structure			With top rate		Welfare change: ΔW			Tax change: ΔR
w_g	h	Position	h	Position	$EV_{\Delta w}$	$EV_{\Delta M}$	EV	
18.4	55.09	s3	54.35	c4	−11.63	11.80	0.17	−4.77
25.0	56.38	s3	55.25	s4	−30.02	50.00	19.98	9.14
30.0	56.99	s3	56.04	s4	−34.87	70.00	35.13	24.14

price of leisure and the value of full (or virtual) income. It is therefore useful to decompose the welfare effect into the price and income effects.

Consider a change in the tax system such that the net wage and full income for an individual change from w_0 and M_0 to w_1 and M_1. The equivalent variation can be decomposed as follows:

$$\begin{aligned} EV &= \{M_1 - M(w_0, U_1)\} + \{M_0 - M_1\} \\ &= EV_{\Delta w} + EV_{\Delta M} \end{aligned} \tag{7.9}$$

where the terms $EV_{\Delta w}$ and $EV_{\Delta M}$ relate respectively to the components arising from the reduction in the price of leisure over the range covered by the top rate and the fall in full income. Thus, $EV_{\Delta w}$ measures the welfare gain because leisure hours have become less costly in terms of after-tax income foregone, and $EV_{\Delta M}$ captures the loss in full income via the reduced net wage, w, associated with the tax increase. The terms in (7.9) are defined so that a positive value indicates a reduction in welfare, while a negative value implies a welfare gain. The absolute value of the first term in curly brackets in the above expressions corresponds to an area to the left of a Hicksian (compensated) leisure demand curve between appropriate 'prices' of leisure.

Examples of labour supply and welfare changes for hypothetical single individuals are shown in Table 7.7. The tax change examined involves a movement from the appropriate structure without a top marginal rate to the one with such a rate, indicated in Table 7.1: the terms s*n* and c*n* indicate either tangency or corner solutions on segment *n* or corner *n* of the corresponding piecewise linear budget constraint. Each individual is assumed to have Cobb–Douglas preferences, with a coefficient on net income of $\alpha = 0.75$. The only difference between the individuals relates to their gross wage rates. Of course, many individuals – those who are not affected by the tax change – experience no welfare changes.

The hypothetical individual with a gross wage of $18.40 per hour

Table 7.8 Examples of couples with children

Initial structure			With top rate		Welfare change: ΔW			Tax
w_g	h	Position	h	Position	$EV_{\Delta w}$	$EV_{\Delta M}$	EV	change: ΔR
22.6	45.23	s4	44.25	c5	−14.11	14.31	0.20	−12.25
25.0	51.89	s4	49.62	s5	−36.31	50	13.69	−19.1
28.2	54.61	s5	53.61	s6	−36.18	62.8	26.62	15.69
30.0	58.91	s5	58.12	s6	−31.83	70	38.17	28.94

reduces labour supply from 55.09 hours per week (on the fourth section of the initial relevant budget constraint) to 54.35 hours, which is at the corner solution introduced by the addition of the top marginal rate. The reduction in hours worked is small, at less than one hour, and the welfare change, $EV = 0.17$, is small, though the change in tax paid is actually negative (the individual is on the wrong side of the Laffer curve). However, the person with an hourly wage of $25 also reduces labour supply by less than one hour but has $EV = 19.98$, composed of a marginal excess burden of $10.85 and additional tax of $9.14, implying a marginal welfare cost of $1.19 – that is, an excess burden per dollar of extra revenue of over a dollar. The higher wage of $30 results in a similarly small labour supply response, a much higher excess burden, but a smaller marginal welfare cost.

Table 7.8 shows hours and welfare changes for hypothetical workers in couple households with children, for the same tax change. In this case the absence of the top marginal rate (of 0.40) means that the initial effective rate structure has rates of 0.15, 0.85, 0.25, 0.55 and 0.35 applying above thresholds of 0, 200, 450, 650 and 1400. The worker with a wage of $22.6 per hour actually has, before the tax change, tangency positions on segments 2 and 4, but the latter is the global maximum. The tax change gives rise to a move to the new corner solution (though the sub-optimal tangency on segment 2 is clearly unchanged). This gives rise to a small labour supply reduction, a small welfare loss, but again a tax reduction, so that again the wrong side of the Laffer curve is relevant. For the two higher wages of $28.2 and $30 per hour, the marginal excess burdens are similar, at $10.93 and $9.23 respectively, but the marginal welfare costs are $0.70 and $0.31 respectively.

These hypothetical examples demonstrate that it is very difficult to generalise about welfare changes, even for individuals with similar preferences. They all display small hours responses but substantial variations in marginal excess burdens and marginal welfare costs.

7.8 CONCLUSIONS

This chapter has considered, within a limited compass, the extent to which economic theory can offer specific policy advice regarding income tax structures. Ultimately, it was seen that many of the results are negative or too broad to offer direct policy guidance. Indeed, much of the theory has clarified instead just why it is very difficult to produce clear-cut arguments. In providing policy advice, the point inevitably arises that the role of the economist is to examine the implications of adopting alternative value judgements – and there are few results which do not depend in some way on the ultimate objectives of a tax system.

The extensive optimal tax literature does not provide, and was never expected to provide, clear guidance, but instead has clarified the precise way in which the optimal tax system depends on a wide range of factors, some of which relate to value judgements while others concern behavioural responses or basic conditions, such as abilities, which display considerable heterogeneity in practice. Clarifying just how certain conclusions rely on strong, and perhaps unrealistic, assumptions is of course part of the role of economists, yet it is understandable that this can provoke impatience in others.

In looking for practical advice, it appears that a more piecemeal approach must be used. That is, it is necessary to consider in turn a number of features, or their implications for particular specified outcomes, rather than hoping to produce a general rule. This chapter has discussed just a few of those factors, mainly in the context of the role of a top marginal income tax rate. Illustrative numerical examples were provided, showing the kind of calculation which may be made. In particular, it was suggested how a behavioural microsimulation model could be used to examine marginal reforms.

It seems almost inevitable that consideration of income tax structures returns yet again to the famous statement made by McCulloch (1845), quoted in the introduction. Modern public finance theorists might argue that the 'cardinal principle' of proportionality involves an unstated value judgment, and that there is now a better understanding of just why a simple 'compass' is not available (in view of the many measurement problems), and a better understanding of constraints imposed on any 'rudder' (or policy instrument) in attempting to achieve a policy objective. However, his argument does provide a timeless reminder that any policy advice must be extremely tentative and will (given sufficient courage) often take the form of explaining just why a stated objective cannot be achieved by a particular policy initiative, given the propensity of politicians to tinker with tax structures.

NOTES

* I am very grateful to Norman Gemmell for discussions and detailed comments. I should also like to thank Angela Mellish for comments on an earlier version.

1. There was some ambiguity here as to whether Smith held a benefit view or a sacrifice view.
2. In particular it was extended by Lord Overstone, who suggested that a tax should be productive, computable, divisible, frugal, non-interferent, unannoyant, equal, popular and uncorruptive. This classification influenced Norman, who added 'unevasibility'. Norman's approach was dominated by his utilitarian view of sacrifice in an ability to pay context; see O'Brien (2009).
3. Later explorations of the concept of 'equal sacrifice', as discussed for example by J.S. Mill (1848), left some ambiguity here, but see below.
4. The income tax structure at the time had a tax-free threshold (and there were no transfer payments), but the 'degressive' rate structure meant that it was proportional for higher-income recipients.
5. And indeed that analysis, at its inception, included the utility treatment of labour supply behaviour, by Jevons (1871). It arises from the emphasis on exchange, that is, selling labour in return for consumer goods.
6. However, the maximisation of a social welfare function itself presupposes a huge amount of information (including net incomes, hours levels and resulting utilities of all individuals).
7. A further example is the result that indirect taxes are not necessary if preferences are separable between goods and leisure (marginal rates of substitution between goods do not vary with the wage rate).
8. For an empirical study of changes in income tax structures in many countries, see Peter et al. (2007). They show how the flattening of rate structures spread from higher to lower income countries, and document the use of flat-rate systems in post-communist counties since the mid-1990s.
9. Indeed, there are familiar theories about the ways in which politicians may wish to exploit the lack of transparency of complex tax structures.
10. On behavioural modelling, see Creedy and Kalb (2006).
11. For an indirect tax, the approximation is one-half of the product of expenditure on the good, the compensated demand elasticity and the square of the tax rate.
12. On the role of exemptions, see Creedy (2001b).
13. Suppose hours worked, expressed as a function of the gross wage, are $h(w) = 0$ for $w \leq w_m$ and $h > 0$ for $w > w_m$. Then if $F(w)$ is the distribution function of wage rates, arithmetic mean earnings are $\bar{y} = \int_{w_m} wh(w)dF(w)$. Even in the special case where $h(w)$ is linear in w (which arises if preferences are Cobb–Douglas), the threshold wage, w_m, is itself a function of preferences and the tax parameters.
14. The optimal rate depends also on the cardinalisation of utility used in the social welfare function, which is not surprising as any monotonic transformation is equivalent to attaching different weights to utility at different levels. When individuals have relevant non-income characteristics (concerning the size and composition of their household) further value judgments are required in relation to the use of adult equivalent scales and the income unit.
15. In fact, they may not be convex, but the discussion here is not affected.
16. Special cases of explicit solutions have been produced, some involving quasi-linear utility functions.
17. For other reviews of policy implications of optimal tax theory see, for example, Stern (1984), Heady (1993), Tuomala (1995) and Bradbury (1999). For a more critical discussion, see Slemrod (1990).
18. See, for example, simulation results reported in Creedy (1998a) and, for wide-ranging discussions of means-testing, see also Atkinson (1995) and Bradbury (1999).

19. On marginal indirect tax reform see, for example, Ahmad and Stern (1984), Madden (1996) and Creedy (1999).
20. This is obviously a simplifying assumption for illustrative purposes. In view of the New Zealand tax and benefit structure, a further (small) mode is generated at the lower end of the distribution of taxable income, and other small modes and antimodes appear as a result of labour supply effects discussed above.
21. These may be compared with estimates of the Gini (G) and Atkinson (A) measures of inequality for New Zealand in 2006/07, by Creedy et al. (2008a), of $G = 0.464$ and $A = 0.190$ (with inequality aversion of 0.5).
22. However, Creedy and Kalb (2005) showed how such changes really need to consider the complete range of the non-linear budget constraint facing each individual.

REFERENCES

Ahmad, E. and N.H. Stern (1984), 'The theory of tax reform and Indian indirect taxes', *Journal of Public Economics*, **25**, 259–98.

Atkinson, A.B. (1995), *Public Economics in Action: The Basic Income/Flat Tax Proposal*, Oxford: Oxford University Press.

Atkinson, A.B. and J.E. Stiglitz (1980), *Lectures in Public Economics*, London: McGraw-Hill.

Besley, T. and S. Coate (1992), 'Workfare versus welfare: incentive arguments for work requirements in poverty-alleviation programs', *American Economic Review*, **82**, 249–61.

Bradbury, B. (1999), *Optimal taxation theory and the targeting of social assistance*, University of New South Wales, Social Policy Research Centre.

Chang, C.H. (1994), 'On the optimum rate structure of an individual income tax', *Southern Economic Journal*, **60**, 927–35.

Cohen-Stuart, J. (1889), *On Progressive Taxation*. Reprinted in *Classics in Public Finance* (ed. by R.A. Musgrave and A.T. Peacock, 1958), London: Macmillan.

Creedy, J. (1996), *Fiscal Policy and Social Welfare*, Cheltenham, UK and Brookfield, USA: Edward Elgar.

Creedy, J. (1998a), 'Means-tested versus universal transfers: alternative models and value judgements', *Manchester School*, **66**, 100–117.

Creedy, J. (1998b), 'The optimal linear income tax model: utility or equivalent income?', *Scottish Journal of Political Economy*, **45**, 99–110.

Creedy, J. (1999), 'Marginal indirect tax reform in Australia', *Economic Analysis and Policy*, **29**, 1–14.

Creedy, J. (2001a), 'Tax modelling', *Economic Record*, **77**, 189–202.

Creedy, J. (2001b), 'Indirect tax reform and the role of exemptions', *Fiscal Studies*, **22**, 457–86.

Creedy, J. and G. Kalb (2005), 'Measuring welfare changes in labour supply models', *Manchester School*, **73**, 664–85.

Creedy, J. and G. Kalb (2006), *Labour Supply and Microsimulation: The Evaluation of Tax Policy Reforms*, Cheltenham, UK and Northampton, MA, USA: Edward Elgar.

Creedy, J. and C. Sleeman (2006), *The Distributional Effects of Indirect Taxes: Models and Applications from New Zealand*, Cheltenham, UK and Northampton, MA, USA: Edward Elgar.

Creedy, J., J. Enright, N. Gemmell and N. McNabb (2008a), *Equity and efficiency measures of tax-transfer systems: some evidence for New Zealand*, New Zealand Treasury, Working Paper No. 08/04. Wellington: New Zealand.

Creedy, J., N. Herault and G. Kalb (2008b), *Welfare change measures in behavioural microsimulation modelling: accounting for the random utility component*, University of Melbourne.

Deaton, A. (1983), 'An explicit solution to an optimal tax problem', *Journal of Public Economics*, **20**, 333–46.

Diamond, P.A. (1998), 'Optimal income taxation: an example with a U-shaped pattern of optimal marginal tax rates', *American Economic Review*, **88**, 83–95.

Edgeworth, F.Y. (1897), 'The pure theory of taxation', *Economic Journal*, **7**, 46–70, 226–38, 550–71.

Edgeworth, F.Y. (1925), *Papers Relating to Political Economy*, Vol. II, London: Macmillan.

Hashimzade, N. and G.D. Myles (2004), *The structure of the optimal income tax in the quasi-linear model*, PEUK Working Paper, No. 2.

Heady, C. (1993), 'Optimal taxation as a guide to tax policy', *Fiscal Studies*, **14**, 15–41.

Hindriks, J. and G.D. Myles (2006), *Intermediate Public Economics*, Cambridge, MA: The MIT Press.

Kanbur, R., M. Keen and M. Tuomala (1994), 'Optimal non-linear income taxation for the alleviation of income-poverty', *European Economic Review*, **38**, 1613–32.

Kanbur, R., J. Pirttilä and M. Tuomala (2004), *Non-welfarist optimal taxation and behavioural public economics*, University of Tampere, Finland.

McCulloch, J.R. (1845), *A Treatise on the Principles and Practical Influence of Taxation and the Funding System* (ed. with introduction by D.P. O'Brien, 1975), London: Longman.

Madden, D. (1996), 'Marginal tax reform and the specification of consumer demand systems', *Oxford Economic Papers*, **48**, 556–67.

Mill, J.S. (1848), *Principles of Political Economy* (reproduced with editorial material by W.J. Ashley), London: Longmans, Green and Company.

Mirrlees, J.A. (1971), 'An exploration in the theory of optimum income tax', *Review of Economic Studies*, **38**, 175–208.

Myles, G.D. (1999), *On the optimal marginal rate of income tax*, University of Exeter.

O'Brien, D.P. (2009), 'Introduction', in *Taxation and the Promotion of Human Happiness: An Essay by George Warde Norman* (ed. by D.P. O'Brien with J. Creedy), Cheltenham, UK and Northampton, MA, USA: Edward Elgar.

Peter, K.S., S. Buttrick and D. Duncan (2007), *Global reform of personal income taxation 1981–2005: evidence from 189 countries*, Georgia State University, Andrew Young School of Policy Studies, International Studies Program, Working Paper 07-21.

Saez, E. (2001), 'Using elasticities to derive optimal tax rates', *Review of Economic Studies*, **68**, 205–29.

Slemrod, J. (1990), 'Optimal taxation and optimal tax systems', *Journal of Economic Perspectives*, **4**, 157–78.

Smith, A. (1776), *An Inquiry into the Nature and Causes of the Wealth of Nations* (Cannan edition reproduced, 1776), Chicago: Chicago University Press.

Stern, N.H. (1984), 'Optimal taxation and tax policy', *IMF Staff Papers*, **31**, 339–78.
Tuomala, M. (1985), 'Simplified formulae for optimal linear income tax', *Scandinavian Journal of Economics*, **87**, 668–72.
Tuomala, M. (1995), *Optimal Taxation and Redistribution*, Oxford: Clarendon Press.
Tuomala, M. (2006), *On the shape of optimal non-linear income tax schedules*, Tampere Economic Papers, No. 49.

8. Modelling labour supply responses in Australia and New Zealand

Guyonne Kalb*

8.1 INTRODUCTION

This chapter discusses the use of labour supply modelling to inform behavioural responses in tax policy microsimulation models and compares New Zealand with Australia. Typically, as in this case, discrete choice structural labour supply models are chosen for their ability to incorporate detailed tax and social security system information. Given the use of these microsimulation models to predict the effect of tax policy changes, this is obviously important.

A distinguishing feature of microsimulation models is the use of a large cross-sectional dataset providing information about the characteristics of individuals and households, including their labour supply, earnings and, in some cases but not in the models discussed in this chapter, expenditure. Therefore an advantage of microsimulation models is that they can replicate to a large extent the heterogeneity observed in the population.

A behavioural microsimulation model predicting labour supply responses to policy changes consists of three components. The first, discussed in section 8.2, is an accounting or arithmetic microsimulation model, sometimes called a static model. This component computes net household incomes for a sample of households, for current, previous or hypothetical tax-benefit regimes.

The second component is a quantifiable behavioural model of individual tastes for net income and labour supply, which is used to simulate individuals' preferred labour supply under a given set of economic circumstances. The third component consists of a procedure to allocate to each individual a preferred supply of hours conditional on the relevant tax-benefit system. Analysing simulated changes in this allocation of labour supply, between a base tax system and a counterfactual regime, forms the essence of behavioural microsimulation. These two components are described in section 8.3.

The microsimulation models for Australia and New Zealand, the Melbourne Institute Tax and Transfer Simulator (MITTS) and TaxMod[1] respectively, are then described briefly in section 8.4. It is useful to compare some aggregated measures regarding labour supply variations in response to wage changes with those available from independent studies. These elasticities summarise the responsiveness of individuals and households to one aspect of financial incentives according to the labour supply models used in the microsimulation. Such comparisons are made in section 8.5 for Australia and New Zealand. Given the relatively scarce number of labour supply studies in New Zealand (and the more extensive and up-to-date evidence for Australia), it is of interest to explore whether labour responses in New Zealand and Australia are likely to be similar. Section 8.6 briefly concludes.

Before discussing microsimulation modelling in this chapter, it is important to mention the limitations of microsimulation models, such as the ones described here. They are supply-side partial equilibrium models in that the behavioural components concentrate on examining the effects on variations in the hours of work that individuals wish to supply of changes in the tax structure. The demand for labour is not taken into account. Hence, depending on what happens to the demand for labour, individuals may in reality not be able to work their desired number of hours and outcomes may be driven to some extent by what jobs are available. Large changes in the tax structure, designed for example to increase the labour force participation of benefit recipients, may also have effects on the demand for labour through wage changes. In partial equilibrium models, there is an assumption that changes in the tax and transfer system have no effect on individuals' wage rates.

Microsimulation models also typically provide a static overview of one point in time and do not allow for life-cycle dynamics. Decisions on labour force participation could be different when only short-term implications are taken into account compared with decisions based on a longer time horizon.

8.2 NON-BEHAVIOURAL MICROSIMULATION

The majority of large-scale tax simulation models are non-behavioural or arithmetic. That is, no allowance is made for the possible effects of tax changes on individuals' consumption plans or labour supplies. It is sometimes said that they provide information about the effects of tax changes on the 'morning after' the change. Tax policy simulation consists of three steps:

- implementing the existing programme rules and regulations for all the units in the sample (taking into account their characteristics), trying to reproduce the pre-reform policy environment;
- implementing the proposed reform by applying the modified programme rules to the same set of units; and
- taking the difference between pre-reform and post-reform values – this is the estimated impact of the reform.

A typical arithmetic microsimulation model is described in section 8.2.1, followed by a discussion of the data required to build this type of model in section 8.2.2. This is followed in section 8.2.3 by discussion of an important component of any tax policy microsimulation model, the tax and transfer system.

8.2.1 A Typical Arithmetic Model

Advantages of non-behavioural models include the fact that they do not involve the need for estimation of econometric relationships. They are relatively easy to use and quick to run, and can therefore be used by a wide range of users. Furthermore, since no econometric estimation is required, they retain the full extent of the heterogeneity available in the survey data used.

When examining the effects of policy changes, these models generally rely on tabulations and associated graphs, nationally and for subgroups, of the amounts of tax paid and social security payments received (and changes in these) at various percentile income levels. In addition, some models may produce a range of distributional analyses and tax progressivity measures, along with social welfare function evaluations in terms of incomes.

Arithmetic models are typically used to generate profiles, again for various household types, of net income at a range of gross income levels. These profiles are useful for highlighting potential discontinuities, and are helpful when trying to redesign tax and transfer systems in order to overcome such discontinuities and/or excessively high marginal tax rates over some income ranges.

8.2.2 The Data

In the introduction, reference is made to the data requirements of tax models. In Australia, the two large-scale household surveys that are potentially useful are the Household Expenditure Survey (HES) and the Survey of Income and Housing Costs (SIHC) both collected by the Australian

Bureau of Statistics (ABS). However, the former does not contain sufficient information about hours worked by individuals while the latter does not contain information about expenditure patterns. The SIHC is a representative sample of the Australian population, containing detailed information on labour supply and income from different sources, in addition to a variety of background characteristics of individuals and households. The measurement of income in the HES is known to be unreliable, so that in developing models for the analysis of direct taxes and transfer payments it is not surprising that reliance has been placed on the SIHC. Therefore, it is not straightforward to include indirect tax in Australian direct tax models.[2] The extension of models to cover consumption taxes would require some elaborate data merging.

When analysing actual or proposed policy changes, it is preferable to use data which are as close to the relevant time period as possible to avoid having a starting point that is too different from reality. This can be difficult to achieve. To update incomes, the Consumer Price Index is used, and to update wage rates, the average male and female wage indices are used. However, if the tax and social security system is substantially different in the year for which the data are obtained from the year for which a change needs to be simulated, the different incentives arising from the different systems in the two years might well have caused labour supply changes. To take this possibility into account, MITTS can also update labour supply in the base dataset if required.

An alternative approach to deal with this issue is to run two simulations instead of one simulation and compare the pre-reform and post-reform systems via a common third system, which is to be used as the base system in both simulation runs. This third system has to be the system in place at the time the data were collected. This approach was used in Buddelmeyer et al. (2004a, b) and in Buddelmeyer, Dawkins and Kalb (2004).

For New Zealand, the Household Economic Surveys (HES), all released by Statistics New Zealand (NZSTATS), were used in TaxMod. In the period relevant to this chapter, these surveys were released on a yearly basis from 1991/92 to 1997/98, but are currently undertaken only once every three years. The survey collects information on the sources and amounts of income received by persons resident in private dwellings throughout New Zealand, along with data on a range of characteristics for all individuals within the household. Individuals in each household are linked by a household number and family number, so that household characteristics such as income and the number and age of children can be derived by using information from other records in the same household. As for Australia, the detailed information on income allows the budget constraint to keep its full complexity. Each surveyed household has a weight associated with it, which represents how common households of that type are in the population. Thus the sample can be weighted to estimate features of the entire private-household population in New Zealand.

Information on household expenditure is also available in the HES but this is not used in TaxMod. The primary focus of TaxMod is tax and benefits. TaxMod uses most of the income data, which includes income from current jobs, from jobs that finished in the last 12 months, from interest, dividends, lottery winnings and so on. TaxMod ignores benefit amounts recorded in HES, but takes note of benefit duration. When projecting the population forward, market incomes are inflated, and the appropriate benefit rates or superannuation rates for the year being modelled are applied, based on length of eligibility. In general, monetary variables can be updated to particular years using the quarterly Consumer Price Index as published by Statistics New Zealand. Furthermore, the observed nominal wages can be adjusted by average wage increases for men or women as relevant.

8.2.3 The Tax and Transfer System

Detailed knowledge of the tax and social security system is required to build a microsimulation model. Actual tax and transfer systems are typically complex and contain a large number of taxes and benefits which, being designed and administered by different government departments, are usually difficult to integrate fully. The complexity increases where several means-tested benefits are available because of the existence of numerous eligibility requirements. It is only when detailed information about individuals is available that it becomes possible to include the complexities of actual tax and transfer systems in a simulation model.

However, it is unlikely that household surveys contain sufficient information to replicate realistic tax systems fully. In some cases, it may be necessary to impute values, which may not always be possible. Furthermore, regulations regarding the administration of taxes and transfers often leave room for some flexibility in interpretation. In particular, the administration of means tests or other benefits may allow a degree of discretion to be exercised by benefit officers who deal directly with claimants. Changes in the interpretation of (possibly ambiguous) rules, or the degree to which some rules are fully enforced, can take place over time. Furthermore, there may be changes in people's awareness of the benefits available, and the eligibility rules, thereby affecting the degree of take-up.

Given these limitations, even large-scale models may not be able to replicate actual systems entirely. Thus they may not accurately reproduce aggregate expenditure and tax levels. Similarly, the same problems may give rise to distortions in measuring the extent to which redistribution occurs.

8.3 BEHAVIOURAL MICROSIMULATION

Behavioural models are often essential when assessing proposed policy changes, because many tax policy changes are designed with the aim of altering the behaviour of individuals. For example, some policies are designed to induce more individuals to participate in paid employment or, for those already working, to increase their hours of work.

The production of behavioural microsimulation tax models, allowing for labour supply variations, represents a considerable challenge and has involved substantial innovations in labour supply modelling. On labour supply modelling in the context of tax simulation models, see, for example, Apps and Savage (1989), Banks, Blundell and Lewbel (1996), Blundell et al. (1986), Creedy and Duncan (2002), Creedy and Kalb (2005), Duncan (1993), Duncan and Giles (1996), Moffitt (2000) and Klevmarken (1997). Examples of behavioural microsimulation analyses using MITTS or TaxMod-B can be found in Buddelmeyer, Creedy and Kalb (2007).

Even where labour supply is not the main focus of a policy, there may be unintended consequences which affect other outcomes. Measures of the welfare losses, for example resulting from increases in taxes, are overstated by non-behavioural models which rely on 'morning after' changes in tax paid, rather than allowing for substitution away from activities whose relative prices increase as the result of the policy change. In addition, estimates of the distributional implications of tax changes may be misleading unless behavioural adjustments are modelled.

This section first describes a typical behavioural microsimulation model, before discussing the issue of modelling non-participation in the labour force.

8.3.1 A Typical Behavioural Microsimulation Model

Existing behavioural microsimulation models are restricted in the types of behaviour that are endogenous. At most, individuals' labour supplies and household demands are modelled. Variables associated with longer-term decisions such as: household formation, marriage and births, along with retirement, labour training and higher education decisions, are considered to be exogenous and independent of the tax changes examined.

A component which evaluates the net income corresponding to any given number of hours worked by each individual is a fundamental component of a behavioural model. This produces, for each individual, the precise budget constraint relating net income to hours worked. The behavioural part of the model can then be used to evaluate which part of the individual's constraint is optimal. This component is in effect an associated non-behavioural model which is applied across the range of possible labour supply for each individual.

Behavioural microsimulation models have, to some extent, a lower degree of population heterogeneity than non-behavioural models. This is because econometric estimation of the important relationships must involve the use of a limited range of categories. For example, in estimating labour supply behaviour, individuals may be divided into groups such as couples, single males and single females, and single-parent households. The number of groups is limited by the sample size, but the estimated functions can be made dependent on variables, such as age, location, occupation and education level. In addition, individual-specific variability may be introduced to ensure that the optimum labour supply in the face of current taxes actually corresponds, for each individual, to the level that is observed in the current period.

8.3.2 Simulating Changes in Labour Force Participation

An important policy issue relates to the nature of tax and transfer changes designed to encourage more people to participate in the labour market. Hence this is likely to provide a focus for behavioural microsimulation studies, but this is also the area that raises the greatest difficulty for modellers. There are several reasons for this. First, there is less information about non-participants in survey data. For example, it is necessary to impute a wage rate for non-workers, using estimated wage equations and allowing for selectivity issues. In addition, variables such as industry or occupation, which are often important in wage equations, are not available for non-workers. A second problem is that there are fixed costs associated with working, irrespective of the number of hours worked. These are usually difficult to estimate due to data limitations. Finally, labour supply models typically treat non-participation as a voluntary decision, giving rise to a corner solution. However, demand-side factors may be important and there may be a discouraged worker effect of unemployment, which is difficult to model.

A choice must be made between continuous and discrete hours labour supply estimation and simulation. Earlier studies of labour supply used continuous hours models, involving the estimation of labour supply functions. In this case, it is important that the results are such that hours worked can be regarded as the outcome of utility maximisation. In other words, it must be possible to recover the indirect utility function by integration.[3] This contrasts with discrete hours estimation and microsimulation, where net incomes, before and after a policy reform, are required only for a finite set of hours points. The discrete hours approach has substantial advantages in estimation, since it allows for the complexity of the tax and transfer system and avoids the problems with endogeneity between the net wage and hours worked which are present when a standard labour supply function is estimated. Furthermore, estimation involves direct utility functions, which may depend on many individual characteristics. The determination of optimal labour supply is easier, since utility at each of a limited number of hours levels can readily be obtained and compared. The use of direct utility functions also means that no integration from estimated supply functions is required in simulation. In addition, modelling the move in and out of the labour market is relatively straightforward in the discrete model compared to the continuous model. The discrete hours approach is used in MITTS and TaxMod-B, which are described in the following section.

8.4 MITTS AND TAXMOD

The specific features of the Australian and New Zealand microsimulation models are described in sections 8.4.1 and 8.4.2 respectively. This is followed by a discussion of the use of labour supply modelling in MITTS and TaxMod-B in section 8.4.3. The same approach is used in both microsimulation models and the specification of the models has been made as similar as possible given the data and differences between the two countries. The type of explanatory variables included in the models is the same.

8.4.1 MITTS

MITTS is a behavioural microsimulation model of direct taxes and transfers in Australia. It was designed to examine tax policy reforms which capture labour supply responses to changes in budget constraints. The results reflect only the supply side of the labour market, and a discrete hours framework is used in which individuals can move between specified discrete hours levels, rather than being able to vary hours continuously.

In the present version of MITTS, SIHC data from 1994/95 to 2003/04 can be used. One set of econometric estimates of preferences underlying the behavioural responses are based on data observed between 1994 and 1998 and another set is based on data observed between 1999 and 2004. Details of the first set of wage and labour supply parameters used in MITTS can be found in Kalb and Scutella (2002) and Kalb (2002). All results are aggregated to population levels using the household weights provided with the SIHC.

In MITTS, the arithmetic tax and benefit modelling component is called MITTS-A (the behavioural component is called MITTS-B). This component also provides, using the wage rate of each individual, the information needed for the construction of the budget constraints that are crucial for the analysis of behavioural responses to tax changes.

The tax system component of MITTS contains the procedures for applying each type of tax and benefit. As mentioned before, it is not possible to include within MITTS all the complexity of the tax and transfer system. However, all major social security payments and income taxes are included in MITTS. Pre-reform net incomes at the alternative hours levels are based on the MITTS calculation of entitlements, not the actual receipt. Hence in the calculation of net income it is assumed that take-up rates are 100 per cent.[4]

The various components of the tax and benefit structure are assembled in the required way in order to work out the transformation between hours worked and net income for each individual under each tax system. Changes to the tax and benefit structure, including the introduction of additional taxes, can be modelled by editing the programmes in this component. MITTS stores several previous Australian tax and transfer systems, which can be used as base systems for the analysis of policy changes.

MITTS-A contains the facility to examine each household, income unit and individual in the selected base dataset in turn and generate net incomes, at the given hourly wage rates, for variations in the number of hours worked. Thus the changes in effective marginal tax rates (EMTRs) and labour supply incentives faced by households at various levels of the wage distribution can be compared, in addition to calculating the aggregate costs of different reform packages. Furthermore, distributions of EMTRs for a variety of demographic groups can be produced for pre-reform and post-reform tax systems, as well as distributions of gainers and losers, for various demographic characteristics. Hypothetical households can also be constructed and examined.

8.4.2 TaxMod

TaxMod is a model of the New Zealand population based on data from Statistics NZ – the Household Economic Survey. TaxMod provides a detailed picture of the New Zealand population, which allows a variety of questions related to the effect of changes in income tax and social security to be answered. The two main strengths of TaxMod are that it accurately models the interactions between various policies and that it allows new policies to be modelled.

TaxMod works similar to MITTS. It reads in one family at a time, calculates market income, adds income from various government programmes (benefits, superannuation, Family Support, Accommodation Supplement) according to eligibility, and calculates tax liability. It can provide output at the personal, family and household level, which can then be processed using a statistical software package such as SAS or STATA. Examples of output include disposable income, unemployment benefit, low income rebate, total tax paid minus benefits received. It also accumulates some figures for the entire population, and these are available directly from TaxMod as standard output tables.

TaxMod can also analyse a single family, whether extracted from HES or hypothetical. Detailed results of the tax/benefit calculation can be displayed for each member of the family, showing results under two sets of tax/benefit parameters. This feature is very useful for understanding surprising results. Another useful feature is that TaxMod allows us to take a family, allow one of the income variables to go through a range of values, and graph a variable of interest. This is useful to understand the effects of a policy change on EMTRs.

Limitations of TaxMod stem primarily from the data on which it is based. Although HES collects a large amount of information from each household, and surveys a large number of households by New Zealand standards, the data has notable shortcomings. The main purpose of HES is to measure CPI accurately and the sample design means that the accuracy of results relating to general questions is not as high as would be ideal.

For example, the numbers of ex-beneficiaries that show up in the HES data are consistently low relative to administrative data collected by the Department of Social Welfare. There are two ways of handling these shortcomings – attempt to compensate for them, or estimate the sampling error. Both techniques have been used with TaxMod. As part of the data preparation, household weights are altered to correct the population totals in various areas, and data for recent years allows estimation of the size of the sampling error for different measures.

Unlike in MITTS, the behavioural and non-behavioural microsimulation models in TaxMod are not integrated. TaxMod is a non-behavioural microsimulation model in which behavioural responses of individuals resulting from a policy change in tax or transfer payments are not accounted for in the modelling process. TaxMod-B is a separate behavioural microsimulation model which can read output data from TaxMod, containing net incomes for each household at a range of predetermined labour supply points. It is designed to provide a tool for additional analysis so that the labour supply effects of the policy changes can be simulated and evaluated. In addition, the effects on government revenue and expenditure while allowing for labour supply responses can also be simulated.

The input for TaxMod-B is based on the HES datasets, but these data need to be run first through TaxMod, the static microsimulation model for New Zealand, before they can be used. TaxMod is needed to calculate net incomes at a range of discrete labour supply levels before and after the reform.[5] In addition to the net incomes, the files contain a range of individual and household characteristics. TaxMod-B contains no social security or tax system information, but only the labour supply parameters on which the behavioural responses are based and a variety of tabulation and graphic facilities. After each simulation, a Gauss output data file is also generated which allows further analysis to be undertaken outside TaxMod-B. The wage and labour supply parameters for New Zealand are reported in Kalb and Scutella (2003, 2004).

8.4.3 Using Labour Supply Modelling in MITTS-B and TaxMod-B

MITTS-B and TaxMod-B examine the effects of a specified tax reform, allowing individuals to adjust their labour supply behaviour where appropriate. Both models use the same approach to obtain behavioural responses of tax policy changes. The behavioural responses generated by MITTS-B and TaxMod-B are based on the use of quadratic preference functions whereby the parameters are allowed to vary with individuals' characteristics. These parameters were estimated for four demographic groups, which include married or partnered men and women, single men and women, and sole parents; see Kalb (2002), and Kalb and Scutella (2003). The joint labour supply of couples is estimated simultaneously, unlike a common approach in which female labour supply is estimated with the spouse's labour supply taken as exogenous.

The framework is one in which individuals are considered as being constrained to select from a discrete set of hours levels, rather than being able to vary labour supply continuously. Other studies using this approach include Van Soest (1995), Duncan, Giles and MacCrae (1999) and Keane and Moffitt (1998).

Some individuals are observed to be working a number of hours such that they are facing very high EMTRs. One explanation for this is that in practice people may not be claiming all the benefits to which they are entitled, especially if the benefits are small, so that their actual EMTR is not as large as it seems from the calculations. An alternative explanation is that people are in practice restricted in their labour supply choice. If people are actually at hours levels that give them marginal rates of 100 per cent or more, this cannot be explained in a continuous hours labour supply framework. Such points could not be the optimal points in the model, since the indifference curves cannot be flat. However, in a discrete hours approach such labour supply points can be optimal, because if people are not free to vary their hours continuously they have to select the best discrete choice available.

Different sets of discrete hours points may be used for each demographic group. Different sets of discrete hours points are used for married men and all other groups. Given that the married males' hours distribution is much less spread over part-time and full-time hours than the other distributions, male labour supply is represented by just six points, whereas female labour supply is divided into 11 discrete points.

Given the aim of simulating policy changes with regard to the tax and transfer system and assessing its effect on labour supply, priority is given to incorporating all possible detail on taxes and transfers. Utility is maximised conditional on the restricted total amount of time available to each adult and the restricted amount of total household income. It is expected that utility increases with an increase in leisure (including home production time) and income. Usually more income means less leisure time for one of the adults, except when more income is obtained through social security benefits. It is assumed that everyone who is eligible for benefits takes them up. Maximising a household's utility involves balancing the amount of leisure and income. It is assumed that all nonparticipants are voluntarily not working and that participants are at their preferred labour supply points. Wage rates, non-labour income and household composition are exogenous in this model.

Restricting the number of possible working hours to a limited set of discrete values means that complex tax and transfer details can be incorporated. The economic model, assuming there are two adults in the household, is specified as follows. The utility function, $U(x, \ell_1, \ell_2)$, is maximised subject to a time restriction for each adult. Let ℓ_i and h_i denote the weekly aggregate of leisure and home production time, and hours of work of partner i, with $\ell_1 + h_1 = T$ and $\ell_1 + h_2 = T$. The time spent in employment is chosen from discrete hours sets. Let x indicate total net income per week, which is assumed equal to household consumption. The gross wage rates of male and female partners are denoted w_1 and w_2 respectively and y_i are the non-labour incomes. Let C refer to household composition, and $B(\,)$ is the amount of benefit for which a household is eligible, given household composition and household income. The tax function indicating the amount of tax to be paid is $\tau(\,)$. The budget constraint is given by:

$$x = w_1h_1 + w_2h_2 + y_1 + y_2 + B(C, w_1h_1 + w_2h_2 + y_1 + y_2) \\ - \tau(B, w_1h_1 + y_1, w_2h_2 + y_2, C) \quad (8.1)$$

The discrete hours choices are given by the sets $[0,h_{11},h_{12},\ldots,h_{1m}]$ and $[0,h_{21},h_{22},\ldots,h_{2,k}]$ for partners 1 and 2 respectively. Using these sets, net income can be calculated for all $(m + 1)(k + 1)$ combinations of h_1 and h_2. For this limited set of hours, the utility each possible combination of hours would generate, according to the specified utility function, can be computed.

The choice of labour supply is simultaneously determined for both adult members of the household. Depending on the form of the utility function, different interactions between household income and labour supply of both adults can be modelled.

Utility is assumed to consist of a deterministic and a random component. Choosing an extreme value specification for the random component results in a multinomial logit model; see Maddala (1983) and Creedy and Kalb (2005). The deterministic component used in MITTS and TaxMod-B is a quadratic specification, following Keane and Moffitt (1998). It is simple but flexible in that it allows for the leisure of each person and income to be substitutes or complements. A fixed cost of working parameter γ is included in the income variable x to indicate the cost of working versus nonparticipation, following Callan and Van Soest (1996). The deterministic component of utility is specified as follows:

$$U(x, h_1, h_2) = \beta_x(x - \gamma_1 - \gamma_2) + \beta_1h_1 + \beta_2h_2 + \alpha_{xx}(x - \gamma_1 - \gamma_2)^2 \\ + \alpha_{11}(h_1)^2 + \alpha_{22}(h_2)^2 + \alpha_{x1}(x - \gamma_1 - \gamma_2)h_1 \\ + \alpha_{x2}(x - \gamma_1 - \gamma_2)h_2 + \alpha_{12}h_1h_2 \quad (8.2)$$

where the αs and βs are preference parameters and γ_1 and γ_2 are the fixed cost of working parameters to be estimated, where the indices 1 and 2 denote the husband and wife respectively. The fixed cost is zero when the relevant person is not working. For one-adult households, the model is simplified by excluding everything related to the second adult.

Observed heterogeneity is included by allowing β_1, β_2, β_x, γ_1 and γ_2 to depend on personal and household characteristics. Unobserved heterogeneity may be added to β_1, β_2, β_x and γ_2, in the form of a normally distributed error term with zero mean and unknown variance. Parameter estimates for all four demographic groups are in Kalb (2002) and Kalb and Scutella (2003).

For those individuals in the dataset who are not working, and who therefore do not report a wage rate, an imputed wage is obtained. This imputed wage is based on estimated wage functions, allowing for possible selectivity bias, as described in Kalb and Scutella (2002, 2004). Some individuals are fixed at their observed labour supply if their imputed wage or their observed wage, obtained by dividing total earnings by the number of hours worked, is unrealistic.[6] Furthermore, some individuals such as the self-employed, the disabled, students and those over 65 have their labour supply fixed at their observed hours.

Simulation is probabilistic, as utility at each discrete hours level is specified as the sum of a deterministic component (depending on the hours worked and net income) and a random component (here, an extreme value type I distribution, which is associated with the multinomial logit model). Hence MITTS and TaxMod-B do not identify a particular level of hours worked for each individual after the policy change, but generates a probability distribution over the discrete hours levels used. Net incomes are calculated at all possible labour supply points. Given a random set of draws from the error term distribution, along with the computed deterministic component of utility at each of the labour supply points, the optimal choice for each draw can be determined conditional on the relevant set of error terms.

A behavioural simulation for each individual begins by setting reported hours equal to the nearest discrete hours level. Then, given the parameter estimates of the preference function, which vary according to a range of characteristics, a set of random draws is taken from the conditional distribution of the error term for each hours level. The utility-maximising hours level is found by adding the random to the deterministic component of utility for each discrete hours level. A user-specified total number of draws is produced. These are drawings which generate the observed hours as the optimal value under the base system for the individual. This process is described as 'calibration'.

For the post-reform analysis, the new net incomes cause the deterministic component of utility at each hours level to change, so using the set of draws from the calibration stage, a new set of optimal hours of work is produced. This gives rise to a probability distribution over the set of discrete hours for each individual under the new tax and transfer structure. Transition matrices showing probabilities of movement between hours levels are computed using these probabilities.

When examining average hours in MITTS-B or TaxMod-B, the labour supply after the change for each individual is based on the average value over the set of draws. This is equivalent to calculating the expected hours of labour supply after the change, conditional on starting from the observed hours before the change. In computing the tax and revenue levels, an expected value is also obtained after the policy change. That is, the tax and revenue for each of the hours points are computed for each individual, and the average of these is obtained using the probability distribution of hours worked.

An alternative to the calibration is to draw from the unconditional distribution of error terms and generate a probability distribution of labour supply in the base and reform system.

8.5 LABOUR SUPPLY ELASTICITIES

In constructing any microsimulation model it is important to ensure that, using the base system, it can generate revenue and expenditure totals for various categories that are close to independently produced aggregates. For a behavioural model, it is also useful to see how summary information about labour supply behaviour compares with results from other studies. Such comparisons are examined in this section, and in particular New Zealand and Australia are compared. Unfortunately, the comparison is limited by what is available from earlier research in which labour supply models were estimated for New Zealand.

Alternative approaches of calculating wage elasticities are first discussed in section 8.5.1, before reporting results for Australia and New Zealand in sections 8.5.2 and 8.5.3, respectively. In section 8.5.4, the two countries are compared with each other and with results from other countries.

8.5.1 The Calculation of Wage Elasticities

It is common in studies of labour supply to provide wage elasticities for various groups, often computed at average values of wages. Elasticities are convenient as a summary measure since the parameters of the utility function themselves, which drive the labour supply responses, are not very informative with regard to the responsiveness to financial incentives that can be expected from the different types of individuals. That is, the discrete hours labour supply model used in MITTS and TaxMod-B simulations of behavioural responses to policy changes does not provide straightforward wage elasticities with regard to labour supply. However, elasticities implied by a discrete choice model can be approximated by comparing the expected labour supply for an individual after an x per cent wage increase with the expected labour supply under the original wage, and expressing the difference as a percentage change divided by x. Applying this to each individual in the sample, the average elasticity across the sample, or population when making use of the weights, can be computed. It should be noted that the change in wage is a change in the gross wage rate and that the change in net wage rate is also affected by the tax and transfer system which is in place.

A range of different concepts is used in the literature. For example, instead of calculating the average elasticity across the sample, an alternative is to calculate the elasticity for a hypothetical person with average values for each of the relevant characteristics.[7] Hence it cannot be expected that the same values will be obtained, but comparisons of orders of magnitude are useful.

In MITTS, elasticities is computed in two different ways, whereas for TaxMod-B only elasticities based on the first approach were computed. First, the wage elasticities are calculated for each individual for whom labour supply responses are simulated. Expected labour supply is computed at the observed and imputed wage levels. It is calculated by drawing 100 random error terms for each individual to add to the deterministic utility level. This allows us to determine the optimal utility level and thus the preferred labour supply for each draw. Expected labour supply is calculated as the average over these 100 draws. The next step is to increase all wage rates by 1 per cent in MITTS (10 per cent for New Zealand) and calculate expected labour supply again using the same draws. The percentage difference in labour supply is the wage elasticity. Weights are used to calculate the average elasticity across all individuals by demographic group. In MITTS, the average of the individual elasticities is taken whereas for New Zealand the average expected hours across the sample (or subgroup) is computed before and after the wage change and the percentage change between those two values is used to approximate the relevant elasticity. The change in participation is calculated by comparing the average weighted probability of being at zero hours before and after the wage increase.

Second, using calibrated labour supply, the wage elasticities are calculated for each individual for whom labour supply responses are simulated and who works positive hours.[8] First, expected labour supply is computed at the observed and imputed wage levels. In this case where calibrated labour supply is used, the error terms are drawn conditionally; that is, only error terms that place the individual at their observed hours are used. Again 100 draws from the error terms are used. Due to the calibration, at the original wage, the expected labour supply equals the observed discretised hours point for each individual. The next step is to increase all wage rates by 1 per cent and calculate expected labour supply again using the same draws from the error terms. Again, the percentage difference in labour supply is the wage elasticity and weights are used to calculate the average elasticity.

For the change in participation, the probability of being at zero hours after the wage change and the observed non-participation before the wage change are used. The change in participation is calculated by comparing the average weighted probability of being at zero hours before and after the wage increase.

Expected hours are never zero in principle, so the first set of wage elasticities is calculated for a larger sample (including workers and non-workers) than the second set of wage elasticities (only calculated for workers). It is expected that workers and non-workers have different elasticities. In fact, even within the workers or non-workers group, values for the elasticities vary widely. Elasticities provide the most information at the disaggregated level, since at the aggregate level a small elasticity can hide a wide variation of responses for subcategories in the population. For all demographic groups, the individual simulated elasticities vary from negative to positive values, with a substantial number being zero.

In interpreting the results, one should keep in mind that elasticities are relative measures. That is, the same elasticity has different implications for absolute labour supply changes at different levels of labour supply. People working low hours could have a large elasticity if their weekly labour supply increased or decreased by one hour. Therefore, a large elasticity for some individuals does not necessarily imply the labour supply response will be large in absolute terms. Individuals working few hours who change their labour supply are going to affect the average elasticity to a lesser extent in the approach used for the New Zealand calculations compared to the approach used in MITTS for Australia.

8.5.2 Wage Elasticities for Australia

The tables with wage elasticities and cross-wage elasticities are presented below. The elasticities are calculated based on samples excluding people over 65, disabled individuals, full-time students and the self-employed, for whom labour supply is not simulated in MITTS. Elasticities are broken down by a number of individual and household characteristics. To compare calibrated and non-calibrated wage elasticities for the same group of individuals the latter wage elasticities are also reported separately for the subgroup of workers in MITTS.

With regard to the participation changes, using calibration means that for each individual the starting point is at the extreme probabilities of 0 and 100 per cent of participation in the labour force, whereas using expected labour supply means the starting point can be anywhere in the range from 0 to 100 per cent. Therefore, at the individual level the scope for change (both increases and decreases) appears larger when using calibrated labour supply. However, because these larger changes can be

Table 8.1 Implied average uncompensated wage elasticities by demographic group based on 1994–98 labour supply estimates (Australia)

Demographic group	Based on expected labour supply			Based on calibrated labour supply	
	Average wage elasticity		Change in participation	Average wage elasticity	Change in participation
	All hours	Observed hours >0	Percentage points	At observed discretised positive hours	Percentage points
Single male	0.22	0.21	0.16	0.04	0.17
Single female	0.38	0.22	0.19	0.07	0.16
Sole parent	1.48	1.49	0.41	0.78	0.24
Married male without children	0.33	0.28	0.20	0.09	0.19
Married female without children	0.42	0.36	0.18	0.23	0.18
Married male with children	0.17	0.16	0.11	0.04	0.11
Married female with children	0.66	0.63	0.22	0.49	0.13
Cross-wage elasticities					
Married males without children	0.06	0.06	0.05	−0.02	0.03
Married females without children	0.08	0.05	0.05	−0.06	0.03
Married males with children	0.02	0.02	0.03	−0.03	0.02
Married females with children	0.12	0.05	0.04	−0.12	0.00

negative or positive, nothing conclusive can be predicted about the resulting participation changes on average. Table 8.1 shows that the changes are fairly small in all groups for both approaches. For single men, single women, married men and married women without children, the calculated changes are similar in both approaches.

Single parents and married/de facto women, particularly those with children, appear most responsive to wage changes. Cross-wage elasticities in couple families are all quite small. The elasticities presented in Table 8.1 are disaggregated by education level in Table 8.2. Disaggregation by age was examined as well but no regular patterns were observed so these results are not reported here.

Disaggregation by education in Table 8.2 shows a tendency for higher wage elasticities amongst individuals at the lowest skill level, except for single parents. For the latter group, only the highest education level displays a clearly lower elasticity compared to the three lower levels of education.

This higher elasticity for people with relatively low skills is at least partly due to the lower participation rate and lower hours of work of this subgroup. Similarly, the cross-wage elasticities (not presented here) also appear slightly higher for the individuals with low skill levels, even turning negative for those with a diploma or degree. Again this is likely to be due to the level of labour supply in the starting point.

In Table 8.3, elasticities based on the most recent set of labour supply parameters for Australia are presented. To allow for easier comparison with the New Zealand elasticities, the same approach as needs to be taken for New Zealand was applied for this table in addition to the approach used in Tables 8.1 and 8.2. Although the actual elasticities have changed compared to those based on the earlier parameters, as in Table 8.1, married/de facto women and single parents are predicted to have the highest wage elasticities. As in Table 8.1, the cross-wage elasticities are small, and negative cross-wage elasticities are observed only when using calibrated labour supply.

The elasticities are clearly sensitive to the moment of averaging across the sample, although the general patterns remain roughly the same. When using expected labour supply applying the same approach as for New Zealand results in somewhat lower elasticities compared to first computing the individual elasticities before averaging these over the sample. The differences between these two approaches are larger and less predictable when the elasticities are based on the calibrated labour supply. This is at least partly due to the fact that more observations can be used when applying the New Zealand approach since those not working before the wage increase can now be included in the calculation based on calibrated labour supply.

8.5.3 Results for New Zealand

Table 8.4 presents the wage elasticities for New Zealand. The elasticities are calculated based on samples excluding people over 65, disabled individuals, full-time students and the self-employed, for whom labour supply is not simulated in TaxMod-B. The information that is available only allows

Table 8.2 Implied average uncompensated wage elasticities by demographic group and education level (Australia)

Demographic group by education level	Based on expected labour supply			Based on calibrated labour supply	
	Average wage elasticity		Change in participation	Average wage elasticity	Change in participation
	All hours	Observed hours > 0	Percentage points	At observed discretised positive hours	Percentage points
Single male					
Year 12 or less	0.25	0.26	0.18	0.05	0.16
Vocational qualification	0.23	0.22	0.18	0.03	0.22
Diploma	0.10	0.12	0.09	0.01	0.23
Degree	0.12	0.11	0.12	0.01	0.10
Single female					
Year 12 or less	0.56	0.32	0.21	0.14	0.18
Vocational qualification	0.21	0.20	0.16	0.03	0.11
Diploma	0.25	0.10	0.21	−0.04	0.35
Degree	0.15	0.10	0.14	0.02	0.11
Sole parent					
Year 12 or less	1.55	1.91	0.38	0.79	0.23
Vocational qualification	1.62	1.67	0.45	0.59	0.16
Diploma	1.70	1.23	0.61	1.58	0.48
Degree	0.83	0.61	0.33	0.54	0.27
Married male without children					
Year 12 or less	0.49	0.46	0.27	0.04	0.23
Vocational qualification	0.27	0.22	0.17	0.20	0.16
Diploma	0.21	0.18	0.16	0.03	0.22
Degree	0.14	0.12	0.11	0.05	0.16
Married female without children					
Year 12 or less	0.51	0.52	0.21	0.15	0.20
Vocational qualification	0.33	0.22	0.15	0.46	0.09

Table 8.2 (continued)

Demographic group by education level	Based on expected labour supply			Based on calibrated labour supply	
	Average wage elasticity		Change in partici-pation	Average wage elasticity	Change in partici-pation
	All hours	Observed hours > 0	Percentage points	At observed discretised positive hours	Percentage points
Diploma	0.41	0.36	0.21	0.23	0.16
Degree	0.26	0.18	0.10	0.15	0.20
Married male with children					
Year 12 or less	0.24	0.23	0.16	0.04	0.16
Vocational qualification	0.15	0.14	0.10	0.04	0.07
Diploma	0.12	0.09	0.07	0.04	0.09
Degree	0.10	0.10	0.06	0.04	0.09
Married female with children					
Year 12 or less	0.75	0.73	0.21	0.45	0.13
Vocational qualification	0.57	0.55	0.21	0.30	0.08
Diploma	0.57	0.66	0.27	0.70	0.11
Degree	0.58	0.48	0.23	0.67	0.19

elasticities to be broken down by age and couple families cannot be further subdivided into those with and without dependent children. In addition, the wage change of 10 per cent is applied across the board which means that the head's and spouse's wages are increased at the same time. The elasticities for couples presented in Table 8.4 are therefore different from those usually presented in that they combine own and cross-wage elasticities. Given the results for Australia, it is expected that the own wage elasticities dominate and that the results are likely to be close to the own wage elasticities.

The order of magnitude of elasticities in New Zealand is comparable to those in Australia, although single men and women in New Zealand appear more responsive to wage increases than singles in Australia and married/de facto women and single parents appear less responsive.

The elasticities by age have to be interpreted cautiously, since no separate labour supply models have been estimated for those close to retirement

Table 8.3 Implied average uncompensated wage elasticities by demographic group based on 1999–2004 labour supply estimates (Australia)

Demographic group	Based on expected labour supply			Based on calibrated labour supply	
	Average wage elasticity		Change in participation	Average wage elasticity	Change in participation
	All hours	Observed hours > 0	Percentage points	At observed discretised positive hours	Percentage points
Single male	0.33 [0.30]	0.33	0.20	0.16 [0.28]	0.19
Single female	0.28 [0.19]	0.24	0.17	0.06 [0.19]	0.17
Sole parent	0.90 [0.70]	0.85	0.29	0.41 [0.59]	0.26
Married male without children	0.49 [0.36]	0.41	0.24	0.31 [0.32]	0.20
Married female without children	0.70 [0.54]	0.58	0.25	0.54 [0.43]	0.19
Married male with children	0.27 [0.25]	0.26	0.15	0.16 [0.16]	0.09
Married female with children	0.86 [0.75]	0.84	0.32	0.90 [0.52]	0.16
Cross-wage elasticities					
Married males without children	0.07 [0.03]	0.04	0.06	−0.03 [−0.01]	0.02
Married females without children	0.07 [−0.02]	−0.00	0.05	−0.12 [−0.07]	0.03
Married males with children	0.03 [0.02]	0.02	0.04	−0.02 [−0.02]	0.01
Married females with children	0.12 [0.01]	0.01	0.06	−0.10 [−0.06]	0.04

Note: [..] indicates the elasticity when using the New Zealand approach of computing average hours across the sample before and after the wage change first, before computing elasticities based on these averages.

age. So for example, health and the amount of assets accumulated by the household are not taken into account in the labour supply decision. These two factors are known to play an important role in retirement decisions. However, eligibility for the superannuation payment, another important factor, was taken into account. In the period over which the models were estimated, an important change to the state-provided superannuation

Table 8.4 Wage elasticities and non-participation rates[a] *by age and demographic group (New Zealand)*

	Married men[b]	Married women[b]	Single men	Single women	Sole parents[c]
Wage elasticities					
All	0.23	0.38	0.63	0.82	0.34
Selection: people < = 30	0.22	0.34	0.55	0.75	
Selection: people 31–50	0.11	0.37	0.65	0.72	
Selection: people > 50	0.40	0.58	1.21	1.34	
Selection: people > 60	0.76	0.83	1.86	1.77	
Change in expected non-participation in percentage points					
All	−1.7	−1.9	−4.1	4.5	−0.8
Selection: people < = 30	−1.7	−1.7	−3.6	−4.3	
Selection: people 31–50	−1.5	−2.0	−4.7	−4.6	
Selection: people > 50	−2.4	−2.3	−5.0	−4.9	
Selection: people > 60	−2.6	−1.6	−2.9	−3.3	

Notes:

[a] Expected labour supply (from which the elasticities are derived) is calculated at the sample characteristics. Average unweighted expected hours of work are computed across the samples. To approximate elasticities, a wage increase of 1% (instead of the 10% used here) would have been better. It would also have made the results more comparable to the Australian numbers.

[b] Wages increase for both partners in a couple at the same time.

[c] The information by age is not available for sole parents.

was taking place. The age of eligibility for the universal superannuation payment was gradually increased from 60 to 65 in the period from April 1992 to April 2001. This large change in financial incentive clearly affected individuals' labour supply decisions despite that it concerned the older age groups only. It helped identify the parameters of the models. It would be of interest to examine the effect of this change in the age eligibility while allowing for the effects of other factors such as health as well.

8.5.4 Comparisons with Other Countries

The range of elasticities published in the literature is fairly wide, with large differences between studies using different data and approaches.[9] The implicit labour supply elasticities in MITTS and TaxMod-B are similar to those generally found within the international literature. The results for married and single men and women are well within the range of results usually found.

The elasticity for single parents is often found to be larger than for other groups and this is also found in MITTS for Australia, but not for New Zealand. Compared to other countries the labour force participation of single parents in New Zealand (and Australia to a lesser extent) is low. To understand whether the relatively low elasticity for single parents in New Zealand is due to differences in behaviour or whether the tax and social security system imposes disincentives which are larger in New Zealand than in Australia, further analysis would be required. For example, a comparison could be made between the EMTRs of single parents in the two countries, examining how the gross wage rate change translates into a net wage rate change. In addition, more up-to-date data could be used to check the persistence of the observed difference in elasticities.

The elasticity for single parents implicit in MITTS is at the higher end of this range internationally. Other evidence of a high labour supply responsiveness for single parents in Australia has been found by Murray (1996), Duncan and Harris (2002) and Doiron (2004). Doiron's paper is of particular interest. She evaluated a policy reform affecting single parents in the late 1980s and found large labour supply effects. She compared the effect obtained through a natural experiment approach with predicted effects of policy changes from the MITTS model, as found in Duncan and Harris (2002) or Creedy, Kalb and Kew (2003). Based on the results from her evaluation, Doiron argued that observed shifts in labour supply of single parents can equal or even surpass the predictions based on behavioural microsimulation.

These results suggest that single parents' labour supply elasticities may be substantial. This is perhaps not surprising, given the low participation rate of single parents and the tendency to work low part-time hours. An increase in labour supply by one hour is a larger percentage increase compared with the same increase for a married man. For the other demographic groups, elasticities of those working few hours are also generally higher than for those in the same group who work greater hours. The single parent group is the smallest demographic group in the population. Thus, a change in their labour supply responsiveness would have a relatively small effect on the overall result.

Another way of validating behavioural results is by comparing the predicted effects of a policy change obtained through a simulation with the estimated effects of the policy change after it has been introduced. The problem with this approach is that it is often difficult to find policy changes that can be evaluated accurately.

Blundell et al. (2004) evaluated a range of labour market reforms in the UK by a difference-in-difference approach at the same time as simulating the effects of these reforms. They found similar results for sole parents and married women, but for married men the estimated effects were opposite.

They suggested that this could be due to a number of reasons related to the analyses, such as differences in sample selection rules, not accounting for other changes that occurred at the same time as the reforms or not accounting for general equilibrium effects changing the distribution of wages.

It has been difficult to find policy changes in Australia which could be used to test MITTS in a similar way. However, for sole parents, Cai et al. (2008) compare the effect of the Australian New Tax System introduced in July 2000 calculated by MITTS with the effect calculated using a difference-in-difference evaluation approach. The results indicate, if anything, that the simulated effects appear to be smaller than the effect of the policy change as estimated through an evaluation approach.

8.6 CONCLUSION

This chapter has made a first comparison between the implied elasticities of two sets of labour supply models: one for Australia and the other for New Zealand. Given that I no longer have access to the New Zealand microsimulation model or data, an in-depth comparison has not been possible. Nevertheless, some information from earlier research was still available and has been used to obtain an indication of the similarity of the two sets of labour supply responses.

The order of magnitude of the elasticities is broadly speaking comparable but there appear to be differences in the groups that are most responsive to financial incentives. In New Zealand, single men and women appear most responsive, whereas in Australia single parents and married/de facto women are most responsive.

More analysis would be needed to confirm whether this difference still holds when using more recent New Zealand data and when applying the same approach to approximate elasticities in both countries, such as using a 1 per cent increase in wage instead of a 10 per cent increase. In addition, if the difference holds, more in-depth analysis would be required to determine whether this is due to differences in behaviour or whether the tax and transfer system imposes more disincentives for some groups in Australia compared to New Zealand or vice versa.

NOTES

* I have used material from earlier work with Hielke Buddelmeyer, Lixin Cai, John Creedy and Rosanna Scutella in the preparation of this chapter. The work on New Zealand was commissioned by the New Zealand Treasury between 2003 and 2005. This chapter has

benefited from the comments of the paper's discussant at the 'New Zealand Tax Reform – Where to Next?' Conference, Malathi Velamuri, and other conference participants. All responsibility for this chapter lies with the author.

1. This is the predecessor of TaxWell, the current microsimulation model developed by the New Zealand Treasury.
2. Indirect tax models for Australia include the Demand and Welfare Effects Simulator (DAWES) developed in Creedy (1999).
3. On the integrability condition in labour supply models, see Stern (1986).
4. Alternatively, it is possible to use a simple rule whereby a benefit is not claimed if it is less than a specified amount.
5. TaxMod had to be adapted to enable these net income calculations at the relevant discrete hours points.
6. The rejection range is less than 4 and more than 100 dollars per hour for Australia and less than 50 per cent of the relevant minimum wage at the relevant time or greater than 100 dollars per hour for New Zealand.
7. This is not very useful in our case. The calculation of net income from gross income is based on actual persons, so, for example, 0.33 children aged between 0 and 2 could not be entered in our tax and transfer calculations. As a result, in the context of discrete choice labour supply modelling, wage elasticities for average persons cannot be derived.
8. At zero hours, the elasticity cannot be calculated.
9. See overviews by Killingsworth (1983), Killingsworth and Heckman (1986), Pencavel (1986) or more recently by Blundell and MaCurdy (1999) or Hotz and Scholz (2003).

REFERENCES

Apps, P. and E. Savage (1989), 'Labour supply, welfare rankings and the measurement of inequality', *Journal of Public Economics*, **47**, 336–64.

Banks, J., R. Blundell and A. Lewbel (1996), 'Tax reform and welfare measurement: do we need demand system estimation?', *Economic Journal*, **106**, 1227–41.

Blundell, R. and T. MaCurdy (1999), 'Labor supply: a review of alternative approaches', in O.C. Ashenfelter and D. Card (eds), *Handbook of Labor Economics, Volume 3*. Amsterdam: North-Holland, pp. 1559–695.

Blundell, R.W., C. Meghir, E. Symons and I. Walker (1986), 'A labour supply model for the simulation of tax and benefit reforms', in R.W. Blundell and I. Walker (eds), *Unemployment, Search and Labour Supply*, Cambridge: Cambridge University Press, pp. 267–293.

Blundell, R., M. Brewer, A. Duncan, H. Reed and A. Shephard (2004), *The Employment Impact of Labour Market Reforms: A Bank of England Report*, London: Institute for Fiscal Studies.

Buddelmeyer, H., J. Creedy and G. Kalb (2007), *Tax Policy Design and Behavioural Microsimulation Modelling*, Cheltenham, UK and Northampton, MA, USA: Edward Elgar.

Buddelmeyer, H., P. Dawkins, A. Duncan, G. Kalb and R. Scutella (2004a), *An analysis of the Australian Labor Party's tax and family benefits package: using the Melbourne Institute Tax and Transfer Simulator (MITTS)*, Report to the Australian Labor Party, 2004.

Buddelmeyer, H., P. Dawkins, J. Freebairn and G. Kalb (2004b), 'Bracket creep, effective marginal tax rates and alternative tax packages', *Mercer–Melbourne Institute Quarterly Bulletin of Economic Trends*, 1.04, 17–28.

Buddelmeyer, H., P. Dawkins and G. Kalb (2004), 'The Melbourne Institute

report on the 2004 Federal Budget' *Mercer–Melbourne Institute Quarterly Bulletin of Economic Trends*, 2.04, 19–23.
Cai, L., G. Kalb, Y.-P. Tseng and H. H. Vu (2008), 'The effect of financial incentives on labour supply: evidence for sole parents from microsimulation and quasi-experimental evaluation', *Fiscal Studies*, **29**, 285–325.
Callan, T. and A. Van Soest (1996), *Family labour supply and taxes in Ireland*, ESRI Working Paper No. 78, Dublin: The Economic & Social Research Institute.
Creedy, J. (1999) *Modelling Indirect Taxes and Tax Reform*, Cheltenham, UK and Lyme, USA: Edward Elgar.
Creedy, J. and A.S. Duncan (2002), 'Behavioural microsimulation with labour supply responses', *Journal of Economic Surveys*, **16**, 1–39.
Creedy, J. and G. Kalb (2005), 'Discrete hours labour supply modelling: specification, estimation and simulation', *Journal of Economic Surveys*, **19**, 697–734.
Creedy, J., G. Kalb and H. Kew (2003), 'Flattening the effective marginal tax rate structure in Australia: policy simulations using the Melbourne Institute Tax and Transfer Simulator', *Australian Economic Review*, **36**, 156–72.
Doiron, D.J. (2004), 'Welfare reform and the labour supply of lone parents in Australia: a natural experiment approach', *Economic Record*, **80**, 157–76.
Duncan, A.S. (1993), 'Labour supply decisions and non-convex budget sets: the case of National Insurance contributions in the UK', in A. Heimler and D. Meulders (eds), *Empirical Approaches to Fiscal Policy*, London: Chapman & Hall, pp. 137–62.
Duncan, A.S. and C. Giles (1996), 'Labour supply incentives and recent family credit reforms', *Economic Journal*, **106**, 142–55.
Duncan, A. and M.N. Harris (2002), 'Simulating the behavioural effects of welfare reforms among sole parents in Australia', *Economic Record*, **78**, 264–76.
Duncan, A., C. Giles and J. MacCrae (1999), *Household labour supply, childcare costs and in-work benefits: modelling the impact of the working families tax credit in the UK*, Unpublished paper, London: Institute for Fiscal Studies.
Hotz, V.J. and J.K. Scholz (2003), 'The earned income tax credit', in R. Moffitt (ed.), *Means-Tested Transfer Programs in the United States*, Chicago: The University of Chicago Press, pp. 141–97.
Kalb, G. (2002), *Estimation of labour supply models for four separate groups in the Australian population*, Melbourne Institute Working Paper No. 24/02.
Kalb, G. and R. Scutella (2002), *Estimation of wage equations in Australia: allowing for censored observations of labour supply*, Melbourne Institute Working Paper No. 8/2002.
Kalb, G. and R. Scutella (2003), *New Zealand labour supply from 1991–2001: an analysis based on a discrete choice structural utility model*, New Zealand Treasury Working Paper No. 03/23.
Kalb, G. and R. Scutella (2004), Wage and employment rates in New Zealand from 1991 to 2001, *New Zealand Economic Papers*, **38**, 21–47.
Keane, M. and R. Moffitt (1998), A structural model of multiple welfare program participation and labor supply, *International Economic Review*, 39 (3), 553–89.
Killingsworth, M.R. (1983) *Labor Supply*, New York: Cambridge University Press.
Killingsworth, M.R. and J.J. Heckman (1986), 'Female labor supply', in O.C.

Ashenfelter and R. Layard (eds), *Handbook of Labor Economics, Volume 1*, Amsterdam: North-Holland, pp. 103–204.

Klevmarken, N.A. (1997), *Modelling behavioural response in EUROMOD*, University of Cambridge Department of Applied Economics Working Paper No. 9720.

Maddala, G.S. (1983), *Limited Dependent and Qualitative Variables in Econometrics*, New York: Cambridge University Press.

Moffitt, R. (2000), 'Simulating transfer programmes and labour supply', in T. Callan (ed.), *Taxes, Transfers and Labour Market Responses: What Can Microsimulation Tell Us?*, Dublin: The Economic and Social Research Institute, pp. 1–22.

Murray, J. (1996), 'Modelling the labour supply behaviour of sole parents in Australia', in M. McAleer, P. Miller and C. Ong (eds), *Proceedings of the Econometric Society Australasian Meeting 1996, Volume 4: Microeconometrics*. Perth: Uniprint, University of Western Australia, pp. 507–46.

Pencavel, J. (1986), 'Labor supply of men', in O.C. Ashenfelter and R. Layard (eds), *Handbook of Labor Economics, Volume 1*, Amsterdam: North-Holland, pp. 3–102.

Stern, N.H. (1986), 'On the specification of labour supply functions', In R.W. Blundell and I. Walker (eds), *Unemployment, Search and Labour Supply*, Cambridge: Cambridge University Press, pp. 143–89.

Van Soest, A. (1995), 'Structural models of family labor supply: a discrete choice approach', *Journal of Human Resources*, **30**, 63–88.

9. Employment incentives for sole parents: labour market effects of changes to financial incentives and support*

Jacinta Dalgety, Richard Dorsett, Steven Johnston and Philip Spier

9.1 INTRODUCTION

The New Zealand Government has used the tax system as a vehicle for delivering family-targeted social assistance since 1986 when Family Assistance Tax Credits replaced other social assistance for families that was paid entirely through the Department of Social Welfare. Although subject to some criticism (see, for example, Kornhauser, 2009; Ventry, 2007), paying social assistance through the tax system reduces costs by using existing administrative structures, allows greater flexibility in payment schedules than traditional welfare systems and increases the take-up of income-tested entitlements (Ventry, 2007). This chapter looks at the impact of family-targeted social assistance paid through the tax system on the employment rates of sole parents, who in recent decades have had relatively low levels of engagement with the labour market.

9.2 POLICY CHANGES AFFECTING SOLE PARENTS

Sole parents are a diverse group: some have the necessary skills and are able to work while others face multiple barriers to employment. National and international evidence indicates that effective support for clients who are not work-ready includes focussing on confidence, raising skill and employability levels, specialist services that increase levels of social participation, and addressing mental health barriers (OECD, 2008; MSD, 2002).

Successful interventions for work-ready sole parents focus on providing financial incentives and reducing external barriers, for example, by improving access to quality childcare and finding jobs with family-friendly hours (OECD, 2008). New Zealand has promoted employment of sole parents though the introduction of:

- the independent family tax credit in July 1996 (later renamed the child tax credit). The independent family tax credit was payable to families who did not receive an income-tested benefit or New Zealand Superannuation payments;
- abatement rate changes, in July 1996, that encouraged sole parents receiving the Domestic Purposes Benefit (DPB) and the Widow's Benefit to work part-time; and
- work-testing requirements that meant sole parents with children over the age of 6 had to be available for and actively seeking employment (following the introduction of this measure there was an 8 per cent decline in the number of DPB recipients) and subsequent replacement of work testing with enhanced case management (following the introduction of this measure there was a 4 per cent decline in the number of DPB recipients).

More recently, in April 2006 the government replaced the child tax credit with the in-work tax credit, an employment-conditional payment for families that is paid through the tax system. In-work benefits similar to the in-work tax credit have been shown by the OECD to effectively improve work incentives. In-work benefits can be a cost-effective mechanism to 'make work pay' as they also reduce in-work poverty (OECD, 2008). In-work benefits are most effective when targeted at groups less engaged with the labour market.

Increased financial support for employment (for example, through in-work benefits) has been shown both nationally and internationally to encourage sole parents into full- or part-time work (MSD, 2002; OECD, 2008). Increased financial support works by providing a financial incentive to work, removing or reducing financial barriers (for example, the cost of childcare, transportation to work, and abatement of other financial entitlements) and reducing the risks of moving from benefit into work by providing a stable source of income. Transfers similar to the in-work tax credit in the United States and the United Kingdom have resulted in an increase in sole parents' employment rates of around five percentage points (pp).

9.2.1 Recent Policy Changes: The Working for Families Package

The in-work tax credit was introduced by the New Zealand government as one of a number of substantial changes to in-work incentives and financial support for families with dependent children. The changes were made as part of the 'Working for Families' (WFF) package, which was implemented between October 2004 and April 2007.

The objectives of the policy changes in the WFF package, as set out by Cabinet, were to (Cabinet Policy Committee, 2004):

- 'make work pay' by supporting families with dependent children so that they are rewarded for their work effort;
- ensure income adequacy with a focus on low- and middle-income families with dependent children to address issues of poverty, especially child poverty; and
- achieve a social assistance system that supports people into work, by making sure that people get the assistance they are entitled to, when they should, and with delivery that supports them into, and to remain in, employment.

Further legislation passed in November 2005 made changes which extended the package to larger numbers of recipients by raising the income threshold and lowering the rate of abatement for income in excess of the threshold.

Low- to middle-income families with dependent children were the key target group for the policy changes (see Appendix). The policy changes impacted several components that were designed to work together (Cabinet Policy Committee, 2004):

- increases in family tax credit rates;
- introduction of the in-work tax credit;
- changes to the abatement regime of WFF Tax Credits (a group of tax credits targeted at families with dependent children including family tax credit, in-work tax credit, parental tax credit and minimum family tax credit);
- increased Childcare Assistance for those eligible;
- an increase in Accommodation Supplement thresholds and rates;
- changes to the Invalid's Benefit to encourage work trials;
- replacement of the Special Benefit with Temporary Additional Support, which is targeted at beneficiaries with higher financial costs; and
- consequential changes to other social assistance.

These changes to financial incentives and support for work were designed to work together to meet the aim to 'make work pay' for all families. The policy changes increased the number of families eligible for the Accommodation Supplement and Childcare Assistance and increased the levels of payments. These changes removed some of the financial barriers to families moving into work. The introduction of the in-work tax credit provided a specific mechanism to increase the financial benefits of employment.

The Ministry of Social Development (MSD) and Inland Revenue (IR) jointly implemented these changes.

9.3 RECENT TRENDS IN SOLE PARENTS' EMPLOYMENT AND BENEFIT RECEIPT

Prior to the policy changes, many low income families were little or no better off in low-paid employment once work-related costs, benefit abatement, other entitlement abatements (for example the Accommodation Supplement, Family Assistance and Childcare Assistance) and tax were taken into account. In particular, those with low earnings potential who needed to use paid childcare were generally worse off in paid work than on benefit. Qualitative interviews with sole parents consistently found that a lack of financial incentives to take up paid work kept some sole parents on benefit (Levine et al., 1993; MSD, 2002).

The extent to which the objective to 'make work pay' has been met for sole parents was assessed by examining changes in two indicators: employment rates and patterns of benefit receipt. If the changes to financial incentives and support for working helped to 'make work pay' for sole parents then their employment rate would be expected to increase. As sole parents can be employed while receiving a benefit, this would not necessarily be reflected in a change in benefit receipt rates. In view of this, this chapter also looks at patterns of benefit receipt explicitly to see if any changes occurred. Examining both employment rates and time spent on benefit gives a more comprehensive picture of the impact of the policy changes in meeting the 'make work pay' objective.

9.3.1 Changes in Sole Parent Employment Rates

Employment rates of sole parents were expected to increase as the in-work tax credit and increases in family tax credit rates removed some of the financial barriers to employment cited by sole parents. Prior to the introduction of WFF the Treasury commissioned an estimate of the expected labour market impact of the WFF package. Buddelmeyer et al. (2007) used

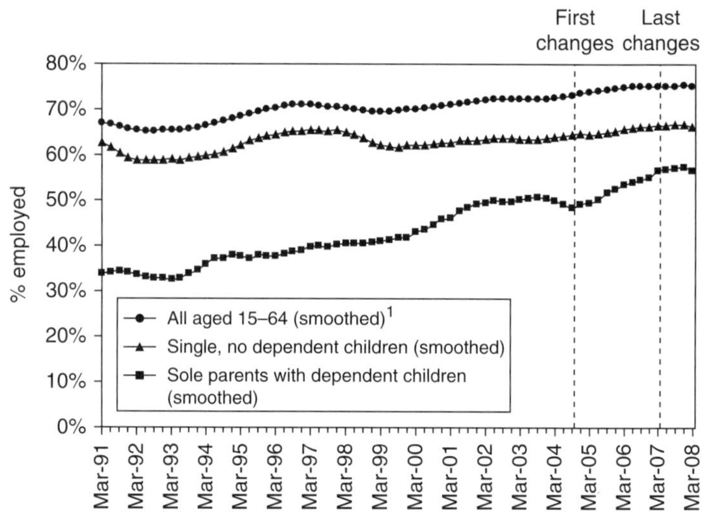

Note: [1] Smoothed by taking the average of the current and previous three quarters.

Source: Statistics New Zealand: Household Labour Force Survey, customised tables for population aged 15–64, annual average rates calculated by MSD.

Figure 9.1 Percentage of sole parents in employment compared to singles and all working-age adults

a micro-simulation analysis to model the labour supply response to the incentives brought about by the WFF package. The largest effects on labour supply were expected for sole parents, with their employment rate expected to rise from 45.7 per cent prior to the introduction of the WFF package to 47.5 per cent after the introduction of WFF – a change of 1.8 pp. Although it was expected that some sole parents already in employment would reduce their hours, the average hours worked by sole parents was expected to increase.

The observed change in employment rates for sole parents was much higher than was estimated by Buddelmeyer et al. (2007). The employment rate of sole parents aged 18–64 increased by 10 pp, from 48.3 per cent in the quarter ending June quarter 2004 to 57.7 per cent in the quarter ending June 2007. Furthermore, Figure 9.1 shows that sole parents' employment rate grew faster than that for all the working-age population.[1]

9.3.2 Changes in Benefit Numbers

The number of sole parents in receipt of a benefit was expected to decrease with the introduction of the policy changes. In-work tax credit provides

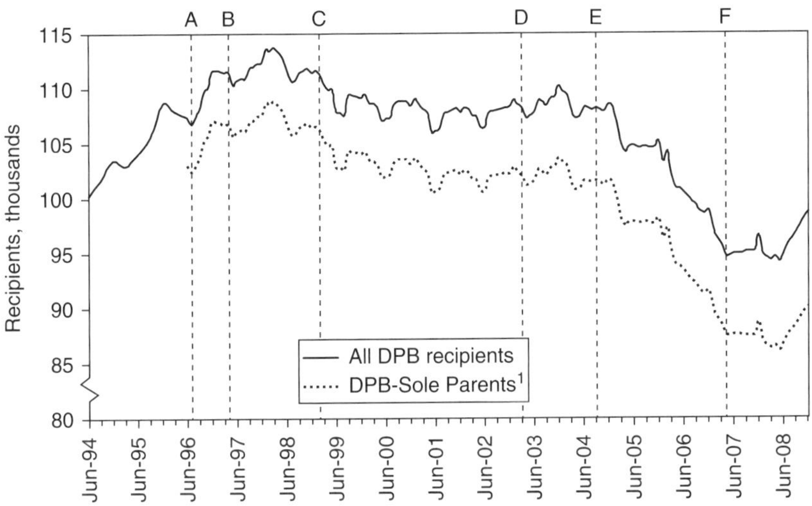

A = Dual abatement introduced (different abatement rates for work tested and non-work tested benefits)
B = Part-time work-or-training test for parents whose oldest child is aged 14 or over
C = Full-time (youngest child aged 14+) part-time (youngest child aged 6–13) work-tests introduced
D = Enhanced case management introduced. Work tests removed
E = First WFF changes
F = Changes to WFF Tax Credits abatements and thresholds and introduction of in-work tax credit

Note: [1] Numbers of DPB-Sole Parent recipients are not available prior to June 1996.

Source: MSD Information Analysis Platform.

Figure 9.2 Domestic Purposes Benefit recipients: all types 1994–2008

an incentive for those who receive a benefit and are also working to leave benefit altogether. Sole parents who work at least 20 hours a week are eligible for in-work tax credit and, in some cases, minimum family tax credit. For example, in April 2008, the weekly family income for a sole parent with two children under the age of 12, where the sole parent is working 20 hours a week for minimum wage, would be $22 greater if the family moved off benefit entirely and received in-work tax credit and minimum family tax credit rather than continue to receive an abated benefit.

Changes in the number of sole parents in receipt of a main benefit are reflected in trends in DPB recipients, most of whom are sole parents.[2] Figure 9.2 shows the changes in numbers of DPB recipients overall and the changes in the number of recipients of DPB-Sole Parent and indicates some of the other key policy changes affecting sole parent families. The changes to WFF Tax Credits, Accommodation Supplement and Childcare Assistance followed more than a decade of reforms aimed at promoting employment among sole parents.

Numbers of sole parents receiving the DPB were fairly stable from 1999 to March 2005. Since then New Zealand has experienced the largest fall in the number of people receiving the DPB since this benefit was introduced in 1973. Numbers of all DPB recipients fell from 107 900 at the end of March 2004 (just prior to the introduction of the first changes to the Accommodation Supplement and Childcare Assistance) to 94 300 at the end of March 2008, a reduction of 13 500 (12 per cent). Despite an increase in the numbers of DPB recipients in the latter part of 2008, numbers are still well below the levels seen in the early 2000s. There were 98 700 DPB recipients at the end of December 2008.

9.4 ECONOMIC CONTEXT

The policy changes were introduced during a period of economic buoyancy. Growth in Gross Domestic Product (GDP) (Statistics New Zealand, 2008a), low unemployment rates (Statistics New Zealand, 2008b) and increased demand for low-skilled workers (New Zealand Institute of Economic Research, 2007) all characterised the period over which the policy changes were implemented. The strong economy and tight labour market are likely to have contributed to the changes in sole parents' benefit receipt patterns and employment. This chapter looks at the extent to which the changes in employment rates and benefit receipt patterns were due to the policy changes over and above the favourable economic and labour market conditions of the time.

9.5 METHODS

The choice of methods to carry out this analysis was preceded by a review of impact methodology by the Policy Studies Institute, United Kingdom (Bryson et al., 2006). The Policy Studies Institute also provided specific guidance on the use of methods. The methods needed to be appropriate to evaluate a programme where most of the eligible families were participating and to control for the strong economic conditions of the time. The two methods chosen were selected because of the data available and their complementary strengths. Each method is described below.

9.5.1 Difference-in-Differences of Employment Rates

The difference-in-differences estimator

Difference-in-differences is a standard non-experimental evaluation approach (Blundell and Costa Dias, 2000). For a policy targeted to a group of interest (the treatment group), it compares the change in an outcome over time for that group with the corresponding change for a group for which the policy should have no effect (the comparison group). The intuition behind difference-in-differences is that, in the absence of the policy, the outcomes for the treatment and comparison groups would have changed in a similar way over time. A difference in the relationship between the treatment and comparison groups following the introduction of the policy can, under certain assumptions, be viewed as an estimate of the impact of the policy on the outcome in question.

To evaluate the impact of the changes to financial incentives and support for working the treatment group was defined as sole parent families with dependent children and the comparison group as single adults without dependent children. The trends of these two groups were used to look at how working-age sole parents' employment changed over the implementation period compared to that of single adults without children. This method was applied to Household Labour Force Survey (HLFS) data over the period June 2004 to June 2007. Outcomes (for example, employment rates and hours of work) from June 2005, June 2006 and June 2007 were compared to June 2004 enabling conclusions to be drawn about the impact of the policy changes that were made between June 2004 and each of these dates. For example for 2007 employment rates the difference-in-differences estimator would be calculated as:

$$DiD = (p_{\text{sole parents, 2007}} - p_{\text{sole parents, 2004}}) - (p_{\text{single adults without children, 2007}} - p_{\text{single adults without children, 2004}}) \quad (9.1)$$

where p is the percentage employed.

The difference-in-differences estimates were calculated using a linear regression model which included other characteristics observed in the HLFS. The estimates controlled for age, highest qualification, ethnicity, region and regional unemployment rate.

The assumptions behind difference-in-differences

Two conditions must be satisfied for the difference-in-differences estimate to have a valid causal interpretation. First, the outcomes of the comparison group should, in the absence of the policy changes, have similar trends to the

Table 9.1 Pre-programme tests comparing changes in employment and hours worked for sole parents with single adults without children (2003–04)

	Employed	Working more than 20 hours
Difference-in-differences estimate (pp)	−4.9*	−5.9*
p-value	0.024	0.007
Sample size	14311	14311

Note: * Statistically significant (at $p < 0.05$) difference-in-differences estimates.

Source: Calculations based on unpublished Household Labour Force Survey data, June quarters.

outcomes of the treatment group. Although it is not possible to observe the extent to which this holds over the period of interest, using data from further back in time means it is possible to explore the extent to which the relationship has held in the past. If the result of a pre-programme test indicates that the relationship has held in the past, this provides reason to believe that, in the absence of the policy, it would also hold in the period of interest.

The 2003 and 2004 HLFS data (which predate the first policy changes) were used to test the stability of the relationship between the treatment and comparison groups before the policy intervention. The pre-programme tests show statistically significant results between 2003 and 2004 (Table 9.1). The estimates are negative because the employment rate and percentage of sole parents working 20 hours or more decreased between 2003 and 2004, whilst for single adults without children these outcomes increased. Although the tests show statistically significant differences, the difference-in-differences method is still of use as during the implementation of the policy changes the sole parents employment rate and the percentage of sole parents working 20 hours a week increased at a faster rate than those of single adults without children (see section 9.6 for further discussion). Consequently, the results of the difference-in-differences analysis are likely, if anything, to be underestimates.

The second condition required for difference-in-differences estimates to be viewed as causal is that the composition of the treatment and comparison groups does not change systematically over time. In the context of these policy changes this means assuming that the policy changes had no effect on fertility and partnering. Although fertility rates have increased in New Zealand in recent years, the rate that single people have their first child has remained relatively static over the implementation period.

9.5.2 Survival Analysis of Time in Receipt of a Benefit

Survival (or duration) analysis is a standard approach used to model the time taken for an event of interest to occur. The central concept in survival analysis is the hazard rate, which is the probability of an event occurring at a particular time given that it has not already occurred. If the hazard rate declines as the length of time in the initial state grows, events are negatively duration dependent. Such duration-dependence is common in labour market processes. For example, benefit exits are often concentrated towards the start of a period of benefit receipt and the longer an individual remains on benefit, the less likely an exit becomes.

Survival analysis was used to evaluate the impact of the policy changes by looking at sole parents in receipt of the DPB-Sole Parent and examining the rate at which they leave benefit entirely (moving from the DPB to another benefit is not regarded as an exit). For those who leave benefits, the rate at which they return to benefit was also examined.

Data used for survival analysis

The survival analysis used a 25 per cent random sample of DPB-Sole Parent recipients from a database containing linked MSD and IR administration information for all families who have received payment of a WFF component, or who have taken part in a WFF evaluation survey, covering most sole parents. Data is held from April 2003 onwards, and the dataset is updated twice a year. Preliminary data for each tax year is available around six months after the end of the tax year and more final data is generally available one year after the end of the tax year. The data used was from the August 2008 update, and included all monthly data from April 2003 to March 2007. For this analysis, benefit receipt in any given month was defined for an individual as 'receiving any income from a benefit during that month'. For sole parents who were in receipt of the DPB-Sole Parent in April 2003 the start date for that period of benefit receipt was also included.

The hazard model

The model is an example of discrete-time survival analysis. It allows the hazard rate to vary with:

- the length of the individual's current period of benefit receipt (the 'baseline hazard');
- individual characteristics;
- the strength of the economy; and
- the stages of the roll-out of the policy changes.

The mathematical form of the model sets the logit of the hazard rate equal to a linear combination of variables representing these explanatory factors. The sets of variables are considered in more detail below.

Baseline hazard

The model allows the hazard rate to change over the length of a period of benefit receipt. To capture the overall pattern of exits in a flexible way, the specification of the baseline hazard avoided restrictive functional form assumptions and instead used a semi-parametric approach whereby the hazard:

- could vary by month over the first quarter of the period of benefit receipt;
- could vary by quarter for the remainder of the first year;
- was constant over the second year;
- was constant at a different rate over years 3 to 5; and
- was constant at a different rate after 5 years.

Individual characteristics

The individual characteristics in the model included age, gender, ethnicity, age of becoming a parent and highest qualification. The model also allows the hazard rate to alter in response to circumstances that changed in the course of a period of benefit receipt. For example, variables were included to capture the effect of being partnered, the effect of having dependent children and the age of the youngest child. This is important as family composition plays an important role in labour supply decisions, for example, those with pre-school-aged children may be less able to consider working. Also, eligibility for DPB-Sole Parent is dependent on an individual having no partner and having dependent children. Consequently, changes to family composition can change eligibility leading to benefit exit.

Controlling for the economy

Real, production-based, seasonally-adjusted GDP was included to control for conditions in the broader economy that might influence benefit receipt.

Capturing the effects of the policy changes

The model allows the hazard rate to change after the implementation of a set of the policy changes. A dummy variable for the period October 2004 to March 2005 captures the effect of the first stage of implementation. A dummy variable indicating the months between April 2005 and September 2005 captures the combined effect of the October 2004 and April 2005 changes. Similarly, the variable indicating the months from April 2006 onwards captures the combined effects of all the policy changes. It is this last variable that captures the key impact of interest (that is, the effect of all the initiatives combined).

Multiple periods of benefit receipt

The benefit history of sole parents can involve multiple periods of benefit receipt as the sole parent moves into employment and off benefit and then back onto benefit receipt. Research published in 1999 showed that 51 per cent of DPB recipients who left benefit due to employment were again in receipt of a main benefit two and a half years later (Wilson, 1999). The hazard model was estimated using all benefit spells of all the individuals. Treating multiple periods as independent may result in biased estimates. To address this, estimation was carried out using the generalised estimating equations (GEE) approach of Liang and Zeger (1986) which allows for exits to be correlated across multiple periods for the same individual.[3]

Benefit re-entry rates

As with changes in the exit rate, survival analysis was used to model how long a DPB-Sole Parent recipient is expected to remain off benefit after they stop a spell of benefit receipt.

9.5.3 Why Two Methods?

The difference-in-differences and survival analysis results capture two different aspects of the impact of the policy changes. The difference-in-differences analysis provides an estimate of the employment impact for all sole parents, whether they received DPB-Sole Parent or not. The survival analysis considers a specific group of sole parents – those receiving DPB-Sole Parent – and looks at the factors influencing changes in their rate of benefit exit and re-entry.

As the survival analysis is based on those in receipt of the DPB, it cannot capture the effect of the policy changes on sole parents not in receipt of the DPB. It is possible that the policy changes may have affected whether sole parents take up benefit. The impact on take up of benefits could be captured in the difference-in-differences analysis but not the survival analysis. However, survival analysis is useful as benefit receipt is not recorded as reliably in the HLFS data (used for the difference-in-differences analysis) as it is in the administrative data used for the survival analysis. Consequently, there is a practical reason for preferring the survival analysis when looking at impacts of the policy changes on benefit receipt. Also, the difference-in-differences analysis only provides an estimate of the overall impact of the

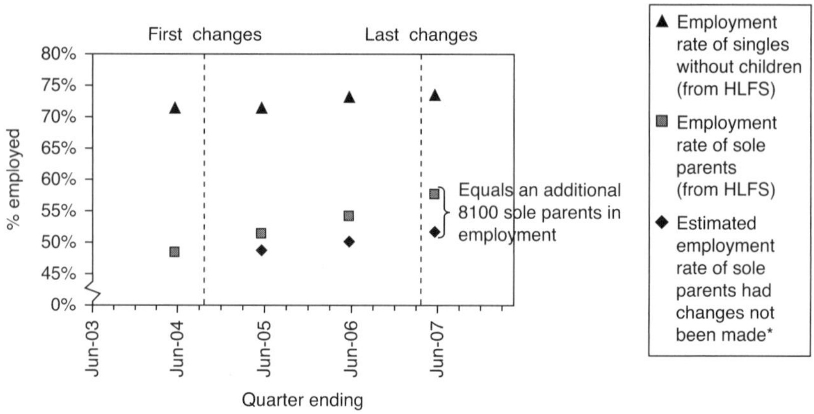

Note: * Calculated as employment rate less difference-in-differences estimate. The estimated employment rates have confidence intervals of ± 4 pp. The only statistically significant effect is that seen in the June 2007 quarter when all the policy changes were implemented.

Source: Calculations based on unpublished Household Labour Force Survey data, June quarters.

Figure 9.3 Percentage of adults aged 18–64 who are working at least one hour a week

policy changes and does not provide insight into how these impacts arose. By considering the impact on benefit exit and benefit re-entry, the survival analysis provides information on the process behind the impacts.

Both methods have their respective strengths and considering them together leads to a greater understanding of the effect of the policy changes.

9.6 RESULTS

9.6.1 Changes in Sole Parents' Paid Employment

Around two-thirds of the increase in sole parents' employment rate is estimated to be due to the changes in financial incentives and support for working (Figure 9.3). This is equivalent to an estimated 8100 additional sole parents in some paid employment.

Over the period of implementation, the employment rate of sole parents aged 18–64 increased from 48.3 per cent in the June quarter of 2004 to 57.7 per cent in the same quarter in 2007, an increase of 9.4 pp. Difference-

Table 9.2 Estimates of the impact of the policy changes on employment for sole parents

	Comparison with 2004		
	2005	2006	2007
Actual change since 2004 (pp)	3.1	5.8	9.4
Impact estimate (pp)	2.6	3.9	6.0*
p-value	0.250	0.097	0.007
Sample size	13 197	12 734	13 629

Note: * Statistically significant (at $p < 0.05$) difference-in-differences estimates.

Source: Calculations based on unpublished Household Labour Force Survey data, June quarters.

in-differences analysis (Table 9.2), estimates that 6.0 pp (± 4.4 pp) of the increase is due to the policy changes. The remaining one-third of this growth would have been seen regardless of the policy changes, capturing the strength of the economy and other employment or policy initiatives.

Although the effect of the policy changes increased throughout the implementation period, the only effect that was statistically significant was the comparison between the June quarters of 2004 and 2007, after the policy changes were fully implemented and the in-work tax credit was introduced. The impacts on changes in employment rates were larger than those anticipated by Buddelmeyer et al. (2007).

Changing hours of work

The growth in employment discussed in the previous section was driven by increased numbers of sole parents working 20 hours or more. Sole parents who work more than 20 hours a week and who are not in receipt of a benefit are eligible for the in-work tax credit.

The percentage of sole parents meeting the eligibility threshold for the in-work tax credit requirement increased from 35.9 per cent in June 2004 to 47.5 per cent in June 2007, an increase of 11.6 pp. Difference-in-differences analysis suggests that around three-quarters (9.2 pp ± 4.5 pp) of this increase was due to the policy changes (Figure 9.4, Table 9.3).

9.6.2 Changes in Benefit Exit and Re-Entry Rates

Survival analysis shows that the policy changes have increased the rate of DPB-Sole Parent recipients' exit from benefit. Estimates of the key survival analysis parameters are presented in Table 9.4. This suggests that

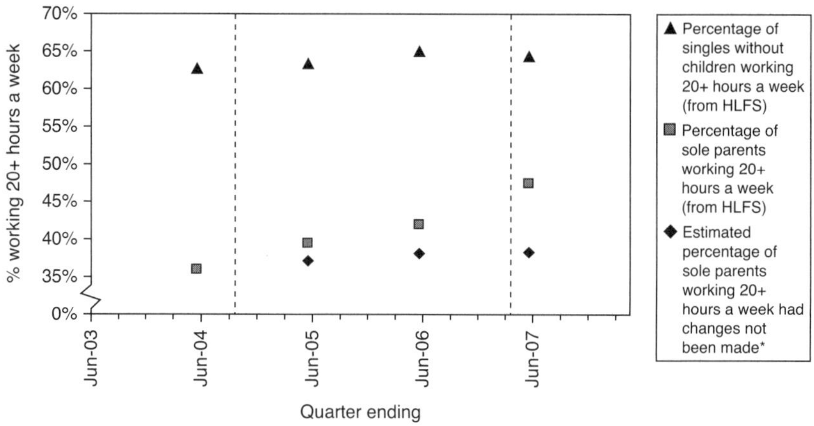

Note: * Calculated as percentage working 20+ hours a week rate less difference-in-differences estimate. The estimated employment rates have confidence intervals of ± 5 pp. The only statistically significant effect is that seen in the June 2007 quarter when all the policy changes were implemented.

Source: Calculations based on unpublished Household Labour Force Survey data, June quarters.

Figure 9.4 Percentage of adults aged 18–64 who are working at least 20 hours a week

Table 9.3 Estimates of the impact of the policy changes on percentage of sole parents working 20 or more hours

	Comparison with 2004		
	2005	2006	2007
Impact estimate (pp)	2.3	3.9	9.2*
p-value	0.304	0.100	0.000
Sample size	13197	12734	13629

Note: * Statistically significant (at $p < 0.05$) difference-in-differences estimates.

Source: Calculations based on unpublished Household Labour Force Survey data, June quarters.

when all the changes are included (April 2006–March 2007) that a significant impact on the hazard rate is found. Table 9.4 also illustrates the significant effect of the economy on benefit exit. Specifically, the rate of exit is higher when the economy is stronger. The effects of the April 2006 policy

Table 9.4 Policy changes and GDP parameter estimates for exits from benefit, sole parents

	Exits from Benefit (n = 44479)	
	Estimate[1]	p-value
Oct 2004–Mar 2005	0.017	0.479
Apr 2005–Sep 2005	0.013	0.684
Oct 2005–Mar 2006	0.013	0.687
Apr 2006–Mar 2007	0.089*	0.013
Real production GDP	0.068*	0.001

Notes:
* Statistically significant (at $p < 0.05$) parameters.
[1] Positive coefficients for benefit exits imply the variable in question is increasing the likelihood of an exit from benefits, with negative coefficients implying a reduction in the likelihood of an exit.

Source: MSD IRD linked Dataset as at August 2008.

changes (including the introduction of the in-work tax credit) remain even after controlling for broad macroeconomic factors.

Using the results presented in Table 9.4, Figure 9.5 plots two survival curves showing how long a sole parent would be expected to remain on benefit. The 'with policy changes' curve corresponds to the situation in which all the policy changes are in place, the 'had policy changes not been implemented' curve corresponds to a hypothetical case where the policy changes have not been introduced. The effect of the policy changes is represented by the difference between the two lines, showing that the effect of the policy changes is to speed up the benefit exit.

Changes in benefit re-entry rates

The policy changes have also decreased the rate of re-entry to benefit for ex-DPB-Sole Parent recipients. Estimates of the key survival analysis parameters are presented in Table 9.5. As with benefit exit rates, the re-entry model shows that it is only when all the changes are considered, including the April 2006 changes, that a significant impact on the hazard rate is seen. Unlike benefit exit rates, GDP was not found to be statistically significant in the re-entry model, although the parameter for GDP had the expected sign, consistent with benefit re-entry being slower when the economy was strong.

The survival curves of the re-entry model show how long a sole parent would be expected to remain off benefit (Figure 9.6). The effect of the policy changes is represented by the difference between the two lines,

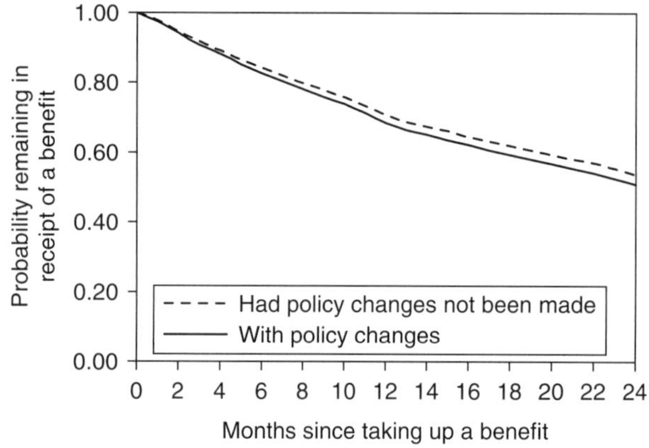

Note: [1] Calculated using a hypothetical DPB-Sole Parent with the average characteristics of the population. Using average characteristics enables conclusions to be drawn about the population of DPB-Sole Parent recipients.

Source: MSD IRD linked Dataset as at August 2008.

Figure 9.5 Probability of a DPB-Sole Parent recipient remaining in receipt of a benefit, by number of months since starting a period of benefit receipt[1]

Table 9.5 Policy changes and GDP parameter estimates for re-entries to a main benefit, sole parents

	Re-entries to benefit (n = 23 803)	
	Estimate[1]	p-value
October 2004–March 2005	−0.033	0.386
April 2005–September 2005	−0.058	0.260
October 2005–March 2006	−0.076	0.161
April 2006–March 2007	−0.191*	0.003
Real production GDP	−0.049	0.114

Notes:
* Statistically significant (at $p < 0.05$) parameters.
[1] Negative coefficients for benefit re-entries imply the variable in question is decreasing the likelihood of re-entering a benefit, with positive coefficients implying an increase in the likelihood of a re-entry.

Source: MSD IRD linked Dataset as at August 2008.

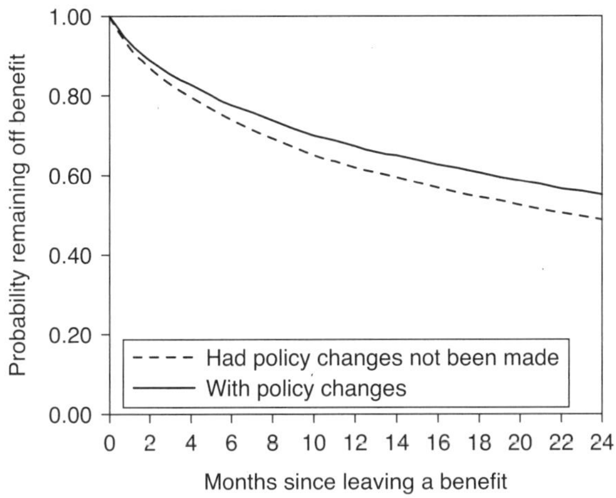

Note: [1] Modelled using a hypothetical DPB-Sole Parent with the average characteristics of the population. Modelling using average characteristics enables conclusions to be drawn about all DPB-Sole Parent recipients.

Source: MSD IRD linked Dataset as at August 2008.

Figure 9.6 Probability of a hypothetical[1] ex-DPB-Sole Parent recipient remaining off benefit, by number of months since ending a spell of benefit receipt

showing that the policy changes have slowed benefit re-entry for sole parents.

9.7 DISCUSSION

The analysis of the impact of the changes in financial incentives and support for work, including subsidised childcare, has found that the policy changes have impacted thousands of sole parents. In June 2007 there were an estimated additional 8100 sole parents engaged in some paid employment as a result of the policy changes.

The policy changes also increased the numbers of sole parents working 20 hours or more per week and therefore meeting the in-work tax credit requirement. Over the period of the implementation of the policy changes the numbers of DPB recipients fell by 12 per cent from March 2004 to March 2008. As a result of the changes sole parents' periods of benefit receipt are shorter and sole parents previously on benefit are staying off benefit for longer.

It is only after the policy changes were fully implemented and the in-work tax credit was introduced that statistically significant results were seen in both the difference-in-differences and survival analyses.

9.7.1 Remaining Barriers

Although the changes in financial incentives and support for work made from 2004 to 2007 have contributed to the achievement of the objective to 'make work pay' for sole parents during the period of implementation, barriers to work still remain for some. A survey completed in September 2007 of low- and middle-income families shows that two out of five sole parents who are not employed consider themselves available for work. For these sole parents the largest barrier they identified was 'finding a job that suits you' (77 per cent). For those who are not available to work, 'preferring to look after my children myself rather than use childcare' (76 per cent) is the primary reason they are not working, followed by 'finding a job that suits you' (65 per cent). For both groups the next most important barriers are 'getting work that paid enough', 'getting enough hours for the job to be worthwhile' and 'having the skills employers want'.

9.7.2 Relevance to Current Economic Situation

The WFF policy changes were implemented during a period of economic growth. Since these changes were made New Zealand has entered into an economic downturn. As a result numbers of DPB recipients have risen to 98 700 in December 2008. Depending on the nature and extent of the recession numbers of DPB recipients may continue to increase.

The findings from this research indicate that financial incentives are effective, over and above a buoyant economy, in supporting sole parents to work. Despite the more difficult economic environment, the findings continue to be relevant as they show that financial incentives will support sole parents, who are able to obtain work, into employment. This research adds to the New Zealand knowledge base about the measures that are effective in encouraging and facilitating labour market attachment for sole parents.

NOTES

* Thanks to Valmai Copeland, Stuart Turner (both at Inland Revenue), Debra Taylor, Denise Stephens, Helen Stott, Debbie McLeod and Moira Wilson (at Ministry of Social Development).

1. Employment rates from HLFS data are typically reported for all adults aged 15+. The analysis carried out in this chapter uses a working age definition of 18–64, which is consistent with the definition applied to beneficiary numbers. Figure 9.1 is based on a customised timeseries of HLFS data, supplied by Statistics New Zealand, which used a different working age definition of 15–64.
2. The different types of Domestic Purposes Benefit payable are: DPB-Sole Parent, DPB-Women Alone, and DPB-Care of Sick or Infirm. Some recipients of the Care of Sick or Infirm DPB benefit are sole parents. Recipients of the Women Alone DPB benefit do not have dependent children. Some sole parents receive other main benefits but the numbers of these are small.
3. Estimation was carried out in SAS using PROC GENMOD.

REFERENCES

Blundell, R. and M. Costa Dias (2000), 'Evaluation methods for non-experimental data', *Fiscal Studies*, **21**(4), 427–68.

Bryson, A., M. Evans, G. Knight, I. La Valle and S. Vegeris (2006), *Methodological Considerations for Evaluating MSD Programmes*, Wellington: Ministry of Social Development.

Buddelmeyer, H., J. Creedy and G. Kalb (2007), *Tax Policy Design and Behavioural Microsimulation Modelling*, Cheltenham, UK and Northampton, MA, USA: Edward Elgar.

Cabinet Policy Committee (2004), *Reform of Social Assistance: Working for Families package*, Office of the Minister of Finance and Revenue and Office of the Minister for Social Development and Employment, available at: http://www.msd.govt.nz/documents/about-msd-and-our-work/work-programmes/policy-development/working for families/rep-04-3-229.pdf, accessed on 1 December 2008.

Kornhauser, M.E. (2009), 'Cognitive theory and the delivery of welfare benefits', *Loyola University Chicago Law Journal*, **40**, 254–96.

Levine, M., H. Wyn and L. Asiasiga (1993), *Lone Parents and Paid Work: A Study of Employment Patterns and Barriers, and Options for Change*, Wellington: Department of Social Welfare and Department of Labour.

Liang, K. and S. Zeger (1986), 'Longitudinal data analysis using generalized linear models', *Biometrika*, **73**, 13–22.

Ministry of Social Development (MSD) (2002), *Evaluating the February 1999 Domestic Purposes Benefit and Widows Benefit Reforms: Summary of Key Findings*, Wellington: Department of Labour and Ministry of Social Development, http://www.msd.govt.nz/publications/2002.html, accessed on 18 February 2009.

New Zealand Institute of Economic Research (2007), *Quarterly Survey of Business Opinion*, June.

Organisation for Economic Cooperation and Development (OECD) (2008), *In-Work Benefits and Making Work Pay in OECD Countries: An Update*, Paris: OECD. Reference No.: DELSE/ELSA/WP1(2008).

Statistics New Zealand (2008a), www.stats.govt.nz/products-and-services/hot-off-the-press/gross-domestic-product/gross-domestic-product-marc08qtr-hotp.htm (Table 6.2 – as published 27 June 2008), accessed on 3 December 2008.

Statistics New Zealand (2008b), www.stats.govt.nz/products-and-services/

hot-off-the-press/household-labour-force-survey/household-labour-force-survey-jun08qtr-hotp.htm, accessed on 3 December 2008.
Ventry, Jr. D.J. (2007), 'Welfare by any other name: tax transfers and the EITC', *American University Law Review*, **56**(5), 1261–280.
Wilson, M. (1999), 'The duration of benefit receipt: new findings from the benefit dynamics data set', *Social Policy Journal of New Zealand*, **13**, http://www.msd.govt.nz/about-msd-and-our-work/publications-resources/journals-and-magazines/social-policy-journal/spj13/duration-of-benefit-recept.html, accessed on 1 December 2008.

APPENDIX 9A: TIMETABLE OF MAJOR CHANGES TO FINANCIAL INCENTIVES AND SUPPORT FOR WORKING*

Oct 2004	**Accommodation Supplement and Childcare Assistance – reduced abatements and increased rates**
Purpose	*Reducing Accommodation Supplement abatements enabled families moving off a benefit to continue to receive support for their housing costs and increased the number of eligible non-beneficiary families. Those earning while in receipt of a benefit no longer had Accommodation Supplement abated.* *Childcare Assistance changes increased the rates by 10 per cent, brought Out-of-School Care rates in line with support for younger children and increased the number of eligible non-beneficiary families.*
April 2005	Family tax credit increased by $25 per week for the first child and $15 per week for additional children **Child component of main benefits moved into family tax credit** Accommodation Supplement areas increased from three to four, and maximum rates increased Family tax credit began to be treated as income for the Special Benefit
Purpose	*Family tax credit changes increased the amount of money families were receiving and increased the number of non-beneficiary families eligible for support.* *Moving the child components of the main benefit aimed to simplify the benefit system. It meant that the net increase in family tax credit for beneficiary families was less than that for working families.* *The new Accommodation Supplement areas acknowledged that there were areas with much higher housing costs than the rest of the country, particularly in Auckland.* *Increased maximum rates of Accommodation Supplement provided more assistance for people with high costs.*
Oct 2005	**Childcare Assistance rates were increased by another 10 per cent**
Purpose	*Increased payments for childcare reduced financial barriers to working.*
April 2006	**In-work tax credit replaced the child tax credit, paying a maximum of $60 per week for eligible working families with up to three children and a maximum of $15 per week for each additional child** **Thresholds raised and abatements standardised to 20 per cent for WFF Tax Credits** Temporary Additional Support introduced to replace the Special Benefit **Minimum family tax credit amount increased**

APPENDIX 9A (continued)

Purpose	*The focus of these later changes was on making work pay with the introduction of the in-work tax credit providing an incentive for families to enter into or remain in work.* *More non-beneficiary families became eligible for WFF Tax Credits and received more money due to both in-work tax credit and changes to abatements.*
April 2007	Family tax credit rates increased by $10 per child per week **Minimum family tax credit increased**
Purpose	*Family tax credit payments increased for both beneficiary and non-beneficiary families.*
Oct 2008	Family tax credit rates and income abatement threshold increased to take account of inflation

Note: * Highlighted changes were specifically designed to contribute to the goal of making work pay.

PART IV

Taxing environmental externalities

10. Carbon taxes vs tradable permits: efficiency and equity effects for a small open economy

John Freebairn

10.1 INTRODUCTION

Economists and some governments, including New Zealand, have debated the relative merits of a tax or a system of tradable permits as a market-based and cost-effective policy intervention to reduce pollution.[1] Actual examples include the pollution of the atmosphere, waterways and the landscape, with greenhouse gases being a key contemporary policy topic. Greenhouse gas emissions associated with the combustion of fossil fuels, deforestation, agriculture and other industrial processes (but with scant attention to human breathing and population growth) are a form of global atmospheric pollution with a high probability of external costs of climate change in the future. In principle, a tax set at the marginal external cost, or a tradable permit with the quota set at the quantity equating marginal social benefits and costs, would result in a net gain in economic efficiency. In response to meeting its target under the 1998 Kyoto Protocol agreement to reduce greenhouse gas emissions, the New Zealand Government initially focused on a carbon tax, then in 2005 switched to a tradable permit scheme, and in 2009 proposes to review the options. Meanwhile, 27 European Union countries have introduced a tradable permit scheme, and Australia proposes to introduce a carbon tax in mid-2011 and then a tradable permit scheme from mid-2012. A global agreement with all the large polluters participating seems some time away. This chapter compares and contrasts the operation and economic effects of a carbon or emissions tax versus a tradable permit scheme to reduce greenhouse gas emissions. In particular, it focuses on the context of a small open trading economy, such as Australia or New Zealand, and on circumstances where these countries implement policy to reduce pollution before other countries with whom they trade join a global greenhouse reduction policy programme.

The rest of the chapter is organised as follows. Section 10.2 sketches the context of the greenhouse gas externality market failure problem, and it describes the carbon tax and tradable permit as correction policy intervention options. Section 10.3 considers the economic incidence and distributional effects, and the efficiency effects, of the two policy interventions. With New Zealand in mind, the section considers the particular cases of petroleum products, electricity products, agriculture, and the second round effects on other industries using electricity and petroleum products as intermediate inputs. Some of the challenges of developing a cooperative policy strategy among most of the world's governments, and the relative properties of the tax and tradable permit options in meeting these challenges, are addressed in section 10.4. On the assumption that Australia and/or New Zealand implement either a tradable permit or a carbon tax scheme to reduce greenhouse gas emissions before many of the key countries from whom it imports or to whom it exports, Section 10.5 investigates the arguments for assistance to the so called trade-exposed energy-intensive industries (TEEI) and the way assistance could be provided. A final section concludes.

10.2 POLICY PROBLEM AND INTERVENTION OPTIONS

This chapter proceeds on a number of assumptions. First, on available scientific evidence there is a high probability that the production of greenhouses gases, including carbon dioxide and methane, as a by-product of many production processes for products we value in consumption are adding to the global stock of greenhouse gas emissions (see, for example, IPCC, 2007). Second, further increases in this global stock of emissions will cause over the coming decades and centuries significant changes in climate, such as warming, changes in rainfall patterns, and more frequent and adverse extreme weather events. Third, the climate changes will bring much higher costs in the future for adaptation of, for example, agriculture, water supply, integrity of infrastructure, loss of biodiversity and population relocation relative to the costs of reducing emissions (see, for example, Stern, 2006; Garnaut, 2008). As is the case with most issues in science and economics there is uncertainty and contested arguments and evidence in the area of climate change. At a minimum, some investment in reducing greenhouse gas emissions is seen as a prudent form of insurance.

From an economic perspective, greenhouse gas emissions are a form of global externality with a very long life. No one owns the atmosphere, and under the current market system it is treated as a public good with the characteristics of non-rival consumption and no enforceable property

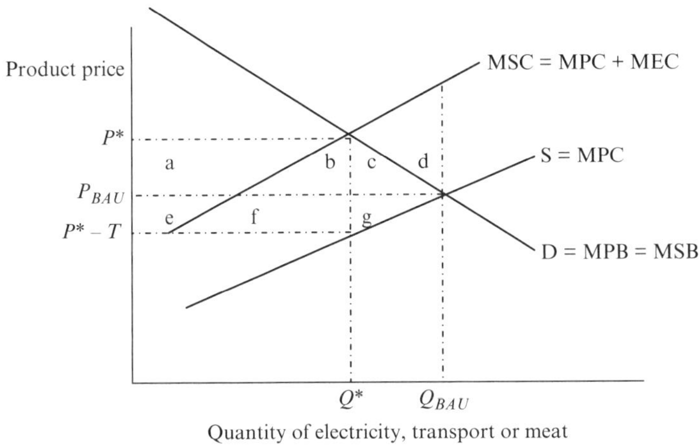

Figure 10.1 Competitive supply and demand model for a desired consumer good

rights. Apart from some regulations designed to reduce local smog, businesses and households ignore the external costs of greenhouse gas emissions. Relative to many other pollution problems for which the external costs are local and short-lived, with greenhouse gas emissions the external costs are associated with the global stock of emissions and the emissions have lives of decades to centuries.

The nature of the market failure with greenhouse gas emissions can be illustrated with two simple diagrams, one for a particular product and a more general one for the greenhouse gas emission product. In Figure 10.1 for a desired consumer good such as electricity, motor transport or beef we have a competitive market supply and demand model. The demand curve, D, represents the marginal private benefit, MPB, of the product. We further assume that MPB equals the marginal social benefit, MSB. The supply curve, S, under competition represents also the marginal private cost curve, MPC, of capital, labour and materials, but it treats the disposal of greenhouse gas emissions as a zero private cost. A competitive market would result in production and consumption of the desired product of quantity Q_{BAU}, and also a quantity of greenhouse gas emissions, and a price of P_{BAU}.

From a social efficiency perspective, we need to recognise the external costs of the greenhouse gas emissions represented by the marginal external cost of emissions per unit of the desired product produced and consumed. In Figure 10.1 this is represented by the marginal external cost, MEC. The marginal social cost, MSC, includes both the MPC and the MEC.

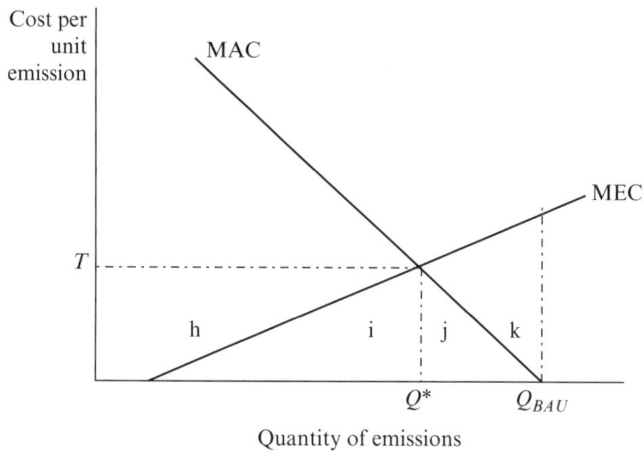

Figure 10.2 Social benefits and costs of the pollution externality

Then, the efficient level of production and consumption of the electricity, transport, meat, and so on falls from Q_{BAU} to Q^*. Also, the quantity of greenhouse gas emissions is lower, but in general not driven to zero. There is a net efficiency gain of area d. The efficiency gain is the argument for correcting the market failure associated with the pollution.

A more general representation for the economy of the social benefits and costs of the pollution externality useful for studying policy intervention options is given in Figure 10.2. Here we aggregate across all products that involve the pollution external cost, including electricity, transport and beef, of Figure 10.1. The horizontal axis shows the quantity of pollution or greenhouse gas emissions for the economy. The marginal abatement cost function, MAC, shows the cost of reducing greenhouse gas emissions from the business as usual output Q_{BAU}, corresponding to Q_{BAU} of Figure 10.1. The MAC aggregates across all greenhouse-gas-emitting activities.[2] As the pollution emissions are reduced, increasing costs per unit of reduced pollution are incurred as consumers switch their purchases from carbon-intensive to carbon-extensive products which are poorer and/or more expensive substitutes, as firms switch to less carbon intensive production methods which are more expensive, and as more research and development (R&D) is outlaid to achieve better substitutes for the carbon-intensive products and production processes. The marginal external cost function, MEC, is shown as increasing with the level of pollution. In Figure 10.2 the efficient level of pollution is at emissions level Q^* where MAC = MEC, or where MSC = MSB for each product (as in Figure 10.1).

Governments have a number of policy instruments to achieve the desired shifts in Figures 10.1 and 10.2 from business-as-usual quantities of products, production processes and pollution at Q_{BAU} to the socially efficient quantities at Q^*. Broadly, these instruments include: establishing a system of property rights over the global atmosphere; regulations, for example renewable energy targets, the use of fluorescent rather than incandescent light bulbs, and on/off days for using a private car; subsidies, for example for solar energy and insulation of buildings; and the market-based instruments of a carbon or emissions tax and a tradable permits scheme. This chapter focuses on the market-based options. They internalise the costs of the current market pollution externality to all producers and consumers, and they are recognised as the more cost-effective ways of tapping into all the available options to cost effectively reduce pollution (see, for example, any of the environmental economics textbooks, including Perman et al., 2003; Tietenberg, 2006).

There are similar design options available for both the tradable permit and carbon tax options. First, consider the point along the production chain at which the permit or tax is applied. All else constant, the preferred point is a direct measure of the pollution (for example tonnes of CO_2) rather than an associated input downstream (for example coal) or output upstream (for example electricity) However, considerations of operating costs, both for businesses and government, may result in choosing an earlier or later stage in the supply chain. The answer varies by source of pollution. In the case of fossil-fuel-fired electricity generators, the generators represent both the most direct measure of the pollution and the least operating cost point on the supply chain for either policy instrument. By contrast, while the combustion of petroleum products results most directly in pollution with the millions of vehicles and other appliance uses, a more concentrated and small number of firms at the petroleum refinery (and importer) stage minimise the compliance and administration costs, and there is a high correlation between the quantity of fuel and the pollution emission. The choice of point on the supply chain for ruminant animals is unclear, and not yet resolved. Individual animals are the direct pollution source, but pollution per animal is likely to vary with animal genetics, feed and management; and there are millions of animals. The correlation between the number of animals slaughtered by a more concentrated industry of meat processors and pollution by ruminants is unlikely to be high,[3] but compliance and administration cost savings are available. Both the tradable permit and emissions tax systems require measurement of the taxable sum or permit measure for legal, operational and general acceptance reasons. Then, for these design and operational cost comparisons criteria the emissions tax and tradable permits schemes are similar.

In making a distributional assessment and to evaluate equity effects, it is important to focus not on the initial or statutory incidence of the policy intervention, but rather on the economic incidence once market prices and quantities have adjusted to the changed set of incentives. Only in the special and unlikely case of no substitution of inputs along the supply chain, that is the Leontief constant input–output technology, is the economic incidence of taxes at different points on the supply chain independent of the point at which a cost for pollution is imposed (Alston and Scobie, 1983).

For a comparison of the operation, efficiency and distributional implications of the carbon tax and tradable permit systems, initially consider a simple one-period situation where we have close to perfect information, and in particular of the MAC and MEC functions. In the context of Figure 10.2, economic efficiency would have a carbon or emissions tax at rate T per unit of pollution, and a tradable permit scheme would limit the quantity of emissions to Q^*. The market price of the tradable permits would also be at price T, and the tax would restrict pollution to Q^*. Further, if government were to auction the tradable permits they would sell at price T, with both systems collecting additional government revenue of area $h + i$. Then, the higher cost of production, namely the additional cost per unit of pollution per unit of desired product produced, becomes reflected in the product supply curves of Figure 10.1. These higher production costs induce businesses to choose less pollution-intensive production methods, the higher product prices induce households to shift consumption away from pollution-intensive products, and there are better incentives and returns from R&D that reduces the carbon footprint, all of which reduce pollution.

Note from Figure 10.1 that much of the extra cost associated with the policy intervention to reduce greenhouse gas emissions is passed forward to consumers as higher prices P^*. The more elastic product supply relative to product demand, the higher will be the proportion of the cost of the carbon tax or of the tradable permits that is passed forward to the households. In the case of a perfectly elastic supply, 100 per cent of the cost increase ultimately is borne by households.[4] Of course, by the same reasoning, most of the benefits of reduced costs of adaptation to climate change (the external costs of pollution) ultimately will be passed on to households. Then, in this static and perfect knowledge world, the carbon tax and tradable permit schemes are essentially the same with identical implications for distribution and for efficiency.

In the more realistic world of imperfect knowledge and when the MAC and MEC curves vary over time, some important differences between the tradable permit system, essentially a quantity-based policy intervention, and a carbon or emissions tax, essentially a price-based policy intervention, become important. Because of imperfect knowledge of the MAC and MEC functions, both in terms of the basic science and in the estimation of social costs and benefits, it is inevitable that the chosen tax rate or tradable permit quantity will not be at the point where MSB = MSC. As a consequence, the full efficiency gain (of area d in Figure 10.1 or of area k in Figure 10.2) will not be achieved. In the extreme cases of too high a tax or too small a tradable quota, the chosen policy can create a social loss relative to business as usual.

Where we have a good idea of the relative slopes of the MAC and MEC curves but are unsure about their position, Weitzman (1974) has shown that for comparable percentage errors (relative to the optimum) the tax or price option will involve smaller efficiency losses than the tradable permit or quantity option when the MEC is flatter than the MAC, and vice versa. If we take a short-term perspective, the MEC is likely to be highly elastic because it is the global stock of greenhouse gases rather than the annual flow which is the link to climate change and pollution costs. In the short term the MAC is likely to be inelastic because of the importance of complementary long-lived capital items, such as power stations and motor vehicles, in the quantity of greenhouse emissions. Both these observations favour the choice of a tax. However, the relevant time-frame is the long run because of the long life of greenhouse gases pollution. Over a longer period the MAC will become flatter with greater opportunities to change the complementary capital stock and to induce and adopt new technology, and the MEC becomes less elastic with a focus on the stock (or cumulative flows) of greenhouses gases. Then, in the appropriate longer-run context, it is difficult on a priori grounds to apply the Weitzman model in judging a tax or a tradable quota as likely to minimise the efficiency loss in the inappropriate choice of the tax rate or quota quantity.

Inevitably the MAC curve will shift from year to year. For example, variations in economic growth over the economic cycle and of climate as it affects cooling and heating demands are important short-term shifters, and over the longer-term population growth, technology and changes in preferences and industry mix will affect longer-term trends. In all cases, knowledge about the magnitudes of these shifts will be imperfect and arrive with lags. Shifts in the MAC curve under the tax and tradable permits policy options will have different implications for the patterns of stability of the decision environment facing businesses, households and governments, as illustrated in Figure 10.3. We start with an initial period MAC with a choice of tax rate T^* or tradable permit Q^*, with each having comparable dual quantity and permit price effects. Shifts in the MAC curve, for example inwards to MAC_1 or outwards to MAC_2, result in different patterns of stability for the price and quantity of emissions. The tax option results in stable extra costs for greenhouse-gas-intensive products

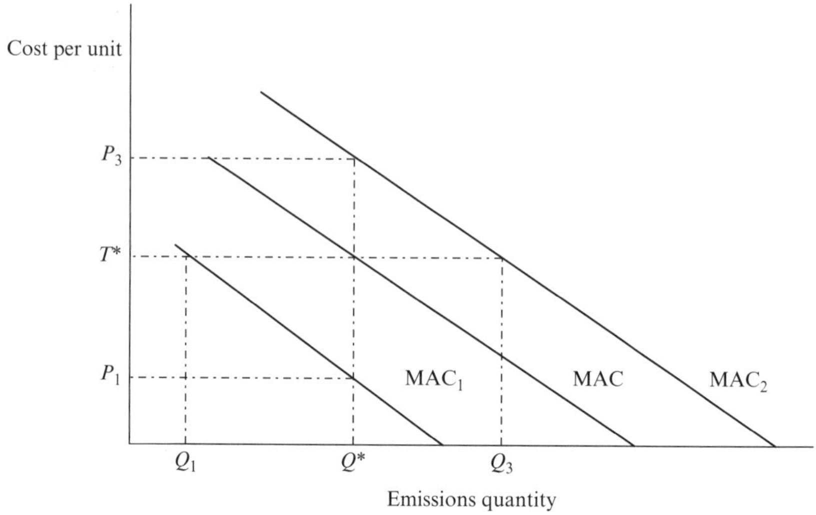

Figure 10.3 Implications of shifts in MAC curve on stability of price and quantity

and production processes and incentives for R&D, but with volatility in the reduction of emissions.

By contrast, the tradable permit system results in the opposite of a stable and guaranteed level of pollution, but with volatility of the permit prices. If the MAC is inelastic, as seems likely in the short run, shifts in the curve will result in much greater volatility of prices with a tradable permit scheme than will be the volatility of the greenhouse gas emissions under a carbon tax; and vice versa. Experiences with the European Union ETS system and the US SO_2 permits system reveal quite extreme volatility of permit prices, and in fact greater volatility than oil prices (Shapiro, 2007).[5]

Of course, if the New Zealand objective is to achieve an internationally agreed greenhouse gas emission country quota, the tradable permit scheme is a more direct and certain policy instrument than an emissions tax.

Two sets of arguments have been advanced in favour of the tax option with its price stability relative to the volatile prices of a tradable permit scheme. While both the tax and tradable permit mechanisms allow markets to find the least costly way of reducing emissions in any given period, Orszag (2008) argues that over a number of periods price stability will reduce the long-term costs of reducing emissions, and he estimates cost savings of up to a fifth. So long as the MAC function is convex to the origin, as seems likely, this inter-temporal cost saving argument in favour of a tax over a tradable permit scheme is compelling. By contrast, given that it is the stock of emissions rather than short-run variations in the flow of emissions that cause the external costs, volatility from year to year in the flow of emissions have minimal social costs. Second, stability of the cost and price increment effects of the tax policy intervention relative to the tradable permit intervention to reduce greenhouse gas emissions reduces the volatility of relative prices. This stability generally contributes to more effective and efficient decision-making by firms and consumers, and also by macroeconomic policy managers.[6]

10.3 SOME DETAILS FOR A SMALL TRADING COUNTRY

This section explores in more detail for the specific context of New Zealand the expected market responses and the efficiency and equity effects of a carbon tax or a tradable permit scheme on the petroleum products, electricity, agricultural and other industries which use energy as intermediate production inputs. Two different contexts are considered: (1), where all countries participate in a global agreement; and (2) where New Zealand plays an early-mover role and reduces greenhouse gas emissions before some of its key trading partners.

In the context of a relatively free world market for nearly homogeneous crude oil, petroleum products and gas, New Zealand and other small trading countries are price-takers. While the petroleum products refinery and distributive industries are highly concentrated, the combination of (a) a homogeneous product and a constant marginal cost curve suggest Bertrand oligopolistic pricing at close to marginal cost (including a normal return on funds) and (b) the regular scrutiny on anti-monopoly pricing by the public and government competition authorities point to 100 per cent pass through of higher marginal costs. Government statistical agencies always assume 100 per cent pass through of excise taxes on petroleum products. Estimates of the incidence of indirect tax changes associated with the GST tax reforms in New Zealand in 1985 and Australia in 2000 (both of which involved a combination of a rationalisation of existing indirect taxes and a tax mix change of more tax on consumption and less on income resulting in a diverse pattern of net indirect tax changes, or of marginal cost changes) assuming 100 per cent pass through were close to actual outcomes (see, for example, Stephens, 1989, for New Zealand; Dixon and Rimmer, 2000; The Treasury, 2003, for Australia).[7] For petroleum products and gas, but not other products discussed below, both New Zealand and Australia have proposed what effectively is a consumption or destination base tax for greenhouse gas reduction policy interventions; namely, to tax or require tradable permits for imports and domestic production but to exempt exports. Then, 100 per cent of the cost increment of emissions associated with petroleum products will be passed forward to domestic buyers, both to final household consumers and to business users of petroleum products as intermediate inputs.

Assessing the market reactions of the cost increment with a carbon tax or tradable permit on the greenhouse emissions of the electricity generation industry is more challenging. As a non-traded product, generators face a downward-sloping demand curve. Electricity is a non-storable and hence a heterogeneous product by time of day and by season. It is produced with a variety of technologies which vary by carbon intensity (from nearly zero for renewables and nuclear, to gas, black coal and brown coal), by cost and then by mix of fixed and variable costs, and by ease and cost of short-term changes in output levels. As a result, pricing involves a complex ranking of technologies by time of day and season. Then, the extent of pass through of the costs of imposts on greenhouse gas emissions on wholesale electricity prices will vary from zero if the renewable sources are the marginal producers to 100 per cent if the fossil-fuel-fired generators are the marginal producers. Taking Europe as a guide for New Zealand,[8] the estimates of Sijm et al. (2006) and Smale et al. (2006) for Europe that between 60 and 100 per cent of the extra permit costs were passed forward as higher prices suggests that most but not all of the costs of greenhouse gas emissions will be passed on as higher electricity prices.

Agriculture, and particularly the production of greenhouse gases by ruminants and fertilisers, is another and different story. Because of measurement and administrative uncertainties, no country, including New Zealand, to date has proposed a specific arrangement for these emissions; rather, inclusion of agriculture has been delayed for several years. Also important is that agriculture is a traded industry. It is a reasonable approximation to assume that New Zealand is a price-taker, both as an importer (for example of grains) and an exporter (for example of meat and dairy products). Then, if New Zealand introduces costs on the production of greenhouse gas emissions by agriculture before some of the major countries with whom it trades, New Zealand agricultural producers will bear most of the additional costs with no ability to pass forward the cost increases as higher prices to either New Zealand households or to export buyers. As other trading countries introduce policies placing an explicit cost on the production of greenhouse gases by agriculture, the relative world prices of agricultural products, and the perfectly elastic export demand and import supply functions facing New Zealand, will rise. These rises will be larger the more greenhouse-intensive the product. Then, the effects of an explicit charge for greenhouse gas emissions by New Zealand agriculture vary from almost 100 per cent absorption of the higher costs by farmers if New Zealand moves before other countries to close to 100 per cent pass through to consumers under a global agreement involving most of the world's agricultural product traders.

All industries use petroleum products and electricity as intermediate or production inputs. That is, with either a carbon tax or a tradable permit scheme on petroleum products, gas and electricity generation described above, most of the extra costs will be passed on to the business buyers as higher input costs (see, for example, Warren et al. (2005); Cornwell and Creedy (1996)). For the industries using energy as an intermediate input, the higher cost of energy effectively has a production or origin base falling on production for domestic and export sales, but not on imports. How much of the extra input costs are passed on to buyers will depend on whether New Zealand is an early mover or is part of a wider global agreement, and then on the trade status of the industry, and perhaps also on the industry structure and conduct.

Consider first the case where there is a global agreement in place, or more narrowly the case of the non-traded industries with limited exports or import substitutes. Much, but clearly not all, of the services sector, the construction sector and some small-scale manufacturers fit the non-traded case. Most of these non-traded industries are characterised by close to constant returns to scale technology and they are price-takers in the factor markets. Together these characteristics result in close to perfectly elastic marginal cost functions. Increases in energy costs with an emissions tax or a tradable permits scheme raise marginal costs. With most industry structures found in these industries, including perfect competition, monopolistic competition and several of the oligopoly models, about 100 per cent of a marginal cost increase, in this case for pollution, will be passed forward to buyers, and ultimately domestic consumers, as higher prices.[9] The magnitude of the price increase will vary across products depending on their direct and indirect input carbon intensity. Effectively, for the non-traded industries the cost increment associated with a carbon tax or tradable permit scheme is the same as the indirect tax changes associated with the GST tax reforms in New Zealand in 1985 and Australia in 2000 (both of which involved a combination of a rationalisation of existing indirect taxes and a tax mix change of more tax on consumption using a destination tax base and less on income). Analyses for both countries assuming constant returns to scale production technology and competitive pricing resulting in a 100 per cent pass forward of the net indirect tax changes corresponded closely with realised outcomes (see, for example, Stephens, 1989, for New Zealand; Dixon and Rimmer, 2000; The Treasury, 2003, for Australia).

However, for industries using energy as intermediate business inputs, the additional marginal cost of energy inputs under proposed tradable permit schemes has a production or origin base, not a consumption base. Then, in a small open trading economy such as New Zealand, facing near perfectly elastic export demand and import supply functions, which introduces an emissions tax or tradable permit scheme before other countries, the ability of firms to pass on the extra costs in the export and import competing industries is effectively zero, as described above for agriculture. In these trade-exposed industries, most of the higher cost will be passed back to the producers, and then to the owners of the quasi-fixed inputs used by these industries.

The foregoing partial equilibrium model assessment of the effects of a carbon tax or a tradable permit scheme on individual products highlights the costs of the policy interventions to reduce pollution and it underplays the benefits. First, the schemes change relative prices, with the prices of those products relatively intensive in their direct and indirect production of greenhouse gases rising relative to those products which are relatively extensive in their direct and indirect production of greenhouse gases. As shown in general equilibrium modelling, for example by Adams (2007) for Australia, while the pollution-intensive industries contract as shown for example in Figure 10.1, the relatively pollution extensive products and production processes expand because their relative prices and costs fall. That is, as required, the composition of employment, capital and natural resource use changes to reduce the aggregate level of pollution. No doubt the structural changes of 'creative destruction' involve adjustment costs, but all modern economies are in a constant state of structural adjustment responding to changes in tastes, technology, relative factor prices, international trade, and so forth. Second, and as a part of this reallocation process, the net tax revenue increase for government allows a fiscal expansion in aggregate demand via a combination of a reduction in other taxes, increased expenditure and a lower deficit. Together, these two sets of offsetting effects mean that in aggregate, the overall economy levels of investment and employment may change very little, if at all. Third, the lower levels of greenhouse gas emissions reduce external costs which provide benefits in the form of lower costs in adapting to a smaller dose of climate change.

10.4 GLOBAL DIMENSIONS AND THE POLICY OPTIONS

The need for a cooperative global agreement to reduce greenhouse gas emissions brings out some interesting comparisons between the carbon tax and tradable permit policy instruments. It is the stock of global emissions rather than the annual flow of emissions from any country which drives the external costs associated with climate change. From an individual country's selfish perspective, free riding is the dominant strategy, with a non-cooperative equilibrium of no active steps to reduce global pollution. For example, in terms of Figure 10.2, an individual country who reduces pollution (in moving from current pollution at Q_{BAU} to Q^*) bears all the costs (of area j) but only gains a minute share of the saved external costs for the globe (of area j + k), most of which goes to other countries incurring no costs; and the individual country who continues with business as usual can gain a share of the benefits of pollution reduction by other countries (of area j + k) while incurring zero costs. In the absence of a global government with power to enforce compliance by individual countries a cooperative agreement among the different countries is required.

In principle, either a well-functioning tradable permit scheme or a harmonised tax scheme will provide a least cost global reduction in greenhouse gas emissions. With a competitive market the world price of the tradable permit will equalise the MAC across countries. A harmonised carbon tax at about the same price as the permits will have the same cost-efficiency property. However, there are some fairness and administrative considerations of the carbon tax relative to a tradable permits scheme which seem more likely to facilitate the negotiation of a cooperative global agreement.

One of the challenges to reaching a cooperative global agreement is to induce the cooperation of developing countries by offering them a 'fair' agreement. Most developing countries in seeking to raise their living standards and to reduce poverty look to embark on an industrial revolution, as did the developing countries before them. The anticipated faster rate of growth of industrial production, even with the benefit of more advanced technology, will result in a faster rate of growth of greenhouse gas emissions than likely for the developed countries. Then, developing countries will be more affected by an historical greenhouse gas emission target than slower growing developed countries. Further, the developing countries argue that the accumulated stock of greenhouse gas emissions largely is from the pollution of developed countries over the past two centuries, whereas they as late industrial developers have made only a small contribution to the stock of pollution. A tradable permit scheme which allocates permits with respect to an historical benchmark (such as the emission levels of the Kyoto Protocol of 1990) or even a per capita quota (as proposed by Garnaut, 2008, and others) does not fully capture history. By contrast, an emissions tax system which automatically recycles money back to the developing country government, and which is robust

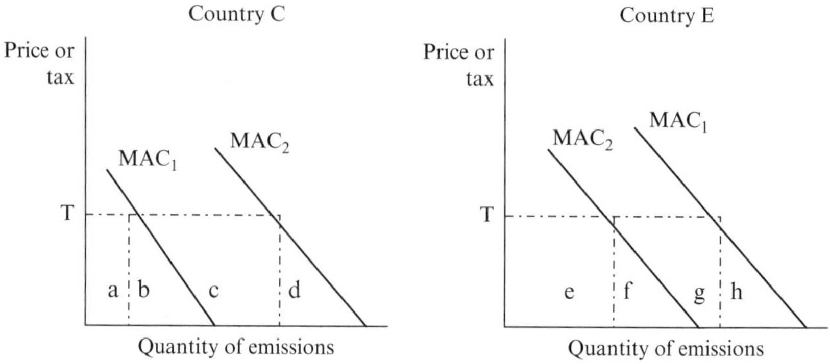

Figure 10.4 Inter-country implications of a tax or tradable permits

to different growth rates, may be more appealing in terms of equity while achieving a similar low cost reduction in the global stock of pollution and external costs of climate change.

By way of illustration, consider Figure 10.4. It shows the MAC functions for two countries as MAC_1 for the current year and MAC_2 for a period in the future. Country C is a developing country and the MAC curve shifts outwards with economic growth. Country E is a developed country, and for dramatic effect the MAC is shown to shift inwards with slow economic growth and technological change. Assume for further simplicity only a negligible change over time in the tax rate or the tradable permit price to emit greenhouse gases, at price *T*. Under the tradable permit system, country C with the shift of MAC_1 to MAC_2 would have to purchase a large number of additional permits at a cost to the developing country of area b + c, and presumably buying from other countries, including from country E which can sell surplus permits and receive revenue of area f + g. It is likely that such a transfer from the developing countries to developed countries will be resented.[10] The prospect of large revenue transfers becomes a reason for the developing countries to resist joining a cooperative international agreement based on a cap-and-trade system, and especially one that initially allocates permits by country based on current emission levels (as underlies the Kyoto Protocol).

By contrast, under the emissions tax scheme, country C would reap an increase in tax revenues, of area b + c, and country E a fall in tax revenues, of area f + g, with no inter-country transfers. At the same time, under both policy intervention strategies the same carbon price incentives are in place to reduce global emissions and the perceived losses to the producers and consumers of each country of the greenhouse-gas-polluting goods are little changed, namely area d versus b for country C and area h versus f for country E (ignoring the external benefits of less global pollution). On this policy strategy comparison, the tax option has more attractive distributional effects across countries over time, and with similar efficiency implications.

A related issue is the perceived integrity across countries with different political persuasions and administrative capacities of a tradable permit scheme versus a carbon tax. With a tax for each country, the government revenue-gaining incentives more closely match the spending incentives. While such desirable incentives also arise if the tradable permits are auctioned, it is less so where some of the permits are gifted. Failures of administration, and even corruption, of one country are largely contained to that country with a pollution tax. By contrast, with a tradable permit scheme, the failures of one country will spread to other countries and then potentially undermine the integrity of a global quota.

10.5 POLICY DESIGN ISSUES FOR AN EARLY MOVER

In the likely event that New Zealand, and/or other countries, implements a tradable permit or an emissions tax to reduce greenhouse gas emissions before other countries with which it trades, the issue of assistance to trade-exposed energy-intensive industries (TEEI) arises. This section explores the effects of such an early-mover strategy on the structure of the economy and on global greenhouse gas emissions, the arguments for and against assistance to the TEEI with a distinction between short-term and longer lags before other countries sign up, and if assistance is to be provided, the options for providing assistance.

The tradable permit systems proposed for Australia and for New Zealand, and the operating European system, primarily impose a production- or origin-based charge on greenhouse gas emissions, with the exception of the petroleum products refinery industries where a consumption or destination base is proposed. Costs of permits to pollute are imposed on the domestic production of electricity and on the domestic production of the rest of the economy that use electricity and petroleum products as inputs, and a production base seems inevitable if and when agriculture is included. Under this production pollution base imports will be exempt and exports will face higher costs, as will domestic production for domestic consumption.

Under a production of pollution base system, the TEEI in an early-mover country, both exporters and import competitors, face additional costs of production for the direct and indirect greenhouse gas emissions in their inputs. But there is no comparable change in costs for their competitors in countries which are yet to place a cost on emissions. The change of relative country competitiveness will lead to a fall in exports and a rise in imports of the early-mover country. For a return to balance of payments equilibrium, the associated rise in the current account deficit will require a depreciation of the currency, and a compensating improvement in the competitive position of the traded sector.[11] In the new equilibrium, the comparative advantages of industries with different (direct plus indirect) carbon intensities will alter. Production of exports and import substitutes of the relatively carbon-extensive products will fall (with the cost increase of the pollution scheme greater than the price increase effect of the depreciation). On the other side, production of exports and import substitutes of the relatively carbon-intensive products will rise (with the price increase of the depreciation greater than the extra cost impost of the scheme). The net effects on aggregate output, employment and investment in the TEEI are ambiguous.

A number of industry structural changes in the early-mover country and the rest of the world may follow. Suppose business decision-makers in the early-mover country regard the initial changes of relatively higher prices for carbon-intensive products and production processes as likely to last some time so as to warrant changes in production and investment decisions. Changes in the early-mover country result in less greenhouse gas emissions. But, the greenhouse intensity in the rest of the world rises so that in a global context, and this is the relevant context for the external costs of greenhouse gases pollution, global pollution may change very little. This offset is referred to as 'carbon leakage'.

With the passage of time as more and more countries implement policies to place an explicit cost on greenhouse gas emissions, the cost disadvantage of the TEEI in the early-mover country will erode and the exchange rate will appreciate. The extent to which this appreciation partly, fully, or more than fully offsets the initial period depreciation will depend on the patterns of comparative advantage in terms of the carbon intensity of the early-mover and laggard counties. Both forces will reverse some of the initial period changes in the comparative advantages of different TEEI in each set of countries. Some reverse industry restructuring in both sets of countries would follow. Nevertheless, with a global agreement to reduce greenhouse gas emissions, relative to the current or business as usual industry structure, the longer run will involve considerable restructuring of the TEEI in the early-mover country to a less carbon-intensive mix of products and production processes.

In the Australian context, the White Paper (Department of Climate Change, 2008) and Garnaut (2008) have argued for interim compensation to the TEEI, but with different forms and levels of assistance. The supporting efficiency arguments have been to partly nullify both carbon leakage and unnecessary industry restructuring and then its reversal with the attendant adjustment costs associated with creative destruction. Political responses to equity arguments for compensation of stranded assets and responding to special interest group lobbying also would seem to lie behind the compensation proposals.

A number of counter arguments to temporary compensation to the TEEI on the efficiency criterion can be noted. They vary and depend on the expected time-lag and confidence that other countries will implement policies to place an explicit charge on greenhouse gas emissions. Consider first the scenario of a high probability that within a few years other countries will follow the early-mover country. This means that the initial loss of cost disadvantage of the TEEI in the early-mover country relative to the rest of the world will be short-lived. Rational and far-sighted businesses would be expected to see through the short term and to the reversal of changes in comparative advantage. Most decisions would be made in the context of the expected longer-run scenario with most countries placing a cost on greenhouse gas emissions. In the short run, because of muffled price effects (because the law of one price does not hold) and because of the sunk cost characteristic of many investments and the associated relatively low elasticity of supply for most TEEI, changes in production and employment of the exporting and import competing industries, and of net exports and the exchange rate, would be relatively small. Then, carbon leakage and unnecessary industry restructuring would be limited, but industry restructuring for a less greenhouse-gas-intensive future world economy begins.

Further, not providing special assistance to the TEEI avoids the costs associated with rent seeking by special interests groups which has dominated much of the Australian debate over the last two years. The case for compensating assistance to the TEEI for efficiency reasons seems weak in this short-run adjustment period scenario.

Consider next the alternative scenario where either many years are likely to elapse before other countries with which the early-mover country competes join a global agreement, or there is much uncertainty about such an agreement being reached, or both. In terms of economic efficiency, this scenario is not unlike the situation of claimed 'unfair competition' with distorted global markets for many agricultural products, or for manufactured products produced with lax environmental regulations or 'undesirable' labour practices. From a global perspective, removing the distortions is first best. But, in the reality of a low probability of changes in other countries, from the perspective of the early-mover country, the rest of the world is as it is. In particular, these other distortions determine the opportunity costs facing the early-mover country. In the greenhouse emissions reduction context, this means the early-mover country accepts that there will be a long time lapse and uncertainty that other countries will adopt policies to increase the price on emissions for industries competing with their TEEI. The provision of compensation to TEEI in the early-mover country inevitably comes with an expensive rent-seeking game, and one that is unlikely to be a one-off game.

A key feature of the proposed system of temporary compensation of the TEEI in Australia (Department of Climate Change, 2008; Garnaut, 2008)[12] and New Zealand provides free permits to pollute to both the emissions-intensive export and import competing industries, but with no impost on imports. A much reduced pollution base than either a production base or a consumption base is one consequence. The Australian scheme for example envisages that about 30 per cent of the permits for pollution on production will be returned to producers in the TEEI. In effect, the compensation scheme distorts the allocation of resources in favour of the traded sector (which bears no cost for pollution) and away from the non-traded sector (whose pollution is taxed). There is no market failure to justify such a reallocation of resources from the non-traded to the traded sector.

A consumption or destination base for a tradable permit or emissions tax scheme to reduce greenhouse gas emissions is another option. Effectively, the early-mover country places a charge on its consumption of greenhouse gas emissions, with a tax on the pollution content of imports and a rebate on the pollution content of exports. The rates of the import tax and export rebate would be linked to the cost differential faced by the early-mover country TEEI. As other countries join a global agreement the rates would fall to zero. Arguably, an emissions tax building on the design of the GST (but with the base being the direct and indirect input pollution content rather than value added) would be more readily applied than a tradable permit system. A consumption base would avoid most of the carbon leakage and unnecessary restructuring with a production base. Comparable administrative challenges and rent-seeking costs of the above proposal to compensate the TEEI under a production base are likely. Also, questions of compatibility of such a scheme with WTO and other international protocols may need to be resolved.

Interestingly, the associated problems with compensating TEEI argue against an early-mover country strategy. A global agreement relative to a staggered system of countries joining over an extended and uncertain time frame reduces efficiency losses associated with carbon leakage, unnecessary restructuring, added administrative and compliance costs, and the deadweight costs of rent-seeking lobbying by special interest groups. The justification for an early move has to put much weight on such uncertain potential gains of early movers speeding up the time of an international agreement and the psychic benefit derived from own country reduction of emissions per se.

10.6 CONCLUSIONS

It has been argued that a carbon tax relative to a tradable permit system to reduce greenhouse gas emissions in a small open economy that takes an early-mover decision, such as Australia or New Zealand, has some advantages and few disadvantages in terms of efficiency, equity and administrative simplicity. Both are market-based policy interventions to internalise pollution costs and both draw on the wealth of businesses and households privately held information to minimise the cost per greenhouse gas reduction.

In a static perfect knowledge world, the two policy strategies are essentially the same. Both place a cost on the greenhouse gas emissions. For non-traded products, and for traded products under a global agreement, most of these cost increments are passed forward to households as a form of an additional indirect tax.

But, if the country is a first mover, producers of export and import substitution products will bear most of the extra costs, although there will be some offset with an equilibriating currency depreciation. Arguments for temporary assistance to the trade-exposed energy-intensive industries (TEEI) to reduce carbon leakage and unnecessary industry structural adjustments require caution. If the time lag to a global agreement is short, these efficiency concerns will be short-lived with rational business decisions. If the time lag to a global agreement is extended and/or uncertain, the assistance is likely to become long term, to ignore the early-mover country's opportunity costs, and to delay necessary structural adjustment. If temporary assistance to the TEEI is to be provided, a consumption or destination base pollution tax or quota better meets the criteria of global pollution reduction and a smoother transition to a long-run equilibrium than the non-tradable products base proposed by Australia. Compensation will incur large rent-seeking and administrative costs. These costs caution against the early-mover option.

Recognition of the reality of imperfect knowledge of both the MAC and MEC functions, and that the MAC function shifts over time and at different rates across different countries, results in different outcomes for the carbon tax and the tradable permits schemes. The carbon tax system results in greater stability and certainty of the cost increment and of absolute and relative prices, but with greater variation and uncertainty about the reduction in emissions. In the context of the long life and stock externality properties of greenhouse gas emissions, and likely convexity of the MAC function, the greater price stability favours the carbon tax above the quantity stability property of the tradable permit. Although, if the overriding country objective is to meet a globally agreed quota level of pollution at the expense of other economic objectives such as stability and growth, the tradable permit system dominates.

Achieving a cooperative agreement among most of the medium and large greenhouse-gas-polluting countries is necessary if the efficiency gains of lower pollution are to be achieved, and in a cost-effective way. A harmonised carbon tax would seem to offer some advantages relative to a tradable permit scheme, even though current policy is following the later option. A tax provides stronger incentives for compliance and better insulates poor administration, and even corruption. The inter-country redistributional effects of different rates of economic growth are automatically limited with a tax system, particularly when compared with a tradable permit scheme where the country allocation of permits is tied to an historical base.

NOTES

1. In the context of greenhouse gas emissions, economists in favour of the tradable permit scheme include Garnaut (2008), and those arguing the superiority of a tax scheme include Cooper (2005), Nordhaus (2005) and Shapiro (2007).
2. In the special case of a single product and a constant ratio of the pollution to the product output, the MAC of Figure 10.2 equals MPB – MPC of Figure 10.1.
3. Say, with a correlation coefficient above 0.8. But more important, a charge per animal slaughtered provides almost no incentive to change animal genetics, feed and management which may be important decision choice options in the future to reduce ruminant pollution, and then relative to reducing the number of ruminants slaughtered.
4. While Figure 10.1 is best interpreted as a perfect competition model, roughly the same distributional story holds for a wide range of imperfect competition models (see, for example, Freebairn, 2008). Most analyses of the incidence of indirect taxes, both by government statistical agencies (for example Australian Bureau of Statistics, 2007) and by academics (for example, Creedy and Sleeman, 2006), use the 100 per cent pass through model of the economic incidence of indirect taxes, of which a carbon tax or a tradable permit is a particular example.
5. Detailed design features of a tradable permit scheme, including the right to bank or carryover permits and perhaps also a limited borrowing right, should help to reduce the price volatility, but these are available with the European ETS and US SO_2 schemes. Establishment of a deep international market in tradable permits should further reduce price volatility, but this development requires much work for an international agreement.
6. Some supporting evidence can be gained from studies of periods within a country and across countries of higher inflation being associated with greater variability of relative prices and lower productivity.

7. And, perhaps contrary to theory, the 100 per cent pass through was observed from day one.
8. Data from the International Energy Agency shows that for Europe about 40 per cent of the electricity generation capacity is non-fossil fuel, and then among the fossil fuels gas is nearly as important as coal. In Australia by comparison, coal provides 84 per cent of the electricity generation capacity and will be the marginal producer for most of the time.
9. In the case of perfect competition the pass through rate will be 100 per cent as price equals marginal cost. For monopolistic competition, Ng (1983) shows more than 100 per cent pass through as the tax increase pushes up both the marginal and average cost curves and firm output falls requiring a further increase in price for the zero profit equilibrium. With the Cournot, Bertrand and Stackelberg oligopoly models, and also the monopoly model, the pass through is less than 100 per cent with linear demand curves and more than 100 per cent with constant elasticity demand curves.
10. Of course, an alternative would be to allocate the permits with some dynamic pattern that recognises likely different patterns of shifts in the MAC curves across countries. The tax option handles this issue endogenously without the need for projections or for political lobbying and compromises.
11. The magnitude of the price effects depends on a number of assumptions, including the robustness of the law of one price linking exchange rate adjusted foreign prices and the domestic price. For agricultural, mineral and energy products, which are fairly homogeneous, the law may be a good approximation, but it may be less so for many manufacturers and services where product heterogeneity is more important.
12. But, details of the compensation scheme in terms of the compensation rates vary between the White Paper and Garnaut. The gifted permits are to be tradable and so businesses have incentives to reduce pollution.

REFERENCES

Adams, P. (2007), 'Insurance Against Catastrophic Climate Change: How Much Will an Emissions Trading Scheme Cost Australia?', *Australian Economic Review*, **40**(4), 339–52.

Alston, J. and G. Scobie (1983), 'Distribution of Research Gains in Multistage Production Systems: Comment', *American Journal of Agricultural Economics*, **65**(2), 353–6.

Australian Bureau of Statistics (2007), *Government Benefits, Taxes and Household Income 2003-04*, Catalogue 6537.0, Canberra.

Cooper, R. (2005), *Alternatives to Kyoto: The Case for a Carbon Tax*, Harvard University, http:///www.economics.harvard.edu/faculty/cooper/files/kyoto_et.pdf, accessed on 15 October 2009.

Cornwell, A. and J. Creedy (1996), 'Carbon Taxes, Prices and Inequality in Australia', *Fiscal Studies*, **17**(3), 21–38.

Creedy, J. and C. Sleeman (2006), 'Carbon Taxation, Prices and Welfare in New Zealand', *Ecological Economics*, **57**(3), 333–45.

Department of Climate Change (2008), *Carbon Pollution Reduction Scheme: Australia's Low Pollution Future (White Paper)*, Canberra: Commonwealth of Australia.

Dixon, P. and M. Rimmer (2000), 'The Government/Democrats' Package of Changes in Indirect Taxes', *Australian Journal of Agricultural and Resource Economics*, **44**(1), 147–58.

Freebairn, J. (2008), 'Some Sectoral and Global Distributional Issues in Greenhouse Gas Policy Design', *Agenda*, **15**(1), 13–28.

Garnaut, R. (2008), *The Garnaut Climate Change Review*, Cambridge: Cambridge University Press.

Intergovernmental Panel on Climate Change (IPCC) (2007), *Climate Change 2007: The Physical Science Basis. Summary for Policymakers*, see http://www.ipcc.ch/ipccreports/index.htm, accessed on 15 October 2009.

Ng, K.Y. (1983), *Mesoeconomics: A Microeconomic–Macroeconomic Approach*, Brighton, Sussex: Wheatsheaf.

Nordhaus, W.D. (2005), *Life after Kyoto: Alternative Approaches to Global Warming*, NBER Working Paper Series, Vol. w11889, 2005, available at SSRN: http://ssrn.com/abstract=872724.

Orszag, P. (2008), *Implications of a Cap-and-Trade Program for Carbon Dioxide Emissions*, Statement of Director of the Congressional Budget Office before the Committee on Finance, United States, Washington, April 24.

Perman, R., M. Yue, J. McGilvray and M. Common (2003), *Natural Resources and Environmental Economics, Third Edition*, Harlow: Pearson.

Shapiro, R. (2007), *Addressing the Risks of Climate Change: The Environmental Effectiveness and Economic Efficiency of Emissions Caps and Tradable Permits, Compared to Carbon Taxes*, The American Consumer Institute, available at: http://www.sonecon.com/docs/studies/climate_021407.pdf

Sijm, J., K. Neuhoff and Y. Chen (2006), 'CO_2 Cost Pass-through and Windfall Profits in the Power Sector', *Climate Policy*, 6, 49–72.

Smale, R., M. Hartley, C. Hepburn, J. Ward and M. Grubb (2006), 'The Impact of CO_2 Emissions Trading on Firm Profits and Market Prices', *Climate Change*, **6**, 31–48.

Stephens, R. (1989), 'New Zealand Tax Reform', in J. Head (ed.), *Australian Tax Reform in Retrospect and Prospect*, Sydney: Australian Tax Research Foundation.

Stern, N. (2006), *Stern Review: Report on the Economics of Climate Change*, Cambridge: Cambridge University Press.

Treasury, The (2003), 'Preliminary Assessment of the New Tax System', *Economic Roundup*, Autumn.

Tietenberg, T. (2006), *Environmental and Natural Resource Economics, Seventh Edition*, Boston: Pearson.

Warren, N., A. Harding and R. Lloyd (2005), 'GST and the Changing Incidence of Australian Taxes: 1994–95 to 2001–02, *eJournal of Tax Research*, **3**(1), 114–45.

Weitzman, M. (1974), 'Prices vs quantities', *Review of Economic Studies*, **41**, 447–91.

11. Improving lake water quality through a nutrient trading system: the case of New Zealand's Lake Rotorua

Suzi Kerr and Kelly Lock*

11.1 INTRODUCTION

This chapter is concerned with how public policy should respond to allocate the social costs of abating water pollution – in this case, Lake Rotorua, one of New Zealand's largest lakes, where water quality is declining due to increasing nutrient run-off. The chapter examines how the social benefits and costs of water quality improvements in Lake Rotorua could be shared. In this case, a simple environmental tax instrument is not likely to be the best option as it does not limit the quantity of nutrient loss, which is what determines the lake's water quality. Rather this chapter proposes a 'nutrient trading system'. This would consist of tradable 'nutrient allowances' which limit allowable nutrient losses into the lake by setting the total allowances equal to an environmental 'goal level'. All potential nutrient loss sources would be monitored and required to surrender allowances to cover the nutrient loss at the end of each trading year.

An interesting aspect of this particular pollution problem is that it can take anything from zero to 200 years for nutrients applied to farmland in the catchment area to reach the lake. This raises especially tricky issues concerned with how pollution costs can, and should, be allocated. We show how different options for allocating nutrient allowances and achieving pollution reductions over time conform with standard cost-sharing principles.

Deciding who should pay for improvements in lake water quality is always a politically challenging issue. Our aim in this chapter is to clarify how benefits and costs are likely to be shared with no free allocation of emissions units, present principles for deciding how costs should be shared, and then show how different options for allocating nutrient allowances and achieving reductions in the target level of nutrient loss (the 'cap') over time conform with those cost-sharing principles.[1]

A 'nutrient tax' is a theoretical alternative to a trading system, although a tax is not currently proposed as a real policy alternative. The issue of incidence arises identically in both regulatory forms (tax and trading systems) because, if they are equally efficient, they imply the same marginal cost on nutrient loss. An additional degree of distributional flexibility is provided in a trading system because allowances can be freely allocated.[2] This allows regulators to more closely determine the net wealth impact of the proposed system. The principles of fairness, however, would apply equally if a tax system were used – alternative forms of compensation may be needed if, for example, it was decided to partly compensate farmers for their costs.

We argue that for Lake Rotorua, there is no 'correct' answer to the question of who should pay. The 'best' answer will depend on what the community thinks is fair and is politically feasible. Cost bearing has direct economic impacts on those affected but also has implications for perceptions of fairness and hence support for the regulation, relationships within the community, and social well-being in a broader sense. If stringent environmental targets are chosen, allowances will be valuable and allocation rules will alter wealth significantly. Any rules for sharing costs and allocating allowances need to be relatively simple and transparent so they are easy to implement and will be perceived to be fair.

The initial allocation of allowances will be important for the efficiency with which we meet environmental goals, but only if the trading market is not operating efficiently. This may be important in the short run as people learn how to use the market. If the allocation of allowances provides significant capital it could also affect economic behaviour by loosening capital constraints that limit land development and mitigation.

In the following sections we consider what a nutrient-trading system is likely to cost (section 11.2), the principles for sharing of those costs (section 11.3), and how those cost-sharing principles can be translated into an allowance allocation system (section 11.4). Sections 11.5 and 11.6 then turn to the question of how and when allowances should be issued and how costs can be shared over time. This is not straightforward both because emissions will need to be controlled over many decades and because scientific changes over time may alter the desired target emission levels in ways that are not currently known. Section 11.7 offers some conclusions and recommendations.

11.2 WHAT WILL THE NUTRIENT-TRADING SYSTEM COST?

The costs of a nutrient trading system arise from setting up the system, ongoing administration and, most importantly, costs associated with reducing nutrient loss. Similar costs would be associated with other types of regulation that achieve the same environmental outcome.

11.2.1 Costs of Nutrient Reductions

The likely costs of nutrient loss reductions have been estimated as part of the Proposed Lakes Rotorua & Rotoiti Action Plan (see Environment Bay of Plenty, EBOP, 2007a). Excluding reductions from changes in land use and management, the costs are expected to be on the order of $10 million per year. This would achieve an ongoing total reduction of the two major pollutants – nitrogen (N) and phosphorus (P) of around 59 tonnes of N per year and 16 tonnes of P per year. The estimated costs per kilo of nutrient reduction vary widely across different possible actions, even among actions confirmed by EBOP (see Table 11.1).

Landowners could also incur costs from a number of actions designed to mitigate nutrient outputs. These include changes in current land use or avoiding a planned future use. The cost of land use change is the difference in profitability between the potential and actual use. Landowners may also change land use management practices, which may require capital investments and a likely loss in profitability. No strongly supported cost estimates are available for the additional 170 tonnes of reductions sought from land use but the per tonne cost is probably much lower than for the options in Table 11.1.

The costs of land-use management options vary widely. Landowners have the best information on the costs of all these actions. Nutrient loss reductions could be achieved through further tightening of the so-called 'Rule 11', a rule in the local government's environmental Action Plan that attempts to freeze nutrient losses through farm management plans. However, the costs of this option are likely to be very high for some properties because they will make some land uses, such as dairy farming, very difficult.

11.2.2 Impact of a Trading System on Costs

A nutrient trading system should reduce the costs of mitigating nutrient loss by allowing mitigation to occur in the places and at the times where it costs least. It should also encourage landowners to be innovative in seeking more profitable and less damaging land uses. The ability of the trading system to reduce costs will depend on how efficient the current farm-level caps on nutrient loss are (under Rule 11) relative to non-land-related mitigation efforts, and how mitigation opportunities are distributed. Assessing this is an empirical question. It also depends on how successful the trading

Table 11.1 Costs of various reduction options

Action	Cost per kg
Lake Rotorua: confirmed actions	
Rotorua Wastewater Treatment Plant upgrade	\$99 (N)
Community wastewater reticulation or OSET upgrade for Rotorua	\$460 (N) max
Storm water upgrades within Rotorua urban	\$348 (N) \$2092 (P)
Tikitere geothermal	\$4 (N)[a]
Phosphorus flocculation in the Utuhina Stream	\$140 (P)
Lake Rotorua: potential actions	
Phosphorus flocculation in two other streams	\$140 (P)
Hamurana Stream diversion to the Ohau Channel	\$57 (N in 2005) \$33 (N in 2005)[b] \$481 (P)
Land use management and land use change	\$6 (N)[c]

Notes:

[a] This cost per kg-N is lower than other actions because the Tikitere geothermal flow has a high nitrogen concentration and low volume, and is close to existing reticulation infrastructure.

[b] The reductions in nitrogen from the Hamurana Stream diversion are expected to increase over time, reaching a 'steady state' in 200 years. This reduces the cost per kg of nutrients over time. For more information see Environment Bay of Plenty et al. (2007b).

[c] \$6 per kg-N is simply a budgeted average for expected costs over 10 years. The nutrient reductions from land use/land use management changes will continue beyond 10 years, but total costs will be capped at \$10 million.

Source: Environment Bay of Plenty et al. (2007b).

system is in facilitating and enabling innovative mitigation options. In previous similar systems, such as the US Acid Rain program, which used emissions trading to reduce sulphur dioxide, the costs within the trading system were much lower than anticipated; see Ellerman et al. (2000).

The person who directly pays the cost of mitigation is not necessarily the one who ultimately bears it. Some costs can be passed on to customers, taxpayers and employees. Where the products are exported, Rotorua farmers are unlikely to have a significant effect on their export price so they probably cannot pass costs on except to employees (for example by no longer employing them) and local suppliers. Costs borne by firms providing local services however are likely to be able to pass on some costs. Examples could include golf courses, and others in the tourism sector.

Costs are likely to affect the values of different land parcels so a disproportionate amount of cost will be borne by those who own the land or other affected assets at the time when the regulations are created. For example, a dairy farm is worth a lot more with no regulation than it is once regulation is introduced.

11.2.3 Interactions with the New Zealand Emissions Trading System

The New Zealand government intends to introduce agricultural greenhouse gas emissions (methane and nitrous oxide) into the national emissions trading system in 2013. This provides an important context for nutrient trading. Many of the mitigation options that will reduce nutrient loss, for example land use change toward less intensive uses and reductions in use of fertiliser, will also reduce greenhouse gas emissions. Those landowners who carry out these options will receive a double benefit because they will need fewer nutrient allowances but also fewer New Zealand emission units (NZ Units). This will lower the additional cost of nutrient management. Some nutrient mitigation options such as riparian boundaries will have no effect on greenhouse gases, while others such as straw bales to catch nutrient run-off could potentially increase greenhouse gas emissions. Kerr and Kennedy (2009) discuss this issue in more depth.

The emissions trading system will also involve some free allocation of NZ Units, which will almost certainly affect landowners in the Lake Rotorua catchment. The form of this allocation to farmers is as yet undecided, but those who own land with indigenous or plantation forests established after 1990 are already eligible to benefit.

11.3 PRINCIPLES FOR COST SHARING

This section explores five different sets of principles for cost sharing: those who benefit from a cleaner lake should pay; those who created the problem should pay; those who pollute now should pay; current emitters have inherent property rights; and an equity-based approach – cost sharing which rewards existing efforts to mitigate and protect the poor and vulnerable.

11.3.1 Those Who Benefit from a Cleaner Lake Should Pay

One potential principle for cost sharing is that those who benefit from the regulation should bear its cost. The benefits are spread both within and outside the catchment and between people alive today and future generations. We discuss the way in which each group receives benefit because these may clarify which groups could bear costs and the shares they may each bear.[3] Some of these benefits will be economic and others will be aesthetic or recreational. Still others will arise from cultural values. Non-human values are also associated with a cleaner lake but these do not have an obvious implication for cost sharing so are not discussed here. They would, however, affect the overall environmental goal that is chosen.

Here we break the beneficiaries into those alive today, both within and outside the catchment, and future generations in order to more closely align later with potential cost-sharing mechanisms.

Within catchment

A number of groups within the Rotorua catchment would benefit from improved lake water quality. Tourists and holidaymakers benefit from recreational activities on the lake such as sports, swimming and fishing, and through the aesthetic values they place on looking at an attractive clean lake. Property owners receive these benefits directly; they also receive benefit through higher property values. Those with views of the lake or good access to the lake will get the most value. Tourism operators near Lake Rotorua, including hotel and restaurant owners and tour companies, benefit because their business derives in part from those who come to enjoy the lake. The local community benefits indirectly from employment and other economic activity associated with tourism and people moving to Rotorua to enjoy the lake.

Distinguishing between locals and visitors to the Rotorua region is important for cost-sharing reasons. Locals will bear cost either as property owners or as local tax ('rate') payers, though shifting tax incidence may mean that visitors also bear some costs while in the catchment.[4]

Beyond the catchment

The benefits of clean lake water for New Zealand's 'clean green' image could be significant but are hard to quantify. The clean green image improves access to agricultural markets and increases product premiums and tourism demand. The Rotorua catchment has a high profile as a tourist destination, which means that activities in the area could affect visitors' perception of New Zealand water quality and our efforts to protect it. The key beneficiaries of the 'clean green' image relating to water quality are exporters (especially farmers) and the tourism sector nationwide: tourism operators, hotel owners, airlines and so on.

A second group of beneficiaries outside the catchment (and potentially outside New Zealand) are those who think they might visit, or who will enjoy products (for example movies) that use the local environment. These values are called 'option values'.

Third, some people both within New Zealand and abroad may never visit but simply like to know that the lakes are clean and that the products they consume are not causing undue environmental degradation. This is called 'existence value' because these people need never directly use the lake. These option and existence values are the fundamental drivers for the value of New Zealand's 'clean green' image.

Finally, other catchments will benefit directly from improved water quality in Lake Rotorua because water flows from Lake Rotorua into Lake Rotoiti and the Kaituna River.

Future generations

Within the lifetimes of the current generation, water quality in the lake may stabilise but is unlikely to improve significantly due to the long groundwater lags. The current generation could avoid the cost of a significantly worse lake but this would increase the cost to future generations.

11.3.2 Those Who Created the Problem Should Pay

The New Zealand Resource Management Act enshrines the principle of 'polluter pays'. This states that 'there is no presumed right to discharge contaminants into the environment' and 'everyone has a duty to avoid, remedy or mitigate any adverse effect on the environment arising from that person's activities'.

One part of 'polluter pays' is that those who created the current predicament should pay. Current and near future water quality is largely determined by historical nutrient loss because of long groundwater lags, as well as the build up of nutrient in sediment in the lake. Should those who were responsible for those nutrient flows pay the cost of clean up?

This is consistent with the Maori concept of 'utu', which is the need to fix historical wrongs done to others. It is very different if the harm is done knowingly rather than unknowingly but even accidental wrongs need to be corrected. Responsibility is passed on from generation to generation. Thus, if the government encouraged farmers in the past to intensify and increase fertiliser application, the farmers are not the perpetrators, even though they may have benefited. Even if the government did not understand the harm that was occurring because of the state of science, they still indirectly caused damage and need to fix the historical wrong. In contrast, adopting a principle based on who benefited economically from the agricultural intensification would impose costs on landowners who have been in the catchment a long time, and on New Zealanders as a whole, particularly those in the Rotorua region who benefited from the agricultural boom.

How far back do we go in assigning responsibility? That depends on groundwater lags and on how the historical emissions are locked up in lakebed sediments that contribute to current fluxes. The lake water itself has a short residence time but nitrates can stay in the groundwater system for up to 200 years. Consequently, a high percentage of current nitrates in the lake is the result of activity more than five years ago.

Some scientists estimate that Lake Rotorua is experiencing sedimentation at a rate of approximately 1 cm per year. These new sediments are deposited in the shallow 'active' layer of the lake bed from which nutrients can be released back to the water column. This layer has been estimated to be approximately 15 cm deep. Nutrients below this depth (based on current scientific understanding) are essentially buried and do not influence water quality. Since the lakebed is increasing at 1cm per year, this suggests that nutrients that entered the lake more than 15 years ago are not involved in sediment cycling, assuming a constant rate of sediment growth.

Since sediment below 15cm is not impacting the lake, it is difficult to argue that the current predicament stems from treated sewage discharged into the lake up until 1991. This 15-year limitation on the impact of nutrient flows is less relevant to rural diffuse nitrogen (N) discharges because of the groundwater delays. It could, however, apply to most of the historical phosphorus (P) inputs to the lake from rural land, which are not transported through the groundwater.

11.3.3 Those Who Pollute Now Should Pay

Current emitters are identified in the local government's Action Plan. Pastoral farming creates 71 per cent of total N and 43 per cent of total P nutrient loss. Of pastoral uses, dairying is responsible for 52 per cent of N exports and 24 per cent of P exports, while sheep and beef together export 40 per cent of N and 61 per cent of P. These high rates for dairying are reinforced when calculated per hectare (ha). Dairy farms produce 50 kg/ha/year of N, alongside 28 kg/ha/year for the catchment as a whole (Lock and Kerr, 2008). Urban sources are currently responsible for just 6 per cent of N and 10 per cent of P outflows – the sewage outflows have largely been cleaned up. This was paid for by local ratepayers with some national taxpayer assistance.

11.3.4 Current Emitters Have Inherent Property Rights

A different set of principles comes from a more legal approach to entitlement. These are often powerful in political debate where losses in asset values as a result of regulation are sometimes referred to as 'takings'.

Many argue that current emitters have an implicit property right that should be upheld. Tighter nutrient regulation lowers the value of land that benefits from the ability to apply nutrients. In particular, dairy farms are likely to fall significantly in value. Owners of property at the time the regulation is announced will bear much of the cost of the loss of future profitability through capitalisation of losses in decreased land values. In some cases, it is argued, the ongoing viability of communities could be threatened.

11.3.5 Other Principles for Cost Sharing

Three other issues are important for deciding socially acceptable cost sharing. The first is that those who have already made efforts to mitigate should be rewarded. To many this simply seems just. It also can encourage people to continue voluntary efforts to enhance lake quality including (but not limited to) supporting widespread compliance with the regulations and efforts to find and disseminate new approaches to mitigation.

Another key equity principle is that poor and vulnerable parts of the community should be protected from harm. In the Rotorua catchment this includes low wage earners, those at risk of unemployment and poor landowners (for example Maori who are dependent on small land blocks). The local Maori communities are distinctive in their roles and responsibilities in the catchment but their specific interests and willingness to assume stewardship role are very community-specific and so the implications for cost bearing are not clear.

Finally, a commonly expressed principle is that landowners with 'similar' properties should be treated similarly. This makes sense but begs the question: 'on what basis should they be regarded as similar: past or potential nutrient loss, property size or land use?' More broadly this argues for rules that are transparent and avoid special treatment of any specific group.

11.4 TRANSLATING COST-SHARING PRINCIPLES INTO ALLOWANCE ALLOCATION OPTIONS

The key instrument for moving costs away from those who bear them directly (for example by directly funding mitigation actions, losing profit through constrained production, or through tax incidence and capitalisation of losses), is the free allocation of nutrient allowances. Once a nutrient loss cap is converted into tradable allowances, those who receive them hold a valuable asset and those who need to buy them face an additional

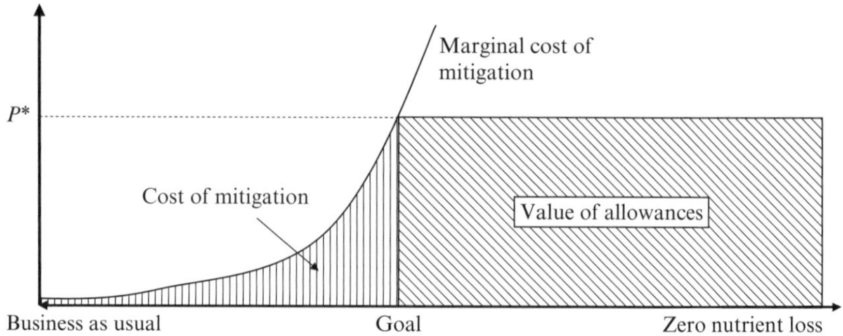

Figure 11.1 Cost of mitigation and value of allowances

cost. Thus the questions of how allowances are initially allocated, and how the costs of reducing the cap over time are managed (for example by proportionately reducing the 'nutrient value' of each allowance or buying back some allowances) are critical to the final distribution of net costs. Who faces these net costs should be determined based on the cost principles discussed in the previous section.

How does mitigation cost relate to allowance values? As Figure 11.1 shows, they are not equal. In the market as a whole, the total value of allowances will be equal to the market price p^* times the total number of allowances in the market. The marginal cost of mitigation curve rises from zero at 'business as usual' (BAU), reaching p^*, the equilibrium 'allowance price' at the goal level of emissions. The total cost of mitigation is the dotted area under the curve.

Every individual emitter will have some opportunities to mitigate at a lower cost per unit than the allowance price. Depending on how great these opportunities are, and how many allowances they were initially allocated, they will then either buy some allowances at full cost or sell them at a profit. The cost to any individual in a nutrient trading system is:

Cost = (BAU Nutrient loss – free allocation) * allowance price
– net change in profit as a result of changed input and output prices
– net change in profit as a result of mitigation actions (11.1)

Full allocation of allowances on the basis of historical (business as usual) emissions could overcompensate all emitters – the introduction of the system could make them wealthier. This suggests that emitters should receive fewer allowances than their business-as-usual emissions. If Rule 11, which constrains current emissions, is effective, landowners will bear some costs of mitigation even at their current emission levels. We also cannot pass costs back to previous landowners so costs that 'should' be borne by them would have to be related to current landownership.

Emitters can be partly compensated for losses through some free allocation of allowances. At the same time, non-emitters who we believe should bear some costs could buy back some allowances from emitters. The balance of free allocation and buy-back, plus any focused efforts to protect vulnerable groups (probably funded directly through local taxes rather than related to allowances) determines the final distribution of cost across current and potential emitters, those who are responsible for historical emissions, and local, national and international beneficiaries of improved water quality.

11.4.1 Sharing Costs Between Emitters and Non-Emitters

While emitters should not be fully allocated allowances to match business-as-usual nutrient loss, neither should they be allocated only the target level of nutrient loss implied by the trading cap, especially if the nutrient loss limit ('the cap') is significantly lower than business as usual. Figure 11.2 shows the various nutrient input levels to the lake against each 'vintage year' (the vintage refers to the year that the nutrients reach the lake).[5] This shows the current level of nutrient inputs, at 547 tonnes of nitrogen per year (tN/y) and three alternative target levels: Rule 11 (746 tN/y); the extreme 'no agriculture' level (200 tN/y) and the 'goal' level of 436 tN/y. The figure suggests that for each vintage emitters could be allocated less than Rule 11 levels with some additional nutrient reductions achieved at the landowners' expense.

The lowest horizontal line in Figure 11.2 illustrates the nutrient levels possible if all activity in the catchment were stopped and land were converted to plantation forestry – emitters should not be responsible for nutrients below this line. Note that all three lower curves peak in the future showing the effect of lags for nutrients already in the groundwater but not yet in the lake. Further reductions in allowances to get down to the level of the trading cap (the regulated 'goal' level of controllable inputs allowed) would be achieved through buy-back by various groups. Imposing some cost on local taxpayers and on specific local sectors for example tourism, fishermen, developers, can be justified by the benefits they would receive from higher lake quality and the historical benefits they have received from the economic activity associated with historical emissions.

These groups could bear some cost through local taxes or through a special levy on tourists or on property owners. For example, it has been suggested that property developers should be required to contribute to lake quality above normal rates. Fishermen could also be charged an

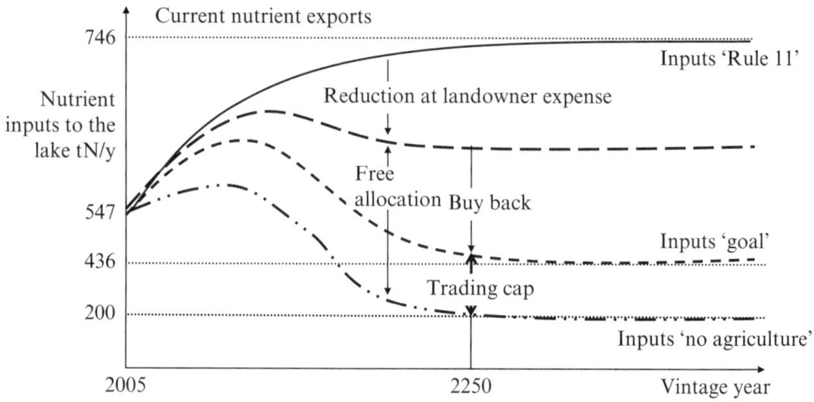

Figure 11.2 Cost sharing, free allocation of allowances and buy-back (illustrative curves only)

additional levy for fishing in Lake Rotorua and tourists could be charged a per night or per attraction fee.

The farming sector throughout New Zealand could contribute in recognition of the value of the clean green image to their exports. To the extent that central government policy is held responsible for historical emissions and that all New Zealand citizens benefited from the prosperity brought by the boom in farming (and fertiliser use), the central government could be expected to contribute. The central government's agreement to pay half the costs of implementing the current action plan (NZPA, 2008) sets one possible precedent for cost sharing between non-emitters. Part of this funding could be used to buy back allowances from emitters as shown in Figure 11.2, though this is not the current intention.

11.4.2 Sharing Costs Among Emitters

Above we discussed the total share of cost to be borne by emitters and how this relates to the total amount of allowances that would be allocated freely to them. The remaining question is how these allowances should be allocated among emitters. We need to balance four issues: long-term equity in cost-bearing; adjustment costs; compensation for stranded assets and a desire not to penalise those who already have low nutrient loss relative to similar land.

Long-term equity

Long-term equity suggests that land with similar long-term development potential (and hence potential nutrient loss) should be treated equally.

This reflects the similar loss in their land value in the long term. This leads towards allocation on the basis of potential nutrient loss: hectares interacted with potential productivity of those hectares. Allocating on the basis of hectares alone (sometimes called averaging) will not correlate well with the loss of land value, as low productivity land that would suffer small losses would receive the same allocation as high productivity, high nutrient loss, high value land.

It has been suggested that land use capability be used as a measure of potential productivity. Two difficulties arise with this. First, land use capability data is not of great quality at fine resolution. Second, land use capability is an ordinal mapping and would need to be translated into potential levels of nutrients in an acceptable way. A simple alternative would be to use carrying capacity (potential stocking rate) maps and apply fixed emission rates to each stock unit. This approach still has data quality issues at fine resolution, however.

For rural properties a formal nutrient loss model, OVERSEER, has been developed to improve monitoring and reporting.[6] For these properties, a better alternative is available. The individual property can be modelled in OVERSEER using best management practices to produce a level of potential nutrient loss. The extra cost of doing this would be negligible, other than the definition of best management, as the model will be calibrated for the property in any case.

Allocation on the basis of any fixed land characteristics will tend to benefit the less developed land and will provide some capital for development. It will not however provide capital to those who need to mitigate – they will face the greatest initial shortfall.

Adjustment costs

Two issues argue for an alternative approach at least initially. First, we want to smooth adjustment costs, minimise economic disruption and protect against initial market dysfunction during a learning period. Not supporting current emitters can increase adjustment costs; the costs arising from rapid changes in economic activity. Adjustment costs may particularly affect poor people with little access to capital and vulnerable employment.

Any allocation other than on the basis of current emissions can cause short-term economic disruption if the allowance market does not work. If landowners find that they own significantly fewer allowances than their current emissions (while others have an excess) and they are unable to purchase allowances, they may have to make rapid and costly changes. Alternatively they may claim (with some justification) that they are unable to comply, thereby weakening the overall regime.

Compensation for stranded assets and rewarding low emitters

Second, we may want to partially compensate those who have invested heavily in improvements to high productivity properties. These investments may now be 'stranded assets' which have low value as a result of the regulation. For example a recent dairy conversion that would optimally be reversed now allowances are required to cover nutrient loss would lose much of its value.

Allocation on the basis of historical emissions, 'grand-parenting', will achieve both of these goals. A grand-parenting system needs to be based on an early date to avoid strategic behaviour. We do not want people to have an incentive to overstate or even increase current emissions to increase their allocation. We want to reward people for past good behaviour rather than penalising or discouraging them. It would be possible also to alter the grand-parenting rule slightly to disallow nutrient loss above a maximum benchmark set per land use type. It cannot, however, be too historical or properties with non-strategic recent growth in nutrient loss would be penalised.

Any grand-parenting system, and particularly one that uses a past date, has issues with data availability. In the Lake Rotorua catchment, data are already being collected for many properties through the Rule 11 benchmarking process. Accurate application of OVERSEER requires several years of historical data but the high costs in using this may not be justified. One advantage of using a grand-parenting approach at least initially is that it makes any errors in monitoring of nutrient loss less important as any errors affect both the initial allocation and early years of compliance monitoring – the real change in monitored losses is what matters for the environmental goal rather than the absolute level of nutrient loss. It reduces the need for external verification of farm-specific parameters – a higher allocation also leads to higher obligations.

If the main motivation for grand-parenting is to protect against allowance market failure rather than to compensate for loss in land and capital value, this could be dealt with by direct intervention in the market to ensure a readily available supply of allowances, possibly at a fixed price. This transfers some risk to government but could provide reassurance to those who will need allowances.

One final argument sometimes raised in the context of allocation is the potential use of allocation of allowances as a way to provide capital for mitigation. This would be aimed at a failure in capital markets, which means that those who should mitigate do not have access to capital. It is difficult to identify these people and this is a very crude and socially expensive way to address this issue.

Government (at all levels) has two roles in the catchment. First, they are a landowner and emitter. Second, they have a responsibility to buy back some allowances as part of the cost-sharing approach. These two roles could be completely separated, with government land allocated allowances on the same basis as any other land. Government efforts to directly mitigate nutrient loss or alter nutrient loads through approaches such as sediment capping could either be used to meet their buy-back requirement or could earn them allowances. These could be used to cover nutrient loss within the cap, or retired to create a lower nutrient cap. The costs of each mitigation or offset activity should be compared with the allowance price to determine whether it is efficient.

11.5 WHAT SHARE OF EACH VINTAGE SHOULD BE ALLOCATED AT WHAT TIME?

The prototype nutrient trading system[7] developed at Motu Economic and Public Policy Research for Lake Rotorua requires allowances to cover nutrients from a property when they enter the lake water. Depending on the property and its characteristics, the time from when a nutrient is applied to the land until it reaches the lake through the groundwater system can be between zero and 200 years. Allowances will each have a declared 'vintage' corresponding to the date the nutrients reach the lake, grouped into date-ranges yet to be determined; see Kerr et al. (2007).

As a consequence of this design, the nutrient trading system needs to define environmental goals and trading caps for lake quality up to 200 years in advance. This does not mean that all allowances for the next 200 years should be allocated immediately, but some of each vintage needs to be allocated, because some of each will be used immediately.

In a world where governments can make binding long-term commitments, with perfect markets and rational fully-informed actors, it would be most efficient to allocate all future allowances now so that those who most want them in their investment portfolio can hold them. Investors could more easily hedge allowance price risk, futures markets would be more likely to develop, and the vested property rights would provide a strong political voice in favour of protecting the system in order to maintain the value of allowances.

In the real world, there are some reasons to issue allowances gradually. More than are immediately required should be issued, but less than all. There are two basic reasons for this: market efficiency and protection of people who may be less well informed. Gradual issuing does not mean that the legal rights to future allowances are not well defined, but it does reduce the ability to trade them in advance.

A burst of trading each time new allowances are allocated will promote liquidity in the market by providing regular price signals. Regular issuing of allowances also provides some protection against some players accumulating a large share of any vintage and exercising market power. If some allowances are issued through an auction, small players would have greater access to allowances. In our proposed system, allowances would be available for auction only if they had been bought back from participants by government because more than the total cap is initially allocated freely to participants.

Gradual issuing has one inefficient effect: it affects who bears the risk of costs from proportional cuts in future vintages. Whoever holds or has legal right to allowances will bear the costs of changes in the environmental goal. Landowners who hold future allowances they do not expect to need may wish to sell to avoid uncertain prices. This risk is not easily transferred away if the landowner has rights to future allowances but they are not yet legally issued.

Gradually issuing allowances in each vintage provides some protection for people who may sell their allowances early and then have regrets. This may be particularly relevant for small Maori trusts but could also affect other unsophisticated landowners. Many owners and trustees may not understand the value of what has been granted to them. They may prematurely sell these units at lower than their long-run value and therefore diminish development options for future generations. If allowances are issued gradually, the extent of these misjudgments will be limited and they will have the chance to make different decisions as they learn how the system operates.

Another option to reduce this risk for some Maori land in particular is to put Maori landowners' allowances into a central pool run by a trust (for example Te Arawa Lakes Trust). This trust could distribute allowances to the well-organised trusts like Ngati Whakaue but the balance of units would remain with the trust. The trust would allocate allowances each year to small units who want to develop and would sell off each year's surplus. The revenue could be used both to run this pool and perhaps to sponsor development or mitigation options. A similar approach has been used for managing fisheries quota; see Lock and Leslie (2007).

11.6 HOW COSTS CAN BE SHARED AS THE SYSTEM EVOLVES

The nutrient trading system will need to evolve over time as new scientific information emerges and as social preferences change. The critical question here is how the distributional implications of these changes should be handled. Should the same principles be applied to changes in the nutrient loss cap and the impacts of changes in scientific knowledge as were used to define initial allocation?

11.6.1 Changes to the Nutrient Loss Cap

Two arguments suggest that the same cost-bearing principles should also apply to costs (or benefits) from changing the environmental target – the cap. The first is that the same agents are gaining similar benefits and sharing similar costs. The second is that it is good to avoid renegotiation of distributional issues unless there is a compelling reason. Renegotiation is costly and induces strategic behaviour, which is costly to society. As an example, anticipating renegotiation could lead farmers to under-invest in mitigation in order to protect their bargaining position. They can continue to claim that they have high mitigation costs. Renegotiation also exacerbates investment uncertainty.

On the other hand, social preferences for cost bearing could change over time. Understanding the true scale of costs and benefits can also alter perceptions of how costs could be shared. Many people are uncomfortable about creating firm property rights to something about which most people have very little understanding. They fear that the powerful will unfairly benefit in the first negotiations over allocation because they better understand the value of the allowances and have the resources to fight for an allocation rule that is favourable to them. Thus renegotiation of cost-sharing rules should not (and in fact cannot under New Zealand law) be ruled out.

To strike a balance, we propose that the same principles used for initial allocation and buy-back are applied to future changes in the cap as the default option. An active change in policy, possibly requiring a change in the local Action Plan, is needed to change this. Specifically we propose that if central government bears 50 per cent of the cost of the initial buy-back, they should similarly bear 50 per cent of future cuts. Reductions shared among allowance holders would be on the basis of proportional reductions in the nutrient loss that can be matched by each outstanding allowance of the vintage affected. The issue of allocation among emitters does not need to be revisited as the reduction is on the basis of who owns the allowances, not who was initially allocated them. The price of allowances should reflect this risk.

Any changes in the caps should be publicised well in advance to minimise uncertainty. They could be incorporated in regular reviews (perhaps each five years). Changes in the caps could be applied with a lag so they do not affect immediate allowance needs.

11.6.2 Scientific Developments

The other likely cause of change in the system, new scientific information on the nutrient impacts of different activities, may require a different set of principles. The driver of change in this situation is new science. This is largely outside of the control of emitters. They cannot easily influence it and cannot be expected to anticipate it. This suggests application of the principle of non-retrospective regulation. Emitters should not be penalised or rewarded for actions they have already taken. To the extent that land use choices are only slowly irreversible, for example forestry, this suggests that if the model that assigns nutrient loss to particular land uses and management changes, the landowners affected should be fully compensated for changes that harm them, and required to provide allowances to match the effects of changes that are in their favour.

If the change in the monitoring model suggests that the catchment as a whole will no longer meet the environmental goal (or will overachieve), the standard mechanism discussed above for adjusting the total cap should be applied.

Full compensation for changes in monitoring does lead to slight overcompensation. This is because mitigation opportunities have changed for actions where the model has changed. As long as landowners cannot affect the process and so respond perversely to the promise of full compensation, this overcompensation has no efficiency impacts and the equity impacts are not likely to be too large.

Some more active participants in the market will however anticipate and cause change in the monitoring model. They will identify mitigation options and push for them to be included and they will search for and promote scientific research that reduces their obligations. The full compensation rule will reduce pressure to change rules in favour of existing land use and management practices. It will however encourage strategic delays in adoption of mitigation actions where the rewards from mitigation are anticipated to rise – agents will thus avoid the need to give up allowances matching the improvement in their position. For example, if a landowner anticipates that wetland enhancement will be added to the monitoring model, they will wait to enhance their wetland. If they enhance it now, when the model changes, it will be regarded as an existing practice and they will have to give up allowances matching the improvement in their compliance position. In contrast, if they delay enhancing it until after the model changes, they will receive the full benefit.

Similarly, anticipated rises in modelled nutrient loss will encourage strategic choices of inefficient land use and practices. Landowners who are in these land uses will anticipate compensation for the increased allowance obligation if they wait. When the rules change they can benefit again by changing their behaviour. For example if a landowner anticipates that the emission coefficient for plantation forestry will rise, even if they would like to convert to native forest, they will delay the conversion until after they receive the compensation. Both sets of strategic behaviour are environmentally damaging and create inequitable gains to those who have inside information or ability to influence the system. One way to reduce this problem is to announce the probability of a change in rule in advance. Only land use and practice at that point in time will be compensated (or required to give up allowances). The uncertainty about mitigation rewards in the period between this announcement and the announcement of the new rule must be offset against the reduction in perverse behaviour.

11.7 CONCLUSION AND TENTATIVE RECOMMENDATIONS

This chapter has proposed that a nutrient trading system is adopted to help deal with the problems of lake water pollution in New Zealand's Lake Rotorua. In particular we have suggested various ways in which this would help to deal with the problem of nutrients from farm land leaching into the lake water over many years. To ease the economic impact of the nutrient trading system's introduction, we propose that allowances are initially allocated to nutrient sources in proportion to their current nutrient loss. Not all nutrient sources will receive the same vintage allowances. The vintage allowances that are received by the nutrient source will depend on their vintage zone: a property with a 50-year groundwater lag will not receive any allowances from the first 50 vintages, as the property will never be required to cover nutrient inputs in these years.

Maintaining current nutrient losses will not achieve water quality goals. Therefore it needs to be decided who will pay for the required nutrient loss reductions. If only the number of allowances equal to the goal level of nutrient loss were allocated, the environmental target would be achieved, but most of the cost of nutrient reductions would be borne by the nutrient sources. In contrast, if sufficient allowances were allocated to cover current nutrient loss, and the government bought back and retired sufficient allowances to meet the goal, taxpayers or local ratepayers would bear all of the cost and nutrient sources would actually profit from the system.[8] Somewhere between these two extremes is likely to be ideal, with nutrient sources and central and local government each bearing some of the cost of achieving reductions. Thus, the nutrient sources are allocated fewer allowances than they need to cover current nutrient loss and central and local government must buy allowances from the market to achieve the remainder of the reduction to achieve the 'goal' level of inputs. The share of the reduction that is paid by each of the parties should be consistent across vintages and explicitly defined. This ensures that all parties bear some of the cost but that the reductions are not too great a burden on any party.

For allowances beyond the vintages that each landowner needs in the first few years of the system, the allocation mechanism will transition to one based on potential nutrient loss, providing a more equitable system. This prevents landowners becoming trapped in their current land use if they do not have sufficient capital to purchase allowances and avoids rewarding high nutrient loss properties indefinitely. To enable this to happen, a measure of potential nutrient loss needs to be determined. Some potential options are land use capability (based on slope, soil type and so on) and potential stocking rates applied through the OVERSEER model with 'standard' management practices.

Both the 'grand-parenting' and 'potential nutrient loss' allocation rules must be as simple as possible and based on readily available data that cannot be challenged to make it as fair as possible (and perceived as such). The same model calibration used to monitor the system should be used for free allocation, to align allocation and obligations to surrender and to reduce participants' risk. This limits the incentives for participants to bias model calibration, as increasing participants' nutrient loss to gain more allowances in the allocation process will also mean that they are required to surrender more allowances each year.

The allocation of allowances should be carried out in stages rather than individuals receiving all future allowances at once. For example, individuals could receive vintage allowances relevant to their first five years in the system. This would protect uninformed allowance holders from selling all of their allowances before they fully understood the system. It would also protect the credibility of the system. This would prevent all of the allowances being used in the first few years of the system, which would severely restrict future nutrient loss from the catchment and lead to increased pressure to increase the trading caps and/or abandon the system. Regular injections of allowances could also lead to periods of increased trading as individuals adjust their allowance holdings. This would provide regular price signals for the market.

Cost-sharing when changing targets should be based on the same principles as reducing nutrient loss when initially allocating allowances. For example, if allowance holders fund 30 per cent of the initial reduction in allowances that were allocated, they should also fund (receive) 30 per cent of any future changes in the nutrient loss cap. This could be deeply embedded in the system by defining each allowance as a share of the target for that vintage rather than as an absolute level of tonnes of nutrients.

Fixing these cost-sharing rules in advance ensures that future decisions are only about the appropriate levels of the caps and not about who is paying for them. This should focus discussion on the optimal social decision rather than being biased by special interests.

When changes are made to the model used to monitor nutrient loss, landowners should not have to enter the market to purchase extra allowances to continue in their current land use/activities. Regulation should not impose retrospective penalties (or rewards) on specific properties for changes that are out of their control and which they cannot anticipate. Imposing costs on a small group of properties would create resistance to science-based improvements to the system.

We propose that landowners' allocation of allowances be adjusted to account for the increase or decrease in allowances now needed to cover their nutrient loss. This involves giving allowances to, or taking allowances from, landowners to ensure that they are no better or worse off. If the new model alters the aggregate level of nutrient loss, the adjustments to allowance levels to restore the environmental goal should use the same mechanism as outlined above to address changes in the trading caps.

NOTES

* We would like to thank Environment Bay of Plenty, the Ministry of Agriculture and Forestry, the Ministry for the Environment and the Foundation for Research Science and Technology through the 'Markets and Water Quality' research programme for their financial support. We greatly appreciate input from members of the Nutrient Trading Study Group. Any opinions expressed are those of the authors and do not reflect the views of the funders or study group. The authors remain responsible for any errors and omissions.

1. For more information on the nutrient trading system, see Kerr and Lock (2009). Other relevant papers are available at www.motu.org.nz/research/group/nutrient_trading.
2. In theory infra-marginal nutrient loss could be exempted but this is not done in reality and would be technically complex.
3. For some existing analysis see Bell and Butcher (2003) and Bell, Thomas and McRae (2004a, 2004b).
4. The New Zealand system of local government finance involves payment of a local property tax: 'property rates'.
5. Due to the long groundwater lags, the inputs to the lake in a given year do not equal the nutrient loss off the land. For example, in areas where there is a 50 year lag, nutrients that are lost off the land in 2009 will not reach the lake until 2059.
6. OVERSEER is a nutrient loss estimating model which distinguishes different types of property based on their geophysical characteristics such as soil type, rainfall, land use and farm management practices.
7. See Lock and Kerr (2009) for more information on the prototype nutrient trading system.

8. The reductions that are funded by central or local government should be used to purchase allowances directly off allowance holders. This could be done via a tender process where allowance holders submit tenders stating how many allowances of each vintage they are willing to sell and for what price. Allowances are purchased from the lowest price bids until the required allowances have all been purchased. A single buy-back process could be used and the funding of the allowances split between the three funders.

REFERENCES

Bell, B. and G. Butcher (2003), *An economic evaluation of land use change options*, Report prepared for Environment Bay of Plenty, available online at http://www.envtop.govt.nz/Environment/Technical-Reports.aspx, accessed on 10 October 2009.

Bell, B., A. Thomas and A. McRae (2004a), *An economic evaluation of water quality induced changes in Rotorua and Rotoiti catchments*, Report prepared for Environment Bay of Plenty, available online at http://www.envtop.govt.nz/Environment/Technical-Reports.aspx, accessed on 10 October 2009.

Bell, B., A. Thomas and A. McRae (2004b), *The Rotorua Lakes: Evaluation of less tangible values*, Report prepared for Environment Bay of Plenty, available online at http://www.envtop.govt.nz/Environment/Technical-Reports.aspx, accessed on 10 October 2009.

Ellerman, A.D., P.L. Joskow R. Schmalensee, J.-P. Montero and E.M. Bailey (2000), *Markets for Clean Air: The U.S. Acid Rain Program*, Cambridge, UK: Cambridge University Press.

Environment Bay of Plenty, Rotorua District Council and Te Arawa Lakes Trust (2007a), *Proposed Lakes Rotorua and Rotoiti Action Plan*, Environment Bay of Plenty, Environmental Publication No. 2007/11.

Environment Bay of Plenty; Rotorua District Council and Te Arawa Lakes Trust (2007b), *Lakes Rotorua and Rotoiti Action Plan – Draft 5*. Environment Bay of Plenty.

Kerr, S. and Kennedy, M. (2009), *Greenhouse gases and water pollutants: Interactions between concurrent New Zealand trading systems*, Motu Economic and Public Policy Research, Note 2.

Lock, K. and Kerr, S. (2008), *Nutrient trading in Lake Rotorua: Choosing the scope of a nutrient trading system*, Motu Economic and Public Policy Research, Working Paper No. 08-05, available online at: http://www.motu.org.nz/publications/working-papers, accessed on 10 October 2009.

Lock, K. and Kerr, S. (2009), 'Nutrient trading in Lake Rotorua: Overview of a prototype system', *RM Theory and Practice*, 74–90.

Lock, K. and Leslie, S. (2007), *New Zealand's quota management system: A history of the first 20 years*, Motu Economic and Public Policy Research, Working Paper No. 07-02, available online at: http://www.motu.org.nz/publications/working-papers, accessed on 10 October 2009.

NZPA (2008), *Govt to pay half of Rotorua Lakes clean up*, available online at: http://www.stuff.co.nz/national/332354, accessed on 10 October 2009.

PART V

Lessons from tax reform episodes

12. Australian tax reforms: past and future

Greg Smith

12.1 INTRODUCTION

This chapter provides a general survey of past tax reform and future reform opportunities in Australia. Section 12.2 deals with the reforms of the past 25 years beginning in 1983.[1] Section 12.3 looks forward from the establishment in 2008 of the Australian Government's Review of Australia's Future Tax System.

Tax reform is often usefully framed by axioms like efficiency, equity, adequacy and simplicity. But the conception and interpretation of these are always in flux as well as conflict. It is probably not possible to make much sense of them outside a clear and continually updated understanding of the emerging social and economic context. Indeed, the history of tax reform is very much a history of struggle to respond to new circumstances – new skills or technologies, new roles of government, new awareness or conceptions of societal needs, and new forms of economic competition. For the most part, it is a struggle to catch up with wider social and economic changes that are well underway. I will attempt to give some flavour of this in the Australian case.

The chapter is structured mainly along thematic rather than chronological lines. It does not seek to define 'tax reform' or to distinguish it from broader 'tax change'. Public policies are always changed for the better in at least someone's mind. It is not unusual to see one tax change undo another, with both called reform in their time. In at least some cases, this is a perfectly sensible policy response to changing circumstances.

12.2 THE PAST 25 YEARS

In 1983 Australia emerged from a severe global economic recession (exacerbated by local droughts) with a new appetite for social, political and economic change. Tax reforms beginning in the 1980s went hand-in-glove with wider economic and financial system reforms; all three were motivated by the depth of concern that Australia had lost its economic way and needed to become more adaptive and dynamic.

Reform directions had already been identified in blueprints drawn up by two major public studies – the Asprey, Taxation Review Committee (1975) and the Campbell, Australian Financial System Inquiry (1981). But neither of these works had prompted significant immediate action. That changed as the 1980s unfolded.

12.2.1 Earlier Foundations

Australia's tax system, like those of other developed countries, was built over the course of the 20th century to meet the public revenue needs of major wars and the steadily expanding welfare state. In essence, by the latter part of the century this meant that the revenue yield of the tax system was ramped up severalfold to about 30 per cent of gross domestic product (GDP); see Figure 12.1. But throughout this period, the Australian tax–transfer arrangements lacked two key features of the template that was established in nearly all other developed economies:

1. Australia had no universal social insurance scheme or associated social security taxes;
2. there was no broad-based consumption tax.

Instead, Australia has relied overwhelmingly on income tax, supported by a ramshackle range of narrowly based sales and transaction taxes.

The burden of income tax is significantly moderated by Australia's extensive use of means tests on pensions and other cash benefits – as a result the Australian system exhibits a comparatively very low rate of tax–transfer 'churn' (that is, those who pay tax receive relatively little in cash benefits and those who receive cash benefits pay relatively little tax).

12.2.2 The Political Economy of Reform

The Australian Constitution, formulated at a time of much smaller government, unintentionally and often through indirect means has resulted in a major imbalance between Commonwealth and State taxing and spending powers. Over the course of the 20th century as social spending increased the Commonwealth has become financially dominant over the States.

The Constitution directly reserves duties of customs and excise to the Commonwealth, and this has been interpreted as preventing the States from imposing volumetric and other taxes based on sales of goods.

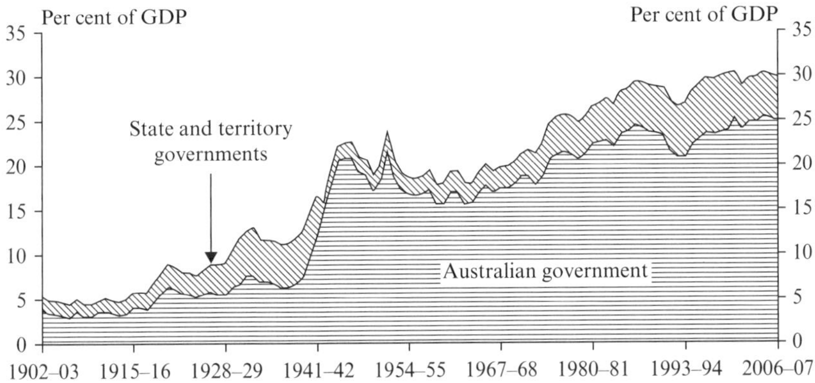

Source: Australian Treasury (2008).

Figure 12.1 Australian Government and state taxation (1902–03 to 2006–07)

Less directly, using other powers, since the Second World War the Commonwealth has also retained sole jurisdiction of the income tax. While both levels of government have shared in the expansion of social spending,[2] only the Commonwealth has had access to the required large tax bases on income and expenditure to fund it.

Overwhelmingly then, the Australian tax system is determined by the Commonwealth, which is a bicameral parliamentary democracy. The executive arm is formed in, and effectively headed by a member of, the lower house. Elected every three years, it is rare for the executive party to have a majority in both houses. The delivery of economic and taxation reform is a leadership task mediated by these arrangements.

The result has been a peculiar political economy in which most reform has been pursued through either of two different pathways. Sometimes it has followed the traditional mode of deliberative analysis and persuasion, with proposals developed by reference to 'public interest' considerations, by expert bodies, using open consultative processes. Other times, the executive has used its bureaucratic advisers to develop behind-doors, in-house reform packages, akin to the semi-secretive budget formulation process. The resulting proposals each then take their chances through the political processes of the parliament, relying on these different sources of momentum. The former relies mainly on the good standing of the preceding deliberative process. The latter depends more on community acceptance of the need sometimes to allow governments a right to set a course and lead through difficult times or challenges.

As in any democratic system, the results are mixed. In Australia, the deliberative persuasion model began with the Asprey and Campbell reports. In 1985 a community tax summit was attempted (following an earlier 'economic summit' in 1983). In the late 1990s, the Business Tax Review committee chaired by John Ralph developed business tax proposals and following that a standing Board of Taxation was established. The Board, in relatively contained spheres determined by the Government, has undertaken a series of successful detailed policy reviews.

The 'in-house secret' package approach featured in three main events. Following the perceived failure of the 1985 tax summit to deliver preferred reform (including a broad-based consumption tax), the Government prepared an alternative 'Reform of the Australian Tax System' package. This brought a personal tax cut, capital gains tax, fringe benefits tax and full dividend imputation. In 1988 a second package was presented, having been developed almost entirely behind closed doors. It brought major reforms to company taxes (including base broadening and a large reduction in the tax rate to 39 per cent) and a new approach to taxing occupational superannuation.

Perhaps the pinnacle of the secretive executive package approach was the development of the 'New Tax System' including the GST in 1998. Although the Government signalled its intent to consider tax reforms, this package was developed in extraordinary secrecy and then launched immediately prior to calling an election. The political shock tactic worked and the resulting mandate for this reform was enough to carry most of it through to implementation in 2000.

12.2.3 The Tax Mix

Throughout, Australia has remained very loyal to the income tax. The income tax provides about 70 per cent of the tax revenues of the national government. In addition, a general revenue payroll tax provides 26 per cent of State–local tax revenues.

When the GST was introduced in 2000, it primarily replaced other indirect taxes, and resulted in only a small net shift from direct to indirect taxes. In the 1970s, both Commonwealth and State governments abandoned estate and gift taxes, although property and property transfer taxes remain significant revenue sources for the States. Sustaining the central role of the income tax has involved much of the tax reform task of the past 25 years. In particular, there has been an active programme of base broadening in relation both to labour and capital incomes. Tax avoidance and evasion have been tackled by a range of measures. Also particularly important have been the fringe benefits and capital gains taxes, both introduced in the mid 1980s.

12.2.4 Business Tax Rates and Base

Income tax collections from companies provide a relatively large share of total tax receipts in Australia – about 20 per cent in 2007–08. This reflects a high share of company income in total income, whereas the effective average tax rate on company income is fairly typical at around the average of other nations.

Effective tax rates have also been relatively stable over the past 25 years. This is despite the reduction in the statutory rate from 46 per cent in the mid 1980s to 30 per cent today. The effective rate has been maintained through imposing a more comprehensive tax base. The main changes have included:

- tax on previously exempt activities (such as gold-mining) and foreign source income;
- capital gains taxes (for companies this is imposed on full nominal gains at statutory rates);
- reduction of accelerated depreciation for most investment in plant and equipment (although depreciation arrangements have changed on several occasions, sometimes in response to the economic cycle).

In addition, company tax collections have likely benefited from stronger anti-avoidance provisions both of general (anti-scheme) and specific kinds. The latter have included thin capitalisation rules for inward foreign investment in Australia, anti-dividend streaming provisions (and other transfer pricing and profit shifting measures) and tight rules preventing tax benefits for public infrastructure investment. In addition, the dividend imputation system has probably had 'integrity benefits' in favouring the recognition of profits in Australia rather than abroad.

The company tax base also retains generally longstanding provisions which are sometimes concessional and sometimes base broadening (relative to commercial measures of profits or many overseas tax bases). The main concessions are for certain classes of capital expenditure, particularly on industrial research and development, mining and petroleum resource exploration, some agri-businesses and film-making. Many of these have been the subject of regular reviews and 'reforms'.

Longstanding provisions that maintain a broad base include limited access to tax benefits for losses (company grouping was introduced in

1984, and fully consolidated assessment of company groups subsequently, but no loss carry-back provisions have been introduced); the absence of write-offs for purchased goodwill; and no deductions for general provisions for bad debts.

Over the past 25 years, Australia has paid considerable attention to strengthening the taxation arrangements for foreign source income, moving from a generally exempt treatment prior to the 1985 reforms to the foreign tax credit system. Strong anti-deferral rules were also introduced for passive investments made overseas. The new international tax arrangements often have been criticised as unduly complex and as standing in the way of Australian companies engaging internationally, or of Australia becoming an attractive place to base regional investments. Concessions have been made over more recent years to reduce the complexity and adverse effects of these provisions, notably following a review of international tax arrangements undertaken by the Treasury and Board of Taxation in 2003.

12.2.5 Personal Income Tax and Transfers

Tax reforms have often set out to reduce personal tax rates. However, with largely unchanged revenue needs and with inflation continually raising the effective rates of tax on a progressive nominal system, the actual changes achieved over the last 25 years have in many respects remained modest. The basic scales currently applying are set out in Table 12.1.

There has been clear progress on reducing the top personal tax rate. This was 60 per cent in the early 1980s and is now 46.5 per cent (including the Medicare levy). Moreover, the income level at which the top rate commences at \$180 000 is now over three times average earnings, about twice the level of the early 1980s.

In the 1985 tax reform, the top personal tax rate was aligned (at 49 per cent) with the company tax rate. However, this alignment lasted only two years – such a high company tax rate proved unsustainable and the rate was reduced to 39 per cent in the 1988 business tax reform (without a matching reduction in personal tax rates).

It has proved more difficult to substantively reduce marginal tax rates on average incomes. For much of the period, governments struggled to ensure that the 30 per cent 'standard' rate applied at average earnings rather than one or other of the higher rates. This was a particular goal of the 1980s reforms and adjustments in the 1990s, but in reality it has not been fully sustained. With the introduction of the GST, income tax rates were cut but of course the GST imposed some additional tax at the time income is spent. Also, the tax scale has been considerably complicated

Table 12.1 Personal tax scales

From July 2008		From July 2009		From July 2010	
Taxable income ($)	Rate %	Taxable Income ($)	Rate %	Taxable Income ($)	Rate %
0–6000	0	0–6000	0	0–6000	0
6001–34 000	15	6001–35 000	15	6001–37 000	15
34001–80 000	30	35 001–80 000	30	37 001–80 000	30
80 001–180 000	40	80 001–180 000	38	80 001–180 000	37
180 001 +	45	180 001 +	45	180 001 +	45

Note: The Medicare levy and low income tax offset are not reflected in this table.

Source: Australian Treasury (2008).

by the increasing use of the low income tax offset (LITO), similar offset devices for pensioners, and the means tested family tax benefit system.

The LITO has the effect of increasing the tax-free threshold to $14 000. This threshold is very similar to that which applied in 1985 – around 23 per cent of average full, ordinary-time earnings. However, the LITO (like many other offsets and benefits) is withdrawn as incomes rise, and this effectively increases the marginal tax rate. The effective marginal tax rate for singles on average earnings is thus 35.5 per cent, and it is higher again for seniors and for many with families.

Another key theme of personal tax reform has been the broadening of the tax base. The 1985 reform abolished tax deductions for business entertainment and introduced a comprehensive fringe benefits tax imposed on employers at the top personal tax rate. Fringe benefits in excess of a $2000 threshold are now also separately calculated for each employee and included in income measures for means tests. Capital gains tax was also introduced, initially on a base indexed for inflation but subsequently on a nominal base reduced by a flat 50 per cent.

One further important factor in the history of the personal tax system has been the increasing emphasis given to family assistance. The tax unit has long been individual rather than family based (although in contrast most means tests operate on family income) and assistance for children shifted from a predominantly tax basis to a transfer basis from the 1970s. The levels of this assistance have increased considerably, with three major programmes – for dependent children, for single income families and for child care.[3] In addition, a cash 'baby bonus' was introduced by the Howard Government (at $5000 it has been means tested by the Rudd Government).

Family assistance is means tested on a family income basis – its payment reduces effective average tax rates but increases (typically by 20 or 30 percentage points) effective marginal tax rates over significant income ranges. For families, effective marginal tax rates very often exceed 50 per cent.

12.2.6 Entities and Integration

Until 1987, Australia had a classical system of company taxation, with company income taxed at the company level and then taxed again when paid as dividends to shareholders. With personal tax rates as high as 60 per cent, and a company tax rate of 46 per cent, not surprisingly this generated many problems, and some equally problematic attempts to legislate to overcome them.

Dividend imputation was introduced in 1987 along with alignment of the company and top personal tax rates. Dividends are franked with credits only to the extent that Australian company tax is paid. Dividend imputation has survived since 1987 but the alignment of tax rates has not. International competitiveness pressures very quickly saw the company tax rate falling, with the first change to 39 per cent coming as early as 1989. Subsequently, further reductions have reduced the rate to its present level of 30 per cent.

Many of the pressures on the original system continue today. The three main forms of entity – partnership, trust and company – each have their own tax features. Partnerships and trusts generally are pass-through entities for income, while companies are not. On the other hand, only partnerships can pass through net tax losses, while trusts and companies cannot. Imputation credits apply only for Australian company tax payments and fully benefit only Australian resident shareholders, generating a new range of arbitrage difficulties.

12.2.7 Retirement Income Policy

Australia introduced a national age pension in 1909. Subsequently, as income taxes developed policy also supported occupational superannuation schemes through income tax concessions. However, the provision of superannuation benefits was essentially an employer prerogative covering only a minority of employees.

In the 1980s, three concerns emerged separately – about the adequacy of the age pension as a retirement income, about the need to restrain nominal wage growth, and about the low apparent level of national savings. Almost by accident, the development of occupational superannuation arrangements emerged as a key policy response to all three concerns.

The longstanding tax concessions for lump sum superannuation benefits were targeted in policy reforms adopted by the new Hawke Government in 1983. This led to trade union objections, and in subsequent consultations superannuation emerged as a policy instrument of renewed interest to both the Government and trade unions, who were closely coordinating policies through a series of 'prices and incomes accords'. Occupational superannuation was extended through awards to nearly all employees. It was seen as a way of improving retirement incomes, of increasing national savings, and as supporting nominal wage restraint (in the then largely centralised wage-setting processes).

Subsequent reforms to superannuation arrangements have essentially built on these initial directions. The Government introduced a tax-based arrangement (termed the 'superannuation guarantee') to better enforce employer contributions and to increase them to 9 per cent of wages. Through several steps the tax treatment of superannuation also changed. A flat rate of 15 per cent tax was applied in 1988 to the income of superannuation funds (including contributions received). This tax brought with it entitlement to dividend imputation credits, strengthening the economic impact of that scheme. Initially, the tax on funds was offset by equivalent reductions in tax on superannuation benefits, but in 2007 the complexity of these arrangements was overcome by abolishing tax on superannuation benefits taken by those aged 60 or more.

Australia is said now to have a three-pillar retirement income system. The first pillar is a means tested age pension as a universal minimum income safety net. The second pillar is a compulsory contributory scheme based on employee earnings. The third pillar is tax-advantaged voluntary saving which is also delivered through superannuation funds.

While the volume of superannuation saving has grown rapidly since the superannuation guarantee (SG) was introduced, the scheme has not to date resulted in any noticeable change in Australia's aggregate national or household savings rates. On the other hand, substantially improved retirement incomes are projected for most Australians as the scheme matures. The age pension alone would deliver an expenditure replacement rate in retirement of about 35 per cent of pre-retirement expenditure for persons on average earnings, but when fully mature, the SG, combined with continuing part pension, delivers nearly double this (Australia's Future Tax System Review Panel, 2008b).

12.2.8 Sectoral Policies

Throughout the past 25 years there have been a considerable number of tax changes directed at particular industries. These are often criticised as adding to tax system complexity, although it is a moot point whether that complexity is any greater than would apply to alternative sectoral policy instruments, or whether such alternatives would work as effectively in other ways.

Among the more notable matters addressed in the period have been:

- Offshore petroleum resources. A resource rent tax was introduced in the 1980s to provide a more economically efficient secondary resource tax than royalties (which still exist for most other natural resource extraction industries).
- Residential real estate. Amortisation deductions for construction costs were introduced in the 1980s, but in addition a brief experiment in limiting access to loss deductions (termed 'negative gearing') was attempted in the 1987–89 period.
- Offshore banking units (OBUs) and venture capital. A range of tax concessions including a 10 per cent tax rate on OBU profits was introduced in the early 1990s. Australian tax policies have displayed considerable ambiguities over the years in approaches to financial system development – sometimes offering concessions while also adopting demanding general rules, particularly for offshore investment.
- Business tax expenditures: Australia publishes annually a statement of tax expenditures (now required under the Charter of Budget Honesty Act). Sectoral business examples include concessions for small business, film production, agriculture and forestry investment schemes, infrastructure investments (now generally abolished), and research and development (most recently both a 125 per cent deduction for expenditures and a premium deduction of 175 per cent for increasing expenditure).

12.2.9 Indirect and State Taxes

Until 2000, Australia imposed wholesale sales taxes at a range of different rates on a large but incomplete range of goods. Like other single stage taxes this had relatively low administrative and compliance costs, but produced economically inefficient cascading effects on prices including exports and import-competing products. Economic costs were increased by the high rates made necessary by the narrow base, the omission of the retail margin from the tax base, and the exclusion of services more generally. The long-run structural shift in the economy from taxable goods to untaxed services meant that revenue was not robust.

The wholesale sales tax was replaced in 2000 by a single rate, 10 per cent goods and services tax (GST) on the value added tax model. The base is broad although there are several exclusions, for certain basic foodstuffs, water, and health and education services. Financial services generally are input taxed. The GST also replaced some inefficient state taxes and was offset by reductions in some other indirect taxes (including fuel and gambling taxes). Thus it was mainly introduced as an indirect tax reform. Its total revenues exceeded that of the taxes it replaced and this allowed for two further types of policy adjustment:

- a modest reduction in personal income taxes; and
- compensation payments for various low-income earners and, for first home-buyers, for the net price effects of the GST on housing.

A range of secondary, specific indirect taxes continue to provide substantial revenues. At the national level excises (or near substitutes) are imposed on road and aviation fuels, tobacco products, alcoholic beverages and the value, above a threshold, of higher priced motor cars. In most cases these are general revenue taxes, with the main exception being the fuel tax paid by large trucks which is a *de facto* road user charge. There are also a range of minor taxes – some hypothecated commodity taxes used for joint industry purposes, some remaining customs duties (although industry protection through protective tariffs has been greatly reduced) and some environmental taxes such as the aircraft noise and oil recycling levies. Each of these taxes has been subject to reviews and reforms over the past 25 years, but few that have greatly changed their basic form or incidence.

The Australian Constitution reserves excises to the Commonwealth and High Court decisions have resulted in the States losing access to fuel, tobacco and alcohol licensing charges (which had been linked to sales). The States have retained taxes only on payrolls, property and a range of stamp duties or similar instruments. The duties on conveyances have grown in revenue significance, and with that in their likely distorting economic effects. Apart from recent efforts to harmonise tax bases and other administrative arrangements (and the abolition of some financial taxes with the introduction of the GST), there has been little substantive reform attempted in relation to these State taxes.

12.2.10 Administration and Compliance

Early in the 1980s, apparently widespread tax avoidance and evasion were central concerns of government. Australia had experienced serious tax evasion in the 1970s and this undermined public trust in the tax system.

Radical changes in tax law emerged from these concerns – including retrospective measures to recover the gains from 'bottom of the harbour' schemes, the enactment of new general anti-avoidance provisions targeting 'tax schemes', and the introduction of new tax-withholding requirements on contractor payments in prescribed industries.

But none of these was ultimately as important as the decision later in the 1980s to shift to a 'self-assessment' system. This change shifted much of the compliance obligation to 'get it right' from the tax authorities to taxpayers. The Tax Office resources previously used to make binding assessments were shifted in large part to alternative compliance enforcement strategies. This set in train a long series of changes in the relationship between tax authorities and taxpayers.

The key features of this change included:

- An increase in real and perceived costs and risks for taxpayers, occasionally balanced by reforms aimed at reducing these costs and uncertainties.
- An increased demand for the Tax Office to clarify requirements – leading to the evolution of large-scale arrangements for both public and private rulings, massively increasing the volume of written tax guidance (and with that the perceived complexity of tax laws).
- The development of large-scale audit and compliance programmes, particularly directed at larger businesses and high-wealth individuals.

In parallel with these changes, the tax system became ever more complex. There were many drivers of these trends, including the problems of tax law drafting in the context of sometimes literalist court interpretations, and the intrinsic compounding problems of increasing policy complexity and multiple objectives. Arguably, too much weight was also placed on the precision of income and other tax base measurements. Policy architecture itself played a key part, with politicians often showing very little interest in the problems of compounding complexity.

12.3 AUSTRALIA'S FUTURE TAX SYSTEM REVIEW

The Australian Government announced a comprehensive review of the tax and transfer systems in the May 2008 Budget speech. The review is being conducted by a panel of five members[4] supported by a secretariat based in the Treasury. The terms of reference are wide although there are two main exclusions, relating to the GST rate and base and the tax treatment of most superannuation benefits. The main report is due in December 2009, but an earlier report on the retirement income system was prepared in March 2009 (ahead of anticipated consideration of pension policies).

12.3.1 Political Economy

A review of the tax system was one of many recommendations emerging from a community summit held in Australia in April 2008. The 'Australia 2020 summit' was convened by the incoming Rudd Labour Government to harness ideas from a wide cross-section of the community for Australia's longer-term public policy goals. The 'economic stream' at the summit called for Australia to aspire to a position in the top five in world per capita income by 2020, and a review of tax policy was seen as one of many requirements to deliver that outcome.

The review was announced shortly after the summit. The inclusion of transfers in its terms of reference in part reflected the increasing integration of the tax and transfer systems and partly a separately emerging debate about the adequacy of pensions. The Government also established a review of the adequacy of the age, carer and disability support pensions, and this was conducted separately by a member (Jeff Harmer) of the broader tax–transfer review panel.

The scope of the review is very wide-ranging. As such it is more akin to the large-scale Asprey and Campbell reviews rather than the narrower assessments that underpinned the development of specific reform packages undertaken over the past 25 years. However, the review process is an unusual amalgam of the two approaches to the delivery of reform proposals outlined in section 12.2 above. The review panel has members both internal and external to the government's advising departments; it is chaired by the Treasury Secretary (Ken Henry) and includes the Secretary of the Department of Families, Housing, Community Services and Indigenous Affairs (Jeff Harmer). The other three members are independently engaged. While the review is consulting widely on issues and broad options, and is releasing discussion papers and commissioned studies, its final recommendations and reports will be developed *in camera* and provided directly to Government.

Australia's Future Tax System Review is still at a relatively early stage. It is currently pursuing research and consultations on the basis of two consultation papers issued in December 2008 – one addressing the whole tax–transfer system and the other the retirement income system (Australia's Future Tax System Review Panel 2008a and b respectively). The Government requested a report on retirement incomes separately so that it could give early consideration to the pension adequacy issue.

Over the next six months or so the review will conduct detailed consultations on issues, receive and publish the results of commissioned studies, and convene a policy conference in mid-year. It will then develop its findings and prepare its main report by December 2009.

At the time of writing (May 2009), it is too early to predict outcomes and the following presents just one view of some of the issues that are likely to be covered.

12.3.2 The Legacies of Past Reform

As described in section 12.2, Australia has pursued an extensive tax (and transfer) reform agenda over the past quarter century, and on that foundation it is perhaps surprising that a comprehensive review is thought necessary at this time. However, there are many features of the tax and transfer systems that have been left substantially untouched by past reform. It is also arguable that some aspects of reform should be revisited in the light of experience and in the context of the new pressures or opportunities presenting in the 21st century.

Among the many legacies of past reform are the following continuing features of the system:

- There has been no substantive change in the aggregate tax burden. Commonwealth tax revenues have been around 25 per cent of GDP throughout the period while the State–local sectors collect a further 5 per cent of GDP.
- There has been no substantive shift from income to consumption tax. The introduction of the GST increased indirect taxes only from 21 per cent to 25 per cent of Commonwealth total revenues. Other aspects of the Commonwealth indirect tax base have been subject to erosion – customs duties have fallen with the continuing shift away from protective tariffs and tobacco, alcohol and fuel excise bases have declined relative to total consumption.
- Income taxes, including capital gains taxes, continue to be considerably distorted by the effects of inflation, and by the effects of longstanding non-neutralities arising from features such as the admixture of accruals and realisations bases for the assessment, the capital–income distinction and international issues.
- There has been no improvement, and probably considerable decline, in overall tax system operating efficiency, and substantial erosion of simplicity, transparency and certainty. This is equally true of the transfer system, particularly its complex array of means testing provisions which for many operate in parallel with income tax obligations.

- High reliance on capital taxes relative to labour taxes has continued, with strong growth in company tax collections associated with the economic fortunes of a long expansion devoted largely to personal tax cuts.
- No meaningful steps have been taken to reform state taxes or to fix jurisdictional imbalances in tax assignment.
- A number of sectoral areas have arguably been neglected and now show signs of stress or of missed opportunities. In particular, there are problems in the way that markets for transport and other public infrastructure, and housing, have developed (or not developed).

Until the recent world financial and economic difficulties, with strengthening terms of trade Australia has enjoyed a very long and strong growth experience, both absolutely and relative to OECD peers. The issues noted above have not been particularly pressing in that context. However, the new and more challenging circumstances that lie ahead, assuming they largely reflect longer-term structural trends and conditions, may expose some of the weaker spots in the Australian policy fabric. This may require that Australia more assiduously seeks to optimise its tax–transfer arrangements, particularly to maintain the high rate of private investment and per capita growth that most Australians aspire to and depend upon – and which may be essential for dealing effectively with the challenges of population ageing, climate change and a range of international pressures.

The potential weak spots that have steadily emerged over the past few decades, while often contested, may include:

- the substantial shortfall in national savings relative to investment, reflected in substantial and increasing net international indebtedness;
- a very large increase in houschold indebtedness;
- a significant decline in housing affordability;
- significant shortfalls and inefficiencies in social and economic infrastructure investment;
- pressures on Australia's attractiveness for foreign direct investment particularly in the terms of trade return to longer-term trends; and
- weaknesses in the performance and outcomes of federal arrangements.

These issues generally have many sources other than the tax transfer system alone. However, they combine to demand more of the tax–transfer system – to improve its social and economic outcomes and to reduce its burden as an administrative and compliance system.

Some of the main issues that are being considered in the Future Tax System Review are discussed briefly in the following sections. At the time of writing, however, apart from its interim report on some retirement income matters, the review panel has not formed any conclusions or made any recommendations about specific reform issues.

12.3.3 Reducing the Aggregate Tax Burden

The terms of reference for the review require that no assumption of smaller government be made but it is left unstated whether this is to be interpreted in absolute or relative terms. It would be possible for the aggregate tax burden to fall while the absolute size of government expenditures is sustained or continues to grow – provided that the aggregate economy (and hence tax bases) grows faster than the rate of government spending. The tax–GDP ratio would then fall over time.

The particular appeal of this observation is that there may be tax structures and arrangements that promote faster economic growth without reducing revenue adequacy. OECD surveys of this issue point strongly to the view that faster economic growth is associated with lower shares of capital taxation in the overall revenue mix, although the same studies caution about the application of this cross-country finding to policies in any individual country (Arnold, 2008).

12.3.4 Securing Adequate Long-Term Revenues

The idea that economic growth could be faster than growth in government spending confronts the evidence of intergenerational studies. The Australian Government has now published two 'Intergenerational Reports', most recently in 2007 (Australian Government, 2007). These studies show that on current demographic trends and policies, aggregate national government spending likely will increase considerably as a share of GDP.

Figure 12.2 shows the latest projected increases in Australian Government spending over the long term, expressed as a share of GDP. There is, of course, considerable uncertainty surrounding projections of this kind. However, it should also be noted that these figures do not include State and local sector spending increases in related areas such as disability services. The main drivers of the increases facing the Commonwealth are:

- population ageing; and
- trends in health spending (particularly pharmaceuticals).

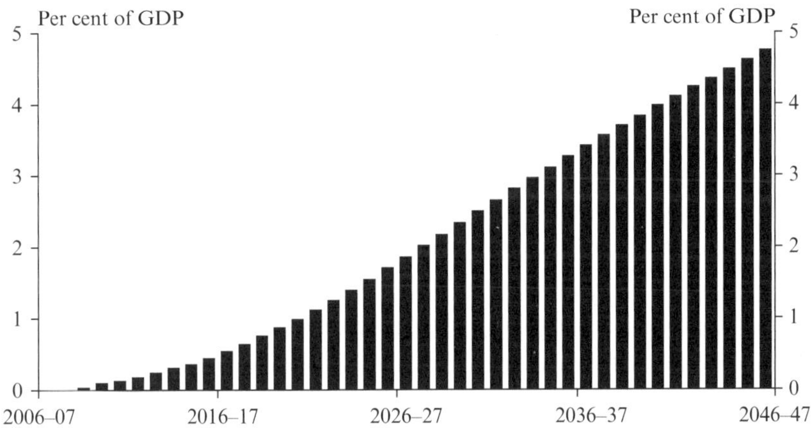

Source: Australian Treasury (2007).

Figure 12.2 Projected increase in Australian Government spending

12.3.5 Business Taxation – Form, Base and Rates

After mixed results from past rounds of business tax reform, considerable ground remains for reconsideration of business taxes in the present review. As noted above, a key driver is evidence that capital taxation is associated with lower economic growth. A specific key driver is the desire to sustain international economic competitiveness.

At the broadest level, there are three interconnected issues.

First, what is the appropriate tax base? In particular, the review is interested in considering the relative merits of income and expenditure (or cash-flow) tax bases. Even if an income base is retained, it is clear that most countries have substantial concessions for physical investment. Moreover, there are large parts of investment spending (particularly relating to intangibles) that are already expensed, raising tax neutrality questions.

Second, what is the appropriate statutory tax rate? The statutory rate particularly affects marginal decisions and issues like profit shifting. Debate on this issue has long focused on international comparisons – not necessarily very helpful given the wide range of rates in place. Some look at international averages: Australia appears to have a rate that is slightly above the unweighted average of OECD countries but below if rates are weighted by economic size.[5]

Third, what tax should apply to distributions of profits? Most company tax systems have moved away from imputation arrangements. A particular point of stress arises in the treatment of the increasingly international operations of companies which reduces franking capacity.

These issues are closely interconnected with one another. In addition they are connected with the design of the personal tax system. Increasingly the common pattern internationally is to set the rate of company tax below the top personal tax rate and to give partial relief, but not imputation, for dividends. The income (rather than expenditure) base is retained in most countries, but with considerable diversity in the detailed specifications of the base.

Australia's Future Tax System Review will look closely at these issues. In doing so, it will be necessary to have regard to international policy settings and tax treaties, and of course Australian choices potentially may have particular relevance in New Zealand and to the Australia–New Zealand economic relationship.

12.3.6 Delivering Radical Simplification

Radical simplification of tax and transfer systems is probably only possible in the context of a very wide-ranging review of the kind now underway. Simplification of the tax–transfer system could serve three main purposes – to reduce the resource costs of administration, compliance and business and financial planning; to improve transparency and hence political understanding of the system; and to reduce risk and uncertainty for taxpayers and transfer recipients.

There are many drivers of complexity. The Australian system is thought to be among the most complex in the world, and perhaps the main reason for this is the very heavy, comprehensive, multiplicative and precise roles given in Australia to income assessment. In part, this reflects the exceptional political focus in Australia on vertical equity questions, even to the point that many horizontal equity measures have vertical equity rules (means tests) imposed upon them. It also reflects the complex objectives and ad hoc development of the various separate elements of the system. In practice, also, income has proven to be a very slippery concept.

Reflecting the 'root and branch' ambitions of the review, the question arises as to whether radical simplification is possible. Any approach to this has to have very strong regard to the three purposes of simplification. It is not desirable to pursue simplification options that merely achieve one purpose at the expense of others. For example, new technologies might mean that complex taxes could be assessed and collected by tax-collecting agencies without much direct work or involvement from taxpayers – but this might mean that the lack of transparency and taxpayer risks are even worse, and that administrative costs are higher.

For individuals and households, the review is looking at the issues from the principal viewpoint of 'client experience'. In doing so, however, the preferred approach is to look at issues as part of the overall assessment of the system rather than to treat it only as a distinct line of work. This aims at ensuring that all of the 'moving parts' of the system are considered in the simplification context. In considering the income base, for example, questions that need to be considered include whether a single base could serve all taxes and transfers, and whether some parts of the system would work better with simplified schedular arrangements rather than the current comprehensive approach.

The complexity of business taxes is also likely to demand considerable further work for the review. Again, an holistic approach is intended, with answers dependent on fundamental questions including the role of capital taxes in the overall system.

12.3.7 The Federation

The Australian federation provides a further range of unique issues. The Australian arrangements are characterised by unusually high levels of both vertical fiscal imbalance and horizontal fiscal equalisation. One of the key effects has been that the States and Territories heavily work some of the few tax bases that they have retained – Australia has high rates of general revenue payroll, insurance and property conveyance taxes. The application of high tax rates on these bases is widely criticised as causing considerable economic inefficiencies.

Some of the more distorting State taxes were abolished as part of the new federal arrangements introduced with the GST in 2000. At issue is whether further progress could be made in addressing the fundamental problems with the revenue bases of the States (and local government, which relies heavily on property based revenues).

12.3.8 Addressing Environmental, Infrastructure and Housing Affordability Issues?

One approach to tax reform is to focus on core principles and to make changes that move policy towards 'first best' economic neutrality outcomes. In practice, however, the application of core principles to tax systems confronts two broad types of constraint:

- Some areas of economic activity are characterised by severe market failure and in these cases there may be a case for designing taxes that seek to correct (not necessarily perfectly) for the failures. The environment provides many case studies, with significant external costs or benefits adversely affecting market performance.

- Another constraint is that the neutrality of taxes, particularly income taxes, is often particularly elusive, for political or practical reasons. For example, no real-world income tax has neutral impacts on housing markets, and none perform neutrally in the presence of inflation. In this setting, the pursuit of first best policies may not always assure first best results.

Compared with tax reform over the past 25 years, tax design in the 21st century may have to take greater account of these constraints and the problems they generate.

In relation to the first, the main current development in Australia is the response to the greenhouse gas problem. The core approach is an emission trading reduction scheme, using the cap-and-trade mechanism. This approach has implications for other areas of tax policy, including petroleum fuel taxes. In addition, other tax issues also arise in relation to the sourcing of fuels, the encouragement of energy conservation measures, or of other 'carbon' pollution-reducing technologies.

The second constraint also suggests that a more flexible 'problem response' approach to tax design may be needed. The nominal income tax appears to work comparatively poorly in relation to certain long-term investments including infrastructure and housing. Part of the problem is that a significant part of the return on these investments is capital growth which is not taxed unless and until realisation, while nominal interest deductions are allowed. A further problem is that housing and many infrastructure markets are characterised by a mixture of taxed and untaxed arrangements, leading to a range of distortions.

It is not certain what part tax arrangements play, but significant problems are now presented in both infrastructure and housing markets in Australia. There are apparent shortages of supply relative to demand in each case. Infrastructure bottlenecks exist in several sectors, and housing affordability has deteriorated considerably. The present review will be looking at areas such as these to see what part, if any, tax reforms could play in delivering better outcomes.

In the case of housing affordability, transfers also play a significant part – rent assistance is provided in a range of forms, separately for private and public tenants, and first home buyers obtain both grants and transfer tax concessions.

12.3.9 Retirement Incomes

The development of Australia's three-pillar retirement income system over the past 25 years leaves several key issues for consideration. The most significant of these relate to adequacy and fiscal affordability.

The adequacy issue relates to three main concerns.

1. Compulsory superannuation obligations apply only to employees. There is a question whether arrangements of some kind should be extended to the self-employed.
2. The notion of retirement income adequacy is based on current policies for public and private consumption. In the future, public consumption spending on health and welfare is projected to grow very rapidly. There is a question whether retirement incomes (or some alternative arrangement) should be sufficient to contribute to that increased cost.
3. Just as the share of the population of retirement age increases, community expectations for retirement living standards is also increasing. In addition, life expectancies continue to rise, and greater longevity means that retirement savings must service a longer period of retirement. These raise the question as to the adequacy of the age pension and of superannuation saving based on the 9 per cent of earnings benchmark. They also raise issues about the forms of retirement income provision that are made available (or perhaps encouraged or mandated).

The affordability issue is also critical. Policy changes over recent years have generally raised fiscal costs. Superannuation has a high tax expenditure cost relative to an income tax benchmark, and the decision to exempt final benefits completely further raised this cost. The Senior Australians Tax Offset effectively raised the tax-free threshold for retirees to very high levels. Age pensions have been increased, and means tests softened, with the income taper rate reduced from 50 to 40 per cent (although inflation and other factors have substantially changed the role of assets tests as well). The income test applying to superannuation savings is unusually concessional, with much of the measure of income derived from superannuation balances excluded from assessment. The future cost of the age pension and of superannuation tax concessions will continue to grow as a share of GDP and in addition projected expenditures on health and welfare costs of the aged will also grow considerably.

The adequacy and affordability issues combine to raise questions about the need for further reform of retirement arrangements. A wide range of parameters could be adjusted to achieve better and more sustainable outcomes. These include the population coverage of the superannuation guarantee, its rate, its taxation arrangements, retirement ages, interaction with the age pension and options for better dealing with health, welfare and longevity costs.

Again, comprehensive review is necessary with an emphasis on looking at the ways in which the tax and transfer elements of the system are integrated, and at the ways in which retirees (and those saving for retirement) actually experience and respond to the system as a whole.

12.3.10 Tax–Transfers Based on Equity, Progressivity and Work Incentives

The Australian tax and transfer systems have evolved complex interactions – complex both to administer and comply with and in their effects on household incentives. The income tax is based on the individual as the unit, but family assistance and some tax provisions have adopted a family (couple) basis, and the family has long been the unit for setting and means testing social assistance payments. The tax scales are no longer a reliable guide to effective marginal tax rates, because a range of tax offsets are effectively means tested as well – clawed back as incomes increase. Such offsets are now more important than the tax scales in delivering tax-free thresholds.

As a result, effective marginal tax rates in the tax–transfer system are both high and complicated, and look very little like a standard progressive structure for many household types. Notwithstanding this, average effective tax rates remain classically progressive. There is concern that these arrangements have adverse impacts on workforce participation. Similarly, there are considerable issues relating to incentives for saving (for example, effective marginal tax rates for retirement saving often exceed 50 per cent).

This raises several potential reform questions:

- Should the tax and transfer systems be fully integrated, administratively and in the measures of income that they use for various purposes?
- Should the current mix of individual and family units for assessing different aspects of the system be retained, or would a family basis (perhaps optionally) serve better across the board?
- Do high effective marginal tax rates matter and if so how can or should they be reduced or smoothed?

- Is there scope (or net benefits) for flat (marginal) rate taxation over considerable ranges, with progressive allowances, given the absence already for many households of a progressive effective marginal rate scale?

12.4 CONCLUDING COMMENTS

Comprehensive policy reviews are worth doing if they open possibilities for beneficial change that incremental processes cannot deliver.

They might do this in a number of ways – improving understanding of the challenges facing the economy and society; renewing the system-wide vision so that programme objectives are clarified and better aligned; reconciling or balancing competing interests through being able to adjust more moving parts; and lengthening policy time horizons to increase focus on investment in critical structural requirements.

While the present review is at an early stage, it is certainly the goal of the Future Tax System Review Panel to contribute in each of these ways. Of course, whether and when such a review ultimately produces any of these results depends both on how well it is done and on the future priorities and circumstances of government.

Circumstances have clearly changed substantially since the review was first proposed and announced. Financial, economic and fiscal conditions are now much more challenging. Yet Australia and New Zealand have relatively strong track records in pursuing major structural reforms in the aftermath of adverse economic times – perhaps a defining feature of Antipodean political economy over much of the last 25 years.

So while circumstances have changed, there does not appear to be any diminution of the motive forces that led to the establishment of the review, or of interest in genuine reform. In that setting, we are looking forward to a very interesting and exciting year.

NOTES

1. 1983 marked the first year of the tax reforming Hawke–Keating Labor Governments, which were succeeded by the similarly reform-minded Howard Coalition Governments of 1996–2007.
2. Generally, the Commonwealth provides most cash pensions and benefits. The States–Territories provide most direct public health (mainly hospitals), school education and welfare services.
3. Maximum payments for young children are $4631 per child, reducing to $1945 for those on middle incomes.
4. Panellists: Ken Henry, Jeff Harmer, John Piggott, Heather Ridout, Greg Smith.

5. Simple OECD averages give undue weight to the large number of small European members. Weighting by economic size increases average tax rate measures because statutory company tax rates at combined levels of government in the largest OECD economies, the US and Japan, are relatively high, both exceeding 30 per cent.

REFERENCES

Arnold, J. (2008), *Do tax structures affect aggregate economic growth? Empirical evidence from a panel of OECD Countries*, OECD Working Paper No. 643, Paris: OECD.

Australian Financial System Inquiry (1981), (Campbell et al.), *Final Report of the Committee of Inquiry*, Canberra: AGPS.

Australia's Future Tax System Review Panel (2008a), *Consultation Paper*, Canberra: Commonwealth of Australia.

Australia's Future Tax System Review Panel (2008b), *Retirement Income Consultation Paper*, Canberra: Commonwealth of Australia.

Australian Government (2007), *Intergenerational Report 2007*, Canberra: Commonwealth of Australia.

Australian Treasury (2007), *Intergenerational Report*, Canberra: Commonwealth of Australia.

Australian Treasury (2008), *Architecture of Australia's Tax and Transfer System*, Canberra: Commonwealth of Australia.

Taxation Review Committee (1975), (Asprey et al.) *Full Report 31 January 1975*, Canberra: AGPS.

13. Company taxation in New Zealand

Matt Benge and David Holland*

13.1 INTRODUCTION

The purpose of this chapter is to examine the role of the company tax as a critical part of the New Zealand income tax system. It does not consider radical reforms such as ACE systems or cash-flow taxes. Rather, it examines tax design issues within the context of a company tax with conventional rates and structure. Nor does it make a detailed examination of the imputation system, which forms a key bridge between company and personal taxation.

The general features of New Zealand's company tax system were established in the reforms of 1989. Since that time, there has been an accumulation of specific policy changes and an evolution of New Zealand's economic context and the broader company tax environment. This has led to pressures on the current regime. This chapter briefly outlines these pressures and considers a number of policy responses to them. Some of these pressures are external and arise from international considerations, in particular downward pressures on the company tax rate. Domestically, they arise principally from the gap between the company and personal tax rates, leading to tax-minimising behaviour by taxpayers – which is sometimes referred to as the 'integrity issue' – and how best to respond to it.

The appropriate response to these pressures must take into account a number of key facts that form the New Zealand context:

1. Company taxation provides a higher level of government revenues than in most other OECD countries. In 2006 New Zealand collected 5.8 per cent of gross domestic product (GDP) in company tax, which was the third highest ratio for the OECD. The OECD average was 3.9 per cent.
2. Company taxation and the imputation system have two key roles in sustaining revenues from the New Zealand tax system:
   (a) application of source-base taxation for profits arising in New Zealand; and
   (b) as a backstop to personal taxation.

3. New Zealand is a relatively open economy but it is geographically isolated.
4. New Zealand has a very mobile labour force. In 2000 about 16 per cent of New Zealanders lived abroad and about 24 per cent of highly-skilled New Zealanders lived abroad. This was the highest ratio in the OECD for highly-skilled individuals living abroad; see Treasury (2009).
5. The proximity and degree of integration with Australia. Statistics New Zealand data indicate that almost 55 per cent of foreign direct investment (FDI) into New Zealand is from Australia; and just over 55 per cent of outbound FDI from New Zealand is into Australia. There is free labour mobility between the two countries.

13.2 THE NEW ZEALAND POLICY PARADIGM

In the 1980s and 1990s many OECD countries implemented reforms of their tax systems that broadened their tax bases and lowered their tax rates. The attempts of the 1970s to use tax incentives to direct economic development and stimulate activity were largely seen to have failed. The promised increases in investment expenditures failed to materialise, tax systems became a miasma of complexity and government revenues were eroded as tax bases narrowed. New Zealand joined in the broad base/low rate reforms and went further than most countries.

The policy thrust of New Zealand's reforms of the late 1980s and subsequent adjustments was to apply a single level of tax on a broad-based definition of income. The five major components of the system are summarised below.

1. *Alignment of top personal and company tax rates.* Alignment of the personal tax top rate and the company tax rate was arguably the cornerstone of the New Zealand system. In combination with the imputation system it eliminated most distortions which arise when income is earned through different entities and allowed New Zealand to avoid many of the complexities that arise in tax systems that apply different rates of tax to the same income earned in different forms. With aligned rates, the company tax provides a backstop to the personal tax system by preventing deferral of tax through shifting personal activity and assets to closely-held companies.
2. *Reasonably flat personal tax system.* Unlike most OECD countries, New Zealand taxed income from the first dollar earned; there was no tax-free threshold. Coupled with a broad base of income, New

Zealand's revenue objectives could be achieved by what was, at that time, a reasonably low rate of company tax by international standards (33 per cent) and a very low (the same 33 per cent) top personal tax rate. Low tax rates, in themselves, contribute to simplification, by reducing incentives to tax plan and consequent anti-avoidance rules, and reducing the tax distortions that inevitably arise from definitions of income that cannot fully reflect economic income (inflation, measurement of depreciation rates and so on).

3. *Broad tax base.* New Zealand broadened its tax base, achieving a greater broadening than most other countries. A welter of tax concessions were removed including export and export-marketing tax incentives, accelerated depreciation and numerous special incentives for farming, forestry and other industries. Under the income tax there were few explicit incentives and a comprehensive definition of income was implemented: for example, the Financial Arrangement rules that impose comprehensive accrual taxation of interest and similar income. The major departure from international norms was that many capital gains are not subject to tax. (Gains earned on revenue account are subject to full tax rates.) New Zealand's goods and services tax (GST) also stands out as very comprehensive, applying a single rate to a broad base of goods and services. In practice, broad-based taxes that enable low rates are likely to reduce the economic costs of taxation and the opportunity and incentives for avoidance.
4. *Imputation system.* New Zealand's imputation system was designed as a practical way to implement an integrated tax system. It ensures that income earned through companies bears a single level of tax. Income retained in the company is subject to the company tax rate, originally equal to the top personal tax rate. This means that companies cannot be used to defer tax for shareholders on the top marginal rate. At the same time, firms can distribute profits and have them taxed at the marginal rates of shareholders if they wish. This is to prevent the over-taxation of company profits where this is material. As a result, New Zealand (and Australia which also has an imputation system) has internationally high distribution ratios of company income and most income ends up being subject to tax at the tax rate of the shareholder.[1] By design, imputation provides a back-up to the company tax since unimputed dividends are subject to full taxation at the personal level, reducing the incentives for tax minimisation for companies that wish to pay imputed dividends.
5. *International taxation.* With some provisos, the basic model underlying the taxation of resident individuals is taxation of worldwide income (that is, on both their domestic-source and foreign-source income).

There is considerable controversy over how best to tax outbound investment income. In principle, it can be in a capital-exporting country's interest to fully tax such income as it accrues, allowing a deduction rather than a credit for any foreign taxes. This would equalise the pre-tax rate of return on domestic investments with the net-of-foreign-tax return on offshore investments. This can be justified on the grounds that the benefit that New Zealand as a whole gets on its domestic investments is the total pre-tax rate of return, which includes taxes paid to fund government expenditures. For offshore investments, the benefit to New Zealand is the post-foreign-tax return, since foreign taxes do not provide any benefit to New Zealand. Thus, taxing individuals on their net-of-foreign-tax offshore income (allowing a deduction rather than a credit for any foreign taxes) will cause individuals to invest in ways which maximise the welfare of New Zealand as a whole.[2]

In practice, at the company level, international tax conventions prevent countries from only allowing a deduction for foreign taxes paid when taxing income from outbound investments. Instead countries are constrained to allow either a credit for foreign taxes or to exempt such income at the company level. However, the imputation system is a step in the direction of reinstating a deduction for foreign taxes. Because not all profits are distributed each year, there will normally be a deferral benefit. Overall, the imputation system is likely to increase the efficiency of offshore investment from a New Zealand perspective. Importantly it also provides a base protection role by reducing incentives for New Zealand companies to transfer-price profits to lower taxed jurisdictions.

Under existing rules, New Zealand taxes the offshore active income earned by subsidiaries of its resident companies as it accrues. Other countries typically defer taxation until dividends are paid, allowing credits at that time, or exempt the income.[3] Under legislation before Parliament in 2009, New Zealand's system of international taxation of the offshore income of companies is expected to be brought into line with international practice, such that active offshore income earned by offshore subsidiaries will be exempted from company tax.

For non-residents, New Zealand taxes their New Zealand-sourced income. In contrast to the taxation of residents, in principle, New Zealand does not seek to tax non-residents on income not sourced in New Zealand.[4] The main way that non-residents are taxed on their New Zealand-source income is through our company tax.

There are theoretical arguments that can be advanced against taxing non-residents on their New Zealand-source income. Taxing this income will tend to drive up the pre-tax rates of return that companies need to make. This has the potential to reduce inbound investment and lower productivity and wage rates. Under certain strong assumptions including the absence of any 'economic rents' from investment in New Zealand, this tax could end up being borne by New Zealand residents but in a less efficient way than if they were taxed directly.

But there are at least two opposing considerations. First, if investment flows into the economy from countries with foreign tax credit systems, lower taxes on income in New Zealand may be offset by higher taxes abroad. In this case, New Zealand taxes need not discourage inbound investment. Second, and much more importantly, foreign investment into New Zealand will often generate economic rents; that is, returns that are higher than the minimum that would be required to justify the investment. In this case the arguments against taxing non-residents on their New Zealand-source income break down. The main effect of taxing this income may be to generate tax revenue and allow lower taxes to be imposed on New Zealanders rather than discouraging investment.

No developed country exempts foreign residents on their domestic-source income, although Ireland has moved in that direction with its low company tax rate and Belgium has an allowance for company equity which exempts foreign residents on domestic-source income up to the level of a risk-free return. On balance, taxation of location-specific returns has led New Zealand to retain full source taxation.

13.3 THE NEW ZEALAND TAX SYSTEM IN 2009

Tax systems, like other complex systems, are subject to deterioration over time. Economic and political cycles come and go. Changes accumulate in response to those cycles. Moreover, changing circumstances can imply that old solutions may no longer address current challenges.

In a review chaired by Robert McLeod, New Zealand undertook a comprehensive examination of its system early this decade (see Tax Review, 2001). While the review made a number of suggestions for change, it reaffirmed the basic paradigm of the New Zealand tax system. Outside commentators commented on the essential soundness of New Zealand's tax policy. However, since that time there have been a number of developments in New Zealand taxation and it is appropriate to reassess the state of the tax system.

New Zealand has done well in avoiding base-eroding tax incentives. The openness of the New Zealand tax policy process and the memory of the chaos of the incentive-riddled tax system of the mid-1980s have led to a consensus among policy makers and most private sector commentators against tax incentives.

In international taxation there has been a further, deliberate retreat from accrual taxation of offshore income. The government has recently proposed the introduction of an offshore active income exemption. This will bring New Zealand's practice more in line with international norms. The exemption responds to concerns that New Zealand-based firms suffer a disadvantage compared to competitors when operating offshore. This could have discouraged otherwise profitable expansion into offshore markets and could have led to migration of firms to other countries (including Australia) to take advantage of more liberal international tax regimes. The policy of allowing only a deduction for foreign taxes remains for dividends distributed to domestic shareholders out of offshore profits. The imputation system effectively taxes back the active income exemption. However, as noted above, deferral can reduce the impact of personal level taxation.

The policy of rate alignment has seen the greatest challenge. Recent tax rate changes include:

- *Company rate*: reduced from 33 to 30 per cent since 2008/09;
- *Top personal tax rate*: increased from 33 to 39 per cent since 2000/01; falls to 38 per cent in 2009/10;
- *Trust tax rate*: has remained at 33 per cent;
- *Portfolio Investment Entity (PIE)*: tax rate capped at company tax rate since 2007; reduced to 30 per cent from 2008/09;
- *Life insurance policyholder income*: taxed at 30 per cent since 2008/09.

Policy pressures arise from this diversity of tax rates because individuals can shelter personal income from higher effective marginal rates using companies, trusts, PIEs and other savings vehicles. Information derived from tax collection data since the introduction of the higher top rate indicates that there has been considerable rearrangement by taxpayers to minimise tax and avoid the full application of the apparent progressivity of the tax system; see Inland Revenue (2008).

There are a number of ways of escaping higher marginal and effective marginal tax rates by diverting income to lower-taxed companies or trusts (see Table 13.1 below). For example, by earning income through a company, an individual can ensure that income is taxed at a 30 per cent rate so long as profits are retained within the company. While income may eventually be taxed at the shareholder's marginal rate when dividends are paid, there can be substantial benefits from tax deferral if income is retained for a number of years in a company before it is distributed as dividends. Figure 13.1 shows a sharp increase in the amount of imputation credits held by closely-held companies. This is likely to indicate that there

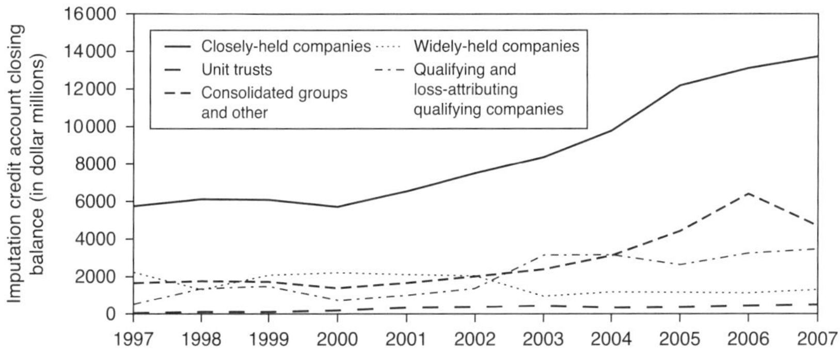

Note: The data for the year ended March 2007 is at August 2008 and incomplete.

Source: Policy Advice Division, Inland Revenue (2008).

Figure 13.1 Imputation credits, 1997–2007

was significant deferral of dividend payouts for such companies in order to avoid the higher personal marginal tax rates.

Trusts can be used to shelter income by having it taxed as trustee income (at a rate of 33 per cent) rather than having it distributed to beneficiaries and taxed as their income. There is continuing evidence of trustee income growing much more quickly than beneficiaries' income.[5]

The effect of these various strategies is illustrated in Figure 13.2 which shows aggregate income of individuals in different income bands for the years 1999, 2002, 2005 and 2007. The year 1999 was before the introduction of the 39 per cent top marginal rate for incomes above $60 000 and Figure 13.2 shows that, at that stage, there was no spike of taxpayers clustered at the $60 000 threshold. Since then, an obvious spike has developed. For example, in 2007 there is much more income attributable to people earning between $59 000 and $60 000 than for other $1000 bands of income on either side. This is likely to be because some of those who would otherwise be facing the top marginal rate are using companies, trusts and other savings vehicles to shelter income from higher rates of personal tax.

This raises concerns about whether it is fair for some taxpayers to be able to escape higher personal rates while others, such as salary and wage earners, face the top statutory tax rate. It also raises efficiency concerns since it is not costless for people to set up tax-efficient entities. From the perspective of the nation as a whole, the money spent doing so is a source of economic waste. Savings and investment can also be allocated inefficiently to take advantage of lower tax rates.

The current tax provisions also raise questions about the achievement

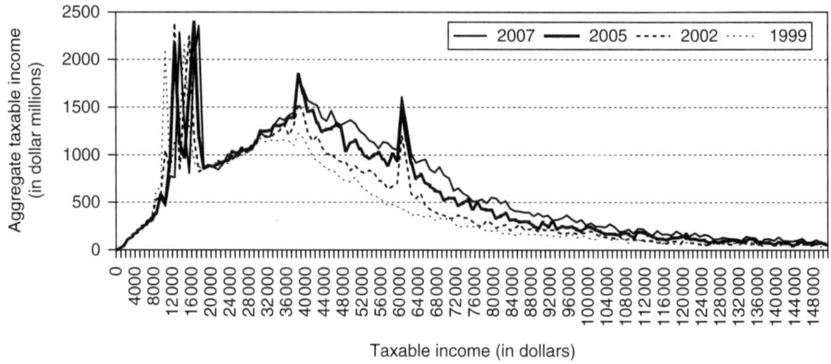

Note: The data for the year ended March 2007 is at June 2008 and incomplete.

Source: Policy Advice Division, Inland Revenue (2008).

Figure 13.2 Aggregate taxation income of individuals by $1000 bands of taxable income

of the objectives underlying the current statutory personal tax rates and thresholds and other measures which also affect effective marginal tax rates (EMTRs), such as abatement of Families Tax Credits, Student Loans and Child Support.[6] These all apply if individual income is received and taxed as personal income, but not if earned in other ways such as through companies, trusts or PIEs. There is therefore considerable variety in the ways in which income is taxed depending on exactly how the income is earned (see Table 13.1).

13.4 DETERMINING POLICY CHOICES

Arguably, a necessary condition for the viability of the current paradigm is maintaining a reasonable correspondence between the company rate and the top personal tax rate. Choosing the right tax structure depends upon predictions of future company tax rates and political choices about the tax mix and progressivity. The government has recently announced a longer term goal of returning to a balanced set of rates, with the company tax, the trust tax and the top personal rates all aligned at 30 per cent. The remainder of the chapter examines the issues relevant to the achievement of this objective.

There are a number of broad questions the answers to which will inform the policy discussion.

Table 13.1 Marginal tax rates (%) by entity

Type of entity	Accumulated at entity level	EMTR after distribution/ attribution of income			
		59% investor*	39% investor*	33% investor*	21% investor*
Direct investment	n/a	59	39	33	21
Trust	33	33	33	33	21
Company/unit trust	30	59	39	33	21
Company owned by trust	30	33	33	33	21
PIE	n/a	30	30	30	21
Widely-held superann. fund	30	30	30	30	30
Life insurance policyholder	30	30	30	30	30

Note: * '*X*% investor' refers to the personal marginal tax rate applicable on an investor's income (including family tax credit abatement where relevant) when this is earned as personal income.

Source: Inland Revenue (2008).

- Does policy of alignment of company and personal tax rates still make sense?
- Are the perceived simplification and efficiency benefits of rate alignment still valid today? Or might growth and productivity considerations drive down the desired company tax rate to a rate that is lower than a government would want to levy on higher personal incomes?
- Is alignment achievable with international pressures on company tax rates?
- Even if alignment of rates remains an appropriate policy objective, is the company tax rate a moving target? Will international rates continue to fall? If so, would New Zealand be forced to follow suit with further reductions in the company tax rate?
- Would a shift from income taxation to increased taxation under the GST be a viable way to achieve alignment even if company tax rates were to fall further?
- Could fairness objectives be maintained by providing an across-the-board cut in personal tax rates to align the top personal rate with the reduced company tax rate? Would a shift toward consumption taxation enhance economic welfare in a manner that complements the efficiency benefits of rate alignment?

- If not, or if achieving alignment takes a considerable time, what is the second best (possibly temporary) alternative?
- Should measures be introduced, as in a number of OECD countries, to prevent certain types of personal income being sheltered in companies or should New Zealand seek to align rates where possible, such as for capital income, as in a Nordic approach?

13.4.1 Whither the Company Tax Rate?

Figure 13.3 shows that in 1987/88, New Zealand's company tax rate was around OECD norms. In 1988/89 the company tax rate fell to 28 per cent and then was raised back to 33 per cent a year later where it remained until 2007/08 with a reduction to 30 per cent in 2008/09. The company tax rate was relatively low compared to rates in other OECD countries from the late 1980s until about 2000. However, since the mid-1980s there has been a downward trend in company tax rates around the world and, even given that New Zealand recently cut its company tax rate, New Zealand's rate is now above the average for OECD countries.

Interestingly, however, as company tax rates have fallen across the world, company tax revenues have not declined as a proportion of GDP (Figure 13.4). Between 1985 and 2005 the average company tax rate fell from 49 per cent to 28 per cent but company tax collections increased from 2.6 per cent to 3.7 per cent of GDP. This is in large part because many countries have broadened their corporate income base while reducing their company tax rates to protect company taxation as a source of revenue.

So while reductions in company tax rates have been characterised by some as a 'race to the bottom', perhaps a more accurate characterisation among OECD countries would be a structural improvement in tax systems towards low rates and broad bases in ways that, to date, have not impaired the company tax as a source of tax revenues, while reducing the distortionary impact of the tax. This raises the question of the future path of company tax rates. Has reducing rates and broadening bases reached a natural limit? It may be that from now on rate reductions would cost significant foregone revenue. Will this slow the race to the bottom among developed economies?

Of particular interest to New Zealand is the future direction of Australia's company tax rate. Australia has announced a review of its tax system, concentrating on issues of competitiveness, among others. The review may well lead to moderate company tax rate reductions in Australia. This raises the question of the extent to which New Zealand's rate can remain higher than Australia's.

A relatively high company tax rate can make it attractive for multinational

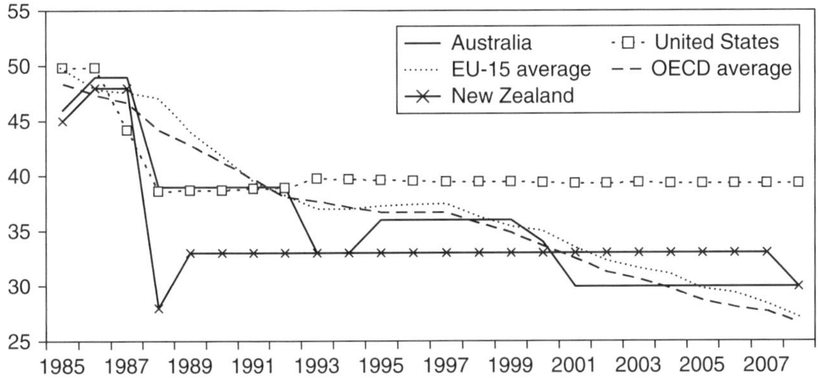

Source: OECD (2008).

Figure 13.3 Corporate tax rate trends 1985–2008

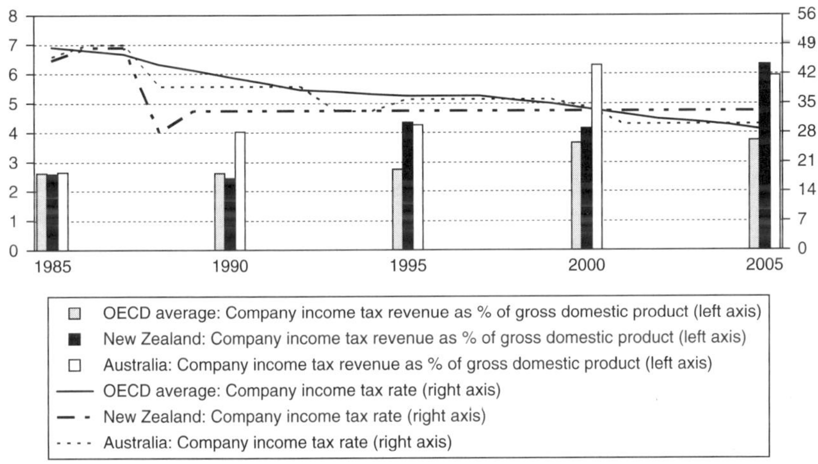

Source: OECD (2008).

Figure 13.4 Company income tax rates and revenues (in per cent), (1985–2005)

firms (especially from Australia with its imputation system) to stream profits away from New Zealand and into lower-tax countries. This might be achieved by firms 'thinly capitalising' their New Zealand operations (that is, financing as much of their New Zealand activities as possible by using debt). Or transfer pricing arrangements may be used whereby

New Zealand entities pay prices that are as high as possible, and charge prices that are as low as possible, on transactions with associated companies overseas. Of course, there are measures to prevent transfer pricing and thin capitalisation but these are not perfectly effective. Incentives to stream profits from New Zealand overseas will tend to arise when the New Zealand company tax rate is higher than that in other countries.

13.4.2 Adopt the Irish System? – Go For Broke!

Independently of international developments, New Zealand could choose to abandon rate alignment and unilaterally reduce company tax rates similar to the Irish system, with the hope of attracting substantial foreign direct investment.

A high company tax rate may discourage capital investment by increasing the user cost of capital and so have a direct negative effect on labour productivity and growth (see OECD, 2008). This is likely to involve a reduction in the level of FDI. This could be important if FDI brings new innovation to New Zealand. There has been much research on the effects of taxes on FDI. A recent authoritative survey reported a median semi-elasticity of −3.3 suggesting that a 1 per centage point reduction in the company tax rate would increase FDI by 3.3 per cent (see de Mooij and Ederveen, 2003). However, there is substantial variation across studies. There is also some evidence that the response may be a less elastic in countries with relatively low tax rates than in countries with relatively high tax rates (Benassy-Quere et al., 2005). This suggests that, at least after a point, further cuts in the company tax rate may have limited ability to increase FDI.

A high company tax rate can also increase investment distortions and reduce capital productivity because, in practice, economic income can never be measured and taxed properly. This can make New Zealand an unattractive place to base a business and has the potential to reduce labour productivity and growth. The 2001 Tax Review proposed a deep cut in the company tax rate for non-resident owned companies to attract FDI.[7] A company tax rate reduction would, in principle, achieve the Irish objective of attracting FDI, without the added revenue cost of lowering taxes on domestic savings.

Could New Zealand, as a small island nation, hope to emulate Ireland? The answer depends greatly on the similarities and differences between New Zealand (today, 2009) and Ireland (in the 1980s at the beginning of the 'Irish miracle'). Some similarities and differences are highlighted in Table 13.2. A short perusal of the list suggests that New Zealand's differences likely outweigh its similarities with Ireland.

Table 13.2 New Zealand and Ireland comparisons

Ireland	New Zealand
Small island economy	Small island economy
Educated English-speaking workforce	Educated English-speaking workforce
Member of EU (GDP $19.2 trillion)	Member of CER (GDP $1.2 trillion)
EU subsidies	No subsidies
On EU's doorstep	Middle of nowhere
Competing against high wage EU countries for FDI	Competing against low wage SE Asian countries for FDI

Moreover, taxing company income is a way of taxing foreign residents on the profits they make through investing in New Zealand. Where foreign-owned firms are making economic rents from their investments in New Zealand, reducing the company tax rate could potentially lead to higher economic profits for their shareholders with little effect on investment. In this case, much of the benefit of a company tax cut could go to foreign residents.

A recent OECD (2008) study has estimated some very large effects of cutting company tax rates on growth of total factor productivity (TFP). The study suggests a reduction in corporate taxation from 35 per cent to 30 per cent would increase average growth of TFP by 0.4 per cent per annum which they argue is likely to be an upper bound estimate. Trend TFP growth in OECD countries only averaged around 1.1 per cent over the period 2000–05. The paper notes that gains in growth are likely to be smaller for lower initial tax rates. That is, reducing company tax rates that are higher than average may have a greater impact than further reductions below the average rate. This latter effect has been reported in other studies.

However, it would be wrong to conclude that these results are necessarily applicable to New Zealand because some of the reasons identified by the OECD why company tax may reduce TFP growth are already substantially mitigated by New Zealand's full imputation system. Moreover there may be other factors in New Zealand's situation which make a substantial rate cut less likely to be welfare enhancing.

In particular, an interesting question is whether location-specific economic rents are likely to be a bigger issue for a small isolated economy like New Zealand's than, say, a country in Europe adjacent to other similar economics. There may often be few location-specific rents when production in one country is closely substitutable for production in another. Consider the choice of whether to establish a new plant in Germany or right across the border in Austria. The choice of country may have relatively little effect on the productivity of the plant or its ability to service the regional market. Here there may be fewer location-specific economic rents because production in one country can be readily replaced with production in another.

Where, however, FDI results in goods or services being produced to service the domestic market, arguably location-specific rents are more likely. Therefore the foregone tax on rents from a cut in tax rates may weigh more heavily on New Zealand than other economies. Typically, FDI into New Zealand seems to be focused on servicing the New Zealand market (for example banks), rather than in producing goods or services to export into the regional market.

The increase in FDI that New Zealand might expect to gain from a cut in tax rates may also be smaller than for countries that are competing within a regional market for FDI. Again consider the choice of whether to establish a new plant in Germany or right across the border in Austria to service the regional market. In that case, it might be expected that the decision of where to invest might be significantly affected by taxes. As the bulk of FDI into New Zealand services the domestic market, inbound FDI into New Zealand may be less sensitive to tax because there are few readily substitutable alternatives for these businesses. It may also be difficult for New Zealand to compete for more footloose manufacturing. For example, it is questionable whether New Zealand would ever be used as a major manufacturing hub to supply the Asian market, irrespective of its tax system.

Company taxes are a high proportion of government revenues in New Zealand. Accordingly, if there were a major reduction in New Zealand's company tax rate, replacement taxes would need to be levied on New Zealanders and this may make New Zealanders as a whole worse off. Finally, a tax preference for income earned by companies, but not other forms of income, leads to inefficiencies in choice of entity, type of investment and financial decisions, such as distribution of profits, which in themselves can impair productivity and growth.

To support major cuts in New Zealand's company tax rate, a case would need to be made that increases in capital stock and productivity, flowing from increases in FDI engendered by the low company tax rate, would be of sufficient net benefit to New Zealand to overcome these various costs.

A deep general rate cut, as in Ireland, would also have profound structural implications for the tax system, including:

- *Integrity measures:* To prevent deferral of taxes on personal income shifted to companies integrity measures would be required. These are outlined in more detail in sub-section 13.5.2 on the 'mind-the-gap' approach.

- *Role of imputation:* With deep cuts in company tax rates, imputation may no longer be considered appropriate. Ireland, for example, has a classical tax system.
- *Capital gains tax:* A classical tax system generally requires capital gains taxation to prevent avoidance or undue deferral of dividend taxation.

A deep cut in the company tax rate would alleviate transfer-pricing and thin-capitalisation concerns by making it attractive for multinational firms to move taxable profits into New Zealand rather than away from New Zealand. However, on balance we would support the general conclusion in New Zealand to date which has been not to introduce a deep company rate cut. Should this conclusion be reconsidered?

13.5 ADDRESSING INTEGRITY PROBLEMS

Integrity problems can be addressed by reducing the variation in tax rates facing taxpayers in different situations. There are a number different ways in which tax rate variation could be reduced. The fundamental decision, which frames other decisions on the rate structure, is the level of the company tax rate relative to the tax rates, particularly the top rate, on personal income.

Choices by government on tax rates applied to the income of individuals will reflect views on the level of revenues required to fund governmental spending programmes, the appropriate progressivity of the tax system, and efficiency considerations related to the impact of taxation on economic behaviour. Choosing the appropriate company tax rate reflects a balance of revenue objectives, international considerations and the structure of taxation of domestic income. Finally, the tax system must be administratively feasible and should strive to minimise compliance costs to the extent possible.

Ideally, the tax system should be flexible so that it can evolve as New Zealand's needs change. For example, fiscal demands may change as there are economic or demographic changes, or particular tax parameters may need to be recalibrated due to external factors; for example, a lowering of the rate of the company tax in response to continued reductions in company tax rates internationally. There is no single best way of balancing these considerations and different countries have chosen different routes to achieving their objectives. These are summarised below as a guide for possible approaches to lessening the current inconsistency in marginal tax rates in New Zealand.

Conceptually, tax rates could be made more consistent in three different ways:

- *Alignment approach*: The top personal and company tax rates would be the same. Alignment would essentially return the tax structure to New Zealand's pre-2000 alignment of the company and top personal tax rates, presumably at the new company tax rate of 30 per cent.
- *Mind-the-gap approach*: Integrity measures would be introduced to prevent current tax deferral and diversion possibilities, while retaining a company tax rate lower than the top personal tax rate.
- *Nordic approach:* A split rate system would be introduced with a lower tax rate applying to income from capital that aligns personal tax rates on investment income with the company tax rate, but continues to tax labour income at full personal tax rates. Variations of this approach have been adopted by the Nordic countries.

13.5.1 Alignment Approach

The most direct return to the New Zealand paradigm would be to align the top personal tax rates with the company rate. The top personal tax rates of 33 and 38 per cent would be set equal to the company tax rate of 30 per cent. This is clearly the simplest way to eliminate the disparity of rates among different entities. It avoids the need to distinguish between active and passive income, as under the mind-the-gap approach, and avoids the practical complications of the Nordic tax system.

Arguably alignment is the preferred option. An individual would be taxed on all forms of income earned through any entity at similar tax rates. Incentives to structure holdings of assets in artificial ways would be eliminated. Marginal tax rates would be reduced, reducing distortions from higher marginal tax rates on decisions to work and save. Complex distinctions required to implement both the mind-the-gap and Nordic approaches would be avoided. The Nordic approach would achieve efficiency benefits with respect to capital income, but would continue to apply high rates of tax on labour income at the top end. Since New Zealand labour (and skilled labour in particular) appears to be particularly mobile, especially between New Zealand and Australia, the efficiency costs of high personal tax rates could be higher than other countries.

There are a number of questions that need to be addressed in assessing the feasibility of the alignment option.

1. *Pressures on the company rate*. Can a company tax rate of 30 per cent be sustained, or will the question of alignment re-emerge if international pressure forces continuing cuts in the company rate? In other words is the system flexible enough to deal with changing circumstances?
2. *Revenue raising*. Reducing the top marginal tax rates is expensive. This requires feasible, base-broadening measures to fill the revenue gap. The obvious candidate to fill the revenue hole, from an efficiency point of view, would be to increase the rate of GST.
3. *Progressivity*. A sharp reduction in the top marginal tax rate would cause concern for those who view progressivity in the personal tax rate structure as necessary to redistribute income and promote fairness.

These fairness issues need to be put in context. Because of the scope that high income earners currently have to shelter their income in companies and trusts, many of the best-off in New Zealand are not necessarily subject to the top personal marginal tax rate. Thus, it is arguable that the current New Zealand rate schedule is less progressive than it appears. Moreover, government spending programmes as well as the tax structure will determine the progressivity of the government's fiscal programme.

If progressivity of the income tax system is of concern, one way to address this would be to make a more dramatic shift from taxes on income to taxes on consumption, that is, the GST. The progressivity of the personal rate structure could be maintained by lowering all personal tax rates by enough to equalise the top personal rate and company rates.

Even so, some may argue that this could be unfair because lower income families typically consume a higher proportion of their income than do higher income families and so are likely to be harder hit by an increase in the GST. As argued in Chapter 2, much of the apparent regressivity of a GST increase would disappear if incidence is measured over the lifetime of individuals. Differences in timing of income and consumption lead to variations of the ratio of consumption to income measured on an annual basis. However, many people consume most of their income over their lifetime, leaving little in the way of bequests. In any event, the poorest in society could be protected by compensating cost-of-living adjustments to low-income benefits and New Zealand Superannuation.

A switch from income to consumption taxes also raises transitional fairness issues to the detriment of individuals with higher savings. Raising the GST effectively imposes a lump sum tax on existing wealth owners though, over a life cycle, reduced taxes on investment income would compensate. However, the current elderly, whose accumulated savings would have borne the previously higher income tax rates, and who do not plan to leave bequests, would be hit hardest. This is only one of a large number of factors which may affect the current elderly including the performance of the share market and interest rates. Nevertheless, this may constrain the size of any increase in GST that might be feasible or provide a case for some other form of compensation for the elderly.

Across-the-board income tax rate reductions would reduce these effective tax rates on income. To the extent that lower marginal income tax rates are offset by a higher rate of GST, theory would suggest that there would not be increased incentives to work. However, the lower marginal income tax rates would be likely to increase the incentive to save and to reduce tax biases between different forms of saving.

Finally, reliance on increases in the GST would provide an avenue to maintain alignment in the future if there are further reductions in the company tax rate in response to international pressures.

13.5.2 Mind-the-Gap Approach

Under this system New Zealand's company tax rate would remain less than the top personal tax rate, with perhaps a modest reduction from current levels.

Most OECD countries have a company tax rate which is considerably less than the top personal tax rate. Some countries have introduced integrity measures to prevent deferral of personal wage and investment income by shifting it to lower taxed closely-held companies. While the concepts behind these measures are reasonably straightforward, their application can be complex in some situations. For example, the rules to maintain personal taxation of investment income on assets shifted to closely-held companies would require an active–passive distinction in the domestic context. The distinction is necessary to allow the business income of companies to benefit from the low company tax rate while preventing tax on income from personal savings to be deferred by transferring passive assets to a closely-held company. Similarly, measures are required to ensure that personal income earned through collective investment vehicles is taxed at the marginal tax rates of individuals. Finally, rules are required to prevent certain personal services being provided through a company from benefitting from the low tax rate.

Rationale and economic incentives

The major rationale for a mind-the-gap system is that it preserves flexibility and independence of the company and personal tax rates. The company tax rate can be set to respond to international tax pressures and growth concerns, while the personal rate structure would be targeted at the redistributive goals of the government. It would reflect a judgment that the company tax rate would not be a stable platform on which to base the personal rate structure. It would represent a major departure from the New Zealand paradigm, as it would allow for a permanent de-linking of the company and personal tax rates.

For non-resident-owned companies, it would represent a permanent reduction in tax. There would be greater flexibility in setting the rate to take account of goals for attracting FDI and minimising international transfer pricing pressures. For domestically-owned companies, incentives depend upon the taxation of dividends at the personal level. If imputation were maintained, the lower company tax rate would provide an explicit tax incentive by allowing deferral of taxation for reinvested income.

The biggest disadvantage of this option is likely to be its effects on economic efficiency. Different rates of tax would be levied on active income earned through companies and by unincorporated businesses, biasing the choice of legal form. Lower tax rates on retained active income would bias high tax rate individuals towards investing in active businesses and away from possibly higher return passive investments.

Maintaining a rate gap also moves away from some of the neutrality goals of an imputation system. Maintaining imputation would avoid double taxation of income passed through companies. This might be considered a particular advantage for closely-held companies versus widely-held. On the other hand, there would be differential tax imposts across companies according to the period that elapses until income is distributed.[8]

Other solutions are possible, such as:

1. Exempting imputed dividends to pass through the active income tax reduction; or,
2. A classical tax system, which double taxes company income and may further discourage distributions.

Other structural issues

A number of other issues are raised, some of which are quite complex. First, there are borderline problems in distinguishing active from passive investment businesses, for example, with rental of real estate. Second, most countries with dividend taxation and a gap between company and personal tax rates have found it necessary to introduce taxation of capital gains. For widely-held companies there is the concern that lack of a capital gains tax could bias the decision to retain or distribute income. For closely-held companies, well known dividend stripping strategies can be used to side-step the taxation of dividends. Thus far New Zealand has avoided introducing taxation of capital gains other than gains that occur on revenue account. Imputation and the relative alignment of company and personal tax rates reduce the structural reasons for having a capital gains tax. If a permanent, perhaps wider, rate differential were expected, this would raise the question: at what rate gap is there a sufficient structural reason to tax capital gains to limit deferral and preserve effective dividend taxation?

13.5.3 Nordic Approach

A Nordic system would apply the lower company rate of tax to all capital income, whether the assets are held by individuals, companies or other entities. Labour income would continue to be taxed at marginal personal tax rates. The Nordic countries introduced their systems for a number of reasons.

Norway has been the leading proponent of split rate systems. In 1992 Norway undertook a reform of its tax system that followed the pattern of tax reforms in the OECD. They replaced a tax system characterised by high tax rates and a distorted base with one with lower tax rates and a broad base. However, unlike most other reforms at that time, they decided to introduce a split rate system with a flat tax rate of 28 per cent on company income and personal income from capital, and a progressive system with higher rates of tax and social security contributions on income from labour. At the time of introduction the top combined (including employers' contributions) rate of tax on labour income was about 50 per cent; by 2003 it had risen to a combined total of 64.7 per cent.

The basic motivation for the reform was to preserve rates of tax on labour income that were high by international standards, while responding to international pressures which made sustaining such high tax rates on capital income impossible. The system also addressed other structural problems such as arbitrage between rates of tax on capital and labour.

The traditional Nordic system requires splitting labour and capital income for unincorporated businesses and closely-held companies. This proved to be the Achilles heel of the system. More recently Norway has replaced its system to fix problems in the traditional split rate model and to respond to ECJ determinations that imputation systems cannot discriminate among EU countries.

The new Norwegian system incorporates a capital gains tax and double taxation of dividends above a standard rate of return. Tax rates on capital and labour are aligned rather ingeniously to prevent deferral of tax on labour income earned through companies and to apply the higher rate of tax to economic rents and not marginal investments. This system obviates the need for rules to distinguish between capital and labour for companies, but such rules are still required for unincorporated businesses.

The New Zealand tax system differs from the Nordic system as it has lower personal tax rates overall and a smaller difference between the top personal tax rate and the company tax rate. Moreover, New Zealand has no payroll tax to fund social security contributions and this makes it more feasible than would otherwise be the case to achieve alignment. Norway's reduced tax rate on capital income is close to the current New Zealand company tax rate. So, while alignment is a potential policy for New Zealand, it is clearly out of reach for Norway. New Zealand does not have a general tax on capital gains, and historically there has never been a political consensus in favour of such a tax. On the other hand, a number of recent policy decisions, such as the capped tax rate for PIEs, have moved New Zealand's system in the direction of a split rate for capital and labour, at least for taxpayers on higher rates of personal tax.

Given these measures, one option would be to adopt a simplified alignment of capital tax rates. PIE income is currently subject to a capped tax rate and is taxed at the lesser of the company tax rate and the statutory tax rate of the individual. A capped tax rate could be extended to all investment income (using a list approach, rather than 'active–passive'), wherever it is earned. The system would not adopt the Nordic separation of labour and capital income for unincorporated and closely-held companies. The capital component of unincorporated business income would face personal marginal tax rates and the labour component of closely-held company income would enjoy the company tax rate. (There would need to be rules to prevent sheltering of salary and wages and perhaps certain forms of personal service income.) Imputation could be maintained, but a capped capital tax rate would apply to dividends. This approach would have much in common with a number of European schedular tax systems which apply lower rates of tax on certain forms of investment income.

Biases would remain because of different rates of tax on business income of companies and unincorporated businesses. Many of the efficiency issues of the mind-the-gap approach would also arise with this simplified Nordic approach. However, investment income would be taxed equally in different entities and so the incentive to hold investments artificially in tax efficient ways would be removed.

The change would exacerbate fairness issues between labour and capital income arising from the current tax-minimising strategies. Since capital income is concentrated among higher income earners, overall progressivity would be reduced. On the other hand, as is well known, the absence of inflation adjustments implies that capital income of individuals is often over-taxed, even at current low inflation rates. A capped tax rate could be seen as a partial *ad hoc* recognition of this over-taxation.

Finally, efficiency and fairness concerns could be lessened if applying a lower tax rate to investment income is seen as a halfway house to eventual full alignment of the company and personal tax rates.

13.6 PRELIMINARY CONCLUSIONS AND QUESTIONS FOR ONGOING DEBATE

This chapter has sought to discuss possible options rather than driving to definitive conclusions in this complex area. However, we would venture some preliminary conclusions and raise questions for further debate. These are:

1. In our view a deep company rate cut is unlikely to be a preferred option for New Zealand in the present international context. There are some important issues that need to be debated in firming up these conclusions:

   - Is there a best rate of company tax rate for New Zealand which trades off the efficiency benefits of lower company rates against the loss of tax on rents?
   - Is investment more sensitive to relatively high tax rates rather than low rates?
   - Is there significant tax base risk from high company tax rates to justify reducing rates to save revenue leakage?

2. In our view so long as it is viable (given any reductions in company tax rates abroad), the preferred option for personal and company income tax rates is the alignment approach, with the company and top personal tax rate equalised, and applied to a broad-based definition of income. But questions for further debate include:

   - Is alignment the best alternative, or is there a case for reducing company tax rates while keeping personal tax rates higher?
   - What is the future direction of the company tax rate in response to international developments? Is alignment sustainable?
   - Could an increase in the rate of GST be used to fund across-the-board personal tax rate cuts to maintain alignment?

3. If rate alignment cannot be achieved, two second best options were outlined: a 'mind-the-gap' approach and a simplified Nordic approach. In our view the choice between these two approaches is less clear-cut. Questions for further debate include:

- Given that New Zealand already has a capped rate of tax for some investment income, could a simplified Nordic system be a way-station toward full alignment?
- A fundamental policy question distinguishing these approaches is, whether an individual's capital income should be subject to the same progressive tax rates as labour income? This has a number of specific aspects:
  Fairness: should all types of personal income face the same rate of tax, or is there a case for lower taxation of savings?
  Trade-offs: do the intertemporal efficiency gains of lower tax rates on savings of the Nordic system outweigh the possible fairness concerns?
  Efficiency: in a small open economy, is it better to target the incentive of a lower tax rate at investment ('mind-the-gap') or extend the incentive to savings (Nordic)?

NOTES

* The views expressed in this chapter are not the views of the New Zealand Inland Revenue Department. We are grateful to Sandra Watson and Iris Claus for the provision of much of the data referred to in this chapter.

1. Self-integration is facilitated by New Zealand's rules allowing taxable bonus issues to be imputed.
2. There are some possible qualifications to the simple national welfare maximisation story. If offshore investment by a New Zealand resident creates scope for additional inbound investment and this inbound investment generates taxable income, this can create a case for a lighter taxation of outbound investment than full taxation with a deduction for foreign taxes. This is the so-called 'seesaw effect' (see Slemrod et al., 1997). However, offshore investment by domestic firms is unlikely to be matched dollar for dollar with inbound investment. Moreover, equity investment is only about one-third of inbound investment and debt is normally subject to only very low rates of tax. This means that for New Zealand the simple national welfare maximisation story is not likely to be qualified much by allowing for the possibility of inbound investment flows.
3. New Zealand also has a grey list of eight countries with comparable tax systems which allows income to be accrued tax-free and an exemption for dividends from affiliates.
4. An exception is that there may sometimes be a non-resident withholding tax (NRWT) impost. Foreign-sourced income passing through a New Zealand company and then to non-resident shareholders as dividends is currently subject to NRWT. This is under review.
5. See Inland Revenue (2008) for more details. Greater tax benefits can be arranged by having companies taxed at 30 per cent held by trusts. Accumulated earnings obtain a deferral advantage by being taxed at 30 per cent, with a final tax of 33 per cent applied when they are distributed to the trust.
6. Income tax rates in 2008 were 21, 33 and 39 per cent. However, many taxpayers receiving family tax credits face an abatement rate of 20 cents per dollar, raising their effective marginal rates to 41, 53 and 59 per cent.
7. This could potentially be achieved in a number of ways: either by trying to define income

earned on behalf of non-residents or by providing refunds of imputation credits as dividends are paid. Either approach would present formidable technical difficulties.
8. This deferral effect happens whenever there is net taxation of the dividend.

REFERENCES

Benassy-Quere, A., L. Fontagne and A. Lahreche-Revil (2005), 'How does FDI react to corporate taxation?' *International Tax and Public Finance*, **12**, 583–603.

Inland Revenue (2008), *Briefing to the Incoming Minister* (November). Policy Advice Division, New Zealand Inland Revenue Department, available at http://taxpolicy.ird.govt.nz/publications/files/IRBIM2008.pdf, accessed on 15 January 2009.

de Mooij, R.A. and S. Ederveen (2003), 'Taxation and foreign direct investment: A synthesis of empirical research', *International Tax and Public Finance*, **10**, 673–93.

OECD (2008), *Tax and economic growth*, OECD Economics Department, Working Paper No. 620, available at www.oecd.org/working_papers, accessed on 15 January 2009.

Slemrod, J., C. Hansen and R. Procter (1997), 'The seesaw principle in international tax policy', *Journal of Public Economics*, **65**, 163–76.

Tax Review (2001), *Final Report* (October), available at www.taxreview2001.govt.nz, accessed on 15 January 2009.

Treasury (2009), *Medium Term Tax Policy Challenges and Opportunities*, New Zealand Treasury (February), available at www.treasury.govt.nz/publications/informationreleases/taxconference, accessed on 15 January 2009.

Index